IPv6 for Enterprise Networks

Shannon McFarland
Muninder Sambi
Nikhil Sharma
Sanjay Hooda

Cisco Press

800 East 96th Street

Indianapolis, IN 46240

IPv6 for Enterprise Networks

Shannon McFarland, Muninder Sambi, Nikhil Sharma, and Sanjay Hooda

Copyright © 2011 Cisco Systems, Inc.

Published by:
Cisco Press
800 East 96th Street
Indianapolis, IN 46240 USA

Printed in the United States of America

First Printing   March 2011

Library of Congress Cataloging-in-Publication data is on file.

ISBN-13: 978-1-58714-227-7

ISBN-10: 1-58714-227-9

Warning and Disclaimer

This book is designed to provide information about the IPv6 deployment options for an Enterprise network. Every effort has been made to make this book as complete and as accurate as possible, but no warranty or fitness is implied.

The information is provided on an "as is" basis. The authors, Cisco Press, and Cisco Systems, Inc., shall have neither liability nor responsibility to any person or entity with respect to any loss or damages arising from the information contained in this book or from the use of the discs or programs that may accompany it.

The opinions expressed in this book belong to the author and are not necessarily those of Cisco Systems, Inc.

Trademark Acknowledgments

All terms mentioned in this book that are known to be trademarks or service marks have been appropriately capitalized. Cisco Press or Cisco Systems, Inc., cannot attest to the accuracy of this information. Use of a term in this book should not be regarded as affecting the validity of any trademark or service mark.

Corporate and Government Sales

The publisher offers excellent discounts on this book when ordered in quantity for bulk purchases or special sales, which may include electronic versions and/or custom covers and content particular to your business, training goals, marketing focus, and branding interests. For more information, please contact: U.S. Corporate and Government Sales   1-800-382-3419   corpsales@pearsontechgroup.com

For sales outside the United States please contact: International Sales   international@pearsoned.com

Feedback Information

At Cisco Press, our goal is to create in-depth technical books of the highest quality and value. Each book is crafted with care and precision, undergoing rigorous development that involves the unique expertise of members from the professional technical community.

Readers' feedback is a natural continuation of this process. If you have any comments regarding how we could improve the quality of this book, or otherwise alter it to better suit your needs, you can contact us through email at feedback@ciscopress.com. Please make sure to include the book title and ISBN in your message.

We greatly appreciate your assistance.

Publisher: Paul Boger

Associate Publisher: Dave Dusthimer

Executive Editor: Brett Bartow

Managing Editor: Sandra Schroeder

Development Editor: Dayna Isley

Project Editor: Seth Kerney

Book Designer: Louisa Adair

Indexer: Tim Wright

Business Operation Manager, Cisco Press: Anand Sundaram

Manager, Global Certification: Erik Ullanderson

Technical Editors: Jim Bailey, Ciprian P. Popoviciu

Copy Editor: John Edwards

Proofreader: Apostrophe Editing Services

Editorial Assistant: Vanessa Evans

Composition: Mark Shirar

About the Authors

Shannon McFarland, CCIE No. 5245, is a corporate consulting engineer for Cisco, working as a technical consultant for enterprise IPv6 deployment and data center design with a focus on application deployment and virtual desktop infrastructure. Over the last 16 years, he has worked on large-scale enterprise campus and WAN/branch network design, data center design and optimization for Microsoft operating systems and server applications, as well as design and optimization of virtual desktop infrastructure deployments. For the past 10 years, Shannon has been a frequent speaker at IPv6 events worldwide (notably Cisco Live [formerly Networkers]), IPv6 summits, and other industry events. He has authored many papers and Cisco Validated Designs (CVD) on IPv6, IP Multicast, Microsoft Exchange, VMware View, and other applications, as well as contributed to many Cisco Press books. Prior to his time at Cisco, Shannon worked as a consultant for a value-added reseller and also as a network engineer in the healthcare industry. Shannon lives with his wife and children in Castle Rock, CO.

Muninder Sambi, CCIE No. 13915, is a manager of product marketing for the Cisco Catalyst 4500/4900 series platform. As a product line manager, he is responsible for defining product strategies on the multi-billion-dollar Catalyst 4500 and 4900 series platforms, which include next-generation product architectures both for user access in Campus and Server access in the Data Center. Prior to this role, Muninder played a key role in defining the long-term Software and Services strategy for Cisco's modular switching platforms (Catalyst 6500 and 4500/4900 series) including a focus on IPv6 innovations. Some of these innovations enabled dual-stack IPv6 deployments in large enterprise and service provider networks. Muninder is also a core member of Cisco's IPv6 development council. Muninder has represented Cisco as part of multiple network design architecture reviews with large enterprise customers. Over the last 12+ years, Muninder has worked on multiple Enterprise Campus, WAN, and Data Center designs. Prior to working at Cisco, Muninder worked as a network consultant for one of India's leading network integrators and was responsible for designing and implementing LAN, WAN, and hosted Data Center networks. Muninder lives with his wife and children in Fremont, California.

Nikhil Sharma, CCIE No. 21273, is a technical marketing engineer at Cisco, where he is responsible for defining new features, both hardware and software, for the Catalyst 4500 product line. Over the last 10 years, Nikhil has worked with various enterprise customers to design and troubleshoot both large and midsize campus and data center networks.

Sanjay Hooda, CCIE No. 11737, is a technical leader at Cisco, where he works with embedded systems and helps define new product architectures. His current focus areas include high availability and messaging in large-scale distributed switching systems. Over the last 14 years, Sanjay's experience spans various areas, including SCADA (Supervisor Control and Data Acquisition), large-scale software projects, and enterprise campus and LAN, WAN, and data center network design.

About the Technical Reviewers

Jim Bailey, CCIE No. 5275 (Routing and Switching; Service Provider) and CCDE No. 20090008, is an AS technical leader at Cisco Systems with over 18 years of experience in networking. As part of the Global Government Solutions Group Advanced Services team, he focuses on the architecture, design, and implementation of large U.S. government civilian agency and military networks. He has focused on IPv6 integration into those networks for the last five years.

Ciprian P. Popoviciu, Ph.D., is director of Cloud and Network3.0 practices in the Enterprise Services Group at Technodyne. Previously he held several leadership roles within Cisco, where over the past eight years he worked in close collaboration with standards bodies and large customers worldwide on the IPv6 protocol and product development, IPv6 strategy and planning, and IPv6-enabled, next-generation architecture and deployment. Ciprian coauthored two extensively referenced Cisco Press IPv6 books, four RFCs, and multiple papers on IPv6 technology, strategy, and adoption. He is a senior member of the IEEE, a member of several research advisory boards, and an active speaker at IPv6 industry events.

Dedications

I want to give thanks to my Savior Jesus Christ—I was once lost but now I am found. This book is dedicated to Linda, Zack, and Carter. I am so blessed to have you all in my life, and I am so proud of the honorable young men my sons have become. Thanks for putting up with me for these many months. I also want to thank my mom for her unconditional love and prayers and my dad for the desire to never quit learning. To my mother- and father-in-law, thanks for bringing Linda into this world and into my life; she is the very best. Bob (dad), thanks for being my friend and mentor and always showing me what hard work really is.

—Shannon McFarland

First of all, I would like to dedicate this book to my grandfather (Gyani Gurcharan Singh) for being an inspiration as an author, poet, and classical musician. I would like to thank my family: Dad (Surinder Singh Sambi), Mom (Sukhdev Kaur), my brother (Dr. Ravinder Singh Sambi), my sister-in-law (Amrit Kaur), and wife (Avnit Kaur) for their unconditional support during the writing of this book. I would also like to dedicate this book to my daughter (Japjot), twins (Kabir Singh and Charan Kanwal Singh) and my nephews (Kanwal and Bhanwra).

—Muninder Singh Sambi

First of all I would like to thank my parents: Dad (Satbir Singh) and Mom (Indrawati) and wife (Suman) for their support during the writing of the book. This book is dedicated to my children Pulkit and Apoorva.

—Sanjay Hooda

I would like to thank my wife Parul for her endless support during the process. This book is dedicated to my daughter Anshi for showing me how small things in life bring true happiness.

—Nikhil Sharma

Acknowledgments

I would like to thank a number of people who have contributed to my knowledge and experience of IPv6 and supported my time spent on it (especially in the early days), and those who have provided me support over these many years: My friends and biggest supporters, Freddie Tsao, Steve Pollock, Chris O'Brien, and Mark Montanez. I have been blessed with many great managers who have been so very patient with me over the years and offered great support, especially on IPv6. A few of the many: Todd Truitt, Vince Spina, Kumar Reddy, Mauricio "Mo" Arregoces, Dave Twinam, and Mark Webb. Additionally, I would like to thank the following individuals at Cisco (past and present) who have contributed to this effort directly or indirectly: Patrick Grossetete, Chip Popoviciu, Eric Vyncke, Gunter Van de Velde, Tarey Treasure, Darlene Maillet, Angel Shimelish, Chris Jarvis, Gabe Dixon, Tim Szigeti, Mike Herbert, Neil Anderson, Dave West, Darrin Miller, Stephen Orr, Ralph Droms, Salman Asadullah, Yenu Gobena, Tony Hain, Benoit Lourdelet, Eric Levy-Abegnoli, Jim Bailey, Fred Baker, and countless others. Finally, I would like to thank John Spence and Yurie Rich for years of great feedback and real-world IPv6 deployment validation.

—Shannon McFarland

First of all, I would like to thank my co-authors Sanjay Hooda, Nikhil Sharma, and Shannon McFarland for all their cooperation during the writing of the book. Special thanks to Shannon for keeping us motivated and guiding us through some of the difficult topics.

Thanks to my mentor and dear friend who introduced me to networking, Sanjay Thyamagundalu, for supporting me through the writing of this book.

I would also like to thank my Director Sachin Gupta for his support and motivation towards completion of the book. I would also thank the technical reviewers, Jim Bailey and Chip Popoviciu, for sharing their technical expertise on IPv6 and for always being available for a follow-up to review the comments.

Finally, I would like to thank the Cisco Press team, especially Brett Bartow and Dayna Isley, for guiding us through the process and being patient as we went through the initial drafts and the review process.

—Muninder Singh Sambi

First of all, I would like to thank my co-authors Muninder, Shannon, and Nikhil, who have been very supportive during the course of writing. Additionally I would like to thank my great friend Sanjay Thyamagundalu and my manager Vinay Parameswarannair for their support during the writing of this book. Sanjay Thyamagundalu has provided not only inspiration, but also thought-provoking insights into various areas.

Thanks as well to Brett Bartow, Dayna Isley, and all the folks at Cisco Press for their patience as I struggled to meet the timelines.

—Sanjay Hooda

First and foremost, I would like to thank my mentor and greatest friend Muninder Sambi for introducing me to networking. Without access to Sanjay Hooda's lab, this book could not have happened. Shannon kept the team motivated by showing us the finish line when at times we saw it far away.

Thanks to my friends who have always answered when I called: Amol Ramakant, Deepinder Babbar, Jagdeep Sagoo, Nitin Chopra, and the 24/7 speed dial on my phone, 1-800-Call-Manu.

—Nikhil Sharma

We would like to give special recognition to technical reviewers Chip Popoviciu and Jim Bailey for providing their expert technical knowledge in reviewing the book.

Finally, we want to thank our fantastic editors, Brett Bartow and Dayna Isley, and the Cisco Press team for all their support, patience, and quality work.

Contents at a Glance

Contents

Icons Used in This Book

Command Syntax Conventions

The conventions used to present command syntax in this book are the same conventions used in the IOS Command Reference. The Command Reference describes these conventions as follows:

- **Boldface** indicates commands and keywords that are entered literally as shown. In actual configuration examples and output (not general command syntax), boldface indicates commands that are manually input by the user (such as a show command).

- *Italic* indicates arguments for which you supply actual values.

- Vertical bars (|) separate alternative, mutually exclusive elements.

- Square brackets ([ ]) indicate an optional element.

- Braces ({ }) indicate a required choice.

- Braces within brackets ([{ }]) indicate a required choice within an optional element.

Introduction

Internet Protocol version 6 (IPv6) is the next version of the protocol that is used for communication among devices of all types on the Internet. IPv6 has been in existence for many years, but recently the deployment of IPv6 has accelerated greatly in the enterprise. IPv6 has been under continuous development and is maturing as real-world deployments expose gaps in either the protocol or the deployment methodology of the protocol.

Enterprises around the world are being exposed to IPv6 by either deploying operating systems and applications that automatically use IPv6 (at times without their knowledge), or they are proactively deploying IPv6 to fill requirements for the following: additional addressing, expansion into emerging markets, dealing with merger-and-acquisition challenges, and leveraging the new capabilities of the protocol for cutting-edge endpoints and applications. Whatever the reason, it is critical for the enterprise to fully understand the deployment options available with IPv6 and to take an aggressive but well-thought-out planning and design approach to their deployment.

IP is pervasive; it is everywhere. So, to properly plan and deploy IPv6 in an enterprise network, the IT staff must break the deployment down into places in their network such as the campus, data center, WAN, and so on and then focus on all the places where IPv4 is used today. Then, based on the business and technical drivers, the staff must implement IPv6 alongside of IPv4. There will be times when IPv6 is deployed in new areas where IPv4 is no longer needed and also times when IPv6 might not be needed everywhere that IPv4 is. This book breaks down the enterprise into various places in the network and gives design and deployment guidance on how to implement IPv6 in these areas.

Goals and Methods

Enterprises often get bogged down in the political issues and business justification of a new project and often end up with a technical design and implementation that is sourced from a "figure it out as we go along" mind-set. The goal of this book is to give the reader a practical and proven way to break down the massive task of IPv6 deployment into consumable sections based on places in the network and to provide the reader with validated configuration examples that can be used to build a lab, pilot, and production network.

This book has a pretty consistent flow to the information that is to provide an introduction to each area of deployment, diagrams to show the example topologies (where applicable), and then various configuration examples to help reinforce the deployment concepts. This book will help you understand the options for IPv6 deployment in the enterprise and see how to implement those deployment options.

Who Should Read This Book

This book is intended to be read by people working in an enterprise IT environment and partners or consultants who support enterprise IT. You should already know the fundamental concepts of IPv6 to include addressing, neighbor and router communication, and routing. While some of the chapters are introductions to certain topics and principles, none of them are in-depth enough to be the sole resource for an IPv6 newcomer as they relate to the basic mechanics of the protocol. This book assumes that the reader has a thorough understanding of networking technologies and network design and deployment. The book will work from long-standing design best practices from Cisco related to Layer 2 and Layer 3 design and is not a primer for network design or an introduction to IPv6.

How This Book Is Organized

Although this book could be read from cover to cover, it is designed to be flexible and to allow you to easily move between chapters and sections of chapters to cover just the material that you need more work with.

An introduction to enterprise IPv6 deployment is given in Chapters 1–4 and covers the following introductory topics:

■   **Chapter 1, "Market Drivers for IPv6 Adoption":** This chapter discusses the common business and technical drivers for IPv6 deployment in the enterprise. Growing deployment trends and common use cases are given.

■   **Chapter 2, "Hierarchical Network Design":** This chapter gives an overview of the well-known and mature hierarchical design model for networks and allows the reader to have a basic foundation for network design principles that will be built on throughout the book.

■   **Chapter 3, "Common IPv6 Coexistence Mechanisms":** This chapter discusses a few of the most common coexistence mechanisms (also called transition mechanisms) used in the enterprise. Dual-stack, ISATAP, 6to4, and others are introduced in this chapter.

■   **Chapter 4, "Network Services":** This chapter examines the common network services used in most IPv6 deployments and includes IPv6 multicast, quality of service (QoS), and routing protocols. Other chapters in the book will show more examples of how these services are deployed.

Chapters 5–12 focus on the actual deployment of IPv6 in an enterprise network and are much more technical in nature:

■   **Chapter 5, "Planning an IPv6 Deployment":** This chapter provides information on the high-level predeployment and deployment considerations and phases. The chapter offers a systematic view of planning for the deployment of IPv6.

■   **Chapter 6, "Deploying IPv6 in Campus Networks":** This chapter covers the deployment options most often used in a campus network environment. Various coexistence mechanisms are discussed in detail as well as the configurations for making a highly available IPv6 deployment a success in the campus. Advanced technologies such as the Cisco Virtual Switching System are also discussed.

- **Chapter 7, "Deploying Virtualized IPv6 Networks":** This chapter discusses various network, device, desktop, and server virtualization solutions and provides configuration examples for some of these solutions to inlcude 6PE and 6VPE.

- **Chapter 8, "Deploying IPv6 in WAN/Branch Networks":** This chapter provides the reader with various design scenarios for the WAN and branch areas of the network and gives detailed configuration examples for different WAN/branch devices and services to include Dynamic Multipoint VPNs and the Cisco ASA.

- **Chapter 9, "Deploying IPv6 in the Data Center":** This chapter covers the common technologies, services, and products in the data center and works from a common design to give the reader various configurations that can be used in his or her own environment. Various data center–focused products, such as the Cisco Nexus 7000, 1000v, and MDS 9000, are discussed along with Cisco NAM, ASA, and other products and technologies.

- **Chapter 10, "Deploying IPv6 for Remote Access":** This chapter discusses the options for enabling IPv6 in a remote-access VPN environment. Examples are shown to allow IPv6 over a legacy VPN (non-IPv6-supported products) and also to use the Cisco ASA and AnyConnect SSL VPN solutions in an IPv6 environment.

- **Chapter 11, "Managing IPv6 Networks":** This chapter covers the common management components used in enterprise IPv6 deployments. These components include management applications and tools, instrumentation, and management information transported over IPv6.

- **Chapter 12, "Walk Before Running: Building an IPv6 Lab and Starting a Pilot":** This chapter discusses the need and purpose of a dedicated lab and the importance of a pilot for IPv6. A practical and systematic view of how to build a lab, perform application testing, and move to a pilot environment is discussed.

Chapter 1

Market Drivers for IPv6 Adoption

This chapter discusses the following:

Internet evolution and the need for IPv6: This section focuses on the existing solutions that extend the life of the Internet and the advantages that IPv6 provides over other solutions. This section also outlines the IPv6 market drivers and the frequently asked questions/concerns about IPv6.

IPv6 in the IETF: As IPv6 goes mainstream, it is important for the standards bodies like IETF to standardize on these capabilities, which can be adopted across all network and computing devices.

Enterprise IPv6 deployment status: While many enterprises are looking to enable IPv6 or establish plans for the deployment of IPv6, some of the enterprise verticals such as Retail, Manufacturing, Web 2.0 and Enterprise IT organizations are leading the adoption both by enabling network and computing devices to support IPv6 and also enabling their business applications over IPv6.

The Internet has evolved from an internal distributed computing system used by the U.S. Department of Defense to a medium that enables enterprise business to be innovative and more productive in providing goods and services to its global customers. The Internet Protocol Suite (TCP/IP) is the underlying technology used to enable this communication.

Although the Internet has no centralized governance, it does have overarching organizations that help implement and maintain policy and operation of key Internet elements such as the IP address space and the Domain Name System (DNS). These critical elements are maintained and managed by the Internet Corporation for Assigned Names and Numbers (ICANN), which operates the Internet Assigned Numbers Authority (IANA). ICANN/IANA assigns unique identifiers for use on the Internet, which include domain names, Internet Protocol (IP) addresses, and application port numbers.

More information can be found at

- ICANN: http://www.icann.org
- IANA: http://www.iana.org

The Internet Engineering Task Force (IETF) (www.ietf.org), a nonprofit organization, standardizes the core protocols based on the technical expertise of loosely affiliated international participants. These protocols are used in all products that provide network connectivity, and individual product manufacturers provide a user interface to configure and use these protocols.

The IETF evaluated the growth of the Internet protocol with emphasis on addressing. The organization evaluated the following:

■ **Address space exhaustion:** The IETF, along with industry participation from the IANA, the Regional Internet Registry (RIR), and the private sector, predict the exhaustion of the public IPv4 address pool by 2011.

■ **Expanding routing tables:** The practice of classifying and allocating IP addresses based on classes has lead to an alarming expansion of the routing tables in the Internet backbone routers.

The next sections describe in more detail some of the issues surrounding IPv4 address exhaustion and options developed as temporary workarounds. You then learn how this lead the IETF to develop IPv6.

IPv4 Address Exhaustion and the Workaround Options

Without sufficient global IPv4 address space, hosts are forced to work with mechanisms that provide the capability for an internal (private) IP address space to be translated to a smaller or single externally routable IP address space. Network Address Translation (NAT) enables multiple devices to use local private addresses (RFC 1918) within an enterprise while sharing one or more global IPv4 addresses for external communications. Although NAT has to some extent delayed the exhaustion of IPv4 address space for the short term, it complicates general application bidirectional communication. These workarounds have resulted in the following:

■ Establishing gateways, firewalls, and applications that require specialized code to deal with the presence of NAT/PATs (for example, NAT transparency using UDP)

■ Mapping of standard ports to nonstandard ports (port forwarding)

Establishment and use of NAT workaround code (STUN, TURN, ICE, and so on)

■ Nested NAT/PAT addresses

■ Complexity of the supporting infrastructure, applications, and security

■ Complexity of installing and managing multiple address pools

■ More time, energy, and money spent coding and managing the workaround

■ Inability to easily identify all connected devices on an organization's network

Note   Sensors, even inline, might not be completely successful at dropping packets of an attack. An attack could be on its way, if only partially, before even an inline sensor starts dropping packets matching a composite pattern signature. The drop action is much more effective for atomic signatures because the sensor makes a single packet match.

Note   It took 40 years for radio to achieve an audience of 50 million; it took 15 years for TV and just 5 years for the Internet!

IPv6 is designed to replace IPv4. It enables an unimaginably large number of addresses and brings with it easier network management, end-to-end transparency, and the opportunity for improved security and mobility, as discussed in the following section.

IPv6 Market Drivers

IPv6 helps open doors for new revenue stream opportunities by enabling new applications and enabling enterprises to expand their businesses globally. The four primary factors driving IPv6 adoption, as illustrated in Figure 1-1, include

- IPv4 address considerations

- Government IT strategy

- Infrastructure evolution

- Operating system support

IPv4 Address Consideration
- IPv4 address depletion
- Globalization: limiting expansion of enterprise into emerging markets
- Mobile devices, inefficient address use, and virtualization
- Mergers and acquisitions

Government Regulated Strategy
- Government regulators: U.S. federal mandate, Japan
- Emerging country government regulations: China, Australia and New Zealand, etc..

- IPv6 "on" and "preferred" by default (Windows 7)
- Specific applications driving IPv6 adoption (Server 2008)

Operating System Support

- Next-generation network architecture requires IPv6
- DOCSIS 3.0, Quad Play
- Mobile SP, Networks in Motion
- Networked Sensors, i.e. AIRS

Infrastructure Evolution

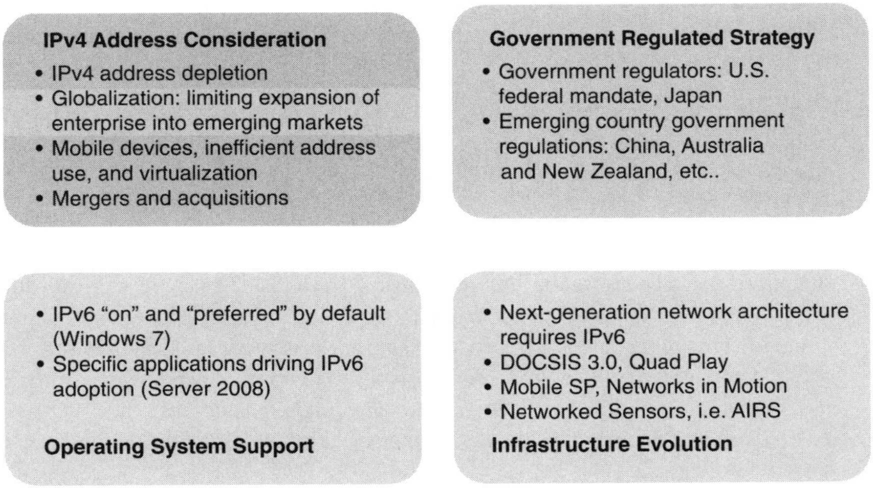

Figure 1-1   *IPv6 Market Drivers*

The following sections describe the key market drivers shown in Figure 1-1.

IPv4 Address Considerations

The following IPv4 address considerations drive the need for IPv6:

- **IPv4 address depletion:** The growing number of applications and global users are fueling the demand for IP addresses. The number of devices that are "always on," such as smartphones, Internet appliances, connected automobiles, integrated telephony services, media centers, and so on, are also increasing. IPv4 provides 4.2 billion (4.294 $\times 10^9$) addresses. In today's global and mobile world, it is only a matter of time before IPv4 addresses are exhausted. Although the primary reason for IPv4 address exhaustion is the insufficient capacity of the original Internet infrastructure, new business drivers including globalization, the explosion of mobile devices, virtualization, and mergers and acquisitions have pushed the IPv4 technology to a limit where we need to evaluate new technologies like IPv6 to further extend the life of the Internet.

- **Globalization:** The network today enables all enterprise business transactions. As enterprises move into emerging markets to expand their business, the network needs to grow, and more IP addresses need to be allocated.

- **Mobile devices:** Because the cost of embedding substantial computing power into handheld devices dropped, mobile phones have become viable Internet hosts and increase the need for addressing.

- **Inefficient address use:** Organizations that obtained IP addresses in the 1980s and early 90s were often allocated far more addresses than they actually required. For example, large companies or universities were assigned class A address blocks with more than 16 million IPv4 addresses each. Some of these allocations were never used, and some of the organizations that received them have diminished in size, whereas other organizations then left out of these large address block assignments have expanded.

- **Virtualization:** A physical system can now host many virtual systems. Each of these virtual systems might require one or multiple IP addresses. One example is with Virtual Desktop Infrastructure (VDI) and the deployment of Hosted Virtual Desktops (HVD).

- **Mergers and acquisitions (M&A):** When one company acquires or merges with another, this often causes a conflict or "collision" in the RFC 1918 IPv4 private addressing scheme. For example, one company might run a 10.x.x.x address space, and the company it acquires might also use this same address space (as seen in Figure 1-2). Many companies deploy a NAT overlap pool for a period of time, where both companies communicate with each other over a nonoverlapping address space such as 172.16.x.x. This enables the hosts at both companies to communicate until one of the sites is readdressed.

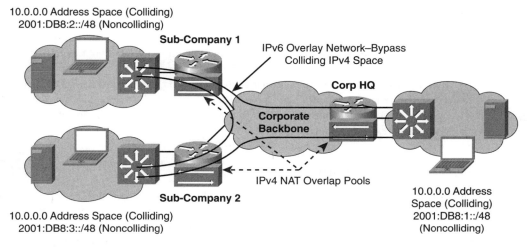

10.0.0.0 Address Space (Colliding)
2001:DB8:2::/48 (Noncolliding)

Sub-Company 1

IPv6 Overlay Network–Bypass
Colliding IPv4 Space

Corp HQ

Corporate Backbone

IPv4 NAT Overlap Pools

Sub-Company 2

10.0.0.0 Address Space (Colliding)
2001:DB8:3::/48 (Noncolliding)

10.0.0.0 Address Space (Colliding)
2001:DB8:1::/48 (Noncolliding)

Figure 1-2 *IPv6 Overlay Model - Resolving M&A Address Collision*

IPv6 is used in this scenario to help ease the M&A burden of colliding address spaces by the deployment of an "overlay" network using IPv6, where critical systems and hosts are enabled for IPv6 operation and communicate with each other over this overlay network. This enables the rapid connection of hosts while buying time for the IT staff to either readdress one company's IPv4 network or to better deploy a dual-stack IPv6 network at both companies.

Government IT Strategy

National IT strategies and government mandates across the globe have caused many enterprises and service providers to implement IPv6 to better support these government agencies (that is, private-sector companies working with government agencies). One example of how a government mandate influences the private sector to deploy IPv6 is when multiple U.S.-based defense contractors rapidly started their planning and deployment of IPv6 to support the U.S. federal IPv6 mandate of June 30, 2008. Many of these companies not only peer with federal agency networks but also provide IP-enabled services and products that would one day require IPv6.

Infrastructure Evolution

The underlying infrastructure for the Internet, and emerging developments in verticals such as energy management, power distribution, and other utility advancements, have matured and grown in size to the point of applying pressure to existing technologies, products, and IPv4. The evolution of technologies in SmartGrid, broadband cable, and mobile operators now require more and more devices to connect to the Internet. Regardless of the use case or technology, all these maturing technologies and use cases either already or soon will depend on IP as their means of communication. IPv4 cannot support these demands, and IPv6 is the way forward for each of these areas of development.

Operating System Support

All widely deployed operating systems support IPv6 by default. These operating systems enable IPv6 addresses by default, thereby accelerating the adoption of IPv6 in enterprises. Key operating systems include Microsoft Windows 7, Server 2008, Apple Mac OS X, and Linux. Many enterprises are finding that IPv6 is used on their networks without their knowledge because of the default preference of IPv6 over IPv4. IT staff realize that they must understand and implement IPv6 in a managed way to control the behavior of IPv6, but also to embrace the capabilities of IPv6.

Summary of Benefits of IPv6

Market drivers or initiatives that often occur externally to the enterprise are at times forced upon an enterprise from the industry they are in or by other external forces (for example, Internet IPv4 address exhaustion), whereas others are beneficial to the enterprise based on business or technical advantages. Table 1-1 summarizes a few of the many benefits for an enterprise to deploy IPv6. Several of these have been talked about in this chapter already, and many will be expanded upon throughout this book.

Commonly Asked Questions About IPv6

IPv6 has been on the way for more than 10 years now, yet for much of the world, it has been irrelevant until recently. Now, as the shortage of IPv4 addresses begins to become obvious to even the most hardened skeptic, awareness and interest are growing.

The following sections address some commonly asked questions or myths that have been created over time with respect to IPv6.

Does My Enterprise Need IPv6 for Business Growth?

This is the most commonly asked question, especially because most organizations continue to connect to the Internet without IPv6 today. There are three key reasons why organizations might need IPv6:

■   Need for a larger address space (beyond IPv4) for business continuity and growing globally.

■   IPv6 is also a generator of new opportunities and a platform for innovation. There are still classes of network applications that aren't possible with IPv4—for example, vehicle-mounted telemetry, which might involve millions of networked sensors on cars.

■   IPv6 is on by default in operating systems like Windows 7 and Linux.

Growth countries like India and China, with huge populations and burgeoning technical competence, will almost certainly move to IPv6 directly. Enterprises that want to be active in those markets but do not use IPv6 will be at a competitive disadvantage.

Table 1-1   *Benefits of IPv6*

Technical Benefits of IPv6	Details
Abundance of IP addresses	This is the most significant benefit that IPv6 provides over IPv4. An IPv6 address is made up of 128-bit values instead of the traditional 32 bits in IPv4, thereby providing approxunately 340 trillion trillion trillion globally routable addresses.
Simpler address deployment	IP address assignment is required by any host looking to communicate with network resources. This IP address has traditionally been assigned manually or obtained through DHCP. In addition to manual and DHCP address assignment, IPv6 inherently enables autoconfiguration of addressing through Stateless Address Autoconfiguration (SLAAC), which can make the deployment of IP-enabled endpoints faster and more simplistic. SLAAC is commonly used for configuring devices that do not need end-user access. These devices include network sensors on cars, telemetry devices, manufacturing equipment, and so on.
	For user-connected hosts including desktops and servers, the lack of DNS information in the router advertisement limits the deployment of SLAAC. The IETF community has put together an experimental draft (RFC 5006) that extends the router advertisement messages (RA messages) to include DNS information. There is also active engagement in the standards body to standardize RA extensions to not only include DNS server information but also to include NTP, BOOTP, and vendor-specific DHCP options.
	Depending on the host operating system implementation, when an IPv6 network adapter is activated, it assigns itself an IP address based on a well-known prefix and its own MAC address. The new host uses its automatic configuration mechanism to derive its own address from the information made available by the neighboring routers, relying on a protocol called the neighbor discovery (ND) protocol. This method does not require any intervention on the administrator's part, and there is no need to maintain a central server for address allocation—an additional advantage over IPv4, where automatic address allocation requires a DHCP server.
End-to-end network connectivity integrity	With IPv4 NAT, a single address masks thousands of non-routable addresses, making end-to-end integrity unachievable. With the larger address space available with IPv6, the need for Network Address Translation devices is effectively eliminated.

Table 1-1   *Benefits of IPv6*

Technical Benefits of IPv6	Details
Opportunity for enhanced security capabilities compared to IPv4	Although rarely deployed today, IPv6 has built-in security capabilities with built-in IPsec support, which can enable end-to-end control packet (routing adjacencies, neighbor discovery) encryption between two or more hosts. For data plane encryption of IPv6 flows, it relies on existing IPv4 mechanisms like IPsec.
Improved attribute extension headers for security, QoS, and encryption	IPv6 has extension attribute headers that are not part of the main packet header. These extension headers, with their own unique packet structures, help provide encryption, mobility, optimized routing, and more. When needed, these headers are inserted between the basic IPv6 header and the payload. The basic IPv6 header includes an indication as to the presence of extension headers through the Next Header field. This vastly speeds the router packet-forwarding rates and improves efficiency.
Improved mobility	Mobile IP (MIP) was developed to ensure that the original gateway is made aware when a host moves from one network segment to another. Originally with MIP (IPv4 based), all the traffic to and from the mobile device needs to go back to the original gateway (home gateway); this is called "triangular routing."
	MIP has been extended in IPv6 to overcome this inefficient triangulation. In MIPv6, a foreign correspondent server is continuously updated as to the network the device is on and which gateway to use to reach the traveling device. The bulk of the packets flow directly between the mobile device and its communicators, and not through the home address. This process is known as *direct routing*. This reduces cost and vastly improves performance and reliability.
Improved flow resource allocation with flow labels	All the Differentiated Services (DiffServ) and Integrated Services (IntServ) quality of service (QoS) attributes from IPv4 are preserved in IPv6. In addition, IPv6 also has a 20-byte Flow Label field that can be used by the end application to provide resource allocation for a particular application or flow type. Even though the standards bodies have defined flow labels in IPv6, not many enterprise applications tend to leverage this capability.

Will IPv6 Completely Replace IPv4?

IPv6 and IPv4 will continue to operate for a long time before the entire infrastructure is moved to IPv6 only. Enterprises and service providers have made significant investments in IPv4 and are well versed with the IPv4 technology.

As IPv6 adoption grows, enterprises need to invest in solutions that enable their legacy IPv4 domains to seamlessly and effectively communicate with IPv6 domains, thereby providing better return on investment. In summary, enterprises looking to adopt IPv6 do not need to discard their IPv4 infrastructure but instead should leverage transition technologies to enable them to coexist.

Is IPv6 More Complicated and Difficult to Manage and Deploy Compared to IPv4?

The larger IP address space provided by IPv6 has created a perception for network architects and administrators that IPv6 is more complicated compared to IPv4; this is not true. The vast address space equips architects to no longer reconfigure their limited address space, making network designs much easier.

All ancillary protocols like DNS continue to work pretty much the same for IPv4 and IPv6. In addition, IPv6 has better autoconfiguration and multicast capabilities (with embedded rendezvous point) that are simpler in implementation compared to IPv4.

There are some new ancillary protocols, such as multicast listener discovery and neighbor discovery, but for the most part, these replace similar mechanisms in IPv4.

Other than IPv6 addressing being in hexadecimal format, it is easier to perform address allocation planning and deployment because the focus is no longer on the number of hosts, but rather on the number of links or "subnets" allocated out of the address block. In many ways, IPv6 is just IP with a higher version number. Similar to IPv4, the IPv6 addressing plan would still need to be designed to ensure that there are natural points of address summarization in the network.

For the entire IT department (including network, computing, storage architects and administrators, application developers, and so on) to leverage IPv6 capabilities, an investment is needed to train them on this upcoming technology.

Does IPv6 continue to allow my enterprise network to be multihomed to several service providers?

Prior to 2007, IPv6 address allocation policies were strictly hierarchical and allowed only enterprises to obtain a network address from a single service provider to avoid overlapping the global routing table.

This has changed since 2007, where enterprises can now get provider-independent (PI) allocations similar to that of IPv4. When an organization applies for PI space, it can obtain IPv6 address space that is not tied to any provider.

By getting provider-independent allocations, enterprises can continue to build redundant, reliable solutions similar to their existing IPv4 designs.

However, many new elements are in development and policy changes are being discussed in the industry that can impact how multihoming is done with IPv6. Today there are unanswered questions related to this topic, and the reader should watch the standards bodies and contact their service providers as time goes on to stay updated on these changes.

Is quality of service better with IPv6?

The only QoS mechanisms built into IPv6 are a few header fields that are supposed to be used to distinguish packets belonging to various classes of traffic and to identify related packets as a "flow." The intention is that these header fields should enable devices such as routers to identify flows and types of traffic and do fast lookups on them. In practice, the use of these header elements is entirely optional, which means that the vast majority of devices don't bother with anything other than the bare minimum support required.

However, IPv4 has similar header elements, intended to be used in similar ways, so the claim that IPv6 QoS is better than that in IPv4 is tenuous.

Is IPv6 automatically more secure than IPv4?

It would be more accurate to say that IPv6 is no less or no more secure than IPv4; it is just different. The main security-related mechanism incorporated into the IPv6 architecture is IPsec. Any RFC-based, standards-compliant implementation of IPv6 must support IPsec; however, there is no requirement that the functionality be enabled or used. This has led to the misconception that IPv6 is automatically more secure than IPv4. Instead, it still requires careful implementation and a well-educated system and network staff.

Does the lack of NAT support in IPv6 reduce security?

This is mostly a myth because NAT increases security. NAT exists to overcome a shortage of IPv4 addresses, and because IPv6 has no such shortage, IPv6 networks do not require NAT. To those who see NAT as security, this appears to mean a reduction in the security of IPv6. However, NAT does not offer any meaningful security. The mind-set of "security through obscurity" is mostly an outdated concept because the vast majority of attacks do not occur through directly routable IP-based methods from the Internet into the inside enterprise but rather through Layers 4–7 attacks. IPv6 was designed with the intention of making NAT unnecessary, and RFC 4864 outlines the concept of Local Network Protection (LNP) using IPv6; this provides the same or better security benefits than NAT.

IPv6 in the IETF

Since 1995, the IETF has actively worked on developing IPv6-related IETF drafts and RFCs in various working groups to include the following:

- Applications area

- Internet area

- Operations and management area

- Real-time applications and infrastructure area

- Routing area

- Security area

- Transport area

Some of the most active areas for IPv6 standardization have occurred in the Internet, operations and management, and transport areas. These areas have been and many still are quite active in the development of standards around addressing, deployment, management, transition, and security of IPv6. It is critical for implementations of IPv6 and its associated architectural components to be based on standards to ensure interoperability between vendors.

The IETF drafts and RFCs are numerous and change or are updated frequently. Research, read, and understand what is happening in the IETF and other standards organizations to be prepared for changes related to IPv6. You an find more information at http://www.ietf.org.

In addition to the IETF, the IPv6 Forum has also developed an IPv6 Ready logo program that certifies IT infrastructure (networking, computing, and storage) with respect to IPv6 conformance and interoperability testing. The key idea of this program is to increase user confidence by demonstrating that IPv6 is available now and is ready to be used. The IPv6 Ready Logo Committee defines conformance and interoperability test specifications to enable different vendors to certify their products toward IPv6 readiness. Additional details of the IPv6 Ready logo and certified products can be found at http://www.ipv6ready.org.

Enterprise IPv6 Deployment Status

With more than 15 years of standards body representation and 10 years of development, IPv6 is now adopted by many large service providers and enterprises. Today, IPv6 is a robust and mature protocol that enables revitalization and innovation of new applications.

IPv6 deployment is happening across many vertical industries, as shown in Table 1-2.

Table 1-2   *IPv6 Deployment Across Vertical Markets*

Vertical Market	Examples
Higher education and research	Building sensors Media services Collaboration Mobility
Manufacturing	Embedded devices Industrial Ethernet IP-enabled components
Government (federal/public sector)	Department of Defense Warfighter Information Network-Tactical (WIN-T) Future Combat System (FCS) Joint Tactical Radio System (JTRS) Global Information Grid Bandwidth Expansion (GIG-BE)
Transportation	Telematics Traffic control Hotspots Transit services
Finance	Merger & acquisition - overlay networks
Healthcare	Home care Wireless asset tracking Imaging Mobility
Consumer	Set-top boxes Internet gaming Appliances Voice/video Security monitoring
Utilities	SmartGrid IP Services over Powerline

Originally, IPv6 was seen only in the research and vendor areas, where the first implementations of IPv6 were worked out. Since then, IPv6 deployment has grown into every vertical, some with specific use cases, such as sensor networks, robotic arms, environment controls, and sensors, whereas other use cases are similar in nature regardless of the vertical.

Most enterprises fall into one of three categories, as shown in Figure 1-3.

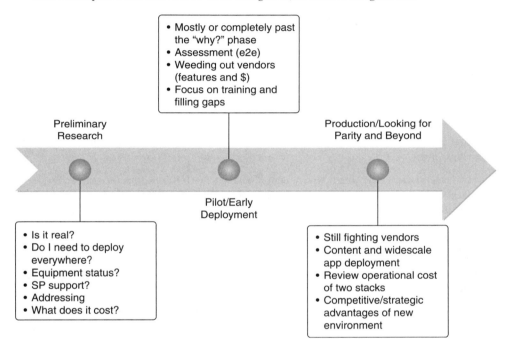

Figure 1-3 *Enterprise Adoption Categories*

The first category is often called the preliminary research phase. Here the enterprise is researching whether IPv6 is real, the advantages of IPv6, how it fits into its environment, preliminary product gaps, and costs of deploying. This phase involves educating the company leadership about the relevance of IPv6 to meet its evolving business needs through online details. For the technical IT group, the research phase involves understanding the IPv6 protocol and its dependencies on its existing infrastructure achieved through working labs, classroom education, and labwork. Many enterprises in this phase are not sure whether IPv6 is relevant to them.

The second category is the pilot/early deployment phase, where most of the "why" has been answered or at least a decision has been made to move forward with IPv6 deployment regardless of a clear business justification for it. Often many consider IPv6 deployment without a clear business case as a "getting our house ready for an unknown guest" undertaking. Many who lived though the early VoIP and IP telephony days recall how unprepared they were for the massive paradigm shift brought on by these technologies and that they did not have their networks enabled for high availability (at least high enough for voice) and QoS. Investing in IPv6 through time, energy, and budget before having a defined business case is often an endeavor in preparing for the unknown or, arguably, the evitable. More serious assessments are made, training has begun, and serious conversations with non-IPv6-compliant product vendors are happening in this phase.

Finally, the third category is the production phase, where the enterprise is looking for a high-quality production IPv6 deployment. At this point, it is moving most, if not all, IT elements to IPv6, and the mind-set is parity with what the enterprise has with IPv4 or is at least good enough to not interfere with the business. The business might still be dealing with noncompliant products or vendors, but most of that has been dealt with by getting rid of those without a strong road map. It is down to doing business as usual but also focusing on using IPv6-enabled applications and services as a competitive advantage.

Throughout the entire process, constant education happens on both the technical and business side, and at each step of the process, there must be continuous buy-in from all groups involved.

Historically there have been deployment challenges with IPv6 adoption, especially because enterprises would not deploy given that there were only a small subset of products supporting IPv6 and not many service providers had IPv6 deployed at their peering points. The service providers would not support it because no enterprises were asking for it, or there were too few products supporting it. Vendors were not building products to support it because there were no enterprises or service providers asking for it. It was and in some cases still is an ugly, vicious circle that can only be broken by innovators and leaders who step out first.

From a content provider perspective, one of the leaders and best deployments for IPv6 is Google, which has launched its "trusted adopter" program: http://www.google.com/ipv6. Other content providers and industry-leading websites are already IPv6-enabled for those hosts who support reaching them through IPv6. Some sites include Google (search and Gmail), YouTube, Netflix, Comcast, and Facebook.

Contrary to trade magazines, blogs, vendors, and skeptics, enterprises have already and are currently deploying IPv6. Many companies do not advertise that they are deploying IPv6, leading to the misconception that deployments are not occurring. Many companies are secretive about IPv6 deployment for security reasons (not knowing what all the attack vectors are and not having robust enough security measures in place), others for financial reasons. The remaining chapters in this book discuss these concerns and outline important deployment considerations.

Summary

IPv6 is the next-generation protocol for the Internet that overcomes the address limitations of IPv4 and removes or reduces the cases for NAT/PAT as they are used today. The key market driver for IPv6 is the abundance of IP addresses. This enables business continuity and opens the door for new applications across the Internet.

The IETF and other organizations continue to evaluate solutions and generate drafts and RFCs to ensure the interoperability of IPv6-enabled hosts.

The majority of service providers and content providers, and many enterprises, are planning, deploying, or have deployed IPv6 within their network infrastructure to future-proof them for new applications.

This book focuses on providing enterprises and service providers with a design framework to assist them in moving to IPv6 through a smooth transition with existing transition technologies and describes ways of integrating IPv6 into their existing infrastructures.

Additional References

Many notes and disclaimers in this chapter discuss the need to fully understand the technology and protocol aspects of IPv6. There are many design considerations associated with the implementation of IPv6 that include security, QoS, availability, management, IT training, and application support.

The following references are a few of the many that provide more details on IPv6, Cisco design recommendations, products and solutions, and industry activity:

Aoun, C. and E. Davies. RFC 4966, "Reasons to Move the Network Address Translator - Protocol Translator (NAT-PT) to Historic Status." http://www.rfc-editor.org/rfc/rfc4966.txt.

Cerf, Vinton G. "A Decade of Internet Evolution." http://bit.ly/cNzjga.

Curran, J. RFC 5211, "An Internet Transition Plan." http://www.rfc-editor.org/rfc/rfc5211.txt.

IANA: http://www.iana.org.

ICANN: http://www.icann.org.

IETF: http://www.ietf.org.

IETF Behavior Engineering for Hindrance Avoidance (behave) drafts: https://datatracker.ietf.org/wg/behave.

IPv6 address report: http://www.potaroo.net/tools/ipv4.

Jeong, J., S. Park, L. Beloeil, and S. Madanapalli. RFC 5006, "IPv6 Router Advertisement Option for DNS Configuration." http://www.rfc-editor.org/rfc/rfc5006.txt.

Rekhter, Y., B. Moskowitz, D. Karrenberg, J. de Groot, and E. Lear. RFC 1918, "Address Allocation for Private Internets." http://www.rfc-editor.org/rfc/rfc1918.txt.

Van de Velde, Hain, Droms, Carpenter, and Klein. RFC 4864, "Local Network Protection for IPv6." http://www.rfc-editor.org/rfc/rfc4864.txt

Chapter 2

Hierarchical Network Design

This chapter covers the following subjects:

- **Network design principles:** This section reviews the three pillars needed to design enterprise networks: modularity, hierarchy, and resiliency. The subsequent sections extend these concepts by segmenting the enterprise network into multiple blocks. The subsequent sections go into details of each of these modules.

- **Enterprise core network design:** This section reviews the need for a core layer and the design considerations for this layer.

- **Enterprise campus network design:** This section reviews different design options in the campus network for the access-distribution blocks.

- **Enterprise network services design:** This section outlines the need for network services as enterprises look into going from a native IPv4 deployment to a dual-stack IPv4/IPv6 design.

- **Enterprise data center network design:** This section reviews the network designs used in a data center network and the features configured in each layer. This section examines the designs used in a storage-area network.

- **Enterprise edge network design:** This section discusses the network design and services of the enterprise edge network, which include head-office WAN aggregation, Internet access, and branch network.

Early computer networks used a flat topology in which devices were added when and where required. These flat network topologies were easier to design, implement, and maintain as long as the number of network devices were small. Adding more and more hosts to this network raised significant challenges in terms of troubleshooting network problems for lack of fault isolation. These flat networks also posed design challenges when it came to connecting a large number of hosts.

Given the challenges with flat networks, enterprises went through iterations of network designs that would not only help them scale as their organizations grew but also provide fault domain isolation. As a result, the network designs became more modular, hierarchical, and resilient. These three concepts hence became the foundation of any good network design.

This chapter outlines the three pillars of a good network design—modularity, hierarchy, and resiliency—and extends these concepts to segment the enterprise network into simpler multiple building blocks, including enterprise core, campus, network services, data center, and edge (Internet, remote Access, WAN, and branch). The chapter also describes design considerations for each of these building blocks, enabling network designers and architects to carefully review the various design options and extend these design principles in their own enterprise network designs. The chapter also provides the foundation for the various network services discussed in Chapter 4, "Network Services."

Network Design Principles

Business applications have evolved over the years from the simplest form of client/server to more user interactive. These business applications now leverage technologies such as voice, video, and wireless. The adoption of collaborative, interactive applications has created a significant shift in the perception and the requirements of the enterprise network. The evolving business landscape now requires the enterprise network to provide the following:

- **User experience for collaboration applications:** The use of collaboration, real-time communication, single-sign-on, and mobility applications is growing, with a positive and engaging user experience being one of the top priorities.

- **Supporting diverse end-user device types:** Enterprises have seen an increased adoption of wireless devices (including Wi-Fi-enabled laptops and smartphones) and thin-client terminals in addition to the traditional personal computers (PC) and IP phones.

- **Network resiliency and improved convergence times:** Business operations that adjust to globalization and continue to operate 24 hours a day, 365 days a year require a resilient network infrastructure that ensures access to business applications during a network upgrade or failure.

- **Pervasive security:** Over the years, security threats have grown in number and complexity, requiring the network security to evolve and support distributed and dynamic application environments. The need for flexible partner and guest access is increasing as business partnerships evolve.

The enterprise network is the infrastructure that interconnects end users and devices. It can span a single floor in a building, multiple floors in a building, or multiple buildings spread across a geographic area. The network is a high-speed fabric that provides basic connectivity and offers a resilient, secure, easy-to-manage network services fabric needed to run business-critical applications. The enterprise network is designed keeping three principles in mind:

- Modularity
- Hierarchy
- Resiliency

The following sections describe each principle in detail.

Modularity

Modularity is one of the fundamental principles of a structured network that defines the enterprise network as an assembly of multiple building blocks designed separately using a systematic approach and applying hierarchy and redundancy where appropriate.

Increased modularity in a network design has self-contained network blocks to support a specific function or set of functions. Therefore, an outage, upgrade, or any change in one module will be limited to its own boundaries. With a modular network design, network services can be selected on a per-module basis but would need to be validated as part of the overall network design. As shown in Figure 2-1, the enterprise network consists of the following modules:

- **Enterprise core:** The enterprise core module is the network backbone that interconnects the campus, data center, edge, and network services modules. Without the core, all other modules would be isolated, requiring that the core of the network provide nonstop 24x7x365 service. The core layer should be designed to have appropriate levels of redundancy and fault tolerance to ensure immediate data-flow recovery in the event of network component failure. Along with fault tolerance, the network core design should also provide fast convergence and load balancing to make optimum use of all the network elements within the core.

- **Enterprise campus:** The campus module contains all network elements for independent operation, providing network connectivity between the end users, devices, and the enterprise core. This module can be further broken into multiple layers based on the required functionality and services. An enterprise can also have more than one campus block within the same geographical location, depending on the number of users within the location.

- **Enterprise data center:** The data center module consists of three key elements: compute (servers), network (Ethernet switches), and storage (Fibre Channel) devices. The data center module has large compute devices in the form of server farms that host business applications. These server farms typically connect to both the Ethernet switching infrastructure and to the Fibre Channel storage network, although the use of a unified storage connection technology such as Fibre Channel over Ethernet (FCoE) is rapidly growing in popularity. The data center network enables users to connect to the business applications hosted on the server farms. The storage network can include Fibre Channel switches that interconnect Fibre Channel hosts, iSCSI devices to the server farms, and/or products that support the Cisco Unified Fabric solution, which supports collapsing Fibre Channel and Ethernet onto the same infrastructure.

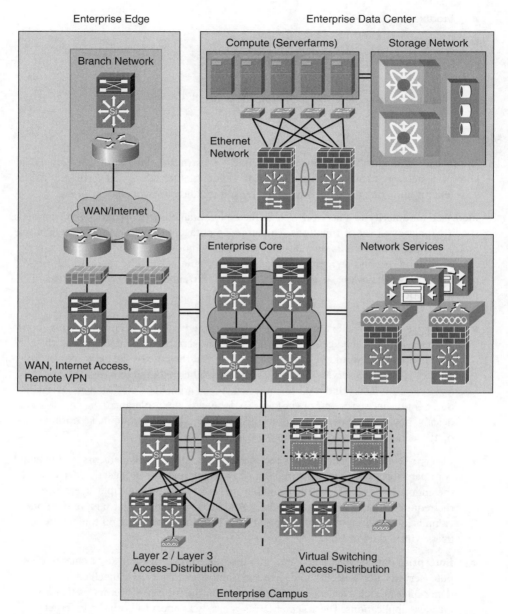

Figure 2-1   *Modular Network Design Example*

- **Enterprise edge:** The enterprise edge module includes the Internet, remote access VPN, and WAN modules that connect the enterprise to a service provider network. The enterprise edge contains all the network elements for efficient and secure communications between the enterprise campus and remote locations, business partners, mobile users, and the Internet. The edge module aggregates the connectivity from various remote sites, filters traffic, and routes the traffic into the enterprise campus.

■ **Network services:** The network services module is relatively a new concept in the enterprise network. The network services module includes both IPv4 and IPv6 services required for unified communication, mobility, and user authentication. Most enterprises typically do not have a dedicated network services block defined, but it is integrated well within the data center. However, the network service module does provide a significant advantage to enterprises deploying IPv6 but cannot fully deploy a dual-stack IPv4/IPv6 network on day one. Those enterprises need to temporarily build and overlay the network as an interim solution to interconnect IPv6 hosts over a non-IPv6-enabled network. By consolidating these services within a single network services module, architects would not require running multiple tunnels across the entire network during the migration to dual-stack.

The smaller building blocks of a modular network design are easy to manage and provide the following benefits:

■ **Ease of management:** With a modular network design, each module can be managed separately, and specific tools can be used to manage all network entities within each module. By having self-contained functionalities in each module, the manageability of each module is contained.

■ **Fault isolation and troubleshooting:** These functional modules provide boundaries that can be aligned with functional or organizational support structures.

■ **Improved flexibility:** Modularity facilitates changes as network devices are required for upgrade. The cost of making an upgrade is contained to a small subset of devices or a user segment requiring the enhanced functionality.

■ **Reduced operational expenses (OpEx):** The modules break down the network into smaller components that are simpler and easier to understand. Simplicity helps expedite the design implementation and reduces training for network operations. Easy validation of network designs can be done because of clear, discrete functionality at every layer.

■ **Simplified product selection:** Modularity enables you to map the purchase of the appropriate network device to the appropriate network layer, thereby avoiding the need to spend capital on unnecessary features.

Because each module is independent of each other, an outage, upgrade, or any change in one module will be limited to its own boundaries.

Hierarchy

Hierarchy is one of the key pillars for a good network design. Each module described in the previous section requires having hierarchy and resiliency built into the network design. For the business environment and underlying communication to continue to evolve, the network designs must be adaptive enough to roll out new end devices and applications, or increase capacity without going through a major forklift upgrade. This network design flexibility has evolved from the traditional flat networks to a hierarchical topology with discrete layers, where each layer has a specific role that enables the network architect to choose the right platform and enables the required functionalities for that layer. These layers have functional characteristics and provide boundaries to failure domains. Each layer has unique functions and separate modules for providing network services.

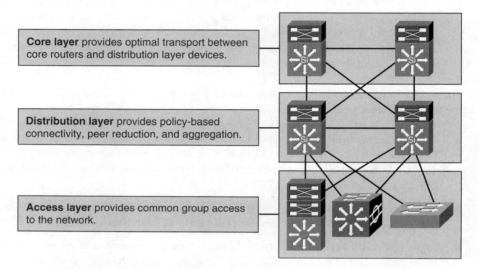

Figure 2-2 *Hierarchical Network Design*

A typical enterprise campus has three layers (as shown in Figure 2-2):

- **The core layer** provides optimal transport between sites and interconnects the different distribution layer resources along with providing connectivity to the data center resources and Internet access through the edge network.

- **The distribution layer** connects network services to the access layer and implements policies regarding security, traffic loading, and routing.

- **The access layer** provides connectivity to the end users and devices.

A hierarchical network design provides a number of advantages, even though the costs of having such a design can be expensive compared to the flat network topologies. These advantages augment the functionality of the network and appropriateness of the model to address network design goals. Key benefits of the hierarchical network design include

- **Scalability:** By having a hierarchical network design, it is easier for the network architects to replicate each of the modules as the enterprise network grows. As shown in the previous models, scalability is frequently limited in network designs that do not use the three-tier model. Although there might still be limitations in the hierarchical model, the separation of functions within the network provides natural expansion points without significantly impacting other portions of the network.

- **Flexibility:** The structured hierarchical design inherently provides a high degree of flexibility because it enables staged or gradual changes to each module in the network independently of the other modules. Changes in core transport can be made independently of the distribution layer. Changes in the design or capacity of the distribution layer can be implemented in a phased or incremental manner. Additionally, as a part of the overall hierarchical design, the introduction of the services block module into the architecture is specifically intended to address the need to implement services in a controlled fashion. Key areas to consider for a hierarchical network design include the following:

    - **Control plane flexibility:** Enable migration between Layer 2 (Spanning Tree) and Layer 3 (routing) protocols.

    - **Forwarding plane flexibility:** The capability to support the introduction and use of IPv6 as a parallel requirement alongside IPv4.

    - **User group flexibility:** Enable network access and associated services within the network to support administration involving acquisition, partnering, or outsourcing of business functions.

    - **Traffic management and control flexibility:** Collaborative applications evolution requires campus designs to provide a simplified mechanism for flow monitoring and troubleshooting.

    - **Flexible security architecture:** The security architecture should adapt to the changing traffic patterns being driven by new applications deployed.

- **Easier implementation:** As the hierarchical model divides the network into logical and physical sections, it is easier for architects to deploy network entities without disrupting the existing infrastructure. For example, in a campus design, new access switches can be deployed and connected to the distribution without any network disruption to the existing access switches and users connected to those access switches.

- **Easier troubleshooting:** It is easier to troubleshoot network issues in a hierarchical network design given that the faults are isolated within a single domain. For example, a routing loop at the distribution block would impact only the connected access switches and not other distribution blocks.

- **Ease of manageability and capacity planning:** Capacity planning is generally easier in the hierarchical model because the need for capacity usually increases as data moves toward the core. Hierarchically designed networks are usually easier to manage because of these other benefits. Predictable data flows, scalability, independent implementations, and simpler troubleshooting all simplify the management of the network.

The enterprise campus and data center sections discuss the three layers of the hierarchical model in more detail.

Resiliency

In addition to building modular and hierarchical network designs, it is important for network architects to consider resiliency along every step of the network design. Integrating resiliency to avoid single points of failure is key for ensuring high availability and business continuity. The coordinated use of resiliency capabilities within the switch, link, and network designs is required across all the different modules and layers that have been discussed previously. For example, enabling redundant supervisors in the access layer can ensure business continuity even when the active supervisor fails. This helps ensure that there is no impact to network convergence on the distribution layer (for both Layer 2 and routed access deployments).

Adding resiliency to the design might require the use of new features, but it is often just a matter of how you choose to implement your hierarchy and how you configure the basic Layer 2 and Layer 3 topologies.

The following sections now take the three guiding principles—modularity, hierarchy, and resiliency—to discuss network designs for each of the different modules: enterprise core, enterprise campus, enterprise network services, enterprise data center, and enterprise edge (head office WAN, Internet access, and branch network).

Enterprise Core Network Design

The *core layer* is the simplest yet the most critical layer. This layer is the backbone of the network. The core needs to be highly reliable and switch high traffic loads as fast as possible. It provides a limited set of services and is highly available using redundant devices and configurations to ensure that software upgrades or hardware changes can be made without disrupting the applications. The core provides a Layer 3 routing module for all traffic in and out of the enterprise network. Routing is critical for the data center core and would need to be configured using built-in robust security mechanism to avoid incorrect neighbor peering, injection of incorrect routes, and routing loops. To prevent this problem, the core layer must include the following:

- Route peer authentication
- Route filtering
- Log neighbor changes
- Antispoofing: Unicast RPF (uRPF) and rate limiting

Table 2-1 shows some of the do's and don'ts that can be used while designing the core of the network.

Table 2-1   *Do's and Don'ts of Core Layer Designs*

Do	Don't
Design the core for high reliability. Consider using 10 GigE and Gigabit Ethernet technologies in port-channel configurations to facilitate high speeds and redundancy.	Use software-based features because they can potentially slow down traffic.
Design core layer devices with little latency.	Support workgroup access in the core layer.
Use routing protocols with low convergence time.	Consider hardware/software upgrades to improve performance when adding new core nodes.

Enterprise Campus Network Design

The campus network architecture is based on the use of two basic blocks or modules connected through the core of the network:

- Distribution layer

- Access layer

The following sections describe both layers in detail.

Distribution Layer

The distribution layer interconnects the access layer switches to the core of the network. A large enterprise campus network can have one or more distribution switches, depending on the number of downstream access layer switches connected to it. Best practices recommend not going beyond 20 access layer switches connected to a single distribution layer. This is mostly limited by the control plane handling of the distribution layer, whether it is a Layer 2 or a routed access design. There are currently three basic design choices for configuring the distribution layer:

- Layer 2 access design

- Routed access design

- Virtual switch design

Layer 2 Access Design

The Layer 2 access is the traditional campus access-distribution design where all the access switches are configured to run in Layer 2 forwarding mode, and the distribution switches act as a demarcation for Layer 2 and Layer 3. In this particular design, the distribution layer switches act as the default gateway for the end hosts.

VLAN-based trunks extend the subnets from the distribution switches down to the access layer. A first-hop redundancy protocol, such as Hot Standby Router Protocol (HSRP) or Gateway Load Balancing Protocol (GLBP), is run on the distribution layer switches along with a routing protocol to provide upstream routing to the core of the campus. One version of Spanning Tree and the use of the Spanning Tree hardening features (such as Loopguard, Rootguard, and BPDUGuard) are configured on the access ports and switch-to-switch links as appropriate. Although these technologies and features are critical to a campus deployment, they are independent of IPv6 and are not discussed in detail.

The Layer 2 access design has two basic variations (as shown in Figure 2-3) that primarily differ only in the manner in which VLANs are defined:

- **Looped design:** One-to-many VLANs are configured to span multiple access switches. As a result, each of these spanned VLANs has a Spanning Tree or Layer 2 looped topology.

- **V (or loop-free) design:** This follows the current best practice guidelines for the multitier design and defines unique VLANs for each access switch. The removal of loops in the topology provides a number of benefits, including per-device uplink load balancing with the use of GLBP, a reduced dependence on Spanning Tree to provide network recovery, reduction in the risk of broadcast storms, and the ability to avoid unicast flooding (and similar design challenges associated with nonsymmetrical Layer 2 and Layer 3 forwarding topologies).

Design and configuration details of each of these designs are covered in Chapter 6, "Deploying IPv6 in Campus Networks."

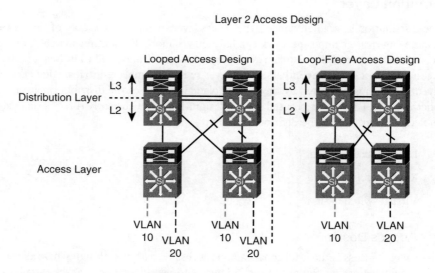

Figure 2-3 *Layer 2 Access Design*

Routed Access Design

An alternative configuration to the traditional multitier distribution block model is one in which the access switch acts as a full Layer 3 routing node (provides both Layer 2 and Layer 3 switching) and the access to distribution Layer 2 uplink trunks is replaced with Layer 3 point-to-point routed links. This alternative configuration, in which the Layer 2/3 demarcation is moved from the distribution switch to the access switch (as shown in Figure 2-4), appears to be a major change to the design, but is actually an extension of the best practice multitier design. Design and configuration details of each of these designs are covered in Chapter 6.

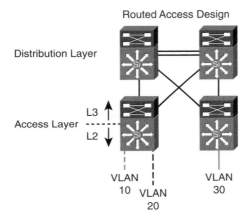

Figure 2-4   *Routed Access Design*

The routed access design has a number of advantages over the multitier design with its use of Layer 2 access to distribution uplinks:

■   It offers common end-to-end troubleshooting tools (such as ping and traceroute), it uses a single control protocol (either Enhanced IGRP [EIGRP] or Open Shortest Path First [OSPF]), and it removes the need for features such as HSRP.

■   Although it is the appropriate design for many environments, it is not suitable for all environments because it requires no VLAN span multiple access switches.

Because routed access designs provide additional advantages, they also pose certain challenges as follows:

■   Implementing routed access design requires careful planning and design to avoid routing loops and requires appropriate route summarization to ensure that the network design can scale as new users and access layer switches are added to the network.

■   With a Layer 2 design, subnets can be easily extended across multiple access layer switches connecting to the same distribution layer. With the routed access design, extending the same subnet across two access switches can lead to overlapping addresses, which can be challenging and require the network designer to carefully implement subnetting and route summarization at the distribution layer.

■ Implementing routed access can be expensive because it might require different hardware and software at each access layer to provide Layer 3 functionalities.

Virtual Switching System Distribution Block

The Virtual Switching System (VSS) distribution block design (as shown in Figure 2-5) is a radical change from the typical Layer 2 or Layer 3 access design. In the past, multiple access switches were connected to two redundant distribution switches, and the configuration of the network control protocols (such as HSRP and 802.1D Spanning Tree) determined the way in which the switches forwarded traffic over each of the uplinks and how the network recovered in the event of a switch or link failure. With the introduction of the virtual switch concept, the distribution switch pair can now be configured to run as a single logical switch.

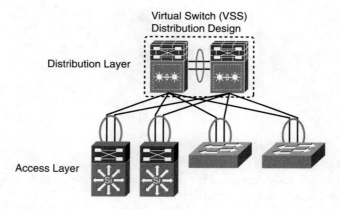

Figure 2-5 *Virtual Switching System Distribution Block Design*

By converting the redundant physical distribution switches into a single logical switch, a significant change is made to the topology of the network. In the other access-distribution block designs, an access switch is configured with two uplinks to two distribution switches and needs a control protocol to determine which of the uplinks to use. In a VSS implementation, the access switch has a single, logical Multichassis EtherChannel (MEC) upstream link connected to a single distribution switch. The VSS architecture is discussed in more detail in Chapter 6.

Comparing Distribution Block Designs

Although each of the three access-distribution block designs provides a viable approach, there are advantages to the virtual switch and routed access designs over the traditional multitier approach. Simpler overall network configuration and operation, per-flow upstream and downstream load balancing, and faster convergence are some of the differences between these newer design options and the traditional multitier approach. Table 2-2 compares the three design options.

Table 2-2 *Comparison of Distributed Block Design Models*

Features	Layer 2 Access Design	Routed Access	Virtual Switch
Access distribution control plane protocols	Spanning Tree (PVST+, Rapid-PVST+ or MST)	EIGRP or OSPF	PAgP, LACP
VLAN spanning access switches	Supported (requires L2 Spanning Tree loops)	No	Supported
Layer 3 boundary	Distribution	Access	Distribution
First-hop redundancy Protocol	HSRP, GLBP, VRRP required	Not required	Not required
Access to distribution per-flow load balancing	No	Yes - Equal Cost Multipath (ECMP)	Yes - MEC
Convergence	900 ms to 50 seconds (dependent on the STP topology and FHRP tuning)	50 to 600 ms	50 to 600 ms

Access Layer

The access layer is the first point of contact or edge of the enterprise network. This layer is the point where end devices attach to access the network. The access layer also serves as the first place where network services can be initiated. PCs, servers, IP phones, wireless access points, cameras, and other PoE/PoE+ devices are examples of a wide variety of devices that can connect to the access layer. Table 2-3 summarizes some services that an access layer switch provides.

Enterprise Network Services Design

The network services module is a relatively new element to the campus design. As campus network planners begin to consider migration to dual-stack IPv4/IPv6 environments, and continue to integrate more sophisticated Unified Communications services, a number of challenges lie ahead. It will be essential to integrate these services into the campus smoothly—while providing the appropriate degree of operational change management and fault isolation. The campus network also needs to continue to maintain a flexible and scalable design. For example, IPv6 services can be deployed through an interim tunnel-based overlay that enables IPv6 devices to tunnel over portions of the campus not yet

IPv6-enabled. Such an interim approach enables a faster introduction of new services without requiring a networkwide, hot cutover. Examples of functions recommended to be located in a services module include

- **Centralized wireless controllers:** These controllers provision and control access points across the entire campus.

- **Centralized IPv6 Intra-Site Automatic Tunnel Addressing Protocol (ISATAP) tunnel termination from the enterprise campus to the network services module:** This creates a tightly controlled overlay tunnel network on top of the existing network. Like all tunneling technologies, running multiple ISATAP tunnels to different segments in the network increases network administration complexity along with making it extremely difficult to manage and troubleshoot.

- **Unified Communications services (Cisco Unified Communications Manager, gateways):** To enable Unified Communications services, enterprises deploy call managers and other voice gateway devices in the services block for centralized management.

- **Policy gateways:** The policy gateways provide user authentication and authorization along with network access control (NAC) functions. Typical policy gateways include authentication, authorization, and accounting (AAA) servers, access control servers (ACS), and NAC profilers.

Table 2-3 *Service and Features Provided by Access Layer Switches*

Service Requirements	Features
Collaboration services	Enabling voice/video applications: Power over Ethernet and QoS marking, policing, queuing Application visibility services: Flexible NetFlow Mobility services: Unified wired/wireless location services Virtualization services: VLAN, VRF-Lite
Automation services	Auto Smartports, Smart CallHome
Security services	Access control: 802.1x and port security Control Plane Policing (CoPP), DHCPv6 Relay, IPv6 Router Guard, IPv6 port access control list (PACL)
Resiliency	Stateful Switchover (SSO), Non-Stop Forwarding (NSF), In Service Software Upgrade (ISSU)
Intelligent network control services	PVST+, Rapid PVST+, EIGRP, OSPF, DTP, PAgP/LACP, UDLD, FlexLink, Portfast, UplinkFast, BackboneFast, LoopGuard, BPDUGuard, RootGuard

Enterprise Data Center Network Design

Data center design is similar to the enterprise campus with a few exceptions, such as a few features and product and performance differences. Other than those, routing is routing and switching is switching. The data center multilayered architecture consists of the following layers:

- **Aggregation layer:** The aggregation layer is the termination point for the access layer and connects the data center network to the enterprise core. In many designs, enterprises consider the core to be also part of the data center, but the design principles still remain the same for the core layer. In the data center, the aggregation layer also serves as a services layer, offering Layer 4 to Layer 7 services including security (firewall), server load balancing (SLB), and monitoring services.

- **Access layer:** The access layer can be a physical access layer using Catalyst and Nexus switches, or it can be virtual access layer by using a hypervisor-based software switch such as the Cisco Nexus 1000v. The access layer connects virtual machines and bare-metal servers to the network. The access layer typically connects to the servers using 10/100/1000 connectivity with uplinks to the distribution at 10 G speeds.

This architecture enables data center modules to be added as the demand and load increase.

Aggregation Layer

The aggregation layer serves as the Layer 3 and Layer 2 boundary for the data center infrastructure. The aggregation layer typically provides 10G connectivity to each access layer switch and to the enterprise core. It acts as an excellent filtering point and first layer of protection for the data center. This layer provides a building block for deploying firewall services for ingress and egress filtering. The Layer 2 and Layer 3 recommendations for the aggregation layer also provide symmetric traffic patterns to support stateful packet filtering.

In these designs, the aggregation layer (highlighted in Table 2-4) also serves as a services layer, providing L4–L7 services including security (firewalls, web application firewall [WAF]), server load balancers (SLB), and monitoring services (network analysis module [NAM]).

Table 2-4   *Layers 4–7 Services in the Aggregation Layer*

Layers 4-7 Services	Functionality
Security	Security is often considered as an afterthought in many designs. In reality, it is easier in the long run if security is considered as part of the core requirements—and not as an add-on. Drivers for security in the data center might change over time because of new application rollouts, compliance requirements, acquisitions, and security breaches. There are three areas of focus for data center security: isolation (VLANs, VRF), policy enforcement, and physical server/virtual machine visibility.
Server load balancing (SLB)	The SLB technology abstracts the resources supporting the service to a single virtual point of contact to ensure performance and resiliency. Abstraction SLB devices mask the server's real IP address and instead provide a single IP for clients to connect over a single or multiple protocols, including HTTP, HTTPS, and FTP.
Web application firewall (WAF)	WAF provides firewall services for web-based applications. It secures and protects web applications from common attacks, such as identity theft, data theft, application disruption, fraud, and targeted attacks. These attacks can include cross-site scripting (XSS) attacks, SQL and command injection, privilege escalation, cross-site request forgeries (CSRF), buffer overflows, cookie tampering, and DoS attacks.
Monitoring	Monitoring services are typically not integrated into the actual data flow but are integrated as passive devices to help with ongoing monitoring of flows and for debugging and troubleshooting purposes. The monitoring services can also be leveraged for capacity planning.

Access Layer

The traditional access layer serves as a connection point for the server farm and application farms. Any communication to and from a particular server/hypervisor-based host or between hosts goes through an access switch and any associated services such as a firewall or a load balancer. There are two deployment models for server access, which are typically deployed separately:

- **End of Row (EoR):** The EoR is an aggregate switch that provides connectivity to multiple racks. The EoR design typically has a single switch that aggregates multiple servers, thereby providing a single point of management.

- **Top of Rack (ToR):** The ToR model has a 1/2RU switch connected within the server rack that connects to the physical servers (both 1 G and 10 G). The ToR switch has 10

G uplinks for upstream connectivity into the aggregation layer switch. Each ToR is an independent switch that needs to be managed separately for software images and configuration.

Security at the access layer is primarily focused on securing Layer 2 flows. Using VLANs to segment server traffic and associating access control lists (ACL) to prevent any undesired communication are best practice recommendations. Additional security mechanisms that can be deployed at the access layer include private VLANs (PVLAN) and port security features, which include IPv4 Dynamic Address Resolution Protocol (ARP) inspection, IPv6 Router Guard, and IPv6 Port Access List (IPv6 PACL). Port security can also be used to lock down a critical server to a specific port.

A virtual access layer refers to the virtual network that resides in the physical servers when configured for virtualization. Server virtualization creates new challenges for security, visibility, and policy enforcement because traffic might not leave the actual physical server and pass through a physical access switch for one virtual machine to communicate with another. Enforcing network policies in this type of environment can be a significant challenge. The goal remains to provide many of the same security services and features used in the traditional access layer in this new virtual access layer.

The virtual access layer resides in and across the physical servers running virtualization software. Virtual networking occurs within these servers to map virtual machine connectivity to that of the physical server.

Data Center Storage Network Design

Storage-area networking (SAN) is used to attach servers to remote computer storage devices such as disk arrays and tape libraries in such a way that they appear to the operating system of the servers to be locally attached devices. The growth of enterprise applications has led to an increased demand of both compute as well as storage space. The SAN offers the following benefits:

- **Application high availability:** Storage is independent of applications and can be accessed through multiple paths.

- **Better application performance:** Processing for data storage is offloaded from servers.

- **Consolidated storage and scalability:** Simpler management, flexibility, and scalability of storage systems.

- **Disaster recovery:** Data can be copied remotely using Fibre Channel over IP (FCIP) features for disaster recovery.

Historically, Fibre Channel has been used as the underlying transport technology for SAN. The Fibre Channel technology is entirely different from Ethernet and is sometimes known as "the network behind the servers." SAN has evolved from the traditional server to storage connections to include switches specially built to transport Fibre Channel Protocol (FCP) commands from one device to another. The switch is also referred to as a "fabric" in the SAN world.

As illustrated in Figure 2-6, the SAN exists independent of the Ethernet LAN. The application clients access the servers through the campus Ethernet network. The servers then use SAN for data I/O.

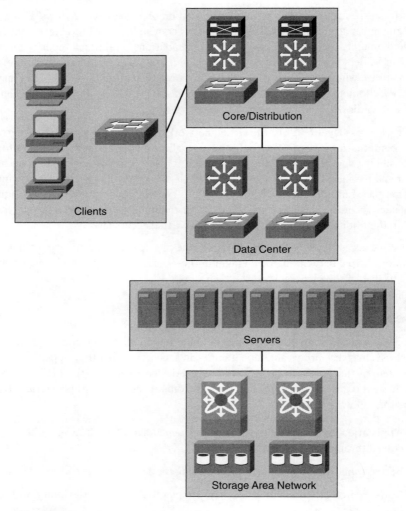

Figure 2-6   *SAN Design*

The SAN design generally fits into two distinct categories:

■   Collapsed core topology

■   Core edge topology

The next sections describe these topologies.

Collapsed Core Topology

In this topology, the host server and storage devices are connected locally on a switch. Multiple switches connect in the fabric using ISLs for interswitch communications.

As the ports are filled on a switch, a new switch is added to the fabric using ISLs. The ISLs by design are used for minimal traffic between the interconnected switches because most of the traffic is local to the switches. As the fabric grows and switches are added, locality of storage is no longer feasible. This situation requires the reevaluation of the ISL bandwidth between switches because they are now more heavily used to host to storage access. Over a period of time, determining ratios for host to storage would be difficult as the fabric grows in this topology.

Figure 2-7 illustrates a collapsed core topology.

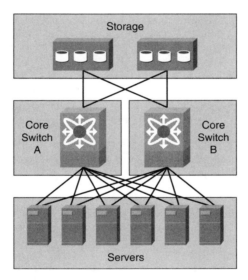

Figure 2-7   *Collapsed Core Topology*

Core Edge Topology

The core edge topology requires two redundant fabrics. Each fabric has a core switch and multiple edge switches. In the core edge architecture, the core switch supports all the storage or target ports in each fabric and ISL connectivity to the edge switches. This topology provides consolidation of storage ports at the core.

In this topology, the hosts connect to edge switches, which connect to the core through ISL trunks. Because storage is consolidated at the core switches in this topology, it can support advanced SAN features on the core switches, which eases management and reduces the complexity of the SAN. This topology also provides a deterministic host-to-storage oversubscription ratio.

Figure 2-8 illustrates core edge topology.

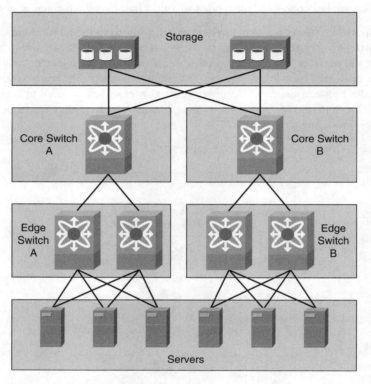

Figure 2-8   *Core Edge Topology*

To connect islands of SANs, perhaps between data centers, technologies such as Fibre Channel over IP (FCIP) can be deployed to encapsulate Fibre Channel into IP and tunnel the traffic between fabric switches, such as the core fabric switches or other FCIP-enabled products.

The combination of Ethernet-based LAN and storage traffic on a common lossless 10-Gigabit Ethernet network is called Unified Fabric or Unified IO. The underlying technology that enables Unified Fabric is called Fibre Channel over Ethernet (FCoE).

Currently, most environments must maintain two physically separate data center networks with completely different management tools and best practices. Moving storage traffic to Ethernet would allow the storage and user application data to flow on the same physical network.

Figure 2-9 illustrates Unified Fabric.

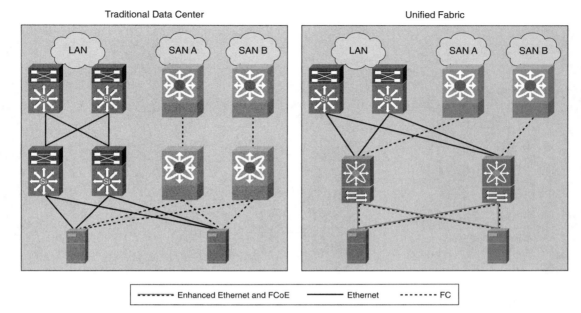

Figure 2-9   *Unified Fabric*

Enterprise Edge Network Design

The enterprise edge module includes the Internet, Virtual Private Network (VPN), and WAN modules that connect the enterprise to a service provider network. The enterprise edge contains all the network elements for efficient and secure communication between the enterprise campus, data center and remote locations, business partners, mobile users, and the Internet. The edge module aggregates the connectivity from various remote sites, filters traffic, and routes the traffic into the enterprise. The modular design of the edge network enables flexibility and customization to meet the needs of different-size customers and their respective business models. The edge network for an enterprise has three key network areas:

- The corporate headquarters, which is commonly known as the WAN aggregation network

- The branch side to connect to the WAN aggregation network

- The area facing the Internet, which serves both remote VPN and regular Internet access

Figure 2-10 illustrates the relationship between different enterprise edge network modules.

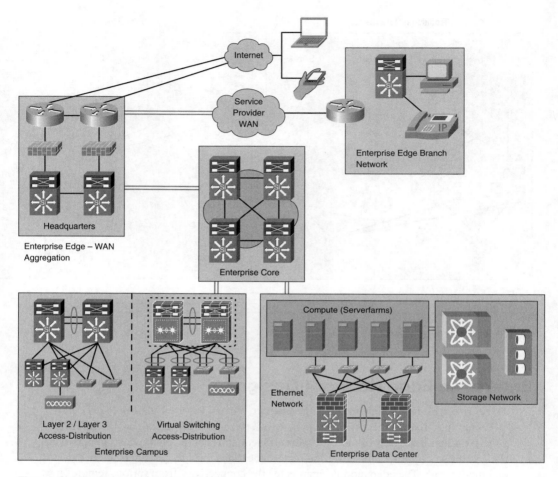

Figure 2-10   *Enterprise Edge Design*

Each module shown in Figure 2-10 has distinct network components and services that fill specific roles. The common components found in the headquarters enterprise edge module are introduced in the following section.

Headquarters Enterprise Edge Network Components

Within the enterprise edge, there are commonly deployed network components that offer distinct functionality. Depending on the size and complexity of the network, these components can be high performing, highly available, and scalable, and offer comprehensive features and security, or they can be consolidated and somewhat minimalistic in function. The enterprise edge network commonly includes infrastructure components as shown in Table 2-5.

Table 2-5   *Enterprise Edge Network Components*

Network Infrastructure	Functionality
Edge router	Basic WAN/Internet connectivity to the service provider. Serves as the first line of protection against spoofing and other network attacks. Collection point for network flow and event information useful for analysis and correlation purposes. Redundancy is achieved by deploying two or more routers and by configuring a First Hop Redundancy Protocol (FHRP).
Outer switch	Provides Layer 2 or Layer 3 connectivity between the firewalls and the edge routers. Two switches are deployed for redundancy. The outer switches provide connectivity to the distributed denial of service (DDoS) mitigation component.
Firewall	Secures the demilitarized zone (DMZ) and WAN aggregation modules by controlling and inspecting all traffic entering and leaving those modules. For redundancy, firewalls are deployed in stateful active/standby failover mode.
Additional security	Implements an intrusion detection system (IDS) with the intent to identify and alert on well-known attacks and suspicious activity. Alerts and alarms generated by the IDS and the endpoint security software are processed by a monitoring and analysis system for analysis and correlation purposes. Identifies DDoS and other network-based attacks, and works with the DDoS mitigation system deployed at the outer switches.

Headquarters Enterprise Edge Network Design

The enterprise edge network infrastructure provides a common infrastructure to enable branch connectivity, Internet connectivity, teleworker connectivity, and communication channels to partners (extranets), thereby reducing capital expenditure and operational expenses. Table 2-6 outlines the design requirements for the edge infrastructure.

Branch Network Architecture

The previous section outlined the network architecture and design considerations for the enterprise edge network at the headquarters site. This section outlines the design components of the edge network in each remote office or branch office for an enterprise. One of the main goals for the branch network architecture is to provide a flexible, scalable, reliable, and secure network infrastructure.

Table 2-6   *Headquarter Enterprise Edge Design Requirements*

Design Requirements	Features
Network resiliency	The edge design needs to ensure that there is no single point of failure, thereby maximizing the availability of the network infrastructure. Any downtime of the edge network can result in bringing down access to data center resources (intranet and extranet resources) and the communication partner channels, contributing to loss of business. The edge design is built out of many platforms and components that can fail or that can be subject to attack. Hence, it is critical to eliminate single points of failure by deploying several layers of redundancy, including redundant interfaces, standby devices, and topological redundancy.
Regulatory compliance	The edge design needs to meet regulatory compliance for standards: Payment Card Industry Data Security Standard (PCI DSS) for the payment card industry. Health Insurance Portability and Accountability Act (HIPAA) for the healthcare industry. Any noncompliance can lead to the revocation of licenses, stiff penalties, and even legal actions.
Modularity and flexibility	The modular design provides a clear demarcation between the network and the services offered for Internet versus branch offices. The design flexibility helps add services (IPsec and WAN optimization services) without impacting the existing design.
Pervasive security	The edge network needs to ensure confidentiality, integrity, and availability of applications, endpoints, and the network.

The branch network architecture has the following key components:

- **Edge routers:** The edge routers (also known as *access routers* or just *branch routers*) are the gateways to enable connectivity between the branch network and head-end enterprise edge network. These routers provide connectivity through one or more WAN or Internet service providers (ISP). These key features are enabled on the edge routers to gain visibility on traffic flows, network activity, and system status: QoS, rate limiting, security (ACLs and uRPF), NetFlow, and SNMP. These routers can have built-in firewalling or can connect to dedicated firewalls to protect branch assets from the external world and to provide a secure communication channel between each branch and the head-end enterprise edge network.

- **Inner switches:** These switches provide connectivity from the edge routers to the remainder of the branch LAN. Smaller branches can have just a few Layer 2 switches connecting to the edge routers. Larger branches can have the same basic design as a larger campus network deployment using the traditional core, distribution, and access layers.

Branch Edge Router Functionality

The branch edge router provides network connectivity between the remote offices and the head-end enterprise edge. Along with basic network connectivity, it also provides firewall and application intelligence services required for a secure and optimized communication channel between the remote sites. The key branch edge router services include

- Optimized application delivery through quality of service (QoS), integrated flow monitoring (NetFlow), and application acceleration (Cisco Wide Area Application Services [WAAS])

- Security, including platform, WAN, and VPN (includes Secure VPN authentication using public-key infrastructure [PKI])

The edge router infrastructure is the foundation upon which the rest of the branch network and advanced services are built. Flexibility and scalability are the two key design requirements for network infrastructure. You need to design a flexible network infrastructure so that advanced network services can be efficiently and seamlessly integrated. You also need to design a scalable network infrastructure so that you can easily add more capacity or more branch sites without disrupting the existing network operations.

The branch edge solution is designed with respect to different requirements such as size, business vertical, location, cost, and so on. The branch design introduces the concept of three profiles: single-tier branch, dual-tier branch, and multitier branch. These three profiles are discussed in more detail in Chapter 8, "Deploying IPv6 in WAN/Branch Networks." The three profiles are outlined in the Table 2-8.

Table 2-8   *Branch Design Profiles*

Branch Design Profiles	Design Considerations
Single-tier branch	The single-tier branch solution consists of a fully integrated, one-box solution. This one device is responsible for LAN and WAN connectivity. This profile is generally deployed where enterprise branches do not require platform redundancy. User capacity is typically between 20 and 30 users in a remote branch office.
Dual-tier branch	The dual-tier branch solution provides a two-layer architecture. The first layer provides dual redundant WAN capabilities, and the second layer provides LAN connectivity. The dual WAN links provide higher availability as compared to the single-tier. A separate Ethernet switch would provide more LAN connections as compared to the single-tier.
Multitier branch	This profile separates network functionality into separate layers. The separate tiers are WAN termination, firewall functionality, services termination, and LAN termination. The significant benefits of this profile are redundancy, availability, and router/switch CPU utilization.

Typical Branch Network Design

Depending on the size of the branch, each branch office would require an external connectivity: up to 1.5 Mbps for small branch offices (up to 100 users) or high-speed (up to 45 Mbps) for larger branches. In some designs, enterprises can use traditional private WAN technologies such as MPLS or Frame Relay, or they can leverage the Internet to connect remote sites using VPN technologies. The branch router hosts the following integrated services:

- **Security services:** Security services such as firewalls and IPsec are either integrated or implemented in a separate appliance depending on the amount of traffic that exits at the branch. Integrated modules inside the edge router can provide services, or a dedicated, standalone device such as a Cisco ASA Firewall can be used.

- **Unified Communications services:** These services include local call control, FXO/FXS ports for direct public switched telephone network (PSTN) connectivity (emergency 911), and backup connectivity

- **Application intelligence services:** One of the key design objectives for the branch solution is to provide branch network users with the same network capabilities and service levels as corporate users. This can be challenging because of the limited bandwidth and inherent delay in WAN links. The typical small branch, which has limited WAN bandwidth, can benefit greatly from application intelligence services, such as WAN optimization/application acceleration using the Cisco WAAS.

The branch also includes a Layer 2 access switch with the following key features:

- Power over Ethernet (PoE)
- Spanning Tree
- Class of service (CoS) on access ports and QoS policing and shaping on edge routers

Additionally, some branch sites can have localized infrastructure services such as a local Microsoft Active Directory server, local DNS, and local DHCP. As it relates to IPv6, the branch edge router can be configured to provide local addressing the Cisco IOS DHCPv6 server or be configured to provide DHCPv6 Relay to forward local DHCP requests to the corporate headquarters site.

Most enterprises find that the enterprise edge design that they use today with IPv4 will most likely be the same design that they use with IPv6.

Summary

The chapter provides a basic overview of a hierarchical enterprise network design. It begins by discussing the three key design principles: modularity, hierarchy, and resiliency. This chapter begins by comparing the flat network designs and the need for hierarchical modular network designs. As networks grew in size and applications' demand for network bandwidth and services grew, new designs for the network were needed.

The network design principle concepts help segment the enterprise network into simpler, multiple building blocks based on the functionality that each module provides. The chapter also summarizes some of the design considerations for each of these building blocks, enabling a network designer and/or architect to review the various design options and extend these design principles in his or her own enterprise network designs.

The enterprise campus section provides connectivity to end users and devices and then introduces and compares the various access-distribution block designs: Layer 2 access (looped or loop-free access design), routed access, and Virtual Switching System distribution block.

The network services block is a new concept that enables network architects to reduce the scope of running tunnels between multiple endpoints required during the transition from IPv4 designs to dual-stack IPv4/IPv6 designs.

The enterprise data center section covers the network design for providing IP connectivity to server farms and the storage network. The SAN design was also reviewed. Although the SAN is agnostic to IPv6, the section brought out the importance of a SAN in an enterprise network and different topologies in a SAN.

The enterprise edge design focuses on how remote locations and teleworkers connect to the enterprise network and discusses some high-level concepts for Internet connectivity. You also reviewed features and security requirements required in a WAN/branch network design.

Additional References

Cisco Enterprise Campus Architecture: Overview and Framework:
http://www.cisco.com/en/US/docs/solutions/Enterprise/Campus/campover.html.

Cisco Data Center Infrastructure Design Guide:
http://www.cisco.com/en/US/docs/solutions/Enterprise/Data_Center/DC_Infra2_5/DCI_SRND_2_5_book.html.

Data Center Design—IP Network Infrastructure:
http://www.cisco.com/en/US/docs/solutions/Enterprise/Data_Center/DC_3_0/DC-3_0_IPInfra.html.

Data Center Service Integration: Service Chassis Design Guide:
http://www.cisco.com/en/US/docs/solutions/Enterprise/Data_Center/dc_servchas/service
-chassis_design.html.

Deploying IPv6 Campus Design:
http://www.cisco.com/en/US/docs/solutions/Enterprise/Campus/CampIPv6.html.

Chapter 3

Common IPv6 Coexistence Mechanisms

This chapter covers the following objectives:

■ **Native IPv6:** This section is for the greenfield deployment and covers the native IPv6 deployment.

■ **Transition mechanisms:** This section covers dual-stack (IPv4/IPv6 coexistence), IPv6 over IPv4 tunnels, and IPv6 over MPLS.

■ **Protocol translation/proxy mechanisms:** This section describes the translation mechanisms generally referred to by the layer at which they operate, for example, from the network layer to the application layer, and focuses on NAT-PT (Network Address Translation - Port Address Translation) and NAT64.

The current IPv4-based addressing scheme will not be enough to accommodate the growing addressing demands of the enterprise networks. IPv6 has been designed to address this shortfall. However, the challenge is how to add IPv6 to an enterprise network effectively and with the least impact. Various mechanisms have been proposed to achieve this. This chapter reviews the common coexistence mechanisms at a high level and includes the following:

■ **Native IPv6 (IPv6-only networks):** Native IPv6 refers to the network where IPv6 is the only transport protocol running.

■ **Dual-stack:** Dual-stack refers to the host/network where both IPv4 and IPv6 protocols are running on the devices.

■ **IPv6 over IPv4 tunnels:** In this transition mechanism, the IPv6 packets are encapsulated within an IPv4 packet. This method is used where IPv6 networks are segregated and IPv4 is the only option to transverse over the existing networks. In this scenario, the IPv6 is at the edge networks only.

■ **IPv6 over MPLS:** In this transition mechanism, the IPv6 domains communicate with peer IPv6 domains over an IPv4 Multiprotocol Label Switching (MPLS) core, providing more dynamic and higher performance.

■ **Translation mechanisms:** These mechanisms allow the communication of the IPv6-only devices with the IPv4-only devices by using translation mechanisms like Socks gateway, Network Address Translation - Port Translation (NAT-PT), TCP-UDP Relay, and NAT64.

Table 3-1 outlines and describes each of these on high level.

Table 3-1   *Coexistence Mechanisms*

Mechanism	Submechanism	Benefits	Challenges
Native IPv6	—	Scalability: IPv6 provides more addresses, thus providing global connectivity and peer-to-peer networking. Improved routing by aggregating routing entries (requires planning and design).	Might require network infrastructure upgrades, OS upgrades, application upgrades, services (DNS, DHCP), network management, and hardware upgrades such as NIC cards.
Transition mechanisms	Dual-stack	Enables connectivity to existing IPv4 applications over IPv4 while providing access to IPv6-enabled applications over IPv6.	Supporting IPv6 and IPv4 simultaneously can be costly because it requires operation and management to support both protocols.
	IPv6-over-IPv4 tunnels	Enables the IPv6 networks to connect with other IPv6 networks over IPv4 backbone.	Large deployments, especially mesh configurations, can be complex and costly.
	IPv6 over MPLS	Enables the IPv6 traffic to be encapsulated and traverse an IP/MPLS network without upgrading all of the MPLS core.	Might require an upgrade in software and hardware in the areas where the IPv6 network meets the MPLS network (for example, PE routers).

Table 3-1   *Coexistence Mechanisms*

Mechanism	Submechanism	Benefits	Challenges
Translation mechanisms	NAT-PT	Provides basic and limited translation between IPv4-only hosts and IPv6-only hosts.	Limited scalability and application support. Some of the other issues include DNS translation, and dual-stack hosts get both native and translated addresses. Limited performance dictated by NAT-PT device.
	NAT64	Provides two forms of translation modes between IPv6-only hosts and IPv4-only hosts: stateless and stateful modes. Stateless is a 1:1 mapping between IPv6 and IPv4. Stateful allows overloading of multiple IPv6 addresses to one IPv4 address.	Some of the same limitations as any NAT device including NAT-PT, such as some application interoperability issues, scale, and performance. However, NAT64 is much better than NAT-PT.

Native IPv6

Native IPv6 is also known as "IPv6-only." It simply means that IPv6 is the only running IP protocol in the network.

In simplistic terms, the IPv6 environments can be thought of in the same way as native IPv4 environments of today, only using a higher version of IP. There will be a time when the operational and capital cost for running a dual-stack network will become unjustifiable. At some point, and that point varies greatly from network to network, it will make sense to turn off IPv4 altogether, or at least in the majority of the network.

There are already customers who deploy native IPv6 networks in "greenfield" or brand-new sites where the network and applications are the latest and greatest and also support IPv6 with few to no gaps in feature richness. These networks are a minority, but they will grow over time.

IPv6 enables organizations to deploy applications addressing specific business needs; however, the biggest challenge facing the deployment of native IPv6 in the near term is that not everyone is taking part in it. Additional challenges include the lack of end-to-end and robust IPv6 support in network, security, management, transport, and applications. Many of the large businesses have built proprietary applications, adding to the operational challenges for the transition to IPv6. This situation is applicable industry-wide, where there are gaps in the overall support for IPv6-only networks. Native IPv6 deployments will grow as support gaps are filled by vendors and service providers.

Figure 3-1 shows the native IPv6 model. The hosts and network devices in this model need to operate in IPv6 end to end for communication between them to be possible.

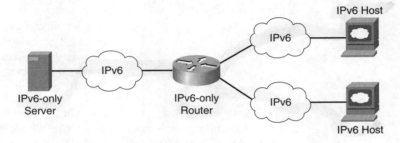

Figure 3-1   *Native IPv6 Topology*

Transition Mechanisms

As the name suggests, transition mechanisms help in the transition from one protocol to another. In the perspective of IPv6, transition basically means moving from IPv4 to IPv6. One day, IPv6 networks will completely replace today's IPv4 networks. For the near term, a number of transition mechanisms are required to enable both protocols to operate simultaneously. Some of the most widely used transition mechanisms are discussed in the following sections.

Dual-Stack

Dual-stack is the foundational and preferred IPv4-to-IPv6 transition mechanism. Dual-stack provides the most natural way for IPv6 hosts and networks to be deployed because no tunneling or translation needs to be performed for end-to-end connectivity. In a dual-stack deployment, both IPv4 and IPv6 are operational on all components (hosts, servers, routers, switches, firewalls, and so on) attached to the network.

The dual-stack mechanism has been used in the past. Previous examples of this mechanism include IPv4 with IPX and/or AppleTalk coexisting on the same node. As with other uses of dual-stack, the IPv4 and IPv6 protocols are not compatible with each other.

The dual-stack model enables the smoothest transitioning from IPv4 to IPv6 environments with minimal service disruptions. This model works by enabling IPv6 in the existing IPv4 environments along with the associated features required to make IPv6 routable, highly available, and secure.

The primary advantage of the dual-stack mechanism is that it does not require tunneling within the network. The dual-stack runs the two protocols as "ships-in-the-night," meaning that IPv4 and IPv6 run alongside one another and have no dependency on each other to function, except that they share network resources. Both IPv4 and IPv6 have independent routing, high availability (HA), quality of service (QoS), security, and multicast policies. Dual-stack also offers forwarding performance advantages because packets are natively forwarded without requiring additional encapsulation and lookup overhead.

The nodes in dual-stack support both protocol stacks (IPv4 and IPv6), enabling them to be configured with both IPv4 and IPv6 addresses. The dual-stack nodes use IPv4 and IPv6 mechanisms such as Dynamic Host Configuration Protocol (DHCP) to acquire their respective configurations like addresses.

Figure 3-2 shows the dual-stack model. The nodes and the networking devices in this model understand and run both IPv4 and IPv6 independently.

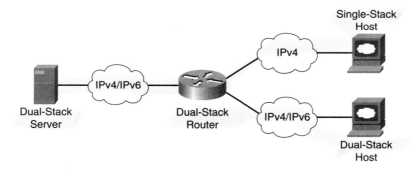

Figure 3-2   *Dual-Stack IPv6 Topology*

IPv6-over-IPv4 Tunnels

IPv4 is the dominant IP protocol deployed in enterprise networks. As the adoption and deployment of IPv6 grow, IPv6 hosts or entire sections of the network might need to communicate over IPv6 end to end, but IPv4-only portions of the network are in the way. This is common in WAN/branch deployments, where the branch and head-end sites are IPv6-enabled, but the WAN in between supports only IPv4. IPv6-over-IPv4 tunnels encapsulate IPv6 datagrams inside of IPv4, enabling end-to-end communication.

Traditionally point-to-point or point-to-multipoint tunnels have been used to "carry" or transport one protocol, in this case IPv6, over another protocol (IPv4). Tunnels have been used for many years to support Novell IPX/SPX, AppleTalk, SNA, and others.

Figure 3-3 shows the basic framework for encapsulating IPv6 inside the IPv4 tunnel header.

There are a variety of tunnel types, and the different tunnel types are used for different purposes. Some of the uses of the tunnel types are based on the termination points (host or router), number of termination points, and in some cases, the operating system version. The tunnel types include

- **Router-to-router:** In router-to-router tunneling, routers connected over IPv4 network infrastructure can transport IPv6 packets by encapsulating these IPv6 packets inside the IPv4 header.

- **Host-to-router:** In host-to-router tunneling, the IPv4/IPv6 hosts can tunnel the IPv6 packets to an IPv4/IPv6 border router. This tunnel terminates at the border router and from there on is sent natively over IPv6 to the end host.

- **Host-to-host:** In host-to-host tunneling, the tunnel exists between the two or more hosts. The IPv6/IPv4 hosts use the tunnel to communicate between themselves by tunneling IPv6 packets within the IPv4 header.

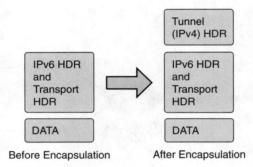

Before Encapsulation   After Encapsulation

Figure 3-3   *IPv6-over-IPv4 Tunnel Encapsulation*

IPv6-over-IPv4 tunneling can be further classified into configured and automatic tunneling mechanisms, based on how the tunnel endpoint address is resolved by the encapsulating node. In manually configured tunneling, the configuration information determines the tunnel endpoint addresses, whereas in automatic tunneling, the tunnel endpoint information is dynamically obtained. Some of these methods include

- Manually Configured Tunnel (MCT)

- IPv6-over-IPv4 generic routing encapsulation (GRE) tunnel

- Tunnel broker

- 6to4 tunnel

- Intra-Site Automatic Tunnel Addressing Protocol (ISATAP) tunnels

- IPv6 over MPLS (6PE)

This chapter provides a high-level overview of these methods. Refer to subsequent chapters for configurations.

Note   Some tunneling technologies such as 6rd, Dual-Stack Lite (DS-Lite), and Teredo are not discussed in this chapter; 6rd and DS-Lite are geared toward service provider (SP) networks. Teredo is a Microsoft-specific, host-based approach and is generally not used in the enterprise.

Table 3-1 outlines and describes the limitations of these methods.

The next sections describe each IPv6-over-IPv4 tunneling method in greater detail.

Manually Configured Tunnel

Manually Configured Tunnels (MCT) are statically defined IPv6-in-IPv4 tunnels. MCT for IPv6 is supported by most of the stacks and routers; RFC 4213 specifies the methodology for manually configured IPv6-over-IPv4 tunnels for transporting IPv6 packets over an existing IPv4 network. This is one of the first transition mechanisms developed to transport IPv6 over an existing IPv4 network.

MCTs use protocol 41 to encapsulate the traffic, and the tunnel encapsulation is determined from the static configuration information present on the tunneling node. The tunneling node could be a dual-stack router or host. For MCTs, additional information such as the packets of interests are found out based on the configuration/routing table in the node.

Figure 3-4 shows the Manually Configured Tunnel. The end hosts in this model run IPv6, while the routers between which the tunnels exist are dual-stack. The network over which the tunnel is formed is an IPv4 network.

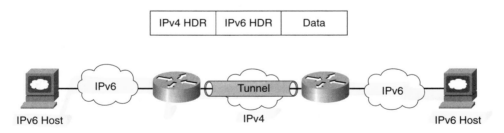

Figure 3-4   *Manually Configured Tunnel*

Example 3-1 shows the packet capture with MCTs. The tcpdump shows the IPv4 HDR in front of the IPv6 header. The outer header (IPv4) shows that the IPv4 tunnel is between 10.1.21.3 and 10.1.21.1 (highlighted), while the inner IPv6 header has addresses 2000:cafe:2::1 and 2000:cafe:2::2 (highlighted).

Table 3-1   *IPv6-over-IPv4 Tunneling Methods*

Method	Description	Limitations (if any)
Manually configured tunnels	Supported by all implementations. Standards-based (RFC 4213).	Difficult to manage as the number of sites increases the operation effort increases exponentially as due to increase in number of sites the number of tunnels increases if fully mesh connections are desired (scalability).
IPv6-over-IPv4 GRE tunnel	Uses IPv4 GRE tunnels. From a tunnel configuration perspective, this is same as Manually Configured Tunnels.	Same as Manually Configured Tunnels.
Tunnel broker	Standards-based (RFC 3053). Requires dedicated tunnel brokers. Dynamic tunnels.	Tunnel broker service needs to accept configuration changes remotely, which leads to security implications.
6to4 tunnel	Standards-based (RFC 3056). Automatic tunneling. Uses IPv4 infrastructure such as a virtual broadcast link. Uses 2002::/16 as a prefix.	Underlying IPv4 address determines the 6to4 IPv6 address prefix, so migration to native IPv6 requires renumbering. Requires public IPv4 addressing. Doesn't support NAT along the path. No multicast support.
ISATAP	Automatic overlay mechanism (RFC 5214). Uses underlying IPv4 as non-broadcast multiaccess (NBMA) link. Easy to configure and can scale to large numbers of hosts.	Transport layer NAT not supported. Delimitation of IPv4 virtual link is required for security reasons. No multicast support.
IPv6 over MPLS	Uses existing MPLS infrastructure to transport IPv6.	Flexible but could be cumbersome to configure based on the underlying method used.

Example 3-1   tcpdump *Output for the Manually Configured Tunnel*

```
root@0[~]# tcpdump -i br0 host 10.1.21.3 -v
tcpdump: listening on br0, link-type EN10MB (Ethernet), capture size
96 bytes
08:58:32.060893 IP (tos 0x0, ttl 255, id 30, offset 0, flags [none],
proto: IPv6 (41), length: 120) 10.1.21.3 > 10.1.21.1: IP6 (hlim 64,
next-header: ICMPv6 (58), length: 60) 2000:cafe:2::1 >
2000:cafe:2::2: ICMP6, echo request, length 60, seq 0
08:58:32.061648 IP (tos 0x0, ttl 255, id 102, offset 0, flags [none],
proto: IPv6 (41), length: 120) 10.1.21.1 > 10.1.21.3: IP6 (hlim 64,
next-header: ICMPv6 (58), length: 60) 2000:cafe:2::2 >
2000:cafe:2::1: ICMP6, echo reply, length 60, seq 0
08:58:32.062063 IP (tos 0x0, ttl 255, id 31, offset 0, flags [none],
proto: IPv6 (41), length: 120) 10.1.21.3 > 10.1.21.1: IP6 (hlim 64,
next-header: ICMPv6 (58), length: 60) 2000:cafe:2::1 >
2000:cafe:2::2: ICMP6, echo request, length 60, seq 1
08:58:32.062437 IP (tos 0x0, ttl 255, id 103, offset 0, flags [none],
proto: IPv6 (41), length: 120) 10.1.21.1 > 10.1.21.3: IP6 (hlim 64,
next-header: ICMPv6 (58), length: 60) 2000:cafe:2::2 >
2000:cafe:2::1: ICMP6, echo reply, length 60, seq 1
```

IPv6-over-IPv4 GRE Tunnel

GRE tunneling has traditionally been used for encapsulating privately addressed IPv4 datagrams or non-IP traffic such as AppleTalk over an existing IPv4 network. Generally with traditional GRE tunneling, the inner IPv4 addresses are not routable over the network over which the GRE tunnel is formed.

An IPv6-over-IPv4 GRE tunnel is another type of manually configured tunneling mechanism that provides the necessary services using a point-to-point encapsulation mechanism. The GRE tunnels in this case carry the IPv6 as the payload. Figure 3-5 shows a sample network with IPv6 over IPv4 using GRE tunnels.

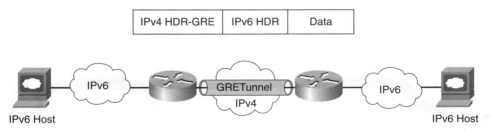

Figure 3-5   *IPv6-over-IPv4 GRE Tunnel*

IPv6-over-IPv4 GRE tunnels require the routers to be dual-stack so that both IPv4 and IPv6 can be processed and routed before, during, and after encapsulation. From the tunnel configuration perspective, this is similar to Manually Configured Tunnels because the GRE tunnel exists between the pair of the routers.

Example 3-2 shows the packet capture for the IPv6-over-IPv4 GRE tunnel. Note the presence of the IPv4 GRE HDR in front of the IPv6 packet.

Example 3-2   tcpdump *Output—IPv6-over-IPv4 GRE Tunnel*

```
root@0[~]# tcpdump -i br0 host 10.1.21.3 -v
tcpdump: listening on br0, link-type EN10MB (Ethernet), capture size
96 bytes
07:21:34.756456 IP (tos 0x0, ttl 255, id 72, offset 0, flags [none],
proto: GRE(47), length: 124) 10.1.21.3 > 10.1.21.1: GREv0, Flags
[none], length: 104) IP6 (hlim 64, next-header: ICMPv6 (58), length:
60) 2000:cafe:2::1 > 2000:cafe:2::2: ICMP6, echo request, length 60,
seq 0
07:21:34.756925 IP (tos 0x0, ttl 255, id 85, offset 0, flags [none],
proto: GRE(47), length: 124) 10.1.21.1 > 10.1.21.3: GREv0, Flags
[none], length: 104) IP6 (hlim 64, next-header: ICMPv6 (58), length:
60) 2000:cafe:2::2 > 2000:cafe:2::1: ICMP6, echo reply, length 60,
seq 0
07:21:34.757319 IP (tos 0x0, ttl 255, id 73, offset 0, flags [none],
proto: GRE(47), length: 124) 10.1.21.3 > 10.1.21.1: GREv0, Flags
[none], length: 104) IP6 (hlim 64, next-header: ICMPv6 (58), length:
60) 2000:cafe:2::1 > 2000:cafe:2::2: ICMP6, echo request, length 60,
seq 1
07:21:34.757581 IP (tos 0x0, ttl 255, id 86, offset 0, flags [none],
proto: GRE(47), length: 124) 10.1.21.1 > 10.1.21.3: GREv0, Flags
[none], length: 104) IP6 (hlim 64, next-header: ICMPv6 (58), length:
60) 2000:cafe:2::2 > 2000:cafe:2::1: ICMP6, echo reply, length 60,
seq 1
```

The limitation of IPv6-over-IPv4 GRE tunnels is that as you add more routers and therefore more tunnels, scaling the solution becomes tedious and time-consuming. As the number of sites increases, troubleshooting and manageability of this solution become difficult.

Tunnel Broker

Initially IPv6 networks started using the transport facilities provided by IPv4 networks using the manual tunnel configurations. Various ideas like automatically configured tunnels with IPv4-compatible addresses and 6to4 have tried to solve the manual configuration issues with automation.

The tunnel broker, as described in RFC 3053, "IPv6 Tunnel Broker," is an alternative approach and uses the dedicated servers to simplify the establishment of tunnels, these servers are called tunnel brokers. The tunnel broker is responsible for the management of the tunnel requests coming from the endpoints. This method fits in scenarios with small, isolated IPv6 sites or IPv6 hosts. These small sites of segregated hosts are interconnected using today's existing IPv4-based infrastructure. Applications on the remote dual-stack systems can access the IPv6 backbone by enabling tunnel broker service.

Figure 3-6 shows the automatic tunnel establishment with a tunnel broker.

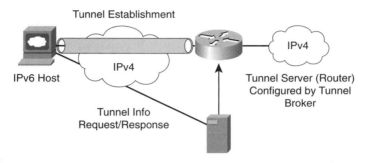

Figure 3-6   *Automatic Tunnel Establishment with Tunnel Broker*

The primary limitation of the tunnel broker service is that the router or tunnel broker service needs to accept a configuration change from a remote server, which might have serious security implications. For example, an enterprise could register the IPv4 address of the router with the service provider on a dedicated website. The service provider delivers a script that builds a tunnel to the IPv6 network, allocates an IPv6 address to the end system, and allocates a network prefix to the router to allow connectivity for the rest of the site. The tunnel broker manages the creation and deletion of the tunnel to the tunnel server. Mistakes or leakage of this information could cause a security exposure to the site.

6to4 Tunnel

The 6to4 tunnel, specified in RFC 3056, "Connection of IPv6 Domains via IPv4 Clouds," is an automatic tunneling mechanism, which is typically implemented on border routers. The 6to4 tunnel mechanism doesn't require any explicit configuration and uses the IPv4 infrastructure like a virtual broadcast link. The tunnel destination is the embedded IPv4 address from the IPv6 destination address in the IPv6 header.

The IPv6 addresses, starting with the 2002::/16 prefix, are known as 6to4 addresses, so to construct the 48-bit 6to4 prefix, 2002 is prepended to the 32-bit IPv4 address for use by a host or a network behind it. For example, using a global IP address of 192.168.10.1 makes the corresponding 6to4 prefix 2002:C0A8:0A01::/48.

While encapsulating the IPv6 packet in an IPv4 packet, the 6to4 tunneling uses protocol number 41. The 6to4 tunneling mechanism provides two deployment scenarios:

- Interconnecting 6to4 domains

- Interconnecting 6to4 and native IPv6 domains using relay routers

Figure 3-7 depicts the 6to4 deployment to interconnect 6to4 domains; this is the simplest deployment scenario to interconnect multiple IPv6 sites. In this deployment scenario, assign only one 6to4 address on the external interface of the router.

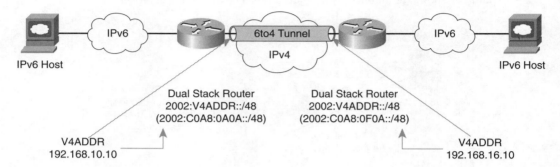

Figure 3-7   *Interconnecting 6to4 Domains*

The second deployment scenario becomes more prevalent when there is a need to communicate between the 6to4 domain and a native IPv6 domain. This communication requires the services of a relay router (which is a standard dual-stack router that uses both 6to4 and native IPv6 addressing). The relay router in Figure 3-8 connects to the IPv4 network, IPv6 native network, and 6to4 IPv6 site network.

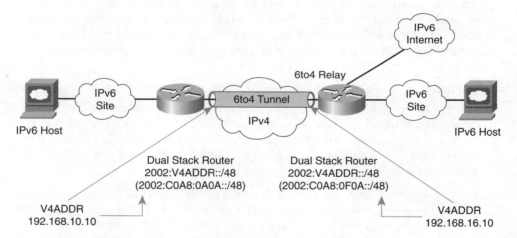

Figure 3-8   *Interconnecting 6to4 domain to native IPv6 domain*

Figure 3-8 shows the interconnection of a 6to4 and a native IPv6 domain.

To make the routing work when interconnecting a 6to4 domain to a native IPv6 domain, an internal routing protocol like Enhanced IGRP (EIGRP) for IPv6 can be used for routing IPv6 within the site. Use a default route pointing to a specific relay router for communicating with the native IPv6 devices. Across the 6to4 tunnel, internal routing protocols cannot be run and the solution is limited to static or Border Gateway Protocol 4+ (BGP4+) routing. According to the specification, the 6to4 relay router must only advertise 2002::/16 and not any subdivisions. Any subdivision must be discarded; this will avoid polluting the IPv6 routing tables with small-prefix routing entries, helping to keep the routing table small.

Publically available 6to4 relays 2002:c058:6301:: (V4ADDR- 192.88.99.1) can be used; this is a special anycast address of the nearest relay router. This address should be used if IPv6 Internet access is desired. Because of the insecure nature of the tunnel between a 6to4 router and a 6to4 relay route, some of the security issues that exist are as follows:

- The data contained in the packets is not checked by the 6to4 relay routers.

- Address spoofing is a major issue, and the IPv6 address of the source can be easily spoofed.

Intra-Site Automatic Tunnel Addressing Protocol (ISATAP)

ISATAP, defined in RFC 5214, is an automatic overlay tunneling mechanism that enables communications among IPv6 hosts within a site. ISATAP uses the underlying IPv4 infrastructure as a nonbroadcast multiple access (NBMA) link layer.

ISATAP tunnels embed the IPv4 address of the interface in the last 32 bits of the IPv6 address. ISATAP tunneling transports IPv6 datagrams at a site where an underlying IPv6 network is not available and where there are a sparse number of dual-stack-enabled hosts that need IPv6 connectivity. To support automatic configuration to the network clients, the ISATAP routers provide network configuration support for the ISATAP site. This enables the IPv6 clients to automatically configure themselves.

As shown in Figure 3-9, the ISATAP address consists of three parts:

Top 64 Bits	32 Bits	32 Bits
Global IPv6 Prefix or Link Local	0000:5EFE	IPv4 Address of the Interface

Figure 3-9   *ISATAP Address Format*

- The first 64 bits are either a link-local or global IPv6 prefix.

- The middle 32 bits are 0000:5EFE (0200:5EFE if using public unicast IPv4 addresses).

- The lowest 32 bits consist of the IPv4 address of the interface identifier.

Figure 3-10 depicts the creation of an ISATAP tunnel by the dual-stack IPv6 hosts with the ISATAP router.

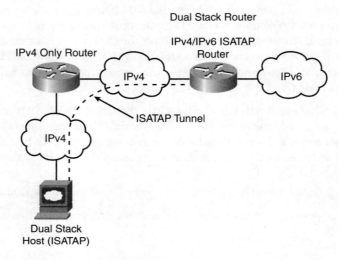

Figure 3-10   *ISATAP Tunnels*

IPv6 over MPLS

While the service providers/large enterprises slowly move their infrastructure to support IPv6, they can use their existing IPv4 MPLS infrastructure to transport IPv6. In this scenario, the provider edge (PE) routers have the IPv6 routing capability, but the provider (P) routers have no IPv6 routing functionality enabled. This enables the service providers to provide IPv6 services (connectivity between the isolated IPv6 domains) without upgrading their backbone networks.

In the following section, you consider the following three concepts to transport IPv6 over MPLS:

■   IPv6 over circuit transport over MPLS

■   IPv6 using IPv4 tunnels over customer edge (CE) routers

■   IPv6 MPLS with IPv4-based core (6PE/6VPE)

Table 3-2 compares these three methods.

IPv6 over Circuit Transport over MPLS

Because the emulation of the circuit is at Layer 2, the underlying circuit transport is fully transparent to IPv6 (Any Transport over MPLS [AToM]). This methodology doesn't need any configuration change at the PE or CE router.

Table 3-2 *IPv6 over MPLS*

Method	Description	Limitations (if any)
IPv6 over circuit transport over MPLS	Service provider (SP) with circuit to CE (forScalability. example, Frame Relay or ATM).	
IPv6 using IPv4 tunnels over CE routers	This is a tunnel-in-tunnel approach and requires CE routers to be dual-stack enabled. No impact on the MPLS infrastructure. IPv6 traffic is encapsulated twice: first in the IPv4 packet and then into an MPLS frame.	Tunnel overhead.
IPv6 MPLS with IPv4-based core (6PE/6VPE)	Standards-based: RFC 4659, 6VPE RFC 4798, 6PE The service is provided over the existing IPv4 MPLS service. Only the PE routers are impacted.	Complexity. MPLS core doesn't know about IPv6. Hard to troubleshoot.

Figure 3-11 shows the IPv6 over circuit transport over MPLS.

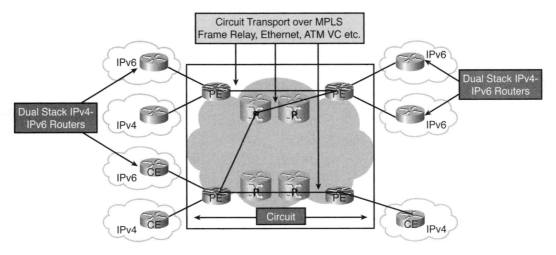

Figure 3-11 *IPv6 over Circuit Transport over MPLS*

AToM can provide both leased line and Layer 2 service emulation such as ATM, Frame Relay, and PPP Ethernet. The only limitation of this approach is scalability—with an increase in CE routers, there will also be an increase in the number of tunnels. If the customer is not worried about the suboptimal routing, the scalability can be overcome by using hubs leading to a partial mesh.

IPv6 Using IPv4 Tunnels on Customer Edge (CE) Routers

With MPLS in the service provider core network, this is a tunnel-in-tunnel approach and requires CE routers to be dual-stack enabled. From the forwarding plane perspective, the IPv6 traffic is encapsulated twice: first in the IPv4 packet and then into an MPLS frame. For the service provider, this approach doesn't impact the operation or infrastructure, so no configuration changes are required to the core or provider edge routers, making this approach simple. However, this design comes with its own scaling limitations because it involves manual configuration and the deployment of a mesh topology at the CE routers.

Figure 3-12 shows IPv6 using IPv4 tunnels on CE routers.

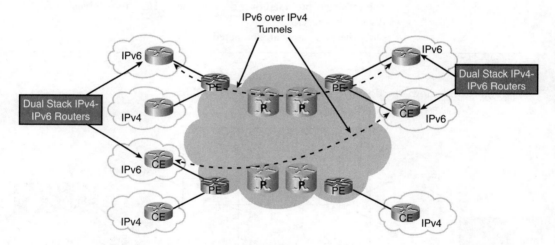

Figure 3-12 *IPv6 Using IPv4 Tunnels on CE Routers*

IPv6 MPLS with IPv4-Based Core (6PE/6VPE)

The following sections deal with the connection between IPv6 sites using 6PE (IPv6 provider edge over MPLS) and 6VPE (IPv6 VPN provider edge) for the MPLS VPN customers.

IPv6 Provider Edge over MPLS (6PE)

6PE is the Cisco implementation of the IPv6 provider edge router over MPLS. 6PE enables the IPv6 sites to communicate with each other using MPLS label switched paths (LSP) over the MPLS IPv4 core network. This feature requires MBGP (Multiprotocol Border Gateway Protocol) extensions on the PE routers to exchange the IPv6 reachability information for the IPv6 prefixes. The PE routers, being dual-stack, can now use the reachability information to apply the appropriate label. Because of the decoupling of the Control Plane and Data Plane in MPLS, it provides this interesting alternative to the transition of IPv4 and IPv6 over a single infrastructure.

On the ingress PE router, the incoming datagrams have two labels. The inner label is assigned to the destination IPv6 prefix through MP-BGP, whereas the outer label is based on the IPv4 address of the PE router providing reachability to the destination IPv6 prefix.

In Figure 3-13, the PEs are dual-stack routers with appropriate configuration of Label Distribution Protocol (LDP) and MBGP. Resource Reservation Protocol (RSVP) is used if MPLS traffic engineering is needed. All PE and core routers are configured with a common interior gateway protocol (IGP).

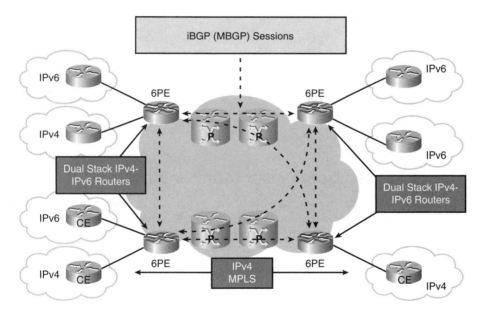

Figure 3-13   *6PE*

IPv6 VPN Provider Edge (6VPE)

6VPE, as specified in RFC 4659, "BGP-MPLS IP Virtual Private Network (VPN) Extension for IPv6 VPN," is for VPN customers. The IPv6 VPN service is the same as the MPLS IPv4 VPN service. This transition mechanism enables services such as "IPv6 VPN access," one carrier supporting other carriers, and so on.

The Cisco 6VPE implementation provides scalability with no IPv6 addressing restriction. This mode is similar to the IPv4 MPLS VPNs, so it enables the enterprises and service providers to deploy the IPv6 MPLS VPN service over their existing IPv4 backbone by just upgrading the PE router to the dual-stack-capable software.

Figure 3-14 shows the 6VPE.

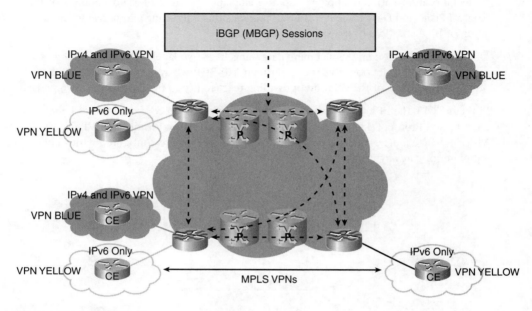

Figure 3-14   *6VPE*

Protocol Translation/Proxy Mechanisms

There are use cases that might require the ability to translate or proxy between IPv4 and IPv6. For example, translation in the data center is necessary to enable communication between IPv6-enabled hosts in the campus/branch and legacy IPv4-only servers in the data center access layer.

An intermediate device or node (for example, router, firewall, or load balancer) can translate from IPv4 to IPv6 and vice versa. Or the operating system can perform translation at each endpoint.

Some examples of mechanisms that perform translation of IPv4/IPv6 include

■   Network Address Translation - Protocol Translation (NAT-PT)

■   NAT64

■   TCP-UDP Relay

■   Bump in the stack (BIS)

■   SOCKS-based IPv6/IPv4 gateway

NAT-PT and NAT64 are discussed because they are the most commonly used mechanisms. The other mechanisms listed previously (TCP-UDP Relay, BIS, and SOCKS-based IPv6/IPv4 gateway) are mentioned only for completeness and are not discussed in the chapter.

Note   NAT-PT has been officially moved to "historic" status via RFC 4966 and is, by most vendors, not a recommended way of performing translation.

NAT-PT

NAT-PT performs translation of the network layer addresses (Layer 3) between IPv4 and IPv6. In this mechanism, end nodes in the IPv6 network are trying to communicate with the nodes in the IPv4 network. This method is primarily used for communication between the hosts that are IPv6-only to the ones that are IPv4-only.

NAT-PT uses a pool of IPv4 addresses and assigns them to IPv6 end nodes/hosts at the IPv4-IPv6 boundaries. This mechanism is similar to today's NAT mechanisms in IPv4 networks.

NAT-PT is based on the Stateless IP/ICMP Translation (SIIT) algorithm, as described in RFC 2765. This algorithm translates between the IPv4 and IPv6 packet headers without requiring any per-connection state.

Similar to NAT with IPv4, NAT-PT enables both static translations and dynamic (pools). In the case of static, one IPv6 address is mapped to one IPv4 address. Using the mapped IPv6 address of the IPv4 address on the NAT-PT router, the IPv6 nodes are able to communicate. Dynamic NAT-PT allocates addresses from the pool to allow multiple NAT-PT mappings.

Figure 3-15 shows the NAT-PT router with the translation table for the addresses.

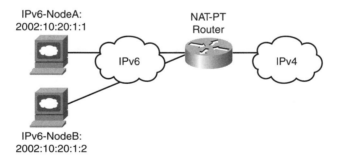

Before Translation		After Translation	
Source Address	Destination Address	Source Address	Destination Address
2002:10:20:1:1	2002:CAF0:1:1	192.168.1.1	10.12.1.1
2002:10:20:1:2	2002:CAF0:1:2	192.168.1.2	10.12.1.2

Figure 3-15   *NAT-PT Example*

The restrictions of this solution are similar to the IPv4 NAT mechanisms, including the following:

■ No support of asymmetrical routing because the traffic for the sessions needs to pass through the same NAT-PT device.

■ Any embedded address translation needs the knowledge of the underlying application/protocol.

NAT64

As the name suggests, the NAT64 transition mechanism refers to the translation of the IPv6 packet to an IPv4 packet. In case of NAT64, the initiator of the packet is always on the IPv6 side. Although NAT64 shares some of the same issues as other NAT mechanisms, it is the best option because it is built upon the years of experience with IPv4 NAT and overcomes some of the issues related to the other mechanisms like NAT-PT. NAT64 provides additional features like NAT mapping, filtering, and TCP simultaneous-open, which are required for the peer-to-peer environment.

NAT64 also provides features such as hairpinning, which enable the IPv6 hosts behind the NAT64 device to communicate with each other. Figure 3-16 shows the network design with the NAT64 device, DNS64, IPv6 clients, and IPv4 servers.

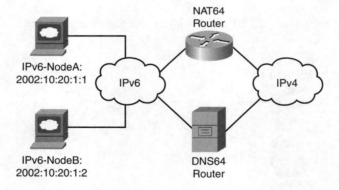

Figure 3-16   *NAT64*

Summary

This chapter dealt with the overview of different transition mechanisms for IPv6, which could be used to prepare a customer to transition from IPv4 to IPv6, depending upon the size and the availability of today's underlying IPv4 infrastructure.

This chapter is meant to provide only a summary look at some of the more popular and supported transition mechanisms. Later chapters, such as Chapter 6, "Deploying IPv6 in Campus Networks," go into more detail on why and how specific transition mechanisms are deployed.

Additional References

Carpenter, B. and K. Moore. RFC 3056, "Connection of IPv6 Domains via IPv4 Clouds." http://www.ietf.org/rfc/rfc3056.txt.

Cisco. Implementing IPv6 over MPLS: http://www.cisco.com/en/US/docs/ios/ipv6/configuration/guide/ip6-over_mpls.html.

Cisco. Implementing Tunnels for IPv6: http://www.cisco.com/en/US/docs/ios/ipv6/configuration/guide/ip6-tunnel.html#wp1055566.

Cisco. IPv6 over MPLS (Cisco 6PE): http://www.cisco.com/warp/public/cc/pd/iosw/prodlit/iosip_an.pdf.

Durand, A., P. Fasano, I. Guardini, and D. Lento. RFC 3053, "IPv6 Tunnel Broker." http://www.ietf.org/rfc/rfc3053.txt.

Carpenter, B. and K. Moore. RFC 3056, "Connection of IPv6 Domains via IPv4 Clouds." http://www.ietf.org/rfc/rfc3056.txt.

Nordmark, E. RFC 2765, "Stateless IP/ICMP Translation Algorithm (SIIT)." http://www.ietf.org/rfc/rfc2765.txt.

Gilligan, R. and E. Nordmark. RFC 2893, "Transition Mechanisms for IPv6 Hosts and Routers." http://www.ietf.org/rfc/rfc2893.

Tsirtsis, G. and P. Srisuresh. RFC 2766, "Network Address Translation - Protocol Translation (NAT-PT)." http://www.ietf.org/rfc/rfc2766.txt.

Nordmark, E. and R. Gilligan. RFC 4213, "Basic Transition Mechanisms for IPv6 Hosts and Routers." http://www.ietf.org/rfc/rfc4213.

De Clercq, J., D. Ooms, M. Carugi, and F. Le Faucheur. RFC 4659, "BGP-MPLS IP Virtual Private Network (VPN) Extension for IPv6 VPN." http://www.ietf.org/rfc/rfc4659.txt.

Templin, F., T. Gleeson, and D. Thaler. RFC 5214, "Intra-Site Automatic Tunnel Addressing Protocol (ISATAP)." http://www.ietf.org/rfc/rfc5214.txt.

Popoviciu, Ciprian P., Eric Levy-Abegnoli, and Patrick Grossetete. *Deploying IPv6 Networks*. Cisco Press. ISBN10: 1-58705-210-5; ISBN13: 978-1-58705-210-1.

Chapter 4

Network Services

This chapter covers the following subjects:

- **Multicast:** This section discusses how multicast is configured in IPv6. Multicast addressing introduces the effectiveness of the IPv6 addressing format. Different IPv6 multicast routing methods is also discussed in this section.

- **Quality of service (QoS):** This section highlights key differences between IPv4 and IPv6 implementations of QoS and then introduces extension headers.

- **IPv6 routing:** This section discusses some of the most widely used routing protocols and describes how they can be used with IPv6.

Enterprise networks today require various network services in addition to data transmission to bring employees, customers, and business partners together. Increasing employee productivity while reducing overall costs for enterprise customers today is achieved by enabling the following network services:

- Multicast

- Quality of Service (QoS)

- IPv6 routing

This chapter provides an overview of these network services. You can find a further in-depth discussion of these services in the Cisco Press book *Deploying IPv6 Networks*, by Ciprian Popoviciu, Eric Levy-Abegnoli, and Patrick Grossetete.

Multicast

In multicast transmissions, a source sends one copy of each packet to a special address that can be used by several receivers interested in that transmission. Those sources and receivers are members of a designated multicast group and can be located anywhere on the network. Multicast-enabled network devices replicate a single copy of the packet to multiple receivers instead of each receiver having a dedicated unicast connection to the source. Using multicast to transmit video traffic reduces the overall network load and minimizes the impact on the source of the video from unnecessary replication of a common data stream. Examples of applications that take advantage of multicast include videoconferencing, corporate communications, distance learning, distribution of software, stock quotes, and news.

Figure 4-1 shows an example in which a single multicast stream is generated by an IP camera and archived by two or more media servers. The IP camera is the source of the multicast transmission, and the media servers are the receivers. The intermediate network components such as switches and routers replicate packets. Packets replicate only where a switch or a router needs to send the multicast stream through multiple egress ports. If unicast were to be used for this application, the IP camera would have generated three individual streams for the three media servers, resulting in unnecessary wastage of compute resources and network overhead.

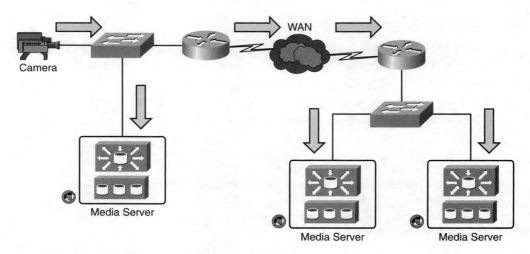

Figure 4-1 *Multicast Being Used for Video Surveillance*

Interested receivers can be members of more than one group and must explicitly join a group before receiving content. Because multicast traffic relies on User Datagram Protocol (UDP), which, unlike TCP, has no built-in reliability mechanism such as flow control or error recovery mechanisms, tools such as QoS can improve the reliability of a multicast transmission. Some edge devices can communicate with the media server using unicast or multicast communications. The use of multicast offers some benefits when a video stream is to be archived by several media servers because only a single stream is required from the IP camera or encoder.

This chapter provides a high-level overview of multicast. For a more in-depth discussion of IP multicast, refer to "Cisco IP Multicast Resources" at http://www.cisco.com/en/US/products/ps6552/products_ios_technology_home.html.

IPv6 Multicast Addressing

IPv6 multicast addresses are defined in RFC 4291. The IPv6 multicast address is composed of an 8-bit address, 4-bit flag, 4-bit scope, and 112-bit group ID field, as illustrated in Figure 4-2.

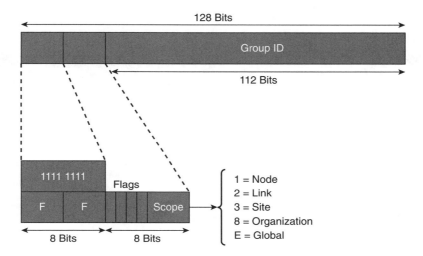

Figure 4-2 *IPv6 Multicast Address Format*

The Flags field distinguishes different address types. Bit T is defined in RFC 4291 and indicates whether the address is permanent by having a value of 0 or if the address is temporary by having a value of 1. Bit P is defined in RFC 3306 and provides a way to derive an IPv6 multicast address from an IPv6 unicast address. The example illustrated in Figure 4-3 illustrates how the RFC 3306 address is built. The Flags field when modified makes two new fields available: Plen (Prefix Length) and the network prefix that is the globally assigned IPv6 unicast prefix. This helps in the allocation of IPv6 multicast addresses, which are known and easy to manage.

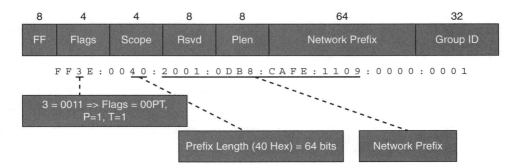

Figure 4-3 *Unicast Prefix Based on IPv6 Multicast Address*

To further help in the allocation of IPv6 multicast addresses, RFC 3956 provides a method to embed the RP (rendezvous point) address within. Using these addresses, the only conflicting addresses would be from the same RP. This is accomplished by setting the R bit in the flags and the P and T bits to 1. This flag configuration of 0111 implies that the reserved field is only 4 bits, and the low-order 4 bits of the reserved field is now the RPAdd field. The address of the RP can be derived from the multicast address using the following two steps, as illustrated in Figure 4-4:

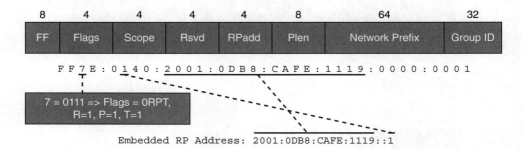

Figure 4-4 *Embedded RP IPv6 Multicast Address*

Step 1.   Copy the first number of bits as defined in the Plen field from the Network Prefix field to a new 128-bit IPv6 address.

Step 2.   Replace the last 4 bits with the contents of the RPAdd field.

Some IPv6 addresses are reserved by the Internet Assigned Numbers Authority (IANA). An updated list of such addresses can be found on the IANA website (http://www.iana.org); however, Table 4-1 shows a partial list of reserved addresses.

Table 4-1 *List of Reserved IPv6 Multicast Addresses Registered with the IANA*

Address	Description
ff02::1	All nodes on the local network
ff02::2	All routers on the local network
ff02::9	Routing Information Protocol (RIP) routers
ff02::a	Enhanced IGRP (EIGRP) routers
ff02::d	Protocol Independent Multicast (PIM) routers
ff02::e	Resource Reservation Protocol (RSVP)
ff02::1:2	All Dynamic Host Configuration Protocol (DHCP) servers and relay agents on the local network site
ff02::1:3	Link-local multicast name resolution

Table 4-1 *List of Reserved IPv6 Multicast Addresses Registered with the IANA*

ff05::1	All nodes on the local network site
ff05::1:3	All DHCP servers on the local network site
ff0x::fb	Multicast Domain Name System (DNS)
ff0x::108	Network Information Services (NIS)
ff0x::114	Experimental

Multicast Listener Discovery (MLD) for IPv6

IPv6 multicast does not use the Internet Group Management Protocol (IGMP) used in IPv4 networks when a receiver signals a router with its desire to receive data from a specific group. IPv6 uses the Multicast Listener Discovery (MLD) protocol, which is a subprotocol of Internet Control Messaging Protocol (ICMP). Table 4-2 provides a summary of MLD message types.

Table 4-2 *MLD Message Types*

Message Type	Description	ICMP Code
Query	General, group-specific, and multicast-address-specific. In a query message, the multicast address field is set to 0 when MLD sends a general query. The general query learns which multicast addresses have listeners on an attached link.	130
Report	In a report message, the multicast address field is that of the specific IPv6 multicast address to which the sender is listening.	131
Done	In a done message, the multicast address field is that of the specific IPv6 multicast address to which the source of the MLD message is no longer listening.	132

MLD uses ICMP to carry its messages. All MLD messages are link local with a hop limit of 1, and they all have the router alert option set. The router alert option implies an implementation of the hop-by-hop option header.

An MLD report must be sent with a valid IPv6 link-local source address or an unspecified address (::) in case the sending interface has not yet acquired a valid link-local address. Sending reports with an unspecified address is allowed to support the use of IPv6 multicast in the Neighbor Discovery Protocol.

General queries (ICMPv6 type 130) are sent by the MLD querier to the all-nodes multicast group (FF02::1). Hosts/receivers will then send replies (ICMPv6 type 131) for the groups they are interested in. A reply for a group is sent to the group address. The hop limit is set to 1, and therefore the packets will never be forwarded. When a receiver wants to start receiving multicast immediately, it should immediately send a report rather than wait for the next periodical query.

When a receiver is no longer interested in a group, it sends a done message (ICMPv6 type 132). This is sent to the all-routers multicast group (FF02::2). The network device checks whether there are other receivers by sending a specific query for that address. The specific query is sent to the group address. If no hosts respond with a reply, the router then assumes that there is no more interest in the group.

Version 2 of the MLD protocol, MLDv2 as defined in RFC 3810, has additional support for source filtering. Source filtering provides the receiver with the option to report interest in listening to packets from a defined group of specific source addresses. Alternatively, source filtering also provides the option for a receiver to listen to all packets except those from a defined group of specific source addresses. MLDv2 is designed to be interoperable with MLDv1.

MLD is primarily configured in the access layer of a network (campus, branch, and data center). The network design and the L2/L3 boundary dictate where MLD is configured.

For in-depth details of MLD, refer to the RFCs in the "Additional References" section, later in this chapter. You can find configuration information at the Cisco website http://www.cisco.com/go/ipv6.

Multicast Routing: Protocol Independent Multicast (PIM)

IP Protocol Independent Multicast (PIM) is the industry de facto standard for building multicast distribution trees. In most cases, the system uses the information learned from PIM to install shared-tree (*,G) and shortest-path-tree (S,G) entries in the multicast routing table.

IPv6 multicast routing is enabled with the following command:

```
ipv6 multicast-routing
```

The following are the main versions of the PIM protocols:

- **PIM Sparse Mode (PIM-SM):** PIM-SM is for one/few-to-many applications, where one or multiple sources transmit to the same group. The typical applications are videoconferencing or peer-to-peer gaming. Routers must join and leave multicast groups explicitly by sending requests to the RP. Upstream routers do not forward traffic unless it has sent a join message to the RP router to receive this traffic. The RP has the responsibility of forwarding multicast data from different sources and receivers as well as serving as the root of the shared multicast delivery tree.

- **PIM Source Specific Multicast (PIM-SSM):** PIM-SSM is a subset of PIM-SM and is a method of forwarding multicast traffic in which the only packets that are delivered to a receiver are those originating from a specific source address requested by the receiver. The typical applications are content delivery such as video or audio programs, including IPTV.

- **Bidirectional PIM (PIM-Bidir):** PIM-Bidir was developed to help deploy emerging communication and financial applications that rely on a many-to-many applications model. PIM-Bidir is the recommended routing protocol for "hoot 'n' holler" applications, which enable any host to send a message to a group it belongs to.

Note PIM Dense Mode (DM) has not been implemented for IPv6.

The following sections describe each of these control plane protocols.

PIM Sparse Mode (PIM-SM)

PIM-SM for IPv6 works in the similar fashion as that of the IPv4 PIM-SM method. PIM-SM builds shared trees and requires the use of at least one rendezvous point (RP) for every multicast group. Different RPs can handle different multicast groups, and for this reason, PIM has to be complemented by a mechanism that allows routers to learn which RP to use for a given group. Such mapping mechanisms are needed both within a PIM domain and between various domains. PIM also builds a Shortest Path Tree (SPT) that is used by default for traffic forwarding.

Only IPv6 PIM provides embedded RP support. This enables the router to learn the RP address using the multicast group destination address. For routers that are the RP, the router must be statically configured as the RP. Routers learn the RP for the group from the group addresses in MLD reports or PIM messages and data packets. It can then use this RP for all PIM activity for the group.

For PIM-SM, a static RP can be configured with the following command:

```
ipv6 pim rp-address 2001:DB8:CAFE:1002::1
```

A virtual unidirectional tunnel interface can send register messages to the RP. A tunnel is automatically created for each RP configured. Example 4-1 shows the IPv6 PIM-SM configuration and virtual tunnel.

Example 4-1 *IPv6 PIM-SM Configuration and Virtual Tunnel*

```
R1(config)# ipv6 multicast-routing
R1(config)# ipv6 pim rp-address 2001:db8:cafe:1002::1
R1(config)#
```

continues

Example 4-1 *IPv6 PIM-SM Configuration and Virtual Tunnel   continued*

```
00:05:17: %LINEPROTO-5-UPDOWN: Line protocol on Interface Tunnel1, changed state
to up
R1# show ipv6 pim tunnel
Tunnel0*
  Type  : PIM Encap
  RP    : Embedded RP Tunnel
  Source: 2001:DB8:CAFE:1001::1
Tunnel1*
  Type  : PIM Encap
  RP    : 2001:DB8:CAFE:1002::1*
  Source: 2001:DB8:CAFE:1001::1
R1# show int Tunnel1
Tunnel1 is up, line protocol is up
  Hardware is Tunnel
  MTU 1466 bytes, BW 100 Kbit/sec, DLY 50000 usec,
      reliability 255/255, txload 1/255, rxload 1/255
  Encapsulation TUNNEL, loopback not set
  Keepalive not set
  Tunnel source 2001:DB8:CAFE:1001::1 (Ethernet0/0), destination
2001:DB8:CAFE:1002::1
   Tunnel Subblocks:
      src-track:
         Tunnel1 source tracking subblock associated with Ethernet0/0
          Set of tunnels with source Ethernet0/0, 2 members (includes iterators),
          on interface <OK>
  Tunnel protocol/transport PIM/IPv6

  Tunnel TOS/Traffic Class 0xE0,  Tunnel TTL 65

<Output omitted for brevity>
```

When the network is divided into several administrative domains, it represents interdomain scenarios. IPv4-based interdomain multicast enabled each PIM domain to manage its own RP. Multicast Source Discovery Protocol (MSDP) was developed to exchange information about sources among PIM domains. Each RP would send PIM (S,G) joins to sources in other domains, provided that the RP has receivers for group G. The operation for MSDP was not scalable for many applications and hence is not supported in IPv6. Interdomain multicast in IPv6 now concentrates around PIM-SSM, discussed in the next section.

PIM Source Specific Multicast (PIM-SSM)

PIM-SSM represents a subset of PIM-SM. In this case, the listener knows a priority of both the group and the source (S,G) it wants to join. PIM-SSM operates similarly to PIM-SM, but it does not build a shared tree and so it does not need an RP. The listener must indicate to its designated router (DR) what (S,G) it is interested in. For this reason,

MLDv2 listener or the SSM MLDv1 mapping router support is required for a PIM-SSM deployment.

Because it builds only (S,G)s, the deployment and management of the service is much easier than for PIM-SM. Moreover, there is no need for additional protocols that help manage the RP. On the other hand, managing the distribution of source information to listeners might represent a challenge. Application layer protocols, independent of PIM, are needed to help hosts automatically discover the source of a given group. Therefore, no additional configuration is needed to configure PIM-SSM apart from mapping MLD, which is discussed in subsequent sections.

The SSM service model requires a host to specify both the multicast group it intends to join and the specific source it intends to listen to. Only MLDv2 supports this functionality on the hosts. Although SSM is a popular deployment model, MLDv2 is not commonly implemented on IPv6 stacks at the time of this writing, so a solution is necessary to make SSM work with MLDv1. This solution is called SSM mapping for MLDv1, and it operates in two modes:

- **Statically configured mapping:** A source (S) is statically mapped to a given group (G) on the router. The router maps any (*,G) MLDv1 report to an (S,G) based on the configured mapping. This mapping feature is off by default on a router. It is enabled with the global command **ipv6 mld ssm-map enable**. The static mapping is configured with the following global commands:

```
ipv6 mld ssm-map static ACL1 source 2001:DB8:CAFE:2001::10
ipv6 access-list ACL1
permit any ff08::1/64
```

    The access control list ACL1 identifies the groups mapped to the source (2001:DB8:CAFE:2001::10).

- **Dynamically configured mapping:** An AAAA record is configured for G in a DNS server. When the router receives an MLDv1 report for (*,G), it does a reverse DNS lookup querying for G's record. The DNS server returns the corresponding S for G. After the SSM mapping has been enabled globally, as previously shown, the dynamic mapping option can be configured using the following commands:

```
ipv6 multicast-routing
ipv6 mld ssm-map enable
ipv6 mld ssm-map static IPv6_SSM_MAP 2001:0DB8:1::1
ipv6 mld ssm-map query dns
```

    In this case, the IP address of the DNS server must be configured on the router. The DNS server can be reached over IPv6 or over IPv4 in a dual-stack network.

This feature, available on Cisco routers, enables IPv6 hosts supporting only MLDv1 to receive SSM-based multicast services.

Bidirectional PIM (PIM-Bidir)

Bidirectional PIM is a more efficient method with a large number of sources and receivers. The difference with PIM-SM is that the router near the source forwards packets back up the tree toward the RP with the RP forwarding multicast using the shared tree. This eliminates the process to create SPTs, and there is no source registration process.

Only static configuration of bidirectional RPs is supported in IPv6 and can be configured as follows:

```
ipv6 pim rp-address 2001:DB8:CAFE:2001::20 bidir
```

This section covers multicast at a high level and provides methods to deploy multicast using IPv6. You can find additional in-depth learning resources of multicast routing for IPv6 at http://www.cisco.com/go/ipv6.

Quality of Service (QoS)

The enterprise networks of today are designed to be complex global communications infrastructures. These networks are the platform to enable a multitude of applications and services. QoS protocols have the task of providing different application streams with priorities and metrics such as

- Bandwidth

- Delay

- Interpacket delay variation (jitter)

- Packet loss

The following sections discuss the differences between IPv6 and IPv4 QoS, extension headers, and IPv4 and IPv6 coexistence. This provides a better understanding of QoS implementation for both protocols, which is useful when planning migration.

Differences Between IPv6 and IPv4 QoS

Differences between implementations of QoS in IPv4 and IPv6 mostly revolve around the traffic-classification process, where packets or flows are differentiated through the use of various parameters such as IP source address, IP destination address, Differentiated Services Code Point (DSCP), or IP precedence values and other higher-level protocol types. After they are classified, the packets can be processed according to a policy that reflects their service level. Table 4-2 summarizes the differences between IPv4 and IPv6 for QoS mechanisms.

Table 4-2 *Differences Between IPv4 and IPv6 for QoS Mechanisms*

QoS Mechanism	Implementation	IPv4	IPv6
Classification	Precedence	Y	Y
	DSCP	Y	Y
Marking	Class-based marking	Y	Y
	Committed Access Rate	Y	Y
	Policy-based routing	Y	Y
Policing and shaping	Rate limiting	Y	Y
	Class-based policing	Y	Y
	Generic traffic shaping	Y	N
	Frame Relay traffic shaping	Y	Y
Congestion avoidance	Weighted Random Early Detection	Y	Y
Congestion management	First In First Out	Y	Y
	Priority queuing	Y	Y (Legacy method not supported)
	Custom queuing	Y	N
	Low-latency queuing	Y	Y

The type of service (ToS) field in the IPv4 packet header is mapped identically to the Traffic Class field in IPv6, and it is used in the same fashion. With IPv6, however, several additional classifiers must be considered, all related to the IPv6 packet header format:

- **Protocol type or version:** Because of the anticipated coexistence of the two protocols, it is worth considering the case where different service levels are applied to IPv4 and IPv6 traffic. The Protocol Type field can distinguish between the two protocols. Additionally, more discrete classifications can be done for the traffic for each protocol type.

- **Flow label:** The flow label is unique to IPv6 and was originally intended for use with resource-reservation-based QoS architectures. It was meant to enable routers to easily recognize a flow for which the resources were reserved. RFC 3697 documents the flow label specifications. This field has the advantage of being located before the Source Address and the Destination Address fields, and that placement helps reduce lookup delays.

Table 4-3 highlights the differences between IPv4 and IPv6 headers.

Table 4-3   *IPv4 and IPv6 Header Comparison*

IPv4 Header Field	IPv6 Header Field
Version	Different version number. Field is the same.
Header Length	Removed in IPv6. Fixed at 40 bytes.
Total Length	Payload Length.
Identification, Flags, Fragment Offset	Removed in IPv6.
Time-to-Live (TTL)	Hop Limit.
Protocol	Next Header.
Header Checksum	Removed in IPv6.
Source Address	Source Address (size is 128 bits).
Destination Address	Destination Address (size is 128 bits).
Options	Removed with IPv6 extension headers.
Type of Service	Traffic Class.

IPv6 Extension Headers

In an IPv6 datagram, one or more extension headers might appear before the encapsulated payload. These headers provide an efficient and flexible method to create IPv6 datagrams. Only special-purpose fields are put into extension headers when needed. The IPv4 header had a provision for options, and it would have been possible to use options for IPv6 as well. However, a better design was needed for certain sets of information, such as fragmenting and other common functions. Options are still needed for IPv6 because they are used to provide even more flexibility. Extension headers are included in an IPv6 datagram; they appear one after the other following the main header, as illustrated in Figure 4-5.

Two IPv6 extension headers can be used for QoS requirements:

■ **The routing extension header** can request a specific route based on the requester's knowledge of the network topology and QoS-sensitive parameters such as possible throughput.

■ **The hop-by-hop header** is the only extension header that must be fully processed by all the devices in the path of the QoS-sensitive data. The use of this header enables faster processing by the network device because there is no analysis of higher-lever protocols. Network devices that cannot recognize this header are required to ignore and continue processing the header. Network devices are not allowed to change this header while the packet is in transit.

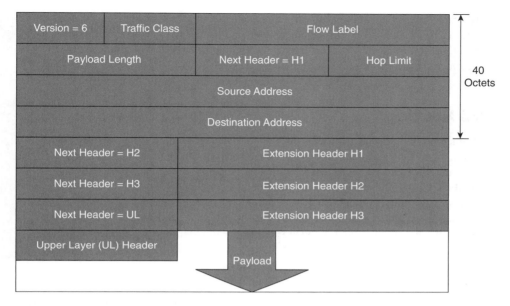

Figure 4-5 *IPv6 Packet with Extension Headers*

IPv4 and IPv6 Coexistence

There are two approaches possible with the coexistence of IPv4 and IPv6:

■ IPv6 traffic is treated differently than IPv4 by using two different QoS policies.

■ IPv6 traffic is treated the same as IPv4 by using a single QoS policy that classifies and matches on both protocols.

The per-hop behaviors (PHB) for the two protocols might be different under the following considerations:

■ IPv4 traffic is revenue generating, and it most likely is more important for the business than the IPv6 traffic, at least in the beginning. In that case, you might choose to prioritize the IPv6 traffic lower than IPv4 and provide fewer resources for it.

■ IPv4 and IPv6 traffic might have to observe different PHBs depending on traffic patterns used by various applications.

In these cases, different classes and policies should be defined for each traffic type.

With transition mechanisms, the IPv6 traffic can leverage the deployed QoS of the traversed IPv4 infrastructure. In some circumstances, the IPv6 traffic might also lose its markings after crossing the IPv4 network.

As applications demand higher performance from an enterprise network, differentiating at the network layer protocol has lost its relevance. End users running a particular application (for example, video) do not care about the network layer being used and expect the same level of network quality irrespective of the network layer protocol. This approach also reduces the management overhead for the QoS deployment. For implementing QoS at Layer 2, it is recommended that no differentiation should be made between the two protocol types.

IPv6 Routing

Numerous IPv4 routing protocols (RP) are available for finding routes between networks, and almost every one of them has an IPv6 correspondent or extension: Routing Information Protocol next-generation (RIPng), Open Shortest Path First version 3 (OSPFv3), Intermediate System–to–Intermediate System (IS-IS), and Enhanced Interior Gateway Routing Protocol (EIGRP). Although an in-depth analysis of routing protocols is beyond the scope of this book, OSPFv3, IS-IS, EIGRPv6, and Border Gateway Protocol (BGP) are discussed in the following sections.

OSPFv3

Open Shortest Path First (OSPF) is a link-state protocol. OSPFv2 is an interior gateway protocol (IGP) used to distribute routing information between routers of a single autonomous system for IPv4 networks. The updates for IPv6 were made in OSPF version 3 (OSPFv3).

Routers running OSPF advertise link state, link prefix/mask, link weight, and other local connectivity parameters in link-state advertisements (LSA). These LSAs are flooded reliably to other routers in the network to ensure that every OSPF router has a complete and consistent view of the topology.

On broadcast and nonbroadcast multiaccess (NBMA) networks, a designated router (DR), elected during neighboring relationship establishment (Hello protocol), can help reduce the amount of control traffic necessary for this operation by acting as a relay between OSPF routers for LSAs. A backup designated router (BDR) is also elected. The BDR picks up the functions of a failed DR with no need of a new election process. See Figure 4-6.

OSPF enables sets of networks to be grouped together into regions called areas. A router maintains a topology database for each area it participates in, and the topology of an area is hidden from the rest of the autonomous system. Areas constitute a useful concept that enables a two-level routing hierarchy, a concept that helps improve scalability. Routers do not need to maintain a topology database for areas they do not belong to, which leads to a significant reduction in routing traffic. Route summarization can occur on the area borders, another way to reduce the routing traffic. See Figure 4-7 for an example of OSPF areas.

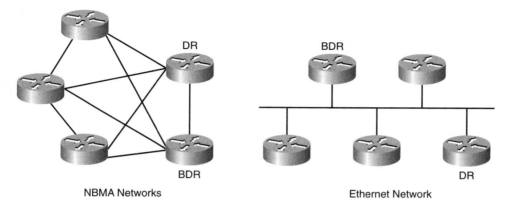

Figure 4-6   *OSPF Network Types with DR and BDR Example*

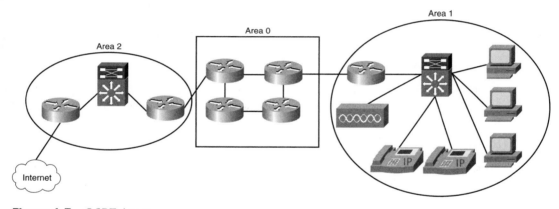

Figure 4-7   *OSPF Areas*

For securing routing distribution and installation, OSPFv2 defines fields AuType and Authentication in its protocol header (RFC 5709).

Finally, OSPF has built-in support for classless interdomain routing (CIDR). (Each route distributed by OSPF has a destination and mask.)

OSPFv3 extends OSPF to provide support for IPv6, as specified in RFC 5340. The basic mechanisms already used by OSPFv2, such as flooding, DR election, area support, SPF calculations, and so on, remain applicable to OSPFv3. Neighboring routers are still identified by the 32-bit router ID in OSPFv3. However, changes in protocol semantics between IPv4 and IPv6, and changes in the address format, have led to significant changes in OSPFv3 compared to OSPFv2.

The two versions of the OSPF protocol operate independently of each other, on disjoint databases. There is no backward compatibility from OSPFv3 to OSPFv2. Example 4-2 illustrates OSPFv3 configuration using NX-OS.

Example 4-2   *Unified OSPF Configuration Example on NX-OS*

```
interface serial1
   ipv6 ospf 1 area 0
   ipv6 ospf cost 12
   ospfv3 cost 22
```

A main goal of OSPFv3 is to create a routing protocol that is independent of any specific network layer. To achieve this, OSPFv3's inter-router messages have been redesigned, and addressing semantics have been removed from OSPF packets and from the basic LSAs. In OSPFv3, LSAs such as router LSAs and network LSAs carry only topology information. The following LSAs have been created to carry IPv6 addresses and prefixes:

■ Link LSAs announce the router's IPv6 link-local address to neighbors on the link, inform these neighbors of a list of IPv6 addresses to associate with the link, and announce the set of options.

■ Intra-area prefix LSAs carry all IPv6 prefix information to all OSPFv3 routers within an area. (This information in IPv4 is carried by the router and network LSAs.)

The following LSAs have been modified:

■ Router link state advertisements and network LSAs no longer carry prefix information. In OSPFv3, these LSAs carry only topology information, making them network-protocol independent.

■ The inter-area prefix replaces the network summary or type 3 LSA. An inter-area prefix LSA advertises internal networks to routers in other areas. With IPv6, those LSAs are expressed as <prefix, prefix length> rather than <prefix, mask>.

■ The inter-area router replaces the Autonomous System Boundary Router (ASBR) summary LSA (type 4). It advertises the location of an ASBR.

OSPFv3 runs on a per-link basis rather than on a per–IP subnet basis as in OSPFv2. When OSPF peering occurs over a physical link, OSPF packets are sent using the interface link-local unicast address as source. The flooding scope for LSAs has been generalized. Authentication has been removed from the OSPF protocol itself, instead relying on IPv6's Authentication Header (AH) and Encapsulating Security Payload (ESP). Most packets in OSPF for IPv6 are almost as compact as those in OSPF for IPv4, even with the larger IPv6 addresses.

OSPFv3 supports the ability to run multiple OSPF protocol instances on a single link. The OSPFv3 packet header includes an 8-bit instance ID used to demultiplex the protocol packets. Each OSPFv3 process sets its configured instance value in the OSPFv3 packets that it sends and ignores received packets with instance values from other OSPFv3 processes.

Instance IDs can control communication between routers sharing a physical network and OSPF area, without relying on complex authentication schemes or access lists, as needed in the past. It enables the providers to run separate OSPF routing domains, even though they have one or more physical network segments in common. For further reading, visit the IPv6 routing section at http://www.cisco.com/go/ipv6.

EIGRPv6

The Cisco-proprietary Enhanced Interior Gateway Protocol (EIGRP) was developed to bridge the gap between the traditional distance vector protocols (IGRP, RIP) and the advanced link-state protocols (OSPF, IS-IS). It integrates some of the proven capabilities of the latter to improve the operation and the scalability of the former. Nevertheless, the intent was to avoid some of the topological constraints that are sometimes associated with link-state protocols. The result is a simple yet fast-converging, resilient, and scalable routing protocol that is largely adopted in many enterprise networks and at the edge of some ISP networks.

EIGRPv6 is a distance vector routing protocol based on IGRP that offers the following improvements:

- Diffusing update algorithm (DUAL) can determine whether a path advertised by a neighbor is loop-free and to identify alternative paths without waiting on updates from other routers.

- It stores all routes learned, not only the best one learned from neighbors.

- It actively queries neighbors when destinations become unreachable, and that leads to competitive convergence times.

- It uses Hello packets to maintain neighbor state, which leads to faster convergence.

- It uses reliable transport protocol for the exchange of updates, which eliminates the need for periodic, full updates.

- It uses complex metrics that provide flexibility in route selection.

To meet the routing needs of enterprise networks, EIGRP has a modular design with protocol-independent core functionality and protocol-dependent modules that enable it to be used for IPv4, IPX, and AppleTalk.

The large deployed base for EIGRP drove the demand for extending its capabilities to support IPv6. The modular implementation of EIGRP simplifies the implementation. It requires the introduction of another protocol-dependent module for IPv6 (protocol identifier 88 was chosen, the same as IPv4) and three new TLVs (IPv6_REQUEST_TYPE [0X0401], IPv6_METRIC_TYPE [0X0402], and IPv6_EXTERIOR_TYPE [0X0403]).

EIGRP for IPv4 and EIGRP for IPv6 have strong similarities. A few differences exist because of some specific aspects of IPv6:

■ The router ID for the EIGRP process remains 32 bits long. It is derived from an IPv4 address found on one of the configured interfaces or is manually configured.

■ On an IPv6-only router, the EIGRP process does not start until the ID is manually configured.

■ The source address (SA) of the EIGRP Hello is the link-local address of the transmitting interface; the destination address (DA) is FF02::A (the all EIGRP routers, link-scope multicast address).

■ The format of the Hello packet implies that two neighbor routers do not have to share the same prefix on the link to see each other's Hellos. Packets sent to specific peers are unicasted, in which case sharing the same prefix on the link becomes relevant.

■ EIGRP for IPv4 uses message digest algorithm 5 (MD5) for authentication, and similar support is provided by EIGRP for IPv6. Although not yet available at the time of this writing, support for IPsec authentication on Cisco routers is in development.

■ Automatic summarization enabled by default in EIGRP for IPv4 is disabled in EIGRP for IPv6 because IPv6 is classless.

■ Unlike EIGRP for IPv4, there is no split horizon in EIGRP for IPv6 because in IPv6, multiple prefixes could be present on the same interface of a router.

EIGRP for IPv6 will be enabled to operate within Virtual Private Networks (VPN) in a similar way as EIGRP for IPv4. Example 4-3 illustrates EIGRP for IPv6 configuration.

Example 4-3 *EIGRPv6 Configuration*

```
interface GigabitEthernet7/1
  ipv6 enable
  ipv6 eigrp 100
ipv6 eigrp router 100
 no shutdown
 eigrp router-id 2.2.2.2
```

The **show** outputs for EIGRPv6 are similar to EIGRP, as illustrated in Example 4-4.

Example 4-4 *EIGRPv6 Output*

```
R1# show ipv6 eigrp topology
EIGRP-IPv6 Topology Table for AS(100)/ID(2.2.2.2)
Codes: P - Passive, A - Active, U - Update, Q - Query, R - Reply,
       r - reply Status, s - sia Status

P 2001:DB8:CAFE:1004::/64, 1 successors, FD is 409600
```

```
          via FE80::A8BB:CCFF:FE01:8700 (409600/128256), Ethernet0/0
P 2001:DB8:CAFE:1001::/64, 1 successors, FD is 281600
        via Connected, Ethernet0/0
P 2001:DB8:CAFE:1002::/64, 1 successors, FD is 128256
        via Connected, Loopback1


R1# show ipv6 eigrp neighbors
EIGRP-IPv6 Neighbors for AS(100)
H    Address                  Interface       Hold Uptime    SRTT   RTO   Q  Seq
                                              (sec)          (ms)         Cnt Num
0    Link-local address:      Et0/0           14 00:01:21    10     200   0  7
     FE80::A8BB:CCFF:FE01:8700
R1#
```

With minor syntax modifications, the commands available for tweaking or troubleshooting EIGRP for IPv4 are available for IPv6 as well.

IS-IS

The Intermediate System–to–Intermediate System (IS-IS) protocol is described in ISO Standard 10589. This link-state, OSI routing protocol was not originally developed for IP but rather to provide the routing functionality between the routers of Connectionless Network Protocol (CLNP)–based networks. With the addition of IPv4 support (RFC 1195), the protocol, sometimes referred to as Integrated IS-IS (I/IS-IS), was widely adopted as the IGP of choice for many ISP and large enterprise networks. (For more information, refer to the book *IS-IS: Deployment in IP Networks*, by Russ White and Alvaro Retana.)

The implementation required a new protocol ID (0X8E) that was set to be used by the IPv6 routers to signal their capability to support ISISv6 and two new TLVs: IPv6_Reachability (0XEC) and IPv6_Interface_Address (0XE8). Extending IS-IS to support IPv6 is an exercise similar to extending it to support IPv4, unlike OSPF, where a new protocol had to be developed. For this reason, IS-ISv6 is operationally similar to IS-ISv4. Few IPv6-specific differences exist. Neighbors are listed in the adjacency table with their link-local address. Because the link-local is used in the Hello packets, adjacencies can be built between neighbors even if they do not share the same prefix. From a user perspective, a new address family was added for IPv6. Most configuration commands available for IS-ISv4 are also available for IS-ISv6 with minimal format changes.

IS-ISv6 uses a single topology and runs the same SPF calculation for all protocols supported. This mode of operation leads to certain deployment constraints. The following sections discuss single topology and multitopology.

Single Topology

By default, IS-ISv6 runs with a single topology for all protocols supported and a single instance of the SPF calculation per level (1 = area, 2 = domain). This could be a benefit because fewer resources are being used by the routers to operate it. On the other hand, the single-topology mode comes with some restrictions:

■ All routers within an area (level 1 or level 2) must support the same set of address families on all interfaces. This ensures topology consistency. It also means that the single-topology mode is not suitable in IPv4 networks where only some islands of IPv6 will be deployed.

■ The interface-configured metric applies to both IPv4 and IPv6.

This need for capabilities consistency raises this question: What will happen when an IS-ISv4 network is migrated to the IS-ISv4+IS-ISv6 network? Because routers are configured with the additional IPv6 address family, the adjacencies will be dropped until the consistency is reestablished. To avoid impacting the operating IPv4 service, you can disable the adjacency checking.

Note   To avoid inconsistencies in the operational network, disable only adjacency checking during the migration process.

Multitopology

IS-IS was enhanced to support independent topologies and SPF calculations for each protocol. In this case, various routers can support different sets of address families. To add multitopology support for IPv6, a new Multi_Topology_Reachable_IPv6_Prefixes TLV was defined. The multitopology operation can be enabled under the IPv6 address family. In this mode of operation, you can set the IPv6 metric independently of the IPv4 one.

To facilitate the migration from single topology to multitopology, you can enable a transition mode. In this case, both types of TLVs are advertised in LSPs. Larger LSPs are thus traded off for a smooth transition.

Configuring IS-ISv6

The simplest way to configure a router to run IS-IS for IPv6 is to enable the protocol on an interface with an IPv6 address. No changes are needed to the configuration of the IS-IS process for IPv4, as illustrated in Example 4-5.

Example 4-5   *IS-IS Configuration Example*

```
isis example-area
net 49.0001.0000.0000.0001.00
!
```

```
interface FastEthernet0/1
 ip address 10.7.1.33 255.255.255.252
 ip router isis example-area
 ipv6 address 2001:FFFF:FFFF::2/64
 ipv6 enable
 ipv6 router isis example-area
```

BGP

Border Gateway Protocol version 4 (BGP4) is the exterior gateway protocol (EGP) used to exchange routes between autonomous systems in the Internet. BGP was designed based on experience gained with EGP, and provides built-in support for CIDR and route aggregation. BGP4 is specified in RFC 1771 and other BGP-related documents: RFC 1772, RFC 1773, and RFC 1774. For in-depth information about BGP, refer to the book *Internet Routing Architectures*, Second Edition, by Sam Halabi.

The BGP basic unit of routing information is the BGP path, a route to a certain set of CIDR prefixes. Paths are tagged with various path attributes, of which the most important are AS_PATH and NEXT_HOP.

The AS_PATH attribute contains a list of autonomous systems a route goes through to get to the destination. Loops are detected and avoided by checking that the router's own ASN is not in the AS_PATHs received from neighboring autonomous systems.

The NEXT_HOP attribute is another important piece of the BGP route advertisement. When the BGP update crosses autonomous system boundaries (see the eBGP discussion that follows), the NEXT_HOP attribute is changed to be the IP address of the boundary router while, as long as updates remain within an autonomous system, the next hop is left unchanged. (See the iBGP discussion that follows.) That ensures that within the autonomous system, the next hop is always the IP address of the external peer that announced the destination prefix, and that internal BGP peers do not have to be on the path to the advertised destination.

BGP can be deployed in two forms: exterior BGP (eBGP) and interior BGP (iBGP). eBGP is used for inter–autonomous system peering, whereas iBGP carries BGP path information inside the same autonomous system. Although some of the information (route, metric) carried by iBGP might be redundant with that advertised by IGPs—such as IS-IS, OSPF, and so on—no IGP is capable of transporting BGP-specific path attributes such as the AS_PATH. Hence, iBGP is necessary to ensure that BGP path attributes received on one edge of the autonomous system, over the eBGP connection, are available on the other edge of the same autonomous system. Example 4-6 illustrates BGP configuration for advertising IPv6 network 2001:100::/24.

Example 4-6 *BGP for IPv6 Configuration on IOS*

```
router bgp 100
 no bgp default ipv4-unicast
 address-family ipv6
  network 2001:100::/24
```

The BGP routing protocol and all its IPv4-based commands work in the same manner, as illustrated in the output of the **show bgp ipv6** command shown in Example 4-7.

Example 4-7   show bgp ipv6 *Output*

```
R1> show bgp ipv6
BGP table version is 8, local router ID is 200.10.10.1
Status codes: s suppressed, d damped, h history, * valid, > best, i - internal,
              r RIB-failure, S Stale
Origin codes: i - IGP, e - EGP, ? - incomplete

   Network            Next Hop          Metric LocPrf Weight Path
*>i2001:200:1::/48    2001:100:1:1::2       0     100      0 200 ?
*   2001:100:1:1::/64 2001:100:1:1::1       0              0 100 ?
*>                    ::                     0          32768 ?
*> 2001:100:2:1::/64  2001:100:1:1::1                      0 100 ?
*> 2001:100:3:1::/64  2001:100:1:1::1       0              0 100 ?
*> 2001:100:3:2::/64  2001:100:1:1::1       0              0 100 ?
*> 2001:100:3:3::/64  2001:100:1:1::1                      0 100 ?
*> 2001:100:3:4::/64  2001:100:1:1::1                      0 100 ?
```

BGP runs over a TCP transport protocol. On connection start, BGP peers exchange complete copies of their routing tables. Then onward, the BGP peers maintain their respective routing database by exchanging only deltas, which makes BGP a very efficient routing protocol.

In addition to BGP attributes, CIDR is used by BGP to aggregate prefixes and reduce the size of the routing tables. When an ISP has been delegated a block of addresses, and has allocated part of this block to its own customers, BGP can aggregate routes received from these customers, and announce the entire block to its BGP peers, allowing a significant reduction in the number of BGP routing tables.

Multiprotocol BGP for IPv6

Multiprotocol BGP4 (MP-BGP), specified in RFC 4760, defines extensions enabling BGP4 to carry routing information for multiple network layer protocols.

In the most typical cases, BGP peering for announcing IPv6 routes will occur over an IPv6 transport, and eventually coexist with a separate BGP session for announcing IPv4 routes, as shown in Example 4-8.

Example 4-8 *Configuring Distinct BGP Sessions for IPv4 and IPv6 Addresses*

```
router bgp 10
 no bgp default ipv4-unicast
 neighbor 2001:db8:cafe:1019::1 remote-as 20
 neighbor 172.16.1.2 remote-as 30
 !
 address-family ipv4
  neighbor 172.16.1.2 activate
  network 172.16.0.0
exit-address-family
 !
 address-family ipv6
  neighbor 2001:db8:cafe:1019::1 activate
  network 2001:db8::/32
exit-address-family
```

Multiprotocol BGP is the only protocol that carries routing information for IPv4 and IPv6 simultaneously. Although this section provided an overview, further detailed configuration examples and guidelines are available at http://www.cisco.com/en/US/docs/ios/ipv6/configuration/guide/ip6-mptcl_bgp.html.

Summary

This chapter provides an overview of multicast for IPv6, in which various methods of implementing multicast protocols (PIM, SSM, PIM-Bidir, and so on) were discussed.

The quality of service (QoS) section provides an overview of how to classify application packets independent of protocol version. Also, a brief comparison between IPv4 and IPv6 is provided along with an overview of extension headers.

Routing protocols such as RIPng, OSPFv3, EIGRP, ISIS, and BGP for IPv6 help in forwarding packets to their right destination. The similarities and differences between IPv4 and IPv6 are discussed for each of these protocols. IPv6 enables the network devices to cope with the growing routing tables; however, the convergence and stability are still challenges just like IPv4 and are areas for future innovations.

Additional References

Bates, T., et. al. RFC 2858, "Multiprotocol Extensions for BGP-4." June 2000.

Deering, S., et. al. RFC 2710, "Multicast Listener Discovery (MLD) for IPv6." October 1999.

Halabi, Sam and Danny McPherson. *Internet Routing Architectures, Second Edition*, August 2000.

Popoviciu, Ciprian, Eric Levy-Abegnoli, and Patrick Grossetete. *Deploying IPv6 Networks*, Cisco Press, February 2006.

Rajahalme, J., et. al. RFC 3697, "IPv6 Flow Specification." March 2004.

Chapter 5

Planning an IPv6 Deployment

The chapter covers the following topics:

- **Determining where to begin:** An enterprise needs to analyze the benefits, costs, risks, and other business factors and technology considerations that, together, all help determine the initial starting point.

- **Planning a pilot:** The pilot phase of an IPv6 deployment is crucial because it exposes training, equipment, design, and technology gaps.

- **Planning an address allocation:** The pilot phase enables experimentation of addressing internally, but at some point, you need to obtain global IPv6 addressing from a regional registry and your service providers.

Moving toward an IPv6 deployment requires careful planning, network design considerations, and training for the network administrators. To deal with many of the challenges of deploying IPv6, you need to perform an assessment of the existing network, which includes product compliance. This chapter provides you with a framework to outline step-by-step predeployment and deployment considerations, thereby reducing the risk involved in integrating IPv6 in the existing infrastructure without much business impact.

Determining Where to Begin

Organizations should identify the reasons to adopt IPv6 in the enterprise, including the drivers and business requirements. It should link IPv6 interoperability to specific business objectives.

Early adoption of IPv6 creates a competitive advantage for an organization. It strengthens its position and increases the flexibility in provisioning innovative services. Other reasons to deploy IPv6 include the following:

- The need for address space to support the explosion of Internet-enabled devices and proliferation of peer-to-peer, always-on applications

- Respond to external pressures of IPv4 address exhaustion

- Business continuity

- Government policies to implement IPv6

- Customer demands

- Global communications

- Migration of supply chains to IPv6

After determining that an enterprise needs to deploy IPv6, some key benefits tasks should be analyzed. This benefit analysis provides better justification of this large-scale effort.

Benefit Analysis

Organizations should analyze the benefits gained by deploying IPv6, including what lines of business and business programs benefit by transitioning to IPv6.

Organizations need to determine whether deploying IPv6 will increase or maintain business revenue. Commonly, enterprises take either a defensive or offensive approach to IPv6. A defensive approach would be if the enterprise cannot realize an immediate benefit from IPv6 deployment, but yet it wants to be prepared if some new business or technology driver comes along. One example of this is when an enterprise wants to ensure that a potential customer, who might end up with an IPv6-enabled or IPv6-only device, can still reach the enterprise's public-facing websites. This is a defensive tactic to ensure business continuity. Offensively, transitioning to IPv6 can increase revenue by introducing new service opportunities or decreasing the cost of maintaining existing services.

On the technical side, deploying IPv6 can eliminate the need to configure "workarounds" such as tunnels and Network Address Translation (NAT). This improves network performance and greatly simplifies operations. IPv6 exhibits numerous technical features that, when compared to IPv4, make it a more powerful and flexible framework to deploy future network applications and services. In brief, the key features of IPv6 protocols are as follows:

- **Increased number of IP addresses:** IPv6 enables billions of new devices to be connected over the Internet, such as mobile devices, consumer electronics, sensors, transportation-monitoring equipment, and so on.

- **Autoconfiguration:** IPv6 standards describe techniques that enable IPv6-ready hosts to set their (networking) operational parameters and automatically can establish communication channels with other hosts.

- **Security:** The standards mandate the support of IP (layer) Security (IPsec) at all IPv6-enabled hosts, enabling the secure exchange of digital information.

- **Mobility:** The Mobile IPv6 (MIPv6) model is simpler than its IPv4 counterpart.

- **Multicast:** Multicasting is widely used in IPv6 networks and improves the efficiency of communications among multiple hosts. Also, the expansion of (IPv6) multicast address space and the explicit address scoping simplify the provisioning of multicast services.

- **Extension headers:** The support of extension headers enables protocol-level information to be carried in addition to the basic IPv6 header.

- **Reduced operational cost:** The deployment of IPv6 protocols can reduce the management overhead of future networks.

The large address space, the removal of NAT gateways, the autoconfiguration features, the integrated support of IPsec, and mobility are some key factors that lead to a reduction in operational costs.

Cost Analysis

Organizations also must analyze what costs are associated with deploying IPv6 transition. For example:

- Designing and engineering (including planning, system engineering, design, testing, implementation, and deployment)

- Changes or upgrades in infrastructure that might include

  - Hardware and software, which include servers, PCs, and possibly all IT equipment

  - Applications

  - Operational support systems

- Recurring cost of training in skills associated with IPv6 and interworking between IPv4 and IPv6

- Operational/support costs after deployment starts

To summarize, the gradual deployment of IPv6 in an organization requires monetary investment. IPv6 features can be added at minimal incremental costs during normal hardware or software replacement cycles. After the IPv6 supporting infrastructure is ready, dual-stack can be used to support a gradual transition from IPv4 to IPv6. In addition to hardware and software, costs can include incremental and recurring expenditures and activities associated with IPv6 deployment.

Investing in an early IPv6 adoption by, for example, upgrading the installed base and increasing the technical expertise in the organization can be high, if not planned for ahead. Similarly, high investments are required when an organization is forced because of market conditions to deploy IPv6 in a short period of time, for example, because of infrastructure upgrades that are not aligned with equipment life cycles. There can be an optimal period of deploying IPv6 in an organization where capital costs are minimized. In most cases, IPv6 can be deployed in a very cost-effective manner as part of a natural procurement cycle, but if IPv6-specific requirements are not included in the procurement process, additional costs can arise if a quick migration is later required.

Risks

Identify risks associated with deploying IPv6, which could include business, legal, or technical risks. For each of the risks identified, there should be mitigating actions that can be used to minimize or prevent those risks, for example:

- **Business risks:** Can we achieve the identified benefits and the return on investment? Can the organization continue to grow with the IPv6 deployment? There is another way to look at the business risk. Deployment of IPv6 can be considered in terms of infrastructure maintenance, much like the upgrade of an old public branch exchange (PBX) that is out of support but still meeting current business requirements. The impact of not maintaining infrastructure is an increase in business risk and sometimes an increase in support costs. Deploying IPv6 is a risk mitigation project. It might not generate revenue immediately, but it might in the future prevent revenue loss.

- **Legal risks:** Unique identifiers exist in IPv6 addresses that can provide the potential to track network activity. This can be privacy risk, and therefore network operators must be aware of any legal requirements to safeguard the privacy of their users.

- **Technical risks:** Security risks can develop if IPv6 and the associated transition mechanisms are not implemented or managed properly. Different transition mechanisms have different technical risks. Some security devices might not provide IPv6 detection or filtering capability, which might open windows of attack. Risk of interoperability needs to be checked for possible interaction issues with other IPv6 stacks, for example, Session Initiation Protocol (SIP) or mobility protocols.

Business Case

Deploying a new technology must meet the following business needs:

- Yield cost savings
- Create or enhance revenue streams
- Generate a competitive or strategic advantage

In the economic climate today, IT decisions are viewed by their return on investment (ROI). While ROI is meant to be a precise measurement, it fails to capture the following factors:

- Risks
- Complexity
- Intangibles

The preceding factors, along with the ROI, need to be captured in the business case to deploy IPv6. The business case also needs to capture financial measures such as cost savings and revenue streams. The business case should highlight major program activities, specific solutions, and impacts.

Transition Team

Establish a team of people, called the transition group, to oversee the IPv6 deployment effort. After it is established, the team can plan, coordinate, and communicate the progress of IPv6 deployment throughout the entire organization. The team can also ensure that resources (for example, staffing, training, budget, and so on) are adequately allocated to complete all identified tasks within schedule. This team is especially critical in large, distributed organizations.

The organization identifies the members of the team and clearly defines their roles and responsibilities. The members can be from different departments such as applications, network, and other business groups. Typically network administrators, system administrators, software developers, and support technicians would be working with a project manager or a team of project managers.

The team also needs to build awareness of IPv6 within the organization. Employees should know what IPv6 is, how it impacts their work areas, and why it is important to the organization as a whole.

The transition group should have executive authority within the organization to sponsor the transition program and set policy. This can provide a significant boost to the overall priority of the transition program when competing for resources.

The team can identify the areas that can be impacted by deploying IPv6 within the enterprise network. This can be achieved by defining milestones to be completed within a schedule and individual owners of tasks.

Individual working groups within the team address separate areas. A lead should be assigned to each group. The transition group can also establish the objectives for the working team and ensure that each working team is staffed and trained appropriately and sufficiently.

Metrics needs to be defined to track transition progress. This would provide the confidence to executive management that milestones outlined in the business case are being achieved.

The transition team needs to develop and communicate clear policy and enforcement procedures to ensure that all impacted areas within an enterprise include IPv6 in their future plans. IPv6 policies should be released and emphasized on a timely basis. Identify methods or tools for review and enforcement of policies. An example of an IPv6 policy could be that all future procurements should be of IPv6-capable/ready assets only. An example of an enforcement procedure could be that only business cases for IPv6-compliant projects will be approved.

An overall comprehensive IPv6 deployment plan needs to be developed for the entire organization to ensure that all IPv6 plans are synchronized, consistent, and prioritized.

After the business plan is executed, the transition team needs to provide periodic communication of the progress of IPv6 transition throughout the enterprise.

Training

In a large enterprise, both the business and technical aspects of deploying IPv6 training might be necessary to initiate and maintain IPv6 readiness. Depending on the role of the personnel in the organization, the type of training can vary. Following is a sample of training categories:

- **Awareness training:** This type of training provides an overview of IPv6 technologies, a basic understanding of the IPv6 technology, and business drivers, deployment issues, and potential applications and devices enabled by IPv6.

- **Architectural training:** This type of training is for individuals who have primary responsibilities in architecting, designing, and deploying IPv6.

- **Operational training:** This training is for individuals who have primary responsibilities in supporting a deployed IPv6 network.

- **Specialized training:** This training is for Subject Matter Experts (SME) who work in a particular technology area (for example, Mobility, Security, and so on).

Planning a Pilot

When introducing a new technology such as IPv6, which is responsible for the underlying connectivity for enterprise applications, it is wise to start a pilot/trial in a lab environment. Testing in a lab environment that mirrors the actual network can help you better understand IPv6 and gain confidence in its potential success in the enterprise network. On successful completion of lab tests, a pilot implementation on a live network should be performed. This pilot can be a small section of the live network.

The following sections provide a high-level overview of some of the activities included an IPv6 pilot. After the pilot is complete, these activities can be revised for a large-scale deployment/migration. An extensive pilot-case study is discussed in Chapter 12, "Walk Before Running: Building an IPv6 Lab and Starting a Pilot."

Assessment

Perform an inventory assessment in the current infrastructure. The result of this analysis provides an initial view of those components that might require an upgrade or replacement. Following is a sample list of the components to inventory:

- **Address allocation planning for both present and future:** This can help map present address allocation practices with IPv6 address allocation.

■ **Networks:** Assess what types of networks are present in the enterprise. Possible network types include IP, wireless, DSL, VoIP, and CPE. A complete network equipment inventory should be done.

■ **Network services:** Determine what network services are running today in the enterprise. For example, DNS, AAA, DHCP, NTP, and so on.

■ **Network management:** Assess how the network would be managed after IPv6 is deployed on the network. Some tools that can be used for network management include NetFlow, MIBS, SNMP, and so on.

■ **Network applications:** Assess how network applications such as VoIP, databases, and so on interact with IPv6. A software and operation system inventory should be done.

■ **Other IP-based/aware services:** Other services, such as location and mobility, will use IPv6 for communications.

Design

Develop an overall IPv6 design for various impacted areas. The IPv6 design plan should be standards-based and should provide as much IPv4 feature parity as applicable to support a smooth transition. The design should take into account any new networks and services as well as traffic growth that an enterprise foresees. The following sections describe areas that can be considered when developing an IPv6 design.

IPv6 Addressing Plan

Understand addressing requirements within the enterprise. As described in this section, the addressing plan should outline the enterprise's IP addressing needs for the next few years and the address allocation, management, and acquisition processes. For example:

■ Examine addressing needs for an enterprise's own infrastructure, its intranet, its extranet, sites not managed by the organization, and services (for example, Layer 3 VPNs) that it supports or offers, and forecast IP address usage.

■ Develop a plan of IPv6 address allocation that outlines how IPv6 addresses should be allocated to support infrastructure and end users and provide efficient and scalable network routing. As part of the allocation, decide whether an enterprise uses Stateless Address Autoconfiguration (SLAAC) or Stateful Configuration for the hosts.

■ Determine the management of IPv6 privacy extensions. This enables hosts to use different IPv6 source addresses with time; for example, using a different IPv6 address daily.

■ Determine the impact of IPv6 routing, its integration, and changes with the existing IPv4 routing.

■ Allocate IPv6 addresses to external connections to the Internet and other sites. This means working with Internet service providers (ISP) on IPv6 peering. Plan end-to-end site connectivity using IPv6 as well.

Chapter 12 provides additional information and a sample of an IPv6 addressing plan.

Transition Mechanisms

Because IPv4 and IPv6 can coexist for a substantial period of time during the transition to IPv6, an organization needs to consider the various transition mechanisms that can facilitate the transition to IPv6 while coexisting with the IPv4 network environment. When selecting a transition mechanism, an organization needs to consider its current network environment, IPv6 traffic forecast, IPv6-capable devices or applications, and IPv6 deployment plan. Transition mechanisms fall into three major categories: dual-stack, tunneling, and translation, as explained in Chapter 3, "Common IPv6 Coexistence Mechanisms." These transition mechanisms also need to be included in the pilot to understand their behavior on the network and provide a learning experience.

Network Services

Network services will be impacted as you deploy IPv6. Understanding these changes is key to having an operational IPv6 network. Network services include Domain Name System (DNS); Dynamic Host Configuration Protocol (DHCP); authentication, authorization, and accounting (AAA); and Network Time Protocol (NTP). For example, an organization might need to decide whether to support autoconfiguration or DHCPv6 or both. It can consider implementing dual-stack DNS to support IPv6 address queries as well as existing IPv4 queries. As part of the pilot, these network services also need to be deployed, especially if their IPv4 counterparts exist in the network today to provide end-to-end services.

Security

In addition to the similar security threats that exist in the IPv4 world, an enterprise needs to protect new threats that arise during the transition to IPv6. For example, existing firewalls and network intrusion detection systems do not provide IPv6 detection or filtering capabilities and might need to be upgraded. Malicious users might be able to tunnel IPv6 traffic through these security devices undetected. Some of the automation features that reduce operational overhead can increase vulnerabilities.

For example, malicious users can spoof solicitation, advertisement, and binding messages. Applications that use automated tunneling can traverse firewalls and therefore expose the network to the outside world. To minimize these problems, mechanisms and policies need to be developed to secure an IPv6 network.

The pilot should include how to secure the network using IPv6, such as using IPsec with IPv6.

New Features in IPv6

IPv6 introduces several new features such as Stateless Address Autoconfiguration (SLAAC), "built in" IPsec, Mobile IPv6, flow label, and more. The pilot presents the perfect opportunity to evaluate these features. Each enterprise can use some or all of these features. A deep understanding of these features will help in determining IPv6 policies for an enterprise.

As an example, SLAAC enables hosts to obtain an IPv6 address automatically when connected to a routed IPv6 network. However, this might be unsuitable for an application, where a stateful configuration using DHCPv6 or static IPv6 address might have to be used.

Scalability and Reliability

As enterprises introduce IPv6 to their existing networks, they must ensure that the IPv6 design itself is a scalable and reliable design. In addition, they must ensure that the IPv6 solution does not introduce negative impacts to the existing network environment.

Dual-stack implies that there would be two protocol stacks running on devices. The overhead that dual-stack brings to devices needs to be looked at. Running dual-stack could, for example, increase CPU utilization on certain devices.

In terms of scalability, the number of routes and neighbors needs to be addressed. This can be worked out with the vendor to determine IPv6 scalability on the device.

Service Level Agreements

Develop service level agreements (SLA) that reflect any new IPv6 policy and include transition mechanisms because they often impact the ability to adhere to a tight SLA. Commonly, enterprises will try to match their existing SLAs and simply add IPv6 to them. This often fails because of the enterprise and service provider(s) having to, for a period of time, use transition mechanisms that introduce additional latency, loss, and jitter to the network.

Lessons Learned and Implementation

After the pilot, it is important to understand the results. Data gathered during the pilot provides information on how an enterprise can migrate to IPv6. The pilot also provides the opportunity for the enterprise to learn IPv6 as a technology. Some features will prove beneficial to use, whereas some features will need to be turned off, depending on the results of the pilot.

Going forward, organizations will need to develop their own IPv6 compliance standard for each device and application in the enterprise. These standards should be based on best industry standards. Some standards/certifications that an enterprise can follow are

USGv6 or the IPv6-ready logo. For those devices and applications that need to transition to IPv6, do the following:

■ **Assess when they will be IPv6-ready.** This step might require contacting vendors for the availability of their IPv6 product road map.

■ **Identify the impact to the supporting services and customers.** This might require establishing a relationship between the systems integrators and vendors. A vendor might provide a product or service that is IPv6 capable. A system integrator would provide different products or applications that would be IPv6 capable. It is important to understand the interaction between applications and devices in an IPv4/IPv6 environment.

After a successful pilot, develop a plan to deploy the IPv6 transition throughout the enterprise. The results of the test plan will play a key role in deciding which IPv6 features are to be used, how they are to be configured, and how they need to be managed.

Start by developing a list of projects to be implemented. Within that list, identify dependencies and prioritize the projects and tasks appropriately. Leverage the IPv6 testing/lab environment to verify architecture, designs, business rules, and so on.

Next, deploy IPv6 during an infrastructure refresh cycle and ensure that all devices procured or developed are IPv6 capable and, more importantly, have the features that the organization needs based on the outcome of the pilot.

Client/Server IPv6 Migration Scenarios

There is certainly no shortage of technology options when deploying IPv6. Selecting the right path will depend on the current environment in terms of end-user devices and operating systems, router models and versions, key applications, budget and resources, and schedule constraints.

The following sections review some starting points of migration scenarios. In reviewing these, the diagram illustrated in Figure 5-1 will be used as a baseline and depicts an all IPv4-only network. Three basic scenarios are discussed. Depending on the complexity of the network, business policies, and various other factors, any of the scenarios can be followed.

Tthis figure has a client with IPv4 applications, IPv4 sockets API and TCP/IPv4 stack, and a server with a comparable configuration. The interconnection network is split into access networks for the client and server, respectively, and a core or backbone network.

This basic diagram illustrates a pair-wise, client/server connection. For a given use case, this could represent an internal client accessing an internal server through an all-internal access and core network as well as over the Internet.

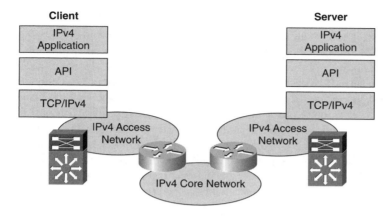

Figure 5-1   *Typical IPv4 Client/Server Model Using IPv4*

IPv6 Core Deployment: "Start at the Core"

This scenario starts by deploying IPv6 in the backbone or core network and slowly moves the IPv6 deployment toward the edges of the network, as illustrated in Figure 5-2.

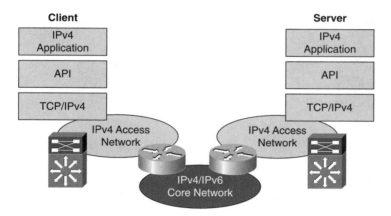

Figure 5-2   *IPv6 Core Deployment Scenario*

This topology requires enabling core routers to support dual-stack IPv4 and IPv6 routing and routing protocols. By enabling a dual-stack core, the enterprise can learn the protocol, routing differences, and many of the other differences with IPv6 without interrupting production IPv4 traffic between endpoints. This is a great option if there is no clear timeline for IPv6 deployment on the endpoints themselves. The core network could be an internal backbone or an IPv6 ISP network, in which case you might need to use 6PE or 6VPE mechanisms.

Localized IPv6 Server-Side Deployment

The localized server-side scenario involves upgrading servers and application hosts to dual-stack implementations. With the server still able to support IPv4 communications and applications, end clients connect as before through IPv4. However, the server would be able to serve IPv6 clients as well when they are dual-stack or IPv6-only enabled. At this point, unless the client is IPv6 enabled, either the client-to-server connection is IPv4-only or a translation or proxy device would have to be deployed. This option works best when a focus needs to be placed on the data center applications, operating systems, and networking components and their support of IPv6. This often occurs before any client connectivity over IPv6 is supported. Many enterprises will start on the server-side simply because it is a more complex area of deployment, and the operating system, applications, and supporting network infrastructure might require a more comprehensive set of IPv6 capabilities than any other area of the network such as the campus. One point to note in this topology is that certain network services, for example, DNS, will be enabled only when end-to-end IPv6 support is available. Figure 5-3 illustrates this configuration.

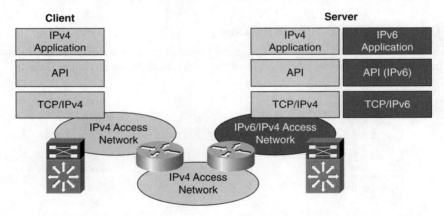

Figure 5-3   *Server-Side IPv6 Deployment Scenario*

Client-Side Deployment

Another scenario is to enable clients for dual-stack operation as well as to access network routers. This is more of a preparation step just like in the server-side scenario. Because end-to-end IPv6 connectivity is not enabled, the clients won't really be accessing an IPv6-enabled service unless they use a tunneling or translation mechanism. This option enables the endpoints to be dual-stack enabled and then, at some point, the end-to-end dual-stack configuration can be made (as seen in Figure 5-5). Existing IPv4 client devices would be supplemented with IPv6 applications, API, and TCP/IP stack. Figure 5-4 illustrates this configuration.

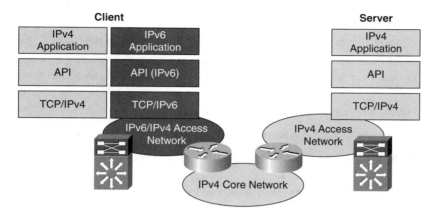

Figure 5-4   *Client-Side IPv6 Deployment Scenario*

Client/Server Deployment: Dual-Stack Configuration

A common approach to deploying IPv6 within an enterprise features upgrading of clients and servers at about the same time, including applications as appropriate. The use of dual-stack deployments, illustrated in Figure 5-5, facilitates the deployment to clients and servers over time.

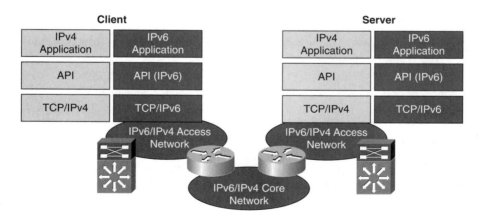

Figure 5-5   *Client/Server IPv6 Deployment Scenario*

Special consideration must be given to application migration, especially for integrated enterprise applications accessed by a large user population. Support of mixed IPv4/IPv6 clients in transition is ideal but might not be practical.

Planning Address Allocation

The Internet Assigned Numbers Authority (IANA) oversees global IP address allocation. IANA delegates allocations of IP address blocks to Regional Internet Registries (RIR). Each RIR represents a geographical area. Some examples of RIRs are as follows:

- ARIN: American IPv6 Registration Services (http://www.arin.net)

- APNIC: Asia Pacific Network Information Center (http://www.apnic.net)

- RIPE: European Regional Internet Registry (http://www.ripe.net)

RIRs allocate IPv6 addresses for local ISPs and end users. Most ISPs follow their RIR's guidelines to allocate single /48 subnets. A typical /48 allocation gives an enterprise 65,536/64 networks. Each /64 subnet has 2^{64} IPv6 addresses.

On receiving an IPv6 subnet, organize the address-space assignments further into enterprise-local subnets for efficient routing and aggregation. The best practices of planning IPv6 addresses are debatable. However, the following standard guidelines exist:

- **Ensure that every LAN subnet is a /64 network.** A good starting point would be to count the VLANs and anticipate how many networks would be needed in the future.

- **Determine the address space needed for network identifiers.** For example, a /56 xxx would provide 256/64 networks and a /52 xxx would provide 4096/64 networks. The 4-bit separation is for easier readability; however, any bit in between can be used.

- **Use /126 networks in the zero address space for link networks (router to router).** This is also recommended in RFC 3627.

Chapter 12 provides additional addressing examples and recommendations.

Summary

In this chapter, IPv6 deployment planning was discussed. The starting points show how the IPv6 deployment process can be started. This includes planning, building a business case, and building a team to oversee the IPv6 deployment.

A trial of IPv6 should be done in a lab environment to gain familiarity with the technology and prepare for a pilot on the live network.

IPv6 address allocation and how to obtain an IPv6 address were discussed toward the end, along with some guidelines that can be used for planning an IPv6 addressing scheme.

Additional References

Cisco. "IPv6 Deployment Strategies."
http://www.cisco.com/en/US/docs/ios/solutions_docs/ipv6/IPv6dswp.html.

Savola, P. RFC 3627, "Use of /127 Prefix Length Between Routers Considered Harmful."
September 2003.

Chapter 6

Deploying IPv6 in Campus Networks

This chapter covers the following subjects:

- **Campus deployment models overview:** A description is given of the three campus IPv6 deployment models that are most commonly used in the enterprise

- **General campus IPv6 deployment considerations:** Details are provided on generic IPv6 considerations that apply to any of the three campus IPv6 deployment models

- **Implementing the dual-stack model:** Detailed configuration examples are shown for the dual-stack model

- **Implementing the hybrid model:** Detailed configuration examples are shown for the hybrid model

- **Implementing the service block model:** Detailed configuration examples are shown for the service block

The book breaks down IPv6 deployment into the various places in the network. This chapter discusses IPv6 in the campus. The campus requirements for IPv6 are different than those in a WAN/branch environment mainly because IPv6 must be forwarded in hardware to support the high-performance requirements such as 10/100/1000 and even 10-Gbps rates commonly seen in the campus network.

When your campus Layer 3 switches cannot support IPv6 in hardware, you can use alternative designs. These options are discussed throughout this chapter.

Campus Deployment Models Overview

The following sections provide a high-level overview of the following three campus IPv6 deployment models and describe their benefits and applicability:

- **Dual-stack model (DSM):** Both IPv4 and IPv6 are deployed simultaneously on the same interfaces.

- **Hybrid model (HM):** Host-based tunneling mechanisms are used to encapsulate IPv6 in IPv4 when needed, and dual-stack is used everywhere else.

- **Service block model (SBM):** This is similar to the hybrid model, only tunnel termination occurs in a purpose-built part of the network known as the service block.

Dual-Stack Model

The dual-stack model (DSM) is completely based on the dual-stack transition mechanism. An interface or link on which two protocol stacks have been enabled at the same time operates in dual-stack mode. Examples of previous uses of dual-stack include IPv4 and IPX or IPv4 and AppleTalk coexisting on the same device.

Dual-stack is the preferred, most versatile way to deploy IPv6 in existing IPv4 environments. IPv6 can be enabled wherever IPv4 is enabled, along with the associated features required to make IPv6 routable, highly available, and secure.

The tested components area of each section of this chapter gives a brief view of the common requirements for the DSM to be successfully implemented. The most important consideration is to ensure that there is hardware support for IPv6 in campus network components such as switches. Within the campus network, link speeds and capacity often depend on such issues as the number of users, types of applications, and latency expectations. Because of the typically high data rate requirements in this environment, Cisco does not recommend enabling IPv6 unicast or multicast layer switching on software forwarding-only platforms. It is important to understand that you can have a platform that can perform IPv4 forwarding in hardware, yet IPv6 forwarding is done in software. Enabling IPv6 on software forwarding-only campus switching platforms can be suitable in a test environment or a small pilot network, but certainly not in a production campus network. It is critical to take an inventory of your campus switching products to ensure that you can perform IPv6 in hardware.

The following section highlights some of the benefits and drawbacks of the DSM and introduces the high-level topology and tested components.

Benefits and Drawbacks of the DSM

Deploying IPv6 in the campus using DSM offers several advantages over the hybrid and service block models. The primary advantage of DSM is that it does not require tunneling within the campus network. DSM runs the two protocols as "ships in the night," meaning that IPv4 and IPv6 run alongside one another and have no dependency on each other to function, except that they share network resources. Both IPv4 and IPv6 have independent routing, high availability (HA), quality of service (QoS), security, and multicast policies. Dual-stack also offers processing performance advantages because packets are natively forwarded without having to account for additional encapsulation and lookup overhead.

Note Customers who plan to or have already deployed the Cisco routed access design will fill find that IPv6 is also supported within that same design.

The primary drawback to DSM is that network equipment upgrades might be required when the existing network devices are not IPv6 capable. Also, there is an operational cost in operating two protocols simultaneously because there are two sets of everything, such as addressing, routing protocols, access control lists (ACL), management, and so on.

DSM Topology

Figure 6-1 shows a high-level view of the DSM-based deployment in campus networks. The environment is using a traditional three-tier design, with an access, distribution, and core layer in the campus. All relevant interfaces that have IPv4 enabled also have IPv6 enabled, making it a true dual-stack configuration. This example is the basis for the detailed configurations that are presented later in this chapter.

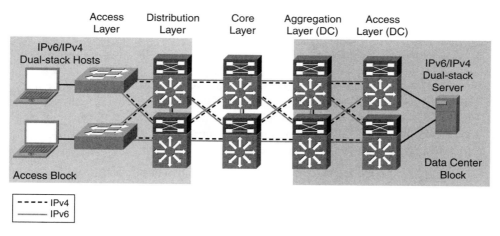

Figure 6-1   *Dual-Stack Model Example*

Note   The data center block is shown here for reference only and is not discussed in this chapter. Chapter 9, "Deploying IPv6 in the Data Center," discusses the deployment of IPv6 in the data center.

DSM-Tested Components

Table 6-1 lists the components that were used and tested in the DSM configuration.

Hybrid Model

The hybrid model (HM) strategy is to employ two or more independent transition mechanisms with the same deployment design goals. Flexibility is the key aspect of the hybrid approach, in which any combination of transition mechanisms can be leveraged to best fit a given network environment.

Table 6-1 *DSM-Tested Components*

Campus Layer	Hardware	Software
Access layer	Cisco Catalyst 3750E/3560E Catalyst 4500 Supervisor 6-E Catalyst 6500 Supervisor 32 or 720	12.2(46)SE 12.2(46)SG 12.2(33)SXI
Host devices	Various laptops: PC and Apple	Microsoft Windows XP, Windows Vista, Windows 7, Apple Mac OS X, and Red Hat Enterprise Linux WS
Distribution layer	Catalyst 4500 Supervisor 6-E Catalyst 6500 Supervisor 32 or 720	12.2(46)SG 12.2(33)SXI
Core layer	Catalyst 6500 Supervisor 720	12.2(33)SXI

The HM adapts as much as possible to the characteristics of the existing network infrastructure. Transition mechanisms are selected based on multiple criteria, such as IPv6 hardware capabilities of the network elements, number of hosts, types of applications, location of IPv6 services, and network infrastructure and end system operating system feature support for various transition mechanisms.

The HM leverages the following three main IPv6 transition mechanisms:

- **Dual-stack:** Deployment of two protocol stacks: IPv4 and IPv6

- **Intra-Site Automatic Tunnel Addressing Protocol (ISATAP):** Host-to-router tunneling mechanism that relies on an existing IPv4-enabled infrastructure

- **Manually configured tunnels:** Router-to-router tunneling mechanism that relies on an existing IPv4-enabled infrastructure

The HM provides hosts with access to IPv6 services, even when the underlying network infrastructure might not support IPv6 natively.

The key aspect of the HM is that hosts located in the campus access layer can use IPv6 services when the distribution layer is not IPv6-capable or enabled. The distribution layer switch is most commonly the first Layer 3 gateway for the access layer devices. If IPv6 capabilities are not present in the existing distribution layer switches, the hosts cannot gain access to IPv6 addressing (stateless autoconfiguration or DHCP for IPv6) and router information, and subsequently cannot access the rest of the IPv6-enabled network.

Tunneling can be used on the IPv6-enabled hosts to provide access to IPv6 services located beyond the distribution layer. HM leverages the ISATAP tunneling mechanisms on the hosts in the access layer to provide IPv6 addressing and off-link routing. Microsoft Windows XP, Windows Vista, and Windows 7 hosts in the access layer need to have

IPv6 enabled and either a static ISATAP router definition or DNS "A" record entry config-ured for the ISATAP router address.

Note   The configuration details are shown in the section "Implementing the Hybrid Model," later in this chapter.

Figure 6-2 shows the basic connectivity flow for the HM.

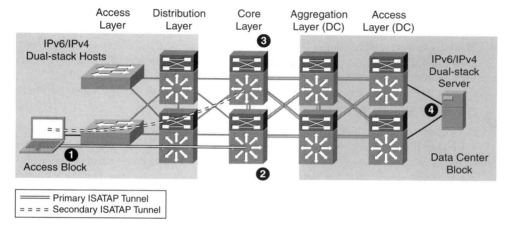

Figure 6-2   *Hybrid Model - Connectivity Flow*

The following list describes the four steps in the HM connectivity flow shown in Figure 6-2:

Step 1.   The host establishes an ISATAP tunnel to the core layer.

Step 2.   The core layer switches are configured with ISATAP tunnel interfaces and are the termination point for ISATAP tunnels established by the hosts. As you can see, this is not ideal because the core layer is designed to be very streamlined and to perform packet forwarding only; it is not a tunnel termination point.

Step 3.   Pairs of core layer switches are redundantly configured to accept ISATAP tun-nel connections to provide high availability of the ISATAP tunnels. Redundancy is available by configuring both core layer switches with loop-back interfaces that share the same IPv4 address. Both switches use this redundant IPv4 address as the tunnel source for ISATAP. When the host con-nects to the IPv4 ISATAP router address, it connects to one of the two switch-es (this can be load balanced or be configured to have a preference for one switch over the other). If one switch fails, the IPv4 Interior Gateway Protocol (IGP) converges and uses the other switch, which has the same IPv4 ISATAP address as the primary. The failover takes as long as the IGP convergence time plus the Neighbor Unreachability Detection (NUD) time expiry. More information on NUD can be found in RFC 4861, "Neighbor Discovery for IP version 6 (IPv6)." With Microsoft Windows Vista and Windows 7 configurations, basic load balancing of the ISATAP routers (core switches) can be implemented. For more information on the Microsoft implementation of ISA-TAP on Windows platforms, see the white paper "Manageable Transition to IPv6 using ISATAP," which is available at the Microsoft Download Center: http://tinyurl.com/2jhdbw.

Step 4.   The dual-stack configured server accepts incoming connection requests and/or establishes outgoing IPv6 connections using the directly accessible dual-stack-enabled data center block.

Many customers simply configure one ISATAP interface for all of their users within the network. This works, but you lose the ability to have control over traffic based on source IPv4 address information. Also, as was described in Chapter 3, "Deployable IPv6 Coexistence Mechanisms," ISATAP creates a large, flat network that might not be what you want, especially with a large number of users.

To help control where ISATAP tunnels can be terminated and what resources the hosts can reach over IPv6, you can use VLAN or IPv4 subnet-to-ISATAP tunnel matching. If the current network design has a specific VLAN associated with ports on an access layer switch and the users attached to that switch are receiving IPv4 addressing based on the VLAN to which they belong, a similar mapping can be done with IPv6 and ISATAP tunnels.

Figure 6-3 illustrates the process of matching users in a specific VLAN and IPv4 subnet with a specific ISATAP tunnel.

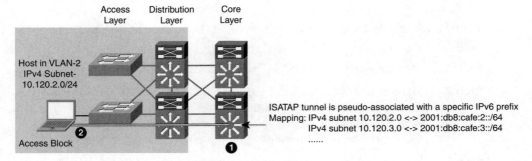

Figure 6-3   *Hybrid Model - ISATAP Tunnel Mapping*

The following list describes the ISATAP tunnel mapping and numbered icons shown in Figure 6-3:

Step 1.   The core layer switch is configured with a loopback interface with the address of 10.122.10.2, which is used as the tunnel source for ISATAP, and is used only by users located on VLAN 2 (that is, the 10.120.2.0/24 subnet).

Step 2.   The host in the access layer is connected to a port that is associated with a specific VLAN. In this example, the VLAN is VLAN-2. The host in VLAN-2 is associated with an IPv4 subnet range (10.120.2.0/24) in the DHCP server configuration.

The host is also configured for ISATAP and has been statically assigned the ISATAP router value of 10.122.10.2. This static assignment can be implemented in several ways. An ISATAP router setting can be defined through a command on the host (**netsh interface ipv6 isatap set router 10.122.10.2**—details provided in the "Tunnel Configuration" section, later in the chapter), which can be manually entered or scripted through Microsoft PowerShell, Microsoft SMS Server, Group Policy, or a number of other scripting methods. The script can determine to which value to set the ISATAP router by examining the existing IPv4 address of the host. For example, the script can analyze the host IPv4 address and determine that the value "2" in the 10.120.2.x/24 address signifies the subnet value. The script can then apply the command using the ISATAP router address of 10.122.10.2, where the "2" signifies subnet or VLAN 2. The 10.122.10.2 address is actually a loopback address on the core layer switch and is used as the tunnel endpoint for ISATAP.

Note   You can find configuration details in the section "Implementing the Hybrid Model," later in this chapter.

A customer might want to provide separate tunnel loopbacks for the following reasons:

■   **Control and separation:** If a security policy is in place that disallows certain IPv4 subnets from accessing a specific resource, and access control lists (ACL) are used to enforce the policy, what happens if HM is implemented without consideration for this policy? If the restricted resources are also IPv6 accessible, those users who were previously disallowed access through IPv4 can now access the protected resource through IPv6. If hundreds or thousands of users are configured for ISATAP and a single ISATAP tunnel interface is used on the core layer device (or wherever the termination point is), controlling the source addresses through ACLs would be very difficult to scale and manage. If the users are logically separated into ISATAP tunnels in the same way they are separated by VLANs and IPv4 subnets, ACLs can be easily deployed to permit or deny access based on the IPv6 source, source/destination, and even Layer 4 information.

■   **Scale:** For years, it has been a best practice to control the number of devices within each single VLAN of the campus networks. This practice has traditionally been enforced for broadcast domain control. Although IPv6 and ISATAP tunnels do not use broadcast, there are still scalability considerations to think about. These include control plane impact of encapsulation/decapsulation, line rate performance of tunneled traffic, and so on. The good news is that the Cisco Catalyst 6500 with Supervisor 720 and Supervisor 32G perform ISATAP tunneling in hardware.

The following are the main solution requirements for HM strategies:

■   IPv6 and ISATAP support on the operating system of the host machines

■   IPv6/IPv4 dual-stack and ISATAP feature support on the core layer switches

As mentioned previously, numerous combinations of transition mechanisms can be used to provide IPv6 connectivity within the enterprise campus environment, such as the following two alternatives to the previous requirements:

■   Using 6to4 tunneling instead of ISATAP if multiple host operating systems such as Linux, FreeBSD, Sun Solaris, and MAC OS X are used within the access layer

■   Terminating tunnels at a network layer different than the core layer, such as the data center aggregation layer

Note   The 6to4 and non-core-layer alternatives are not discussed in this chapter and are listed only as secondary options to the deployment recommendations for the HM. There are additional considerations with 6to4 because the design, security, and scale components do change.

Benefits and Drawbacks of the HM

The primary benefit of the HM is that the existing network equipment can be leveraged without the need for upgrades, especially the distribution layer switches. If the distribution layer switches currently provide acceptable IPv4 service and performance and are still within the depreciation window, the HM can be a suitable choice.

It is important to understand the drawbacks of the hybrid model:

■   IPv6 multicast is not supported within ISATAP tunnels.

■   Terminating ISATAP tunnels in the core layer makes the core layer appear as an access layer to the IPv6 traffic. Network administrators and network architects design the core layer to be highly optimized for the role it plays in the network, which is often to be stable, simple, and fast. Adding a new level of intelligence to the core layer might not be acceptable.

■   Granular VLAN or IPv4 subnet-to-ISATAP tunnel mapping can introduce a lot of operational overhead through a tremendous amount of configuration. You should land somewhere between a single ISATAP tunnel interface for the entire organization and the granular mapping examples discussed in this chapter. Your goal should be to deploy enough ISATAP isolation to meet your needs without it becoming too much to maintain. Dual-stack should be pursued aggressively to relieve the HM overhead.

As with any design that uses tunneling, considerations that must be accounted for include performance, management, security, scalability, path MTU, and availability. The use of tunnels is always a secondary recommendation to the DSM design.

HM Topology

Figure 6-4 shows a high-level view of the campus HM. ISATAP tunnels are established from hosts in the access layer and terminate on the core layer switches. The solid lines indicate the primary tunnel. If the core layer switch that terminates the primary tunnel fails, the host will reestablish the tunnel to the other core layer switch. ISATAP high availability will be discussed in detail later in this chapter. This example is the basis for the detailed configurations that follow later in this chapter.

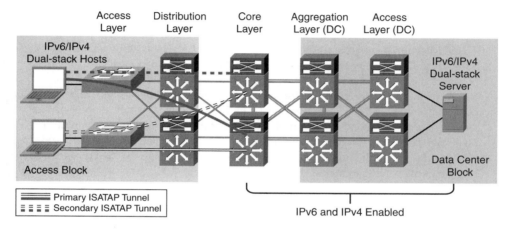

Figure 6-4 *Hybrid Model Topology*

HM-Tested Components

The following are the components used and tested in the HM configuration:

- Campus layer: Core layer

- Hardware: Catalyst 6500 Supervisor 720

- Software: 12.2(33)SXI

Note that the only Cisco Catalyst components that need to have IPv6 capabilities are those terminating ISATAP connections and the dual-stack links in the data center. Therefore, the software versions in the campus access and distribution layer roles are not relevant to this design.

Service Block Model

The service block model (SBM) is significantly different compared to the other campus models discussed in this chapter. Although the concept of a service block design is not new, the SBM does offer unique capabilities to customers facing the challenge of providing access to IPv6 services in a short time frame. A service block approach has also been used in other design areas such as Cisco Network Virtualization, which refers to this concept as the services edge. The SBM is unique in that it can be deployed as an overlay network without any impact to the existing IPv4 network, and it is completely centralized. This overlay network can be implemented rapidly while allowing high availability of IPv6 services, QoS capabilities, and restriction of access to IPv6 resources with little or no changes to the existing IPv4 network.

As the existing campus network becomes IPv6 capable, the SBM can become decentralized. Connections into the SBM are changed from tunnels (ISATAP and/or manually configured) to dual-stack connections. When all the campus layers are dual-stack capable, the SBM can be dismantled and repurposed for other uses.

The SBM deployment is based on a redundant pair of Catalyst 6500 switches with a Supervisor 32 or Supervisor 720. If the SBM is being deployed in a pilot, lab, or small production environment, Cisco ISR or other Cisco Software forwarding-based routers can act as the termination device. The key to maintaining a highly scalable and redundant configuration in the SBM is to ensure that a high-performance switch, supervisor, and modules are used to handle the load of the ISATAP, manually configured tunnels, and dual-stack connections for an entire campus network. As the number of tunnels and required throughput increase, it might be necessary to distribute the load across an additional pair of switches in the SBM.

There are a few similarities between the SBM example given in this chapter and the hybrid model. The underlying IPv4 network is used as the foundation for the overlay IPv6 network being deployed. ISATAP provides access to hosts in the access layer, similar to the hybrid model. Manually configured tunnels are used from the data center aggregation layer to provide IPv6 access to the applications and services located in the data center access layer. IPv4 routing is configured between the core layer and SBM switches to allow visibility to the SBM switches for the purpose of terminating IPv6-in-IPv4 tunnels. In the example discussed in this chapter, however, the extreme case is analyzed where there are no IPv6 capabilities anywhere in the campus network (access, distribution, or core layers). The SBM example used in this chapter has the switches directly connected to the core layer through redundant high-speed links.

Benefits and Drawbacks of the SBM

From a high-level perspective, the advantages to implementing the SBM are the pace of IPv6 services delivery to the hosts, the lesser impact on the existing network configuration (no termination of tunnels, command-line entries), and the flexibility of controlling the access to IPv6-enabled applications.

In essence, the SBM provides control over the pace of IPv6 service rollout by leveraging the following:

- Configuring per-user and/or per-VLAN tunnels through ISATAP to control the flow of connections and allow the measurement of IPv6 traffic use by allowing interface-specific monitoring and specific source/destination pairing in network monitoring tools such as in NetFlow.

- Controlling access on a per-server or per-application basis through ACLs and/or routing policies at the SBM. This level of control allows access to one, a few, or even many IPv6-enabled services while all other services remain on IPv4 until those services can be upgraded or replaced. This setup enables a "per-service" deployment of IPv6.

- Allowing high availability of ISATAP and manually configured tunnels as well as all dual-stack connections.

- Allowing hosts access to the IPv6-enabled Internet service provider (ISP) connections, either by allowing a segregated IPv6 connection used only for IPv6-based Internet traffic or by providing links to the existing Internet edge connections that have both IPv4 and IPv6 ISP connections.

- Implementing the SBM does not disrupt the existing network infrastructure and services.

As mentioned in the case of the hybrid model, there are drawbacks to any design that relies on tunneling mechanisms as the primary way to provide access to services. The SBM not only suffers from the same drawbacks as the HM design (lots of tunneling), but it also adds the cost of additional equipment not found in the HM. More switches (the SBM switches) and line cards are needed to connect the SBM and core layer switches, and any maintenance or software required represents additional expenses.

Because of the list of drawbacks for the HM and SBM, Cisco recommends to always aim for dual-stack deployment.

SBM Topology

Two portions of the SBM design are discussed in this chapter. Figure 6-5 shows the ISA-TAP portion of the design, and Figure 6-6 shows the manually configured tunnel portion of the design. These views are just two of the many combinations that can be generated in a campus network and differentiated based on the goals of the IPv6 design and the capabilities of the platforms and software in the campus infrastructure.

Figure 6-5 shows the redundant ISATAP tunnels coming from the hosts in the access layer to the SBM switches. The SBM switches are connected to the rest of the campus network by linking directly to the core layer switches through IPv4-enabled links. The SBM switches are connected to each other through a dual-stack connection that is used for IPv4 and IPv6 routing and HA purposes.

Figure 6-6 shows the redundant, manually configured tunnels connecting the data center aggregation layer and the service block. It is also common to see servers in the data center use ISATAP to connect to either the HM or SBM termination points. Hosts located in the access layer can now reach IPv6 services in the data center access layer using IPv6. Refer to the section "Implementing the Service Block Model," later in this chapter, for the details of the configuration.

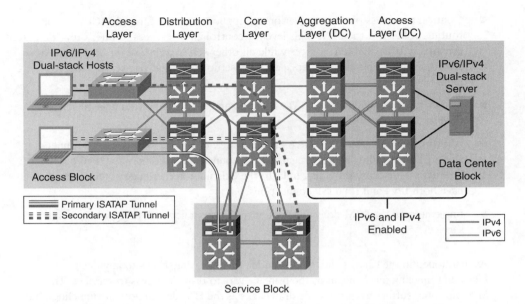

Figure 6-5 *Service Block Model - Connecting the Hosts (ISATAP Layout)*

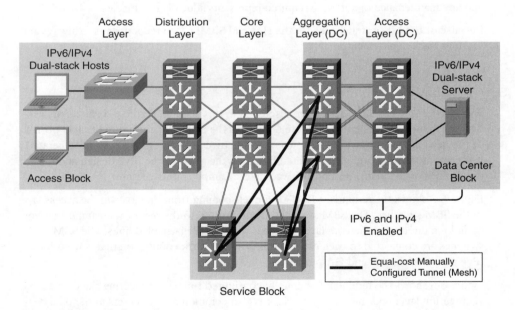

Figure 6-6 *Service Block Model - Connecting the Data Center (Manually Configured Tunnel Layout)*

SBM-Tested Components

The following are the components used and tested in the SBM configuration:

- Campus layer: Core layer

- Hardware: Catalyst 6500 Supervisor 720

- Software: 12.2(33)SXI

General Campus IPv6 Deployment Considerations

Many considerations apply to all the deployment models discussed in this chapter. The following sections focus on the general ones that apply to deploying IPv6 in a campus network, regardless of the deployment model being used. If a particular consideration must be understood in the context of a specific model, this model is called out along with the consideration. Also, the configurations for any model-specific considerations can be found in the implementation section of that model.

All campus IPv6 models discussed in this chapter leverage the existing campus network design as the foundation for providing physical access, VLANs, IPv4 routing (for tunnels), QoS (for tunnels), infrastructure security (protecting the tunnels), and availability (device, link, trunk, and routing). When dual-stack is used, nearly all design principles found in Cisco campus design best practice documents are applicable to both IPv4 and IPv6.

It is critical to understand the Cisco campus best practice recommendations before jumping into the deployment of the IPv6 campus models discussed in this chapter. The Cisco campus design best practice documents can be found at the following URL:
http://www.cisco.com/en/US/netsol/ns815/networking_solutions_program_home.html.

Addressing

As mentioned previously, this chapter is not an introductory chapter and does not discuss the basics of IPv6 addressing. However, it is important to discuss a few addressing considerations for the network devices, specifically for links.

Table 6-2 lists the options related to the use of various prefix lengths on links.

Notes for Table 6-2:

- **/64:** On VLAN interfaces, it is recommended to use a /64 prefix because it is easy and consistent for address management. This is required for Stateless Address Autoconfiguration (SLAAC), Secure Neighbor Discovery (SEND), and privacy extension use.

Table 6-2   *Prefix Length Considerations*

64 Bits	Greater Than 64 Bits	Less Than 64 Bits
Recommended by RFC 5375 and IAB/IESG	Address space conservation	Enables more hosts per broadcast domain
Consistency makes management easy	Special cases: - /126 - Valid for p2p - /127 - Valid for p2p if aware of overlapping addresses (RFC 3627) - /128 - Loopback	Considered bad practice
/64 required for SLAAC, SEND, and Privacy extensions	Complicates management	64 bits offers more space for hosts than media can support efficiently
Significant address space loss	Must avoid overlap with specific addresses: - Router Anycast (RFC 3513) - Embedded RP (RFC 3956)	No real justifiable use case for this option

- **Greater than 64:** Many in the networking community think that a /64 prefix for p2p links is a waste of space. The debate rages on regarding the use of various prefix lengths on p2p links, and the reader is encouraged to balance the legalistic RFC stipulations with real-world deployment considerations. In many deployments, it is common to use a /64 on VLANs (or links where hosts reside), /126 on p2p links, /127 on p2p links if you are aware of the potential overlap with specific addresses (at the time of this writing, an IETF draft exists for the safe use of /127, "Using 127-bit IPv6 Prefixes on Inter-Router Links), and /128 on loopbacks. In this chapter, /64 is used everywhere except for loopback interfaces, where a /128 is used.

- **Less than 64:** There are no real use cases where a site needs more addressing on a link than a /64 can provide and is considered a bad practice.

RFC 3627, "Use of /127 Prefix Length Between Routers Considered Harmful," discusses the reasons why the use of a /127 prefix can cause address overlap with special use addresses..

Physical Connectivity

Considerations for physical connectivity with IPv6 are the same as with IPv4, with the addition of the following elements:

- **Ensuring that there is sufficient bandwidth for both existing and new traffic:** This is an important factor for the deployment of any new technology, protocol, or application.

- **Understanding how IPv6 deals with the maximum transmission unit (MTU) on a link:** This book is not an introductory book for basic IPv6 protocol operation or specifications. A good starting point for understanding MTU and Path MTU Discovery (PMTUD) for IPv6 is with RFC 2460, "Internet Protocol, Version 6 (IPv6) Specification," and RFC 1981, "Path MTU Discovery for IP version 6."

- **Operating IPv6 over wireless LANs (WLAN):** IPv6 should operate correctly over WLAN access points in much the same way as IPv6 operates over Layer 2 switches. However, you must consider IPv6 specifics in WLAN environments, including managing WLAN devices (access points [AP] and controllers) through IPv6 and controlling IPv6 traffic through AP or controller-based QoS, VLANs, and ACLs. IPv6 must be supported on the AP and/or controller devices to take advantage of these more intelligent services on the WLAN devices.

In addition to the preceding considerations, Cisco recommends a thorough analysis of the existing traffic profiles, memory, and CPU utilization on both the hosts and network equipment. Also complete the Service Level Agreement (SLA) before implementing any of the IPv6 models discussed in this chapter.

VLANs

VLAN considerations for IPv6 are the same as for IPv4. When dual-stack configurations are used, both IPv4 and IPv6 traverse the same VLAN. When tunneling is used, IPv4 and the tunneled IPv6 (protocol 41) traffic traverse the VLAN.

IPv6 on data VLANs that are trunked along with voice VLANs (behind IP phones) is fully supported. Depending on the configuration of the data and voice VLANs, you might experience an issue where the Layer 2 multicast router advertisements from the Layer 3 data VLAN interface might bleed over to the attached host (connected to the IP phone or a voice VLAN–enabled switch port). Basically, a PC connected to an IP phone can receive RAs for both the data and voice VLANs. This is an issue that can be manifest regardless of vendor and switch/phone version. Stay tuned for updated best practices on how to properly deal with this on the Layer 3 VLAN configurations or through a possible setting in the Cisco IP Phones that prevents flooding of IPv6 router advertisements on the data VLAN.

For the current VLAN design recommendations, see the references to the Cisco campus design best practice documents in the "Additional References" section, later in this chapter.

Routing

The decision to run an IGP in the campus network is made based on a variety of factors such as platform capabilities, IT staff expertise, topology, and size of network. In this chapter, the IGP for IPv4 is Enhanced IGRP (EIGRP), but Open Shortest Path First version 2 (OSPFv2) for IPv4 can also be used. The IGP configurations for IPv6 can either be

EIGRP or OSPFv3. These IGPs are interchanged in some sections to show the reader what the basic configuration looks like for either IGP.

There are many similarities in how the IGPs function between IPv4 and IPv6, so you end up with similar behavior and expectations. As a rule of thumb, most deployments will start by using the same IGP as is used with IPv4. This allows a smaller learning curve because the staff already understands that IGP. However, in some cases, this is the time when some deployments can use a different IGP for IPv6. This is a greenfield deployment as it relates to IPv6, so it is up to you to figure out whether you want to go in a different direction for the IGP choice. Perhaps you stick with the same IGP but do a better job of summarization or use different functions within the IGP such as a distribution list—or whatever makes sense in your network. The bottom line is to use what works and what you are familiar with, but if the business or technical drivers within your environment dictate a change, make the change.

As previously mentioned, every effort has been made to implement the current Cisco campus design best practices. Both the IPv4 and IPv6 IGPs have been tuned according to the current best practices where possible. It should be one of the top priorities of any network design to ensure that the IGPs are tuned to provide a stable, scalable, and fast-converging network.

High Availability

Many aspects of high availability (HA) are not applicable to or are outside of the scope of this chapter. Many of the HA requirements and recommendations are met by leveraging the existing Cisco campus design best practices. The following are the primary HA components discussed in this chapter:

- **Redundant routing and forwarding paths:** These are accomplished by using EIGRP or OSPFv2 for IPv4 when redundant paths for tunnels are needed, and EIGRP for IPv6 or OSPFv3 for IPv6 when dual-stack is used, along with the functionality of Cisco Express Forwarding (CEF).

- **Redundant Layer 3 switches for terminating ISATAP and manually configured tunnels:** These redundant Layer 3 switches are applicable in the HM and SBM designs. In addition to having redundant hardware, it is important to implement redundant tunnels (ISATAP and manually configured). The implementation sections illustrate the configuration and results of using redundant tunnels for HM and SBM designs.

- **High availability of the first-hop gateways:** In the DSM design, the distribution layer switches are the first Layer 3 devices to the hosts in the access layer. Traditional campus designs use first-hop redundancy protocols such as Hot Standby Routing Protocol (HSRP) and Gateway Load Balancing Protocol (GLBP). In this chapter, configurations are shown with HSRP for IPv6. The configuration for first-hop routing protocols such as HSRP are discussed in the section "Implementing the Dual-Stack Model," later in this chapter.

QoS

With DSM, it is easy to extend or leverage the existing IPv4 QoS policies to include the new IPv6 traffic traversing the campus network. Cisco recommends that the QoS policies implemented be application- and/or service-dependent instead of protocol-dependent (IPv4 or IPv6). If the existing QoS policy has specific classification, policing, and queuing for an application, that policy should treat equally the IPv4 and IPv6 traffic for that application.

Special consideration should be provided to the QoS policies for tunneled traffic. QoS for ISATAP-tunneled traffic is somewhat limited. When ISATAP tunnels are used, the ingress classification of IPv6 packets cannot be made at the access layer, which is the recommended location for trusting or classifying ingress traffic. In the HM and SBM designs, the access layer has no IPv6 support. Tunnels are being used between the hosts in the access layer and either the core layer (HM) or the SBM switches, and therefore ingress classification cannot be done.

QoS policies for IPv6 can be implemented after the decapsulation of the tunneled traffic, but this also presents a unique challenge. Tunneled IPv6 traffic cannot even be classified after it reaches the tunnel destination, because ingress marking cannot be done until the IPv6 traffic is decapsulated (ingress classification and marking are done on the physical interface and not the tunnel interface). Egress classification policies can be implemented on any IPv6 traffic now decapsulated and being forwarded by the switch. Trust, policing, and queuing policies can be implemented on upstream switches to properly deal with the IPv6 traffic.

Figure 6-7 illustrates the points where IPv6 QoS policies can be applied when using ISATAP in HM. The dual-stack links shown have QoS policies that apply to both IPv4 and IPv6. Refer to the "Additional References" section, later in this chapter, for more information about the Cisco campus QoS documentation.

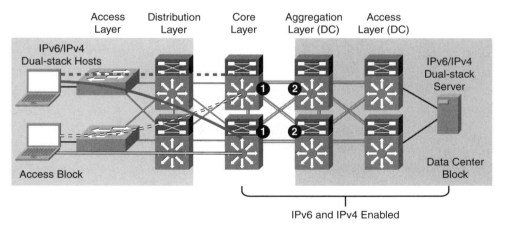

Figure 6-7   *QoS Implementation - The Hybrid Model*

The following list explains the two steps illustrated in Figure 6-7:

Step 1.   In the HM, the first place to implement classification and marking is on the egress interfaces on the core layer switches. As was previously mentioned, the IPv6 packets have been tunneled from the hosts in the access layer to the core layer, and the IPv6 packets have not been "visible" in a decapsulated state until the core layer. Because QoS policies for classification and marking cannot be applied to the ISATAP tunnels on ingress, the first place to apply the policy is on egress.

Step 2.   The classified and marked IPv6 packets (see item 1) can now be examined by upstream switches (for example, aggregation layer switches), and the appropriate QoS policies can be applied on ingress. These polices can include trust (ingress), policing (ingress), and queuing (egress).

Figure 6-8 illustrates the points where IPv6 QoS policies can be applied in the SBM when ISATAP manually configured tunnels are used.

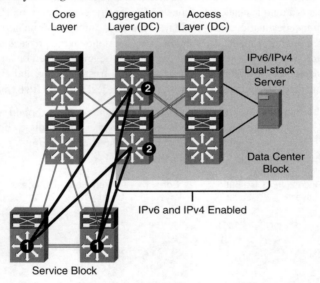

Figure 6-8   *QoS Policy Implementation - SBM (ISAT-AP/Manually Configured Tunnels)*

The following list explains the two steps illustrated in Figure 6-8:

Step 1.   The SBM switches receive IPv6 packets coming from the ISATAP interfaces, which are now decapsulated, and can apply classification and marking policies on the egress manually configured tunnel interfaces.

Step 2.   The upstream switches (aggregation layer and access layer) can now apply trust, policing, and queuing policies after the IPv6 packets leave the manually configured tunnel interfaces in the aggregation layer.

Note   At the time of this writing, microflow policing of IPv6 multicast packets on the Catalyst 6500 Supervisor 32/720 is not supported. In the SBM design, as of the release of this chapter, the policing of IPv6 packets must take place on ingress, and the ingress interface must not be a tunnel. For more information, see the PFC3 QoS documentation at the following URL: http://tinyurl.com/2ewv7mp.

The key consideration for Modular QoS CLI (MQC) is the removal of the **ip** keyword in the QoS **match** and **set** statements. Modification in the QoS syntax to support IPv6 and IPv4 allows new configuration criteria, as shown in Table 6-3.

Table 6-3   *QoS Configuration Changes - IPv4/IPv6*

IPv4-Only QoS Syntax	IPv4/IPv6 QoS Syntax
match ip dscp	match dscp
match ip precedence	match precedence
set ip dscp	set dscp
set ip precedence	set precedence

Some QoS features work for both IPv6 and IPv4 but require no modification to the command-line interface (CLI), for example, weighted random early detection (WRED), policing, and weighted round robin (WRR).

The implementation section for each model does not go into great detail on QoS configuration in relation to the definition of classes for certain applications, the associated mapping of differentiated services code point (DSCP) values, and the bandwidth and queuing recommendations. Cisco provides an extensive collection of QoS recommendations for the campus, which is available on Cisco.com as well as in the Cisco Press book *End-to-End QoS Network Design*. Refer to the "Additional References" section, later in this chapter, for more information about the Cisco campus QoS recommendations and Cisco Press books.

Security

Many of the common threats and attacks on existing IPv4 campus networks also apply to IPv6. Unauthorized access, spoofing, routing attacks, viruses/worms, denial of service (DoS), and man-in-the-middle attacks are just a few of the threats to both IPv4 and IPv6.

With IPv6, many threat possibilities do not apply or at least do not apply in the same way as with IPv4. There are inherent differences in how IPv6 handles neighbor and router advertisement and discovery, headers, and even fragmentation. There are numerous efforts, both within Cisco and in the industry, to identify, understand, and resolve IPv6 security threats. This chapter points out some possible areas to address within the campus and gives basic examples of how to provide protection for IPv6 dual-stack and tunneled traffic. The section "Implementing the Dual-Stack Model," later in this chapter, discusses first-hop security in a dual-stack deployment.

> **Note**   The examples given in this chapter are in no way meant to be recommendations or guidelines, but rather are intended to challenge you to carefully analyze your own security policies as they apply to IPv6 in the campus. You can find detailed IPv6 security information in the book *IPv6 Security*, published by Cisco Press.

The following sections describe general security guidelines for network device protection that apply to all campus models.

Making Reconnaissance More Difficult Through Complex Address Assignment

Addressing of campus network devices (Layer 2 and 3 switches) should be well planned. Many security professionals recommend that the global or unique local addressing (ULA) address of the switch is a value that is not easily guessed. An example of a well-known interface ID for a switch is if VLAN 2 has an address of 2001:db8:cafe:2::1/64 and VLAN 3 has an address of 2001:db8:cafe:3::1/64, where ::1 is the interface ID of the switch. This address is easily guessed and allows an attacker to quickly understand the common addressing for the campus infrastructure devices. Another option is to randomize the interface ID of all the devices in the campus. Using the VLAN 2 and VLAN 3 examples from the previous example, a new address can be constructed by using an address such as 2001:db8:cafe:2::a010:f1a1 for VLAN 2 and 2001:db8:cafe:3::c801:167a for VLAN 3, where "a010:f1a1" is the interface ID of VLAN 2 for the switch.

The addressing consideration described in this section introduces significant operational challenges. For the sake of easing operational management of the network devices and addressing, you should balance the security aspects of randomizing the interface IDs with the ability to deploy and manage the devices through the semirandomized addresses.

Controlling Management Access to the Campus Switches

To more tightly restrict access to a particular switch through IPv6, an ACL is used to permit access to the management interface (line vty) by way of the loopback interface. The permitted source network is from the enterprise IPv6 prefix. To make ACL generation more scalable for a wide range of network devices, the ACL definition can permit the entire enterprise prefix as the primary method for controlling management access to the device instead of filtering to a specific interface on the switch. The IPv6 prefix used in this enterprise site (example only) is 2001:db8:cafe::/48.

Example 6-1 illustrates how a basic ACL can be constructed to restrict VTY access to the switch.

Example 6-1   *Line VTY Access Control List*

```
ipv6 access-list MGMT-IN

 remark Permit MGMT only to Loopback0
```

```
permit tcp 2001:DB8:CAFE::/48 host 2001:DB8:CAFE:6507::A111:1010

deny ipv6 any any log-input

!
line vty 0 4

 session-timeout 3
 access-class MGMT-IN-v4 in
 password 7 08334D400E1C17
 ipv6 access-class MGMT-IN in

 logging synchronous
 login local
 exec prompt timestamp
 transport input ssh
```

The security requirements for running Simple Network Management Protocol (SNMP) are the same as with IPv4. If SNMP is needed, a choice should be made on the SNMP version and then access control and authentication/encryption. In the campus models discussed in this chapter, SNMPv3 (AuthNoPriv) is used to provide polling capabilities for the Cisco NMS servers located in the data center.

■ Example 6-2 shows the SNMPv3 configuration used in the campus switches in this chapter.

Example 6-2 *SNMP Configuration*

```
snmp-server contact John Doe - ipv6rocks@example.com
snmp-server group IPv6-ADMIN v3 auth write v1default
snmp-server user jdoe IPv6-ADMIN v3 auth md5 cisco1234
snmp-server host 2001:DB8:CAFE:100::60 version 3 auth jdoe
```

At the time of this writing, Cisco Catalyst switches do not support the use of IPv6 HTTP ACLs to control access to the switch. This is very important because switches that currently use **ip http access-class** ACLs for IPv4 do not have the same level of protection for IPv6. This feature gap means that subnets or users that were previously denied access through HTTP/HTTPS for IPv4 now have access to the switch through IPv6. It is recommended that the HTTP/HTTPS server is disabled unless direct management access to the device over these protocols is required.

IPv6 Traffic Policing

Traffic policing can be considered a QoS and/or security function. There might be existing requirements to police traffic either on an aggregate or per-user microflow basis (that is, flows defined by a source/destination address pairing and/or source/destination port pairing). In the campus models discussed in this chapter, certain places are appropriate for implementing IPv6 policing, specifically per-user microflow policing:

- **DSM:** The per-user microflow policing of IPv6 traffic is performed against ingress traffic on the Catalyst 6500 distribution layer switches (ideal).

- **HM:** The per-user microflow policing of IPv6 traffic is performed against ingress traffic (from the hosts in the campus access layer) on the Catalyst 6500 data center aggregation layer switches. This situation is not ideal. It is preferred to perform ingress microflow policing on the core layer switches, but in this model, the ingress policing cannot be applied to tunnel interfaces, so it has to be done at the next layer.

- **SBM:** The per-user microflow policing of IPv6 traffic is a challenge in the specific SBM example discussed in this chapter. In the SBM, the service block switches are Catalyst 6500s and have PFC3 cards. The Catalyst 6500 with PFC3 supports ingress per-user microflow policing, but it does not currently support IPv6 egress per-user microflow policing. In the SBM example in this chapter, IPv6 passes between the ISATAP and manually configured tunnel interface on the service block switches. Because ingress policing cannot be applied to either ISATAP tunnels or manually configured tunnel interfaces, there are no applicable locations to perform policing in the service block.

Example 6-3 gives a sample implementation of IPv6 per-user microflow policing. In this example, a downstream switch has been configured with a QoS policy to match IPv6 traffic and to set specific DSCP values based on one of the Cisco-recommended QoS policy configurations. The configuration for this particular switch (shown as follows) is configured to perform policing on a per-user flow basis (based on IPv6 source address in this example). Each flow is policed to 5 Mbps and is dropped if it exceeds the profile.

Example 6-3 *Sample Configuration for Microflow Policing*

```
mls qos
!
class-map match-all POLICE-MARK
  match access-group name V6-POLICE-MARK
!
policy-map IPv6-ACCESS
  class POLICE-MARK
     police flow mask src-only 5000000 8000 conform-action transmit exceed-
     action drop
  class class-default
   set dscp default
!
```

```
ipv6 access-list V6-POLICE-MARK
 permit ipv6 any any
!
interface GigabitEthernet3/1
 mls qos trust dscp
 service-policy input IPv6-ACCESS
```

At the time of this writing, the Catalyst 6500 Supervisor 32 and 720 do not support IPv6 per-user microflow policing and IPv6 multicast routing in hardware if enabled together. The supervisor supports policing in hardware or IPv6 multicast routing/forwarding in hardware, but not at the same time. If the **ipv6 multicast-routing** command is already configured on the switch and an IPv6 per-user microflow policing policy is applied, the system returns a message indicating that the IPv6 packets are software switched. Inversely, if an IPv6 per-user microflow policing policy is applied to an interface on the switch and the **ipv6 multicast-routing** command is enabled, the same warning message appears, as follows:

```
006256: *Aug 31 08:23:22.426 mst: %FM_EARL7-2-
IPV6_PORT_QOS_MCAST_FLOWMASK_CONFLICT: IPv6 QoS Micro-flow policing configuration
on port GigabitEthernet3/1 conflicts for flowmask with IPv6 multicast hardware
forwarding on SVI interface Vlan2, IPv6 traffic on the SVI interface may be
switched in software
006257: *Aug 31 08:23:22.430 mst: %FM_EARL7-4-FEAT_QOS_FLOWMASK_CONFLICT: Features
configured on interface Vlan2 conflict for flowmask with QoS configuration
on switch port GigabitEthernet3/1, traffic may be switched in software
```

More information on microflow policing can be found in the "Additional References" section, later in this chapter.

Using Control Plane Policing (CoPP)

In the context of the campus models discussed in this chapter, CoPP applies only to the Catalyst 6500 Supervisor 32/720. CoPP protects the Multiswitch Feature Card (MSFC) by preventing DoS or unnecessary traffic from negatively impacting MSFC resources. Priority is given to important control plane/management traffic. The Catalyst 6500 with PFC3 supports CoPP for IPv6 traffic. The configuration of CoPP is based on a wide variety of factors, and no single deployment recommendation can be made because the specifics of the policy are determined on a case-by-case basis.

More information on CoPP can be found in the "Additional References" section, later in this chapter.

Controlling Ingress Traffic from the Access Layer

You can filter which prefixes are allowed to source traffic. This is most commonly done on ingress on the VLAN interface of the distribution layer switches (DSM), but it can also be applied to the ingress on the ISATAP tunnel interfaces in the HM or SBM. Controlling IPv6 traffic based on source prefix can help protect the network against basic spoofing.

Example 6-4 shows a basic ACL permitting only the IPv6 prefix for a VLAN.

Example 6-4 *Basic IPv6 Ingress ACL*

```
ipv6 access-list VLAN2-v6-INGRESS
remark PERMIT ICMPv6 PACKETS FROM HOSTS WITH PREFIX 2001:DB8:CAFE:2::/64
permit icmp 2001:DB8:CAFE:2::/64 any
remark PERMIT IPv6 PACKETS FROM HOSTS WITH PREFIX 2001:DB8:CAFE:2::64
permit ipv6 2001:DB8:CAFE:2::/64 any
remark PERMIT ALL ICMPv6 PACKETS SOURCED BY HOSTS USING THE LINK-LOCAL PREFIX
permit icmp FE80::/10 any
remark DENY ALL OTHER IPv6 PACKETS AND LOG
deny ipv6 any any log-input
!
interface Vlan2
 ipv6 traffic-filter VLAN2-v6-INGRESS in
```

> **Note** Cisco IOS IPv6 ACLs contain implicit permit entries for IPv6 neighbor discovery. If **deny ipv6 any any** is configured, the implicit neighbor discovery entries are overridden. It is important to remember that if a manually configured catch-all **deny** statement is used for logging purposes, the following two permit entries must be added back in:
>
> **permit icmp any any nd-na**
>
> **permit icmp any any nd-ns**

In the VLAN2-v6-INGRESS sample given in Example 6-4, a more permissive entry (**permit icmp FE80::/10 any**) is made to account for the neighbor discovery requirement as well as any other ICMPv6 services that are needed for link operation on VLAN2. There are RFCs, drafts, and IPv6 deployment books that specifically discuss the various ICMPv6 types that should or should not be blocked. Refer to the section "Additional References," later in this chapter, for links to the Internet Engineering Task Force (IETF) and Cisco Press book that discusses the filtering of ICMPv6 packets.

First-Hop Security

Today, Cisco provides a variety of security capabilities that help prevent rogue DHCP servers, man-in-the-middle attacks, and other access layer threats specific to IPv4. These same attack vectors exist with IPv6 but lack both industry and vendor solutions to the problem. Cisco generically groups these security capabilities into a single area known as "first-hop security." One of several efforts under way is router advertisement, or RA, Guard. RA Guard helps prevent rogue RAs (rogue routers or hosts acting as routers) on a VLAN/link. Secure Neighbor Discovery (SEND), RA Guard, and other upcoming innovations will go a long way in helping secure IPv6 hosts and devices at the access layer. Solutions such as RFC 3971, "SEcure Neighbor Discovery," and RA Guard are IETF-supported efforts. The status of RA Guard and other operationally focused standards for IPv6 should be tracked at the IETF. Also, additional information such as platform support and configuration examples for RA Guard, port ACLs, and other features can be found in the "Additional References" section, later in this chapter.

Blocking the Use of Microsoft Teredo

Teredo is used to provide IPv6 support to hosts that are located behind Network Address Translation (NAT) gateways. Teredo introduces several security threats that need to be thoroughly understood. Until well-defined security recommendations can be made for Teredo in campus networks, the reader might want to ensure that Teredo is disabled on Microsoft Windows XP SP2 and higher, Windows Vista, and Windows 7. As a backup precaution, the reader might also want to consider configuring ACLs (which can be done at the access layer or further upstream, such as at the border routers) to block UDP port 3544 to prevent Teredo from establishing a tunnel outside the campus network. Information on Teredo can be found in the "Additional References" section, later in this chapter.

The "Additional References" section also lists more resources for IPv6 security.

Multicast

IPv6 multicast is an important service for any enterprise network design, and IPv6 multicast requirements might cause you to reconsider the models discussed in this chapter. The most important issue to understand with IPv6 multicast and the various models is that IPv6 multicast is not supported over ISATAP. This lack of support is not a limitation of equipment or software, but rather a shortcoming of the ISATAP tunneling mechanism (See Section 6.3 of RFC 5214, "Intra-Site Automatic Tunnel Addressing Protocol [ISATAP]").

One of the most important factors to consider in IPv6 multicast deployment in the campus network is to ensure that host/group control is handled properly in the access layer. Multicast Listener Discovery (MLD) in IPv6 is the equivalent to Internet Group Management Protocol (IGMP) in IPv4. Both are used for multicast group membership control. MLD Snooping is the feature that enables Layer 2 switches to control the distribution of multicast traffic only to the ports that have listeners. Without it, multicast traffic meant for only a single receiver (or group of receivers) is flooded to all ports on an access layer switch. In the access layer, it is important that the switches support MLD Snooping for MLD version 1 and/or version 2. Note that this requirement applies only to dual-stack or IPv6-only access/distribution layer deployments. If the host is tunneling past these layers (for example, HM or SBM), IPv6 multicast is not being actively streamed into these hosts natively, so the requirement for MLD Snooping is not present.

Note   Various Linux and BSD implementations support MLDv2, as does Microsoft Windows Vista and Windows 7. MLDv2 is important in PIM-SSM-based deployments. The use of MLDv2 with PIM-SSM is an excellent design combination for a wide variety of IPv6 multicast deployments. Cisco IOS provides a feature called SSM mapping that maps MLDv1 reports to MLDv2 reports to be used by PIM-SSM. You can find more information about Source Specific Multicast (SSM) mapping at the following URL (as well as in the Cisco Press book *Deploying IPv6 Networks*):

http://www.cisco.com/en/US/docs/ios/ipv6/configuration/guide/ip6-multicast_ps10591_TSD_Products_Configuration_Guide_Chapter.html#wp1058805.

In this chapter, IPv6 multicast-enabled applications are supported in the DSM because no ISATAP configurations are used there. The multicast-enabled applications tested in this design are Windows Media Services and VideoLAN Media Client (VLC) using Embedded rendezvous point (Embedded-RP) and protocol independent multicast - source specific multicast (PIM-SSM) groups. The multicast sources are running on Microsoft Windows Server 2003, Windows Server 2008, and Red Hat 5.0 servers located in the data center access layer.

Basic IPv6 multicast concepts are discussed in Chapter 3. Also, several documents on Cisco.com and within the industry discuss IPv6 multicast in detail. No other configuration notes are made in this chapter except for generic references to the commands to enable basic IPv6 multicast functionality. For more information, see the Cisco IPv6 multicast webpage at the following URL:

http://www.cisco.com/en/US/products/ps6594/products_ios_protocol_group_home.html.

Network Management

Many of the traditional management tools used today support IPv6. However, most management tools and instrumentation for IPv6 have a long way to go. In this chapter, the only considerations for management of the campus network are related to basic management services (Telnet, Secure Shell [SSH], and SNMP). SNMP over IPv6 transport is supported on the latest versions of the software, depending on the Catalyst platform. Refer to the platform documentation for support for SNMP over IPv6 transport. If the reader uses a platform that does not yet support SNMP over IPv6 transport, the management of IPv6-specific MIBs/traps/informs is supported on the Catalyst platforms using SNMP over IPv4 transport. Chapter 11 describes management for IPv6 in more detail.

Address Management

Another area of management that you must thoroughly research is that of address management. Deploying large hexadecimal addresses on many network devices should, at some point, be automated and made as simple as possible.

Today, one way to help with the deployment of address prefixes on a campus switch is through the use of the general prefix feature. This feature enables the customer to define a prefix or prefixes in the global configuration of the switch with a user-friendly name. That user-friendly name can be used on a per-interface basis to replace the usual IPv6 prefix definition on the interface. Example 6-5 shows how to use the general prefix feature.

Example 6-5 *Configure the General Prefix*

```
!Define the General Prefix
6k-agg-1(config)#ipv6 general-prefix DC-1 2001:DB8:CAFE::/48

!Configure the general prefix named "DC-1" on a per-interface basis:
6k-agg-1(config-if)#ipv6 address DC-1 ::10:0:0:F1A1:6500/64

!Verify that the general prefix was correctly assigned to the interface:
6k-agg-1#show ipv6 interface vlan 10
Vlan10 is up, line protocol is up
  IPv6 is enabled, link-local address is FE80::211:BCFF:FEC0:C800
  Description: VLAN-SERVERFARM-WEB
  Global unicast address(es):
    2001:DB8:CAFE:10::F1A1:6500, subnet is 2001:DB8:CAFE:10::/64
```

Tip   The general prefix feature is useful where renumbering is required, because changing the general prefix value can renumber a router or switch quickly.

More information on the general prefix feature can be found at the Cisco IOS IPv6 documentation page (see the "Additional Resources" section at the end of this chapter).

IPv6 address allocation to hosts located in the campus access layer can be assigned through SLAAC, static assignment, or DHCPv6. DHCPv6 assignment is the predominant method that is desired by most enterprise campus administrators. Until support for DHCPv6 Relay was available on the Catalyst products, the administrator had no other choice but to rely on SLAAC as the primary means of allocating IPv6 addressing to hosts in the access layer. With DHCPv6 Relay Agent support now available, the administrator can allocate and manage addresses in much the same way as it is done with DHCP for IPv4. SLAAC and DHCPv6 can be used simultaneously throughout the network, depending on your requirements. For example, you could use SLAAC to address IP phones on the voice VLAN and use DHCPv6 for hosts on the data VLAN such as PCs.

Figure 6-9 shows that the DHCPv6 Relay is placed on the campus distribution layer switches, which is the same place as the IP helper used in DHCP for IPv4.

The configuration of the DHCPv6 Relay feature is straightforward. Implement the configuration shown in Example 6-6 on the VLAN interface facing the access layer hosts.

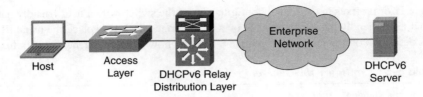

Figure 6-9 *DHCPv6 Relay Placement in the Campus*

Example 6-6 *DHCPv6 Relay Configuration*

```
interface Vlan2
 description ACCESS-DATA-2
 ipv6 address 2001:DB8:CAFE:2::A111:1010/64
 ipv6 nd prefix 2001:DB8:CAFE:2::/64 no-advertise
 ipv6 nd managed-config-flag
 ipv6 dhcp relay destination 2001:DB8:CAFE:102::9
```

The **ipv6 dhcp relay destination** command in Example 6-6 defines the unicast address of the DHCPv6 server. The **ipv6 nd managed-config-flag** command sets the "managed address configuration" flag in the RA so that the host knows to use a stateful address configuration mechanism, such as DHCPv6. You can find more information about DHCPv6 Relay Agent at the Implementing DHCP for IPv6 webpage: http://tinyurl.com/24kb5qy.

Having DHCPv6 Relay Agent support in the network is only part of the equation. The client must support DHCPv6 (such as Microsoft Windows 7), and there must be a DHCPv6 server. Currently, there are three DHCPv6 servers that have been tested by Cisco in the campus:

■ **Cisco Network Registrar:**
  http://www.cisco.com/en/US/products/sw/netmgtsw/ps1982

■ **Cisco DHCPv6 Server in IOS:** http://tinyurl.com/24kb5qy

■ **Microsoft Windows Server 2008:** http://technet.microsoft.com/en-us/library/cc896553%28WS.10%29.aspx

Cisco supports the management of IPv6-enabled network devices through a variety of network management products to include DNS, DHCPv6, device management, and monitoring, as well as network management, troubleshooting, and reporting. Chapter 11 discusses IPv6 management. For more information on the various Cisco Network Management solutions, refer to the Network Management and Automation webpage: http://www.cisco.com/en/US/products/sw/netmgtsw/index.html.

Scalability and Performance

The discussion of scale and performance focuses on general considerations when planning and deploying IPv6 in the campus versus a platform-specific view. This chapter is not meant to analyze scalability and performance information for the various platforms tested.

In general, you should understand the link, memory, and CPU utilization of the existing campus network. If any of these aspects are already stressed, adding IPv6 or any new technology, feature, or protocol into the design could cause a disruption to traffic traversing the device. However, in IPv6 implementations, it is common to see a change in traffic utilization ratios on the campus network links. As IPv6 is deployed, IPv4 traffic utilization is very often reduced as users leverage IPv6 as the transport for applications that were historically IPv4-only. There is an increase in overall network utilization that usually derives from control traffic for routing and also tunnel overhead when ISATAP or manually configured tunnels are used.

The following sections describe scalability and performance considerations for DSM, HM, and SBM.

Scalability and Performance Considerations for the DSM

This section describes scalability and performance considerations for the DSM access layer, distribution layer, and core layer.

One of the primary scalability considerations is that of running two protocols on the access and distribution layer switch. In the access layer (Layer 2 or routed access) or distribution layer, the switch must track both IPv4 and IPv6 neighbor information. Similar to Address Resolution Protocol (ARP) in IPv4, neighbor cache exists for IPv6. The primary consideration here is that with IPv4, there is usually a one-to-one mapping of IPv4 address to MAC address. But with IPv6, there can be several mappings for multiple IPv6 addresses that the host might have (for example, link-local, unique-local, and multiple global addresses) to a single MAC address in the neighbor cache of the switches. Following is an example of ARP and neighbor cache entries on a Catalyst 6500 located in the distribution layer for a host with the MAC address of 000d.6084.2c7a.

The ARP and IPv6 neighbor cache entries for the host in the distribution layer follows:

```
Internet   10.120.2.200          2          000d.6084.2c7a  ARPA    Vlan2

The IPv6 neighbor cache entry is:

2001:DB8:CAFE:2:2891:1C0C:F52A:9DF1      4 000d.6084.2c7a  STALE V12
2001:DB8:CAFE:2:7DE5:E2B0:D4DF:97EC     16 000d.6084.2c7a  STALE V12
FE80::7DE5:E2B0:D4DF:97EC               16 000d.6084.2c7a  STALE V12
```

The IPv6 neighbor cache shows that there are three entries listed for the host (in this case, a Windows host that, by default, does not use an EUI-64-based interface ID). The first address is one of two global IPv6 addresses assigned and reflects the global IPv6 address generated by the use of IPv6 privacy extensions. The second address is another global IPv6 address that is assigned by stateless autoconfiguration (it can also be statically defined or assigned through DHCPv6), and the third address is the link-local address generated by the host. The number of entries can decrease to a minimum of one (link-local address) or increase to a multitude of entries for a single host, depending on the address types used on the host.

Another performance and scalability consideration for the campus network deals with IPv6 multicast. As mentioned previously, it is important to ensure that MLD Snooping (similar to IGMP Snooping in IPv4) is supported at the access layer when IPv6 multicast is used to ensure that IPv6 multicast frames at Layer 2 are not flooded to all the ports.

In addition to the ARP/neighbor cache issues listed previously, there are two other considerations for the distribution layer switches in the DSM:

- Layer 3 IPv6 forwarding must be performed in hardware.

- The processing of ACL entries must be performed in hardware. IPv6 ACLs in the distribution layer are primarily used for QoS (classification and marking of ingress packets from the access layer), for security (controlling DoS, snooping, and unauthorized access for ingress traffic in the access layer), and for a combination of QoS and security to protect the control plane of the switch from attack.

In the core layer, the considerations for scale and performance are the same as with the distribution layer.

Scalability and Performance Considerations for the HM

Scalability and performance considerations for the HM are as follows:

- **Access layer:** IPv6 is not supported in the access layer in the HM. You might need to consider link utilization because there might be an additional amount of traffic (tunneled IPv6 traffic) present on the links. As mentioned previously, however, as IPv6 is deployed, there might be a replacement of link utilization ratios from IPv4 to IPv6 as users begin to use IPv6 for applications that were historically IPv4-only.

- **Distribution layer:** The distribution layer is affected by the same considerations as the access layer.

- **Core layer:** When using the HM, hundreds or more ISATAP tunnels can terminate on the core layer switches. You should consult closely with partners and Cisco account teams to ensure that the existing core layer switches can handle the number of tunnels required in the design. If the core layer switches are not going to be able to support the number of tunnels coming from the access layer, you might need to either plan to move to the DSM or use the SBM instead of the HM so that dedicated switches can be used just for tunnel termination and management until the DSM can be supported. Two important scale and performance factors for the core layer are as follows:

- **Control plane impact for the management of ISATAP tunnel interfaces:** This can be an issue if there is a one-to-one mapping between the number of VLANs and the number of ISATAP tunnels. In large networks, this mapping results in a substantial number of tunnels that the CPU must track. The control plane management of virtual interfaces is done by the CPU.

- **Link utilization:** There is an increase in link utilization coming from the distribution layer (tunneled traffic) and a possible increase in link utilization by adding IPv6 (now dual-stack) to the links from the core layer to the data center aggregation layers.

Scalability and Performance Considerations for the SBM

Scalability and performance considerations for the SBM are as follows:

- **Access layer:** The access layer is IPv4-only in the SBM and requires no specific scale or performance considerations.

- **Distribution layer:** The distribution layer is IPv4-only in the SBM and requires no specific scale or performance considerations.

- **Core layer:** The core layer is IPv4-only in the SBM and requires no specific scale or performance considerations.

- **Service block:** Most of the considerations found in the core layer of the HM apply to the service block switches. The one difference is that the service block is terminating both ISATAP and manually configured tunnels on the same switch pair. The advantage with the SBM is that the switch pair is dedicated for tunnel termination and can have additional switches added to the service block to account for more tunnels, and therefore can allow a larger tunnel-based deployment. Adding more switches for scale is difficult to do in a core layer (HM) because of the central role the core has in connecting the various network blocks (access, data center, WAN, and so on).

Implementing the Dual-Stack Model

The following sections focus on the configuration of the DSM. The configurations are divided into specific areas, such as VLAN, routing, and HA configuration. Many of these configurations, such as VLANs and physical interfaces, are not specific to IPv6. VLAN configurations for the DSM are the same for IPv4 and IPv6, but are shown for completeness.

Note Example configurations are shown for only two switches (generally the pair in the same layer or a pair connecting to each other) and only for the section being discussed, for example, routing or HA.

Network Topology

The diagrams in this section are used as a reference for all DSM configuration examples. Figure 6-10 shows the physical port layout that is used for the DSM.

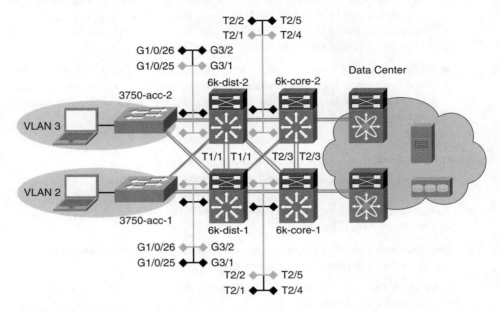

Figure 6-10   *DSM Network Topology - Physical Ports*

Note   Only the details of the campus are shown. You can find the data center portion in Chapter 9.

Figure 6-11 shows the IPv6 addressing plan for the DSM environment. To keep the diagram as simple to read as possible, the /48 prefix portion of the network is deleted. The IPv6 /48 prefix used in all the models in this book is 2001:db8:cafe::/48.

Note   The IPv6 addressing used in this book is by no means meant to be used as a best practice. The addressing used in this book has a focus on simplicity for the sake of easier flow and readability. You should carefully plan the IPv6 address assignment before fully implementing it. A lot can be learned from an existing IPv4 addressing plan—taking advantage of lessons learned, and perhaps, starting from scratch as the IPv6 address plan is a "greenfield" opportunity to do addressing fresh and clean.

In addition to the physical interfaces, IPv6 addresses are assigned to loopback and VLAN interfaces. Table 6-4 shows the switch, loopback/VLAN interface, and IPv6 address for the interface.

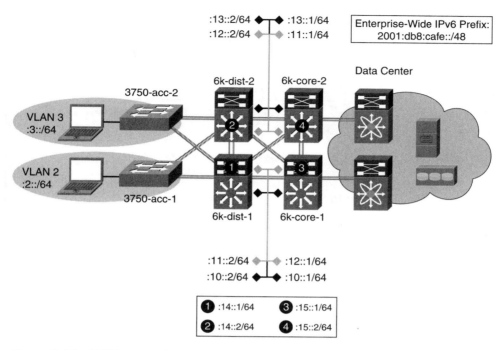

Figure 6-11   *DSM Network Topology - IPv6 Addressing*

Table 6-4   *Switch Loopback/VLAN Addressing*

Switch	Interface	IPv6 Address
3750-acc-1	Loopback	2001:db8:cafe:1f3::5/128
	VLAN2	2001:db8:cafe:2::4/64
3750-acc-2	Loopback	2001:db8:cafe:1f3::6/128
	VLAN3	2001:db8:cafe:3::4/64
6k-dist-1	Loopback	2001:db8:cafe:1f3::3/128
	VLAN2	2001:db8:cafe:2::2/64
	VLAN3	2001:db8:cafe:3::2/64
6k-dist-2	Loopback	2001:db8:cafe:1f3::4/128
	VLAN2	2001:db8:cafe:2::3/64
	VLAN3	2001:db8:cafe:3::3/64
6k-core-1	Loopback	2001:db8:cafe:1f3::1/128
6k-core-2	Loopback	2001:db8:cafe:1f3::2/128

Physical/VLAN Configuration

Physical point-to-point (p2p) links are configured in much the same way as IPv4. Example 6-7 is the p2p interface configuration for the link between 6k-dist-1 and 6k-core-1.

Example 6-7   *6k-dist-1 P2P Link Configuration*

```
ipv6 unicast-routing              !Globally enable IPv6 unicast routing

ip cef distributed                !Ensure IP CEF is enabled (req. for IPv6 CEF)
ipv6 cef distributed              !Globally enable IPv6 CEF.

!
interface TenGigabitEthernet2/1
 description to 6k-core-1
 dampening
 load-interval 30
 carrier-delay msec 0
 ipv6 address 2001:DB8:CAFE:10::2/64      !Assign IPv6 address

 no ipv6 redirects                         !Disable IPv6 redirects
```

The configurations include the **no ipv6 redirects** command. This turns off the default capabilities for sending ICMPv6 redirects (signaling a better route to a host), which are not needed on these links. It is a best practice to disable unneeded services on networking and host devices, especially those that might be used as a security attack target.

Example 6-8 shows the IPv6-specific configuration for the core-to-distribution link.

Example 6-8   *6k-core-1 P2P Link Configuration*

```
ipv6 unicast-routing
ip cef distributed
ipv6 cef distributed
!
interface TenGigabitEthernet2/4
 description to 6k-dist-1
 dampening
 load-interval 30
 carrier-delay msec 0
 ipv6 address 2001:DB8:CAFE:10::1/64

 no ipv6 redirects
```

Example 6-9 shows the 6k-dist-1 VLAN2 configuration. The configuration shows a trunk link to the access layer and a data VLAN (VLAN2). In this example, DHCPv6 relay is enabled for the hosts attached to this VLAN. The line with **no-advertise** is used to prevent the prefix listed from being sent in an RA. This is most often used to prevent non-DHCPv6-capable clients that are on the link from using SLAAC. If you have a mixed environment of DHCPv6-capable and non-IPv6 DHCPv6-capable hosts and want to receive addressing regardless of method, do not use this command. The **managed-config-flag** command signals the client to use stateful address configuration (DHCPv6).

Example 6-9   *6k-dist-1 VLAN2 Configuration*

```
vtp domain ese-dc
vtp mode transparent
!
spanning-tree mode rapid-pvst
spanning-tree loopguard default
spanning-tree vlan 2-3 priority 24576
!
vlan 2

  name ACCESS-DATA-2

!

interface GigabitEthernet3/1
 description to 3750-acc-1
 switchport
 switchport trunk encapsulation dot1q
 switchport trunk allowed vlan 2

 switchport mode trunk
 switchport nonegotiate
 no ip address
 spanning-tree guard root
!
interface Vlan2

 description ACCESS-DATA-2

 ipv6 address 2001:DB8:CAFE:2::2/64

 ipv6 nd prefix 2001:DB8:CAFE:2::/64 no-advertise !Don't send RA for this prefix

 ipv6 nd managed-config-flag         !Enabled managed address configuration
                                      flag
 ipv6 dhcp relay destination 2001:DB8:CAFE:102::9   !Define DHCPv6 server address

 no ipv6 redirects
```

On the Catalyst 3750 and 3560 switches, you must enable the correct Switch Database Management (SDM) template to allow the ternary content addressable memory (TCAM) to be used for different purposes. The 3750-acc-1 and 3750-acc-2 have been configured with the "dual-ipv4-and-ipv6" SDM template using the **sdm prefer dual-ipv4-and-ipv6 default** command (this requires a reboot). For more information about the **sdm prefer** command and associated templates, refer to the following URL: http://tinyurl.com/28qj5lk.

The access layer uses a single VLAN per switch; other VLANs such as management or voice VLANs are not discussed. The VLANs do not span access layer switches and are terminated at the distribution layer. Example 6-10 shows the 3750-acc-1 configuration.

Example 6-10 *3750-acc-1 VLAN Configuration*

```
vtp domain ese-dc
vtp mode transparent
!
spanning-tree mode rapid-pvst
spanning-tree loopguard default
spanning-tree portfast bpduguard default
!
vlan 2                               !VLAN2 - Data VLAN for 3750-acc-1

  name ACCESS-DATA-2

!
interface GigabitEthernet1/0/25
 description TRUNK TO 6k-dist-1
 switchport trunk encapsulation dot1q
 switchport trunk allowed vlan 2

 switchport mode trunk
 switchport nonegotiate
!
interface Vlan2                      !VLAN2 with IPv6 address

  ipv6 address 2001:DB8:CAFE:2::4/64

 no ipv6 redirects
!
interface GigabitEthernet1/0/10
 description TO PC
 switchport access vlan 2

 switchport mode access
 switchport port-security maximum 2
 switchport port-security aging time 20
 spanning-tree portfast
```

Although stacks are not used in any of the models discussed here, they are commonly used on the Catalyst 3750 and 3560 switches in the access layer. IPv6 is supported in much the same way as IPv4 when using switch stacks. For more information on IPv6 with switch stacks, refer to the following URL: http://tinyurl.com/32324vo.

Routing Configuration

As previously mentioned, the routing for the DSM is set up using EIGRP for both IPv4 and IPv6. The EIGRP configuration follows the recommended Cisco campus designs as much as possible.

The configuration for EIGRP for IPv6 is shown for the 6k-dist-1 switches in Example 6-11.

Example 6-11   *6k-dist-1 Routing Configuration*

```
key chain eigrp
 key 100
   key-string 7 1111
!
interface Loopback0
 ip address 10.122.10.9 255.255.255.255          !Address used for RID on EIGRP

 ipv6 address 2001:DB8:CAFE:1F3::3/128

 ipv6 eigrp 10

!
interface TenGigabitEthernet1/1
 description to 6k-dist-2
 ipv6 address 2001:DB8:CAFE:14::1/64

 ipv6 eigrp 10

 ipv6 hello-interval eigrp 10 1

 ipv6 hold-time eigrp 10 3

 ipv6 authentication mode eigrp 10 md5

 ipv6 authentication key-chain eigrp 10 eigrp

!
interface TenGigabitEthernet2/1
 description to 6k-core-1
```

continues

Example 6-11   *6k-dist-1 Routing Configuration*   *continued*

```
 ipv6 address 2001:DB8:CAFE:10::2/64

 ipv6 eigrp 10

 ipv6 hello-interval eigrp 10 1

 ipv6 hold-time eigrp 10 3

 ipv6 authentication mode eigrp 10 md5

 ipv6 authentication key-chain eigrp 10 eigrp

!
interface Vlan2
 description ACCESS-DATA-2
 ipv6 address 2001:DB8:CAFE:2::2/64

 ipv6 eigrp 10

!
ipv6 router eigrp 10

 router-id 10.122.10.9            !RID using Loopback0

 no shutdown                      !IPv6 EIGRP process is by default shut down

 passive-interface Vlan2

 passive-interface Vlan3

 passive-interface Loopback0
```

EIGRP is configured on a per-interface basis. Per the Cisco campus design guides, the EIGRP hello and hold timers are modified for faster convergence and EIGRP authentication is enabled. The router ID for the EIGRP process remains 32 bits long and is derived from an IPv4 address found on one of the configured interfaces or manually defined. Additionally, it is recommended to configure an IPv6 EIGRP summary range that would be advertised towards the core. This is done by using the command **ipv6 summary-address eigrp**. If the router is IPv6-only, the EIGRP router ID must be manually configured.

The configuration for EIGRP for IPv6 is shown for the 6k-core-1 switches in Example 6-12. Only a portion of the configuration is shown because redundant links between the distribution and core layers share identical configurations as they relate to routing.

Example 6-12   *6k-core-1 Routing Configuration*

```
key chain eigrp
 key 100
   key-string 7 1111
!
```

```
interface Loopback0
 ip address 10.122.10.3 255.255.255.255
 ipv6 address 2001:DB8:CAFE:1F3::1/128
 ipv6 eigrp 10
!
interface TenGigabitEthernet2/4
 description to 6k-dist-1
 ipv6 address 2001:DB8:CAFE:10::1/64
 ipv6 eigrp 10
 ipv6 hello-interval eigrp 10 1
 ipv6 hold-time eigrp 10 3
 ipv6 authentication mode eigrp 10 md5
 ipv6 authentication key-chain eigrp 10 eigrp
!
ipv6 router eigrp 10
 router-id 10.122.10.3
 no shutdown
 passive-interface Loopback0
```

It is important to read and understand the implications of modifying various IGP timers. The campus network should be designed to converge as fast as possible. The campus network is also capable of running much more tightly tuned IGP timers than in a branch or WAN environment. The routing configurations shown are based on the Cisco campus recommendations. You should understand the context of each command and the timer value selection before pursuing the deployment in a live network. Refer to the "Additional References" section, later in this chapter, for links to the Cisco campus design best practice documents.

First-Hop Redundancy Configuration

The HA design in the DSM consists of running two of each switches (applicable in the distribution, core, and data center aggregation layers) and ensuring that the IPv4 and IPv6 routing configurations are tuned and completely fault-tolerant. All distribution pairs in the reference campus configuration are running HSRP for both IPv4 and IPv6. Optionally, GLBP can be used.

HSRP is defined on a per-interface basis and is mostly configured like HSRP for IPv4. The configuration in Example 6-13 shows both HSRP for IPv4 and IPv6 for comparison. The IPv6 for HSRP configuration shown has HSRP version 2 enabled and is used to take advantage of several new features such as the advertisement and learning of millisecond timer values, expanded group range, and IPv6 support.

When configuring a standby virtual IPv6 address, there are two options: a manually defined link-local address (FE80::/10 prefix) or autoconfig. Note that depending on the platform and version of code, a global IPv6 address can be defined as the standby address. The **ipv6 autoconfig** command is used to generate a link-local address (from the FE80::/10 prefix) that is created from the HSRP virtual MAC address. The HSRP IPv6 virtual MAC address range is 0005.73A0.000–0005.73A0.0FFF.

Both HSRP IPv4 and IPv6 are using lowered hello timers for faster failover as well as adjusted priority values to establish an active/standby role between the 6k-dist-1 and 6k-dist-2 switches. Preemption is configured so that the switch will take back the role of ACTIVE from the lower-priority 6k-dist-2. Preempt delay is configured for 180 seconds because this is a Catalyst 6500 with many line cards. It is a best practice to configure a delay so that the switch does not go ACTIVE for HSRP before all the line cards have been powered on and activated. A delay of 180 seconds gives enough time from power-up for the line cards to be powered on and activated.

Finally, HSRP authentication has been configured between both distribution layer switches for added security. More information about HSRP for IPv6 can be found at http://www.cisco.com/en/US/docs/ios/ipv6/configuration/guide/ip6-fhrp.html#wp1055254.

The configuration for HSRP for IPv4 and IPv6 on the 6k-dist-1 switch is shown in Example 6-13.

Example 6-13   *6k-dist-1 HSRP Configuration*

```
interface Vlan2
description ACCESS-DATA-2
standby version 2                              !Required

standby 1 ip 10.120.2.1
standby 1 timers msec 250 msec 750
standby 1 priority 110
standby 1 preempt delay minimum 180
standby 1 authentication ese
standby 2 ipv6 autoconfig

standby 2 timers msec 250 msec 750

standby 2 priority 110

standby 2 preempt delay minimum 180

standby 2 authentication ese
```

QoS Configuration

The QoS configurations for the DSM are based on the recommendations found in the Cisco Campus QoS Solutions Reference Network Design (SRND) located here: http://www.cisco.com/en/US/docs/solutions/Enterprise/WAN_and_MAN/QoS_SRND_4 0/QoSCampus_40.html. As was mentioned in the "General Campus IPv6 Deployment Considerations" QoS section, earlier in this chapter, the primary consideration for altering or creating a QoS policy to act on both IPv4 and IPv6 is to ensure that the **ip** keyword is removed from the **match** and **set** statements in the policy configuration. The policy criteria are the same for IPv4 and IPv6 unless it is determined that a special set of QoS policies is needed for IPv6 because of the fact that a completely different set of applications might be used for IPv6. The policies for classification, marking, queuing, and policing vary greatly based on customer requirements. The types of queuing and number of queues supported also vary from platform to platform and line card to line card. The reader should ensure that QoS is thoroughly understood before deploying it for either IPv4 or IPv6 because there are many elements to understand and, in many cases, configurations are platform-dependent.

This chapter is not meant to be a primer for QoS but simply a reference to show a snippet of the overall QoS policy used. A summarized configuration for the 6500-E series switch is shown in Example 6-14 and is for reference only. For the sake of brevity, not all interfaces and per-interface configurations are shown.

Example 6-14   *QoS Example for Catalyst 6500-E*

```
mls ipv6 acl compress address unicast     !Enable HW compression of address/ports

mls qos                                   !Enable QoS

!
class-map match-all BULK-DATA             !Associate IPv6 ACL with class-map

  match access-group name BULK-DATA
class-map match-all TRANSACTIONAL-DATA
  match access-group name TRANSACTIONAL-DATA
!
policy-map PER-PORT-MARKING               !Policy used for setting DSCP value

  class TRANSACTIONAL-DATA
   set dscp af21
  class BULK-DATA
   set dscp af11
  class class-default
   set dscp default
!
ipv6 access-list TRANSACTIONAL-DATA       !IPv6 ACLs used for classifcation
```

continues

Example 6-14   *QoS Example for Catalyst 6500-E   continued*

```
 remark HTTPS
 permit tcp any any eq 443
!
ipv6 access-list BULK-DATA
 remark FTP
 permit tcp any any eq ftp
 permit tcp any any eq ftp-data
!
interface GigabitEthernet3/1
 description to Access
 service-policy input PER-PORT-MARKING          #Apply marking policy
```

Some features do not require any configuration to get them to see and act on IPv6 traffic. Queuing is an example of when IPv6 traffic is dealt with on a per-interface basis without any special configuration changes. Example 6-15 gives an example of a per-interface queuing configuration that equally applies to IPv4 and IPv6.

Example 6-15   *QoS Queuing Example on a 10-Gigabit Ethernet Interface*

```
interface TenGigabitEthernet2/1
 description Uplink
 wrr-queue bandwidth 5 25 15 15 5 5 15        !Per-interface queueing

 wrr-queue queue-limit 5 25 15 15 5 5 15
 wrr-queue random-detect min-threshold 3 80 100 100 100 100 100 100 100
 wrr-queue random-detect min-threshold 4 80 100 100 100 100 100 100 100
 wrr-queue random-detect min-threshold 5 80 100 100 100 100 100 100 100
 wrr-queue random-detect min-threshold 6 80 100 100 100 100 100 100 100
 wrr-queue random-detect max-threshold 1 100 100 100 100 100 100 100 100
 wrr-queue random-detect max-threshold 2 100 100 100 100 100 100 100 100
 wrr-queue random-detect 4
 wrr-queue random-detect 5
 wrr-queue random-detect 6
 wrr-queue random-detect 7
 wrr-queue cos-map 1 1 1
 wrr-queue cos-map 2 1 0
 wrr-queue cos-map 3 1 2
 wrr-queue cos-map 4 1 3
 wrr-queue cos-map 5 1 6
 wrr-queue cos-map 6 1 7
 wrr-queue cos-map 7 1 4
 mls qos trust dscp                           !Trust previously marked DSCP values
```

Multicast Configuration

IPv6 multicast is fully supported in the DSM. One thing to understand is the lack of CLI input required to enable IPv6 multicast when using PIM-SSM or Embedded-RP. If PIM-SSM is used exclusively, it is only required to enable **ipv6 multicast-routing** globally, which automatically enables PIM on all IPv6-enabled interfaces. This configuration also automatically enables PIM-SSM and its associated group range. This process is a dramatic difference from what is required with IPv4 multicast, where all multicast elements must be configured manually.

In the 3750-acc-1 switch example, the switch needs to have IPv6 multicast awareness to control the distribution of multicast traffic only on ports that are actively listening. This awareness is accomplished by enabling MLD Snooping. IPv6 multicast routing is globally enabled on each Layer 3 device all the way to the source located in the data center.

Although IPv6 multicast design is outside the scope of this chapter, configurations are shown for IPv6 multicast on the 3750-acc-1, 6k-dist-1, and 6k-core-1 switches, and the application is leveraging PIM-SSM. After **ipv6 multicast-routing** has been configured, PIM is enabled, PIM tunnel interface(s) for the source registration process are automatically created, and a PIM-SSM group range is automatically configured by the device. All that needs to be done is to have an MLDv2-capable host access the source application that is configured for the appropriate multicast group.

Most of the configuration examples are trivial, but are shown from the access layer to the aggregation layer for operational consistency:

- **3750-acc-1:** Globally enable MLD Snooping.

  ```
  ipv6 mld snooping
  ```

- **6k-dist-1:** Globally enable IPv6 multicast routing. Remember that with IPv6 multicast with PIM, after multicast is globally enabled, IPv6 support for PIM is automatically enabled on any interface that has IPv6 enabled (through static configuration or through IPv6 address assignment).

  ```
  ipv6 multicast-routing
  ```

- **6k-core-1:** Globally enable IPv6 multicast routing.

  ```
  ipv6 multicast-routing
  ```

After IPv6 multicast has been enabled globally, you can use the **show ipv6 pim range-list** command to ensure that the automatic group range for SSM is available, as shown in Example 6-16.

Example 6-16   *6k-core-1 - PIM-SSM Range List*

```
6k-core-1# show ipv6 pim range-list
Static SSM Exp: never Learnt from : ::
  FF33::/32 Up: 00:00:05
```

continues

Example 6-16   *6k-core-1 - PIM-SSM Range List   continued*

```
FF34::/32 Up: 00:00:05
FF35::/32 Up: 00:00:05
FF36::/32 Up: 00:00:05
FF37::/32 Up: 00:00:05
FF38::/32 Up: 00:00:05
FF39::/32 Up: 00:00:05
FF3A::/32 Up: 00:00:05
FF3B::/32 Up: 00:00:05
FF3C::/32 Up: 00:00:05
FF3D::/32 Up: 00:00:05
FF3E::/32 Up: 00:00:05
FF3F::/32 Up: 00:00:05
```

The output shown in Example 6-17 on the 3750-acc-1 switch illustrates that the switch can see both distribution layer switches (indicated by the information in the "ports" column) as locally attached multicast routers.

Example 6-17   *3750-acc-1 IPv6 Multicast PIM Router Status*

```
3750-acc-1# show ipv6 mld snooping mrouter
Vlan    ports
— —     — —.
   2    Gi1/0/25(dynamic), Gi1/0/26(dynamic)
```

When a group is active on the access layer switch, information about the group can be displayed, as shown in Example 6-18.

Example 6-18   *3750-acc-1 IPv6 Multicast Group Output*

```
3750-acc-1# show ipv6 mld snooping address
Vlan      Group        Type       Version     Port List
— — — — — — — — — — — — — — — — — — — — — — — — — —.
2         FF35::1111   mld        v2          Gi1/0/25, Gi1/0/26
```

Note   There may be scenarios where the host operating system does not support MLDv2 and therefore cannot natively participate in PIM-SSM environments. Cisco has functionality that allows an MLDv1-only host to participate through a feature known as PIM-SSM mapping. More information on this feature can be found at the following URL:
http://www.cisco.com/en/US/docs/ios/ipv6/configuration/guide/
ip6-multicast_ps10591_TSD_Products_Configuration_Guide_Chapter.html#wp1058805.

On 6k-dist-1, information about PIM, multicast route, reverse path forwarding (RPF), and groups can be viewed in much the same way as with IPv4. Example 6-19 shows the output of an active group using PIM-SSM (FF35::1111). This stream is coming in from the 6k-core-1 switch and going out the VLAN2 (3750-acc-1) interface.

Example 6-19   *6k-dist-1 IPv6 Multicast Route Output*

```
6k-dist-1# show ipv6 mroute
Multicast Routing Table
Flags: D - Dense, S - Sparse, B - Bidir Group, s - SSM Group,
       C - Connected, L - Local, I - Received Source Specific Host Report,
       P - Pruned, R - RP-bit set, F - Register flag, T - SPT-bit set,
       J - Join SPT
Timers: Uptime/Expires
Interface state: Interface, State

(2001:DB8:CAFE:105:2E0:81FF:FE2C:9332, FF35::1111), 19:58:58/never, flags: sTI
  Incoming interface: TenGigabitEthernet2/1
  RPF nbr: FE80::215:C7FF:FE24:7440
  Immediate Outgoing interface list:
    Vlan2, Forward, 19:58:58/never
```

Routed Access Configuration

When using the routed access design, the primary change to the campus implementation applies to the access and distribution layer configurations. With the routed access design, the access layer performs routing, whereas the previous (traditional) design had the access layer as a Layer 2–only component and the first Layer 3 component was in the distribution layer. This chapter is not meant to discuss the advantages and disadvantages of the routed access design. However, the failover performance improvements realized, along with the important fact that spanning tree is not an active component, make this design attractive to many customers. Because of customer demand, performance, and operational advantages with the routed access design, this chapter discusses implementing IPv6 in this design.

Extending the DSM to now be a routed access design is quite easy. The removal of dependency on a redundant first-hop protocol is also a major improvement in the access layer. Basically, the access layer switches enable IPv6 routing and change the trunk links to routed links, and the distribution layer switches remove the trunks and VLANs for the access layer.

Figure 6-12 shows the updated DSM topology that has the routed access component included. Because nothing has changed upstream of the distribution layer, this diagram includes only the changed layers, which are the access and distribution layers. Also note that the 2001:DB8:CAFE portion of the prefix is removed for clarity in the diagram. Only the subnet identifier (A, B, C, or D) and the interface ID are shown.

Figure 6-12 shows that the links between the access layer and distribution layer are now routed links instead of trunked Layer 2 links. IPv6 addressing and routing are configured

on the new links, and the hosts in the VLANs use the IPv6 address of the VLAN interface on the access switch as the default gateway.

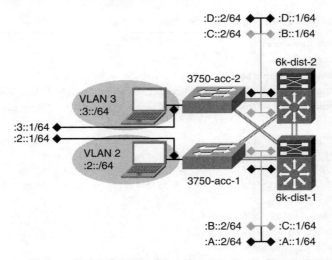

Figure 6-12   *DSM Topology - Routed Access Design*

Note   For those of you using OSPF in their network, the following IGP configuration is
shown using OSPFv3. This is a sample of what the configurations would look like in the
campus for OSPFv3 in the routed access model. This is an effort to help you see the IGP
configurations for both EIGRP for IPv6 and OSPFv3 in a campus network.

The configuration in Example 6-20 shows the relevant routed access configurations for
the 3750-acc-1 switch.

Example 6-20   *Routed Access Layer - 3750-acc-1*

```
ipv6 unicast-routing                          !Globally enable IPv6 unicast routing

!
interface GigabitEthernet1/0/25
 description To 6k-dist-1
 ipv6 address 2001:DB8:CAFE:A::2/64           !Link is now a routed link

 ipv6 ospf network point-to-point
 ipv6 ospf hello-interval 1

 ipv6 ospf dead-interval 3

 ipv6 ospf 1 area 2                           !Link is in area 2
```

```
 no ipv6 redirects
 mls qos trust dscp
!
interface Vlan2
 load-interval 30
 ipv6 address 2001:DB8:CAFE:2::1/64              !VLAN2 on this switch becomes the

                                                 !first layer 3 point for the hosts

                                                 !in VLAN2 - the link-local address

                                                 !on VLAN 2 will be the default

                                                 !gateway for the hosts

 ipv6 ospf 1 area 2                              !VLAN2 is in area 2

 ipv6 nd managed-config-flag

 ipv6 dhcp relay destination 2001:DB8:CAFE:102::9

 no ipv6 redirects
!
ipv6 router ospf 1

 router-id 10.120.2.1
 log-adjacency-changes
 auto-cost reference-bandwidth 10000
 area 2 stub no-summary               !Per the Routed Access Design guide - the

                                      !area (area 2) for the access layer

                                      !prefix is a totally stubby area

 passive-interface Vlan2
 timers spf 1 5
```

Example 6-21 shows the configuration for the 6k-dist-1 switch.

Example 6-21   *Routed Access Layer - 6k-dist-1*

```
interface GigabitEthernet3/1
 description to 3750-acc-1
 ipv6 address 2001:DB8:CAFE:A::1/64              !Link is now a routed link

 no ipv6 redirects
```

continues

Example 6-21 *Routed Access Layer - 6k-dist-1   continued*

```
 ipv6 ospf network point-to-point

 ipv6 ospf hello-interval 1

 ipv6 ospf dead-interval 3

 ipv6 ospf 1 area 2

!
ipv6 router ospf 1

 router-id 10.122.10.9
 log-adjacency-changes
 auto-cost reference-bandwidth 10000
 area 2 stub no-summary

 area 2 range 2001:DB8:CAFE:2::/64 cost 10          !Send a summary into area 0 for

                                                    !prefix "2" in area 2

 passive-interface Loopback0
 timers spf 1 5
```

The summary output of the **show ipv6 route** command for the 3750-acc-1 in Example 6-22 shows a default route coming from the two distribution layer switches. (The default is injected by the upstream switches where the Internet edge connects to the core layer.)

Example 6-22 *3750-acc-1 IPv6 Unicast Route Output*

```
3750-acc-1# show ipv6 route
IPv6 Routing Table - 13 entries
Codes: C - Connected, L - Local, S - Static, R - RIP, B - BGP
       U - Per-user Static route
       I1 - ISIS L1, I2 - ISIS L2, IA - ISIS interarea, IS - ISIS summary
       O - OSPF intra, OI - OSPF inter, OE1 - OSPF ext 1, OE2 - OSPF ext 2
       ON1 - OSPF NSSA ext 1, ON2 - OSPF NSSA ext 2
OI  ::/0 [110/11]

    via FE80::213:5FFF:FE1F:F840, GigabitEthernet1/0/26     !6k-dist-2

    via FE80::215:C7FF:FE25:9580, GigabitEthernet1/0/25     !6k-dist-1

C   2001:DB8:CAFE:2::/64 [0/0]
    via ::, Vlan2
L   2001:DB8:CAFE:2::1/128 [0/0]
    via ::, Vlan2
```

The other configuration change that is made in the DSM when using the routed access design is with IPv6 multicast. Now that the access layer switch is actually routing, the switch needs to be configured to support PIM of whatever variety is used in the rest of the network. The previous multicast configurations shown for the 6k-dist-1 would be deployed at the access layer switches. Note that the customer needs to validate which access layer platforms have IPv6 multicast routing support and in which code version.

Additional information on the Cisco routed access design can be found in the "Additional References" section, later in this chapter.

Cisco Virtual Switching System with IPv6

This section gives descriptions and examples of using the Cisco Virtual Switching System (VSS) with IPv6 in the campus.

Most enterprise networks deploy switches in pairs at the distribution and core layer to provide high availability in cases of chassis failure. The challenges of this design are that it increases the number of network management points (network nodes) as well as requires running protocols like Spanning Tree Protocol (STP) and HSRP. Additionally, to have a loop-free topology, STP blocks half of the links going to the access layer switches, leading to inefficient use of bandwidth.

VSS solves these challenges by combining a pair of Catalyst 6500 series switches into a single network/management element. VSS looks like a single logical switch to the peer switches (see Figure 6-13). Peering switches (that is, access/core switches) connect to the two physical chassis used in a VSS pair with a single ether-channel, called MEC (Multi-chassis Ether-channel). The MEC allows the network designer to come up with a redundant but loop-free Layer 2 network topology without using protocols like STP and HSRP.

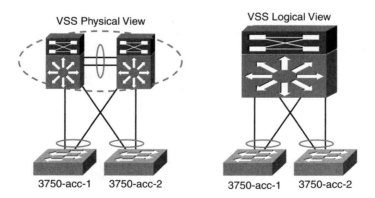

Figure 6-13 *VSS Physical and Logical Views*

The two switches in VSS are in an active-active mode from a data-plane perspective and active-standby mode from a control-plane perspective. In case of failure of one of the chassis, the active-active data-plane model keeps the traffic forwarding intact while the control plane is converging.

Figure 6-14 shows a deployment of VSS using most of the previously discussed DSM topology; only now, the core and distribution layers are using VSS.

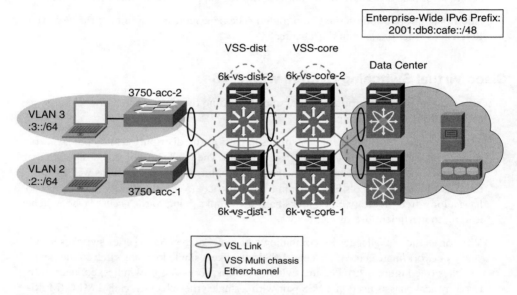

Figure 6-14   *VSS with IPv6 Deployment - Distribution/Core*

From a logical network perspective, the topology appears as a chain of single switches when in reality they are deployed in physical pairs. Other than the loop-free Layer 2 capability and the singular logical configuration of VSS, all other elements of DSM for the distribution and core layers apply.

From a redundancy perspective, the VSS provides stateful switchover (SSO) across the chassis, so in the case of a failure with a single chassis in a VSS pair, peering switches see the failure as a link failure in the MEC and not a topology change. This results in the surviving chassis forwarding the traffic. Additionally, because the switchover across the chassis was SSO, there is no need for routing protocol reconvergence because the routing topology remains intact.

The same IPv6 addressing that was used in the previous DSM examples is used here. One difference with VSS and IPv4 and IPv6 addressing is that each VSS pair uses one address versus one per chassis in a non-VSS configuration. Table 6-5 illustrates the IPv6 addressing used in the VSS example configurations.

Table 6-5 *Switch Loopback/VLAN Addressing for VSS Example*

Switch	Interface	IPv6 Address
VSS-dist	Loopback	2001:db8:cafe:1f3::3/128
	VLAN2	2001:db8:cafe:2::2/64
	VLAN3	2001:db8:cafe:3::2/64
VSS-core	Loopback	2001:db8:cafe:1f3::1/128

VSS Configuration

VSL (Virtual Switch Link) is the technology behind the VSS. The VSS pair exchanges configuration and state information across the VSL. The standby chassis monitors the active chassis over the VSL.

To form a VSS, two standalone switches need to follow the standalone-to-VSS conversion process. The following summarizes the three-step conversion process:

Step 1.   Choose a virtual switch domain number (unique in the same Layer 2 network).

Step 2.   Choose a switch number for each of the switches (in the example, switch #1 for 6k-vs-dist-1 and switch #2 for the 6k-vs-dist-2).

Step 3.   Choose a VSL link (ports connecting the two switches with a unique ether-channel number on each side).

The frames over the VSL link are encapsulated with a special 32-byte header that provides information for the VSS to forward the packet on the peer chassis. The VSL link carries the control and data; the following configuration example uses port-channel 10 and 20 on the two sides of the VSL link. The VSL-specific configuration after the conversion is shown in Example 6-23.

Example 6-23 *Conversion to VSS (6k-vs-dist-1 and 6k-vs-dist-2)*

```
Chassis Example: 6k-vs-dist-1
6k-vs-dist-1(config)# hostname VSS-dist
VSS-dist(config)# switch virtual domain 100
VSS-dist(config-vs-domain)# switch 1                    !switch number 1

VSS-dist(config-vs-domain)# exit

VSS-dist(config)# interface Port-channel10
VSS-dist(config-if)# no switch virtual link

VSS-dist(config-if)# interface TenGigabitEthernet3/5
VSS-dist(config-if)# channel-group 10 mode on
```

continues

Example 6-23   *Conversion to VSS (6k-vs-dist-1 and 6k-vs-dist-2)   continued*

```
VSS-dist(config-if)# interface TenGigabitEthernet3/6
VSS-dist(config-if)# channel-group 10 mode on

VSS-dist# switch convert mode virtual            !Enter yes when prompted

!Output removed for brevity

Chassis Example: 6k-vs-dist-2

6k-vs-dist-2(config)# hostname VSS-dist
VSS-dist(config)# switch virtual domain 100
VSS-dist(config-vs-domain)# switch 2              !switch number 2

VSS-dist(config-vs-domain)# exit

VSS-dist(config)# interface Port-channel20
VSS-dist(config-if)# no switch virtual link

VSS-dist(config-if)# interface TenGigabitEthernet4/5
VSS-dist(config-if)# channel-group 20 mode on

VSS-dist(config-if)# Interface TenGigabitEthernet4/6
VSS-dist(config-if)# channel-group 20 mode on

VSS-dist# switch convert mode virtual            !Enter yes when prompted

!Output removed for brevity
```

Note   For details about the conversion from a standalone to a virtual switch, refer to the Migrate Standalone Cisco Catalyst 6500 Switch to Cisco Catalyst 6500 Virtual Switching System documentation at http://www.cisco.com/en/US/products/ps9336/products_tech_note09186a0080a7c74c.shtml.

After the conversion to VSS, the configuration on each of the distribution switches is as shown in Example 6-24.

Example 6-24   *Distribution Switch VSL Configuration (6k-vs-dist-1)*

```
Chassis: 6k-vs-dist-1                            !The VSL config before merge
switch virtual domain 100

 switch mode virtual
```

```
!
interface Port-channel10
 no switchport
 no ip address
 switch virtual link 1

 mls qos trust cos
 no mls qos channel-consistency
!
interface TenGigabitEthernet1/3/5
 no switchport
 no ip address
 mls qos trust cos
 channel-group 10 mode on

!
interface TenGigabitEthernet1/3/6
 no switchport
 no ip address
 mls qos trust cos
 channel-group 10 mode on
```

After the conversion to VSS, when both switches come up, the VSL-specific configuration shown in Example 6-25 will be dynamically merged, resulting in the same configuration on both switches.

Example 6-25 *Distribution Switch VSL Configuration (6k-vs-dist-2)*

```
Chassis: 6k-vs-dist-2                          !The VSL config before merge

switch virtual domain 100

 switch mode virtual

!
interface Port-channel20
 no switchport
 no ip address
 switch virtual link 2

 mls qos trust cos
 no mls qos channel-consistency
!
interface TenGigabitEthernet2/4/5
 no switchport
```

continues

Example 6-25 *Distribution Switch VSL Configuration (6k-vs-dist-2)   continued*

```
 no ip address
 mls qos trust cos
 channel-group 20 mode on


!
interface TenGigabitEthernet2/4/5
 no switchport
 no ip address
 mls qos trust cos
 channel-group 20 mode on
```

Note In VSS, the interface naming convention has an extra prefix of 1 or 2 based on the switch number. For example, interface TenGigabitEthernet2/4/5 means that the switch number is 2, the slot number is 4, and the port number is 5.

VSS Physical Interface IPv6 Configuration

Physical point-to-point links are configured in much the same way as the standalone Catalyst 6500 case, except that now the two switches at the distribution and the core layers act like a single logical switch. Therefore, only one IPv6 address is used on the port channel interfaces (instead of one for each port channel to each switch in a non-VSS model). Example 6-26 is the point-to-point interface configuration for the VSS distribution layer.

Example 6-26 *VSS Distribution Layer Configuration (Port-Channel)*

```
ipv6 unicast-routing
ip cef distributed
ipv6 cef distributed
!
interface Port-channel30
 description to VSS-core
 ipv6 address 2001:DB8:CAFE:10::2/64
!
interface GigabitEthernet1/7/1
 no switchport
 no ip address
 channel-group 30 mode desirable
!
interface GigabitEthernet2/7/1
 no switchport
 no ip address
 channel-group 30 mode desirable
```

Example 6-27 is the point-to-point interface configuration for the VSS core layer.

Example 6-27 *VSS Core Layer Configuration (Port-Channel)*

```
ipv6 unicast-routing
ip cef distributed
ipv6 cef distributed
!
interface Port-channel30
 description to VSS-dist
 ipv6 address 2001:DB8:CAFE:10::1/64
!
interface GigabitEthernet1/7/1
 no switchport
 no ip address
 channel-group 30 mode desirable
!
interface GigabitEthernet2/7/1
 no switchport
 no ip address
 channel-group 30 mode desirable
```

As with the standalone switch, the access layer uses a single VLAN per switch. The VLANs do not span access layer switches and are terminated at the distribution layer.

All other configurations, such as routing and VLANs (including access layer switches), remain the same as with the non-VSS deployment.

Implementing the Hybrid Model

The purpose of the HM is to provide campus users access to IPv6-based applications, even though parts of the campus might not have IPv6 support. Because of this lack of support, most of the campus network in the HM is IPv4-only. The IPv6 part of the campus network begins in the core layer. The following sections show the core layer configuration as well as the basic ISATAP configuration on the host. As mentioned previously, the HM uses dual-stack from the core layer into the data center. Those configurations are not relevant to the HM because the configurations are the same as those in the DSM. As with the DSM implementation section, configuration snippets for each aspect of the deployment are shown in these sections.

Network Topology

One difference in the HM topology is that the distribution layer is using a pair of Catalyst 3750 switches instead of the Catalyst 6500. This change is not because of any particular issue or recommendation; it is just the way the test lab is configured. Although the Catalyst 3750 does support IPv6 unicast forwarding in hardware, no IPv6 functionality is enabled so that it can simulate an IPv4-only platform for the sake of illustrating the HM configuration. Figure 6-15 shows the network topology for the HM.

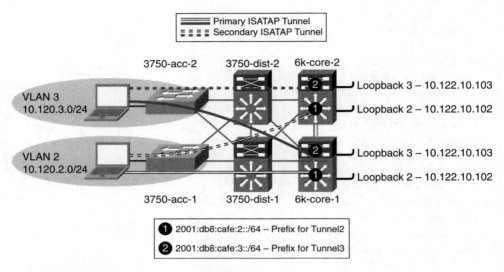

Figure 6-15 *Hybrid Model Network Topology*

The topology is focused on the IPv4 addressing scheme in the access layer (used by the host to establish the ISATAP tunnel), core layer (used as the termination point by the host for ISATAP), and also the IPv6 addressing used for the ISATAP tunnel prefix. In the HM, the core-to-core links and the core–to–data center links are dual-stack. The IPv6 addressing is not shown for these links because they use the same configuration as the DSM. The configuration shows that the ISATAP access high availability is accomplished by using redundantly configured loopback interfaces that share the same IPv4 address between both core switches. To maintain prefix consistency for the ISATAP hosts in the access layer, the same prefix is used on both the primary and backup ISATAP tunnels.

Physical Configuration

The configurations for both core layer switches are shown and include only the distribution-facing interfaces. These configurations are shown only for reference because their addressing can help you when the ISATAP high-availability validation output is shown. Note that everything between the access and core layers is IPv4-only, so nothing special is required other than a redundant and fast-converging IPv4 network.

Example 6-28 shows the 6k-core-1 configuration for the core-to-distribution links.

Example 6-28   *6k-core-1 Interface Configuration*

```
interface GigabitEthernet1/1
 description to 3750-dist-1

 ip address 10.122.0.41 255.255.255.252

 ip hello-interval eigrp 10 1
 ip hold-time eigrp 10 3
!
interface GigabitEthernet1/2
 description to 3750-dist-2

 ip address 10.122.0.45 255.255.255.252

 ip hello-interval eigrp 10 1
 ip hold-time eigrp 10 3
```

Example 6-29 shows the 6k-core-2 configuration for the core-to-distribution links.

Example 6-29   *6k-core-2 Interface Configuration*

```
interface GigabitEthernet1/1
 description to 3750-dist-1

 ip address 10.122.0.49 255.255.255.252

 ip hello-interval eigrp 10 1
 ip hold-time eigrp 10 3
!
interface GigabitEthernet1/2
 description to 3750-dist-2

 ip address 10.122.0.53 255.255.255.252

 ip hello-interval eigrp 10 1
 ip hold-time eigrp 10 3
```

Tunnel Configuration

The ISATAP configuration at the tunnel level is relatively straightforward, but the potentially confusing part relates to the high-availability design for the ISATAP tunnels. The basic configuration of ISATAP on a host consists of enabling IPv6 and configuring the ISATAP router name or IPv4 address. By default, Microsoft Windows XP, Vista, and Windows 7 perform a DNS query of "isatap.domain.com," where "domain.com" is the assigned domain name. If a DNS "A" record for "isatap" has been configured, the host begins to establish an ISATAP tunnel to the address resolved in the record. This default configuration works fine until something happens to the ISATAP router or the path to that router and the end systems have to find the alternate ISATAP router. All the configurations discussed in this chapter include the ability to provide fault tolerance of IPv6 services as optimally as possible.

Providing high availability for ISATAP is crucial in the HM environment. Several methods provide redundancy of the ISATAP routers. The method discussed in the HM implementation uses the two core layer switches to provide fast failover of the ISATAP tunnels. The other method commonly used relies on DNS. Although the DNS method is faster to implement, it is also the most limiting in the overall IPv6 campus design and is the slowest for failover.

You must ensure that the tunnel destination (from the host point of view) is redundant across both core switches and ensure that both IPv4 and IPv6 routing is configured properly.

Two questions commonly asked are, Should there be deterministic routing from the distribution layer (IPv4) to one ISATAP router? Also, is there any value in load balancing? The following considerations apply:

■ The only host operating systems that support the outbound load balancing of ISATAP tunnels are Microsoft Windows Vista and Windows 7.

■ Using customer deployments and detailed testing as a baseline, it has been found that there are few to no benefits in load balancing ISATAP hosts to the ISATAP routers. Testing shows that load balancing from the host side when using redundant IPv6 prefixes for the ISATAP tunnels causes return routability issues, meaning that the return traffic does not take the same return path as the traffic that was sent. The core layer switches in this example can take the load for all the ISATAP tunnels in this design. If the primary core layer switch fails, the secondary can take all the tunnels with no issue. Load balancing in this design provides no improvement in performance, load, or availability and further complicates the management for the operator because troubleshooting the flow of traffic for ISATAP is made even more difficult. Implementing a design that is deterministic for ISATAP eases the burden of traffic management and troubleshooting as well as eliminates the return routability issues.

To maintain low convergence times for ISATAP tunnels when a core layer switch fails, it is important to provide redundant and duplicated tunnel addressing across both core switches. When this duplication is done, only one ISATAP router address or name is needed on the host, and DNS round-robin is not required. The following steps describe this process:

Step 1.   Configure both core layer switches with the same loopback address (for example, 10.122.10.102). Loopback interfaces are used for their stable state and are perfect for tunnel termination. Take care in ensuring that this address is not used as the Router ID (RID) because you will have duplicate RID issues and will also impact CEF.

Step 2.   Configure both core layer switches with a single ISATAP tunnel that uses the loopback as a source (for example, Loopback2—10.122.10.102). The ISATAP

IPv6 prefix is the same on both switches, so it does not matter which switch the host is terminated on; it uses the same prefix for connectivity. This lack of state is a critical element for fast convergence. If the host has to obtain a new prefix for each failover, the recovery time is impacted for this address process. Also, the client keeps all past (old ISATAP prefix) and new IPv6 addresses for the duration of their lifetimes. Using a single prefix for all ISATAP connections for the host greatly reduces convergence time for the host and allows a single IPv6 address entry for ISATAP in any failure scenario.

Step 3. Configure both core layer switches to advertise the loopback address through the IPv4 IGP. The primary switch (6k-core-1) uses default IGP metrics for the loopback address. The secondary switch (6k-core-2) alters the IGP metric (delay value on EIGRP) to make the loopback address on this switch be less preferred. Cisco recommends having a deterministic flow for the tunnels because load balancing between the tunnels using the same prefix is not desirable.

Step 4. Configure both core layer switches to advertise the ISATAP IPv6 prefix through the IPv6 IGP. The primary switch (6k-core-1) uses the default IGP metrics for the IPv6 prefix on the ISATAP tunnel. The secondary switch (6k-core-2) alters the IGP metric (cost value on OSPFv3) to make the ISATAP prefix on this switch be less preferred. This configuration is optional. It is used in this document because a deterministic flow for both IPv4 (see Step 3) and IPv6 is desired.

Step 5. Configure the host with a manually defined ISATAP router address or name (which correlates to a DNS "A" record).

Note   In this section, EIGRP is used as the IGP for IPv4 and OSPFv3 is used as the IGP for IPv6. Using OSPF for both IPv4 and IPv6 or EIGRP for both versions is fully supported. EIGRP for IPv6 was shown in the DSM, and to give the reader a look at OSPFv3 configurations, it has been included here as reference.

To keep the ISATAP tunnels, HA, and routing configurations simple to understand, they are shown together. For the sake of simplicity, the only configuration shown is that of the tunnels for VLAN2. The tunnels for VLAN3 are the same except for addressing specifics.

The following configurations illustrate the preceding five steps described. The configuration is comprised of a loopback interface that is used as the ISATAP tunnel source on 6k-core-1. The tunnel interface has an IPv6 address defined and an OSPFv3 configuration. The IGP definition is not used to establish adjacency *through* the tunnel but is used to advertise the IPv6 prefix of the tunnel interface. By default, on tunnel interfaces, router advertisements are not sent on tunnels because they are point-to-point, and normally there is no reason to send an RA. However, ISATAP is a semiautomatic multipoint tunnel, which implies that both ends of the tunnel are not known. Because of this somewhat dynamic process, you must disable RA suppression (enable RAs). Again, in this example,

EIGRP is used for IPv4 and OSPFv3 for IPv6. You must advertise the IPv4 address of the loopback so that clients can reach the interface for tunnel connectivity. Similarly, the IPv6 ISATAP tunnel prefix must be advertised to the rest of the IPv6-enabled network.

Example 6-30 shows the 6k-core-1 ISATAP configuration. Again, a loopback is configured and is used as the anchor for the ISATAP tunnel. The tunnel definition needs to have an IPv6 address configured, default suppression of RAs on tunnel interfaces is disabled (we want RAs sent), an IGP is enabled to advertise the IPv6 prefix to the rest of the network, and the tunnel source (loopback) and mode are defined.

Example 6-30   *6k-core-1 ISATAP Configuration*

```
interface Loopback2
 description Tunnel source for ISATAP-VLAN2
 ip address 10.122.10.102 255.255.255.255    !Address that will be used as the

                                             !ISATAP tunnel2 source

!
interface Tunnel2
 description ISATAP VLAN2
 no ip address
 no ip redirects
 ipv6 address 2001:DB8:CAFE:2::/64 eui-64    !Tunnel prefix used for ISATAP

                                             !hosts connecting to this tunnel.
                                             !Interface-ID address for this
                                             !switch will be generated using
                                             !EUI-64
 no ipv6 nd suppress-ra                      !Tunnel interfaces disable the

                                             !sending of RA's. This command
                                             !re-enables RA's on this interface.
 ipv6 ospf 1 area 2                          !Just like the VLAN in the DSM,

                                             !this interface is part of area 2
 tunnel source Loopback2                     !Tunnel2 uses loopback2 as the

                                             !source
 tunnel mode ipv6ip isatap                   !Define the tunnel as ISATAP
!
router eigrp 10
 passive-interface Loopback2
 network 10.0.0.0                            !Ensure that the 10.122.10.102 address is
                                             !advertised to the rest of the network
 no auto-summary
```

```
 eigrp router-id 10.122.10.9
!
ipv6 router ospf 1
 router-id 10.122.10.9
 area 2 range 2001:DB8:CAFE:2::/64 cost 10   !Advertise summary for the prefix on

                                             !Tunnel2 - just like a VLAN prefix
                                             !would be sent in the DSM
 passive-interface Loopback2
 passive-interface Tunnel2
 timers spf 1 5
```

Example 6-31 is basically the same configuration with the exception of unique IPv4 and IPv6 addressing. Also, the IGPs are tuned so that the 6k-core-2 switch is less favorable as a path to the ISATAP tunnel interface.

Example 6-31   *6k-core-2 ISATAP Configuration*

```
interface Loopback2
description Tunnel source for ISATAP-VLAN2
ip address 10.122.10.102 255.255.255.255

delay 1000                          !Delay adjusted for EIGRP (IPv4)

                                    !in order to adjust preference
                                    !for the 10.122.10.102 host
                                    !route. This ensures that
                                    !6k-core-2 is SECONDARY to 6k-core-1
!
interface Tunnel2
 description ISATAP VLAN2
 no ip address
 no ip redirects
 ipv6 address 2001:DB8:CAFE:2::/64 eui-64

 no ipv6 nd suppress-ra
 ipv6 ospf 1 area 2
 tunnel source Loopback2
 tunnel mode ipv6ip isatap
!
router eigrp 10
 passive-interface Loopback2
 network 10.0.0.0
 no auto-summary
 eigrp router-id 10.122.10.10
```

continues

Example 6-31   *6k-core-2 ISATAP Configuration   continued*

```
!
ipv6 router ospf 1
 router-id 10.122.10.10
 area 2 range 2001:DB8:CAFE:2::/64 cost 20     !Cost for prefix adjusted so that

                                               !the route from 6k-core-2 is not
                                               !preferred or equal to 6k-core-1

 passive-interface Loopback2
 passive-interface Tunnel2
 timers spf 1 5
```

Figure 6-16 shows the IPv4 routing view from the distribution layer switches to the ISAT-AP tunnel's interfaces (loopbacks on core switches). Loopback2 on 6k-core-1 is set as the primary ISATAP router address for the host. As shown in the previous IPv4 IGP configuration, 6k-core-2 is configured to have the host route of 10.122.10.102 have a higher delay and therefore is not preferred. When a packet arrives from the host in VLAN2 for the ISATAP router (10.122.10.102), a lookup is performed in the distribution layer switch for 10.122.10.102 and the next hop for that address is 6k-core-1.

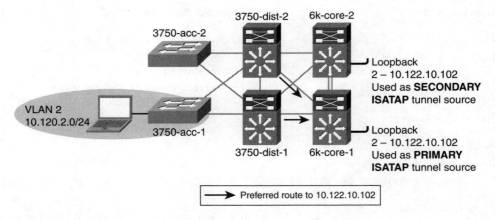

Figure 6-16   *Hybrid Model - Preferred Route for 6k-core-1*

The routing table entry for 10.122.10.102 on the 3750-dist-1 switch is shown in Example 6-32. There is a single entry for 10.122.10.102, which is learned through 10.122.0.41 (6k-core-1).

Example 6-32   *3750-dist-1 IPv4 Route Output - Path to Core*

```
3750-dist-1# show ip route ¦ b 10.122.10.102/32
D       10.122.10.102/32
[90/130816] via 10.122.0.41, 00:09:23, GigabitEthernet1/0/27
```

The router table entry on the 3750-dist-2 switch also shows a single route for 10.122.10.102 with a next hop of 10.122.0.45 (6k-core-1), as shown in Example 6-33.

Example 6-33 *3750-dist-2 IPv4 Route Output - Path to Core*

```
3750-dist-2# show ip route ¦ b 10.122.10.102/32
D        10.122.10.102/32
[90/130816] via 10.122.0.45, 00:10:03, GigabitEthernet1/0/27
```

Figure 6-17 shows that 6k-core-1 has failed, and therefore the route to Loopback2 (10.122.10.102) is no longer available. When the 6k-core-1 route is removed, the new route for 10.122.10.102 is used and packets are then forwarded to 6k-core-2.

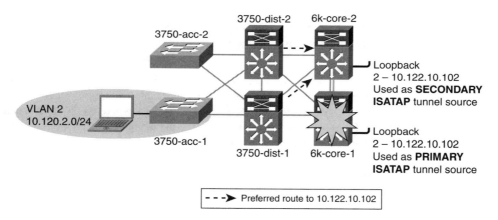

Figure 6-17 *Hybrid Model - Preferred Route 6k-core-2 After Failure*

The updated routing table entry for 10.122.10.102 on the distribution layer switches shows that there is now a change in the routing entry with a next hop of the 6k-core-2 switch (see Example 6-34).

Example 6-34 *3750-dist-1 IPv4 Route Output - Post 6k-core-1 Failure*

```
!3750-dist-1
!output omitted for brevity
3750-dist-1# show ip route ¦ b 10.122.10.102/32
D        10.122.10.102/32
    [90/258816] via 10.122.0.49, 00:00:08, GigabitEthernet1/0/28

!3750-dist-2
3750-dist-1# show ip route ¦ b 10.122.10.102/32
D        10.122.10.102/32
[90/258816] via 10.122.0.53, 00:00:08, GigabitEthernet1/0/28
```

The following two ways enable the host for ISATAP communication in the HM environment:

- Manual definition of the ISATAP IPv4 router address
- Manual definition of the ISATAP IPv4 DNS name (requires DNS record entries)

Using the ISATAP IPv4 router address method is straightforward but difficult to scale without some kind of script or host management tools. As previously mentioned, various tools such as Microsoft Group Policy, Windows PowerShell, and Microsoft SMS Server can be used to run the command locally on the host at login or another predetermined time.

On the Microsoft Windows host in VLAN 2, ISATAP is enabled and the IPv4 ISATAP router address is defined (IPv6 is enabled by default on Windows Vista and 7). As previously mentioned, the HM design maps the host in a VLAN/subnet to a specific ISATAP router address. This configuration is not a requirement but it is recommended if the existing security policy enforces ACLs based on the source IP address of a given VLAN.

Here the host is in VLAN 2, which is in the 10.120.2.0/24 subnet and is therefore configured to use the ISATAP router of 10.122.10.102, where the **2** in 102 signifies VLAN or subnet **2**. The same would happen for VLAN **3** or 10.120.3.0/24, where the ISATAP router is 10.122.10.103. The following configuration is through the **netsh** command interface on the Microsoft Windows client and is used to manually set the ISATAP router:

```
C:\> netsh interface ipv6 isatap set router 10.122.10.102 enabled
Ok.
```

The command in Example 6-35 can be used to verify that the address has been accepted.

Example 6-35 *Microsoft Windows NETSH Output for ISATAP Router - Address*

```
C:\> netsh interface ipv6 isatap show router
Router Name          : 10.122.10.102
Use Relay            : enabled
Resolution Interval  : default
```

The host has successfully established an ISATAP connection to the primary core layer switch (6k-core-1) and received a valid prefix 2001:db8:cafe:2:0:5efe:10.120.2.101 (through an RA—DHCPv6 is not used with ISATAP). ISATAP uses the IPv4 address on the host as the rightmost 32-bit portion of the 64-bit interface ID. ISATAP "pads" the leftmost 32 bits of the 64-bit interface ID with 0000:5efe or 0200:5EFE (if using public unicast IPv4 addresses). The IPv4 address (10.120.2.101), which is assigned to the host through DHCP (or could be static), is used as the tunnel source on the host side of the tunnel, and Loopback2 (10.122.10.102) on the core layer switches is used as the tunnel destination (previously configured ISATAP router address) for the host.

The tunnel adapter automatic tunneling the pseudointerface is as shown in Example 6-36.

Example 6-36 *Microsoft Windows IPv6 Address Summary*

```
Connection-specific DNS Suffix  . : cisco.com
IP Address. . . . . . . . . . . . : 2001:db8:cafe:2:0:5efe:10.120.2.101
IP Address. . . . . . . . . . . . : fe80::5efe:10.120.2.101%2
Default Gateway . . . . . . . . . : fe80::5efe:10.122.10.102%2
```

Using the ISATAP IPv4 router name method is also straightforward but requires DNS entries. If separation of host-to-ISATAP tunnels is desired, such as the configuration described in the previous example, it is difficult to scale, even with DNS, without some kind of script or host management tools. As previously mentioned, various tools such as Windows PowerShell and Microsoft SMS Server can be used to run the command locally on the host at time of login or another predetermined time. Group Policy can also be used as a means to set the ISATAP values.

In this example, a name is used for the ISATAP router instead of an ISATAP IPv4 address. The default DNS name that ISATAP tries to resolve is "isatap" along with the domain suffix. For example, if this host is in domain "cisco.com," the host attempts to resolve "isatap.cisco.com." The user can alter this name similarly to altering the address selection. The configuration on the Microsoft Windows host shown in Example 6-37 shows that the name "vlan2-isatap" has been used as the DNS name.

Example 6-37 *Microsoft Windows NETSH Output for ISATAP Router - DNS*

```
C:\> netsh interface ipv6 isatap set router vlan2-isatap enabled
Ok.

C:\> netsh interface ipv6 isatap show router
Router Name            : vlan2-isatap
Use Relay              : enabled
Resolution Interval    : default
```

On the DNS server, the following entries were made for the two VLANs shown in this section:

- **vlan2-isatap:** Host (A) 10.122.10.102

- **vlan3-isatap:** Host (A) 10.122.10.103

QoS Configuration

The QoS policies for the HM should match the existing IPv4 policies. As previously mentioned, the HM model presents a challenge with respect to where the IPv6 packets are classified and marked. The IPv6 packets are encapsulated within ISATAP tunnels all the way from the host in the access layer to the core layer, and IPv6 QoS policies cannot see the packets inside the tunnel. The first point where the IPv6 packets can have policies applied is at the egress interfaces of the core layer switches. The configuration in

Table 6-6 *IPv6 QoS - Class Map, Match ACL, and DSCP Setting*

Application	Access Group Name	DSCP Setting
FTP	BULK-DATA	AF11
Telnet	TRANSACTIONAL-DATA	AF21
SSH	TRANSACTIONAL-DATA	AF21
All others	N/A	0 (default)

Example 6-38 is meant as a simple example only. In this policy, class maps are used to match against IPv6 access lists, as listed in Table 6-6.

The service policy is applied on egress (output) interfaces (upstream from the access layer). Upstream switches can trust these DSCP settings and also apply queuing and policing as appropriate (refer to the section "Implementing the Dual-Stack Model," earlier in this chapter).

Example 6-38 shows the HM QoS example for 6k-core-1. The QoS policy is very basic and has two class-maps used to classify IPv6 applications: FTP, Telnet, and SSH traffic leaving (output) the 10-Gbps interfaces. Traffic that matches the policy will have a DSCP value set. These values are trusted upstream, and appropriate queuing and policing can be applied.

Example 6-38 *Hybrid Model - QoS Example 6k-core-1*

```
mls ipv6 acl compress address unicast
mls qos
!
class-map match-all CAMPUS-BULK-DATA
  match access-group name BULK-DATA

class-map match-all CAMPUS-TRANSACTIONAL-DATA
  match access-group name TRANSACTIONAL-DATA

!
policy-map IPv6-ISATAP-MARK

  class CAMPUS-BULK-DATA
   set dscp af11

  class CAMPUS-TRANSACTIONAL-DATA
   set dscp af21

  class class-default
   set dscp default

!
```

```
ipv6 access-list BULK-DATA

 permit tcp any any eq ftp

 permit tcp any any eq ftp-data

!

ipv6 access-list TRANSACTIONAL-DATA

 permit tcp any any eq telnet

 permit tcp any any eq 22

!
interface TenGigabitEthernet2/3
 description to 6k-core-1
 mls qos trust dscp
 service-policy output IPv6-ISATAP-MARK

!
interface TenGigabitEthernet3/1
 description to 6k-agg-1
 mls qos trust dscp
 service-policy output IPv6-ISATAP-MARK

!
interface TenGigabitEthernet3/2 description to 6k-agg-2
 mls qos trust dscp
 service-policy output IPv6-ISATAP-MARK
```

Infrastructure Security Configuration

You might want to further tighten IPv6 access control for ISATAP tunnels at the access layer. An access list can be applied to either a host port or an uplink/trunk port at the access layer. It is easier to manage the ACL at the uplink rather than configuring ACLs on each host port.

One access list that can be used is an ACL to permit tunnels from the hosts on the access switch to the ISATAP router address for that VLAN. For example, the following ACL permits the ISATAP tunnels (through protocol 41) only if the destination is 10.122.10.102 (the ISATAP router address previously configured). The ACL ends with a permit for all other IPv4 traffic (this is a dual-stack configuration so IPv4 must be permitted). Again, this ACL can be applied on a specific host port on input (**ip access-group 100 in**) or an uplink trunk or routed port (**ip access-group 100 out**).

```
access-list 100 remark Permit approved IPv6-Tunnels
access-list 100 permit 41 any host 10.122.10.102
access-list 100 deny   41 any any
access-list 100 permit ip any any
```

Implementing the Service Block Model

The ISATAP deployment on the SBM is nearly identical to that of the HM. Both models deploy a redundant pair of switches used to provide fault-tolerant termination of ISATAP tunnels coming from the hosts in the access layer. The only difference between the SBM and HM is that the SBM is using a new set of switches that are dedicated to terminating connections (ISATAP, configured tunnels, or dual-stack), while the HM uses the existing core layer switches for termination.

The following sections focus on the configuration of the interfaces on the service block switches (physical and logical) and the data center aggregation layer tunnel interfaces (shown only for completeness). The entire IPv4 network is the same as the one described in the HM configuration.

Also, the host configuration for the SBM is the same as the HM because the ISATAP router addresses are reused in this example. Similar to the HM configuration section, the loopback, tunnel, routing, and high-availability configurations are all presented.

Network Topology

To keep the diagrams simple to understand, the topology is separated into two parts: the ISATAP topology and the manually configured tunnel topology.

Figure 6-18 shows the ISATAP topology for the SBM. The topology is focused on the IPv4 addressing in the access layer (used by the host to establish the ISATAP tunnel), the service block (used as the termination point for the ISATAP tunnels), and also the IPv6 addressing used in the service block for both the p2p link and the ISATAP tunnel prefix. The configuration shows that the ISATAP availability is accomplished by using loopback interfaces that share the same IPv4 address between both SBM switches. To maintain prefix consistency for the ISATAP hosts in the access layer, the same prefix is used on both the primary and backup ISATAP tunnels.

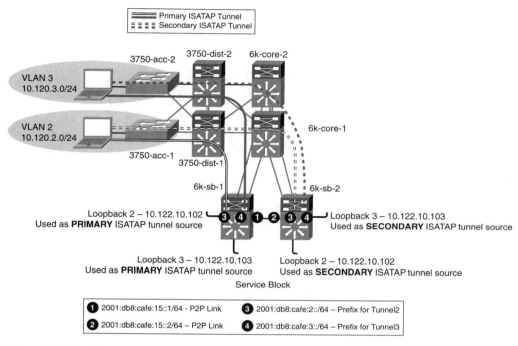

Figure 6-18   *SBM ISATAP Network Topology*

Figure 6-19 shows the point-to-point tunnel addressing between the SBM and the data center aggregation layer switches. The p2p configuration is shown for completeness and is a reference for one way to connect the SBM to data center services. Alternatively, ISATAP, 6to4, or manually configured tunnels could be used to connect each server in the data center that provides IPv6 applications to the SBM. Also, dedicated IPv6 links could be deployed between the data center aggregation/access layers to the SBM that would bypass non-IPv6-capable services in the aggregation layer. Basically, there are many ways to achieve end-to-end connectivity between the hosts in the campus access layer to the services in the data center.

The topology diagram shows the loopback addresses on the service block switches (used as the tunnel source for configured tunnels) and the IPv6 addressing used on the manually configured tunnel interfaces.

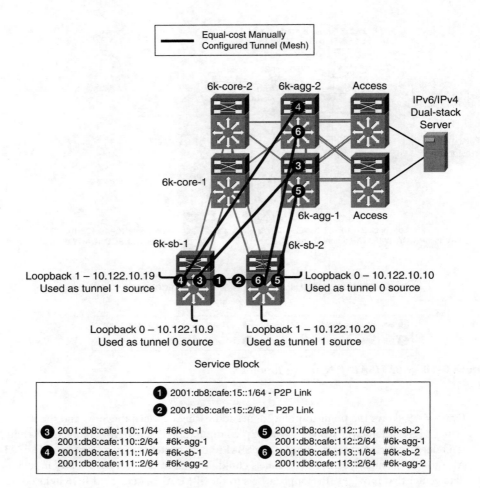

Figure 6-19 *SBM Manually Configured Tunnel Topology*

Physical Configuration

The configurations for both service block switches are shown, including the core layer–facing interfaces. Configurations for the IPv4 portion of the previous topology are shown only for the service block switches. All other IPv4 configurations are based on existing campus design best practices and are not discussed in this section. Also, as was mentioned before, EIGRP for IPv6, OSPFv3, and other IPv6 routing protocols are fully supported. The following configurations use EIGRP for IPv4 and OSPFv3 for IPv6. EIGRP for both IPv4 and IPv6 was tested and is supported with no special considerations.

Example 6-39 shows the 6k-sb-1 IPv4 configuration to the core and also the dual-stack interface configuration to 6k-sb-2.

Example 6-39 *IPv4-IPv6 Link Configurations for 6k-sb-1*

```
interface GigabitEthernet4/1
 description to 6k-core-1
 ip address 10.122.0.78 255.255.255.252          !IPv4-only connections to Core

 ip hello-interval eigrp 10 1
 ip hold-time eigrp 10 3
 ip authentication mode eigrp 10 md5
 ip authentication key-chain eigrp 10 eigrp
 mls qos trust dscp
!
interface GigabitEthernet4/2
 description to 6k-core-2
 ip address 10.122.0.86 255.255.255.252
 ip hello-interval eigrp 10 1
 ip hold-time eigrp 10 3
 ip authentication mode eigrp 10 md5
 ip authentication key-chain eigrp 10 eigrp
 mls qos trust dscp
!
interface GigabitEthernet4/3
 description to 6k-sb-2
 ip address 10.122.0.93 255.255.255.252
 ip hello-interval eigrp 10 1
 ip hold-time eigrp 10 3
 ip authentication mode eigrp 10 md5
 ip authentication key-chain eigrp 10 eigrp
 ipv6 address 2001:DB8:CAFE:15::1/64             !p2p link between SBM switches

 ipv6 ospf network point-to-point

 ipv6 ospf hello-interval 1

 ipv6 ospf dead-interval 3

 ipv6 ospf 1 area 0

 mls qos trust dscp
```

Example 6-40 is the configuration for 6k-sb-2. The configuration is nearly identical with the exception of addressing.

Example 6-40 *IPv4-IPv6 Link Configurations for 6k-sb-2*

```
interface GigabitEthernet4/1
 description to 6k-core-1
 ip address 10.122.0.82 255.255.255.252
```

continues

Example 6-40   *IPv4-IPv6 Link Configurations for 6k-sb-2   continued*

```
  ip hello-interval eigrp 10 1
  ip hold-time eigrp 10 3
  ip authentication mode eigrp 10 md5
  ip authentication key-chain eigrp 10 eigrp
  mls qos trust dscp
!
interface GigabitEthernet4/2
 description to 6k-core-2
 ip address 10.122.0.90 255.255.255.252
 ip hello-interval eigrp 10 1
 ip hold-time eigrp 10 3
 ip authentication mode eigrp 10 md5
 ip authentication key-chain eigrp 10 eigrp
 mls qos trust dscp
!
interface GigabitEthernet4/3
 description to 6k-sb-1
 ip address 10.122.0.94 255.255.255.252
 ip hello-interval eigrp 10 1
 ip hold-time eigrp 10 3
 ip authentication mode eigrp 10 md5
 ip authentication key-chain eigrp 10 eigrp
 ipv6 address 2001:DB8:CAFE:15::2/64          !p2p link between SBM switches

 ipv6 ospf network point-to-point

 ipv6 ospf hello-interval 1

 ipv6 ospf dead-interval 3

 ipv6 ospf 1 area 0

 mls qos trust dscp
```

Tunnel Configuration

The tunnel and routing configuration for ISATAP is exactly the same as the HM. To avoid repeating information presented in previous sections, none of the configurations for the ISATAP tunneling and routing are explained, but the configuration is shown (see the HM example explanations).

The manually configured tunnel configurations are shown in Example 6-41 for the service block switch 6k-sb-1. The tunnel configurations for the data center aggregation switches (6k-agg-1/6k-agg-2) are identical to the service block except for address specifics.

Example 6-41 *6k-sb-1 SBM Manual Tunnel Configuration*

```
interface Loopback0
 description Tunnel source for 6k-agg-1
 ip address 10.122.10.9 255.255.255.255
!
interface Loopback1
 description Tunnel source for 6k-agg-2
 ip address 10.122.10.19 255.255.255.255
!
interface Tunnel0
 description Manual Tunnel to 6k-agg-1
 no ip address
 ipv6 address 2001:DB8:CAFE:110::1/64
 ipv6 ospf network point-to-point
 ipv6 ospf hello-interval 1
 ipv6 ospf dead-interval 3
 ipv6 ospf 1 area 0
 tunnel source Loopback0                    !Anchor p2p tunnel to Lo0

 tunnel destination 10.122.10.1             !10.122.10.1 is loopback0 on 6k-agg-1
 tunnel mode ipv6ip                         !IPv6-in-IPv4 tunnel

!
interface Tunnel1
 description Manual Tunnel to 6k-agg-2
 no ip address
 ipv6 address 2001:DB8:CAFE:111::1/64
 ipv6 ospf network point-to-point
 ipv6 ospf hello-interval 1
 ipv6 ospf dead-interval 3
 ipv6 ospf 1 area 0
 tunnel source Loopback1

 tunnel destination 10.122.10.2             !10.122.10.2 is loopback0 on 6k-agg-2
 tunnel mode ipv6ip
```

Example 6-42 shows the ISATAP configuration for 6k-sb-1. The configurations for 6k-sb-2 are not shown for brevity; the configurations are identical except for address values.

Example 6-42 *6k-sb-1 SBM ISATAP Tunnel and Routing Configuration*

```
interface Loopback2
 description Tunnel source for ISATAP-VLAN2
 ip address 10.122.10.102 255.255.255.255
!
```

continues

Example 6-42   *6k-sb-1 SBM ISATAP Tunnel and Routing Configuration*   *continued*

```
interface Tunnel2
 description ISATAP VLAN2
 no ip address
 ipv6 address 2001:DB8:CAFE:2::/64 eui-64
 no ipv6 nd suppress-ra
 ipv6 ospf 1 area 2
 tunnel source Loopback2
 tunnel mode ipv6ip isatap
!
ipv6 router ospf 1
 router-id 10.122.10.9
 log-adjacency-changes
 auto-cost reference-bandwidth 10000
 area 2 range 2001:DB8:CAFE:2::/64 cost 10
 area 2 range 2001:DB8:CAFE:3::/64 cost 10
 passive-interface Loopback0
 passive-interface Loopback1
 passive-interface Loopback2
 passive-interface Loopback3
 passive-interface Tunnel2
 passive-interface Tunnel3
 timers spf 1 5
```

QoS Configuration

The same QoS configurations and discussions from the "Implementing the Dual-Stack Model" section, earlier in this chapter, apply to the SBM. Based on the example configuration shown in the case of the HM, the only change relates to the interfaces where the classification and marking policies are applied. In the SBM, the service policy is applied to the egress on the manually configured tunnels toward 6k-agg-1 and 6k-agg-2.

Example 6-43 shows that for 6k-sb-1, the service policy would be applied to Tunnel0 and Tunnel1.

Example 6-43   *6k-sb-1 Apply QoS Policy Egress on Tunnel*

```
interface Tunnel0
 description tunnel to 6k-agg-1
 service-policy output IPv6-ISATAP-MARK

!
interface Tunnel1
 description tunnel to 6k-agg-2
 service-policy output IPv6-ISATAP-MARK
```

The security considerations and configurations discussed in the DSM and HM sections apply directly to the SBM.

Summary

This chapter analyzes various architectures for providing IPv6 services in campus networks. The DSM should be the goal of any campus deployment because no tunneling is performed. The HM is useful because it allows the existing campus infrastructure to provide IPv6 access for endpoints in the campus access layer through ISATAP tunnels. The SBM is a great interim design to provide end-to-end IPv6 between the campus access layer hosts and IPv6-enabled applications on the Internet or data center without touching the existing campus hardware.

The models discussed are certainly not the only ways to deploy IPv6 in this environment, but they provide options that can be leveraged based on environment, deployment schedule, and targeted services specifics.

Table 6-7 summarizes the benefits and challenges with each of the models discussed in this document.

Table 6-7 *Benefits and Challenges of Various Models*

Model	Benefit	Challenge
Dual-stack model (DSM)	No tunneling required No dependency on IPv4 Superior performance and highest availability for IPv6 unicast and multicast Scalable	Requires IPv6 hardware-enabled campus switching equipment Operational challenges with supporting dual protocols - training/management tools
Hybrid model (HM)	Most of the existing IPv4-only campus equipment can be used (access and distribution layer) Per-user or per-application control for IPv6-service delivery Provides high availability for IPv6 access over ISATAP tunnels	Tunneling is required; increase in operations and management Scale factors (number of tunnels, hosts per tunnel) IPv6 multicast is not supported Tunnel termination at core
Service block model (SBM)	Highly reduced time to delivery for IPv6-enabled services Requires no changes to existing campus infrastructure Similar to the HM in other advantages	New IPv6 hardware capable, campus switches are required All cons from the HM

Additional References

Many notes and disclaimers in this chapter discuss the need to fully understand the technology and protocol aspects of IPv6. There are many design considerations associated with the implementation of IPv6 that include security, QoS, availability, management, IT training, and application support.

The following references are a few of the many that provide more details on IPv6, Cisco design recommendations, products and solutions, and industry activity:

Arkko, J., ed., Kempf, J., Zill, B., and Nikander, P. RFC 3971, "SEcure Neighbor Discovery (SEND)."

Cisco. "Catalyst 3750-E and 3560-E IPv6 and Switch Stacks." http://www.cisco.com/en/US/docs/switches/lan/catalyst3750e_3560e/software/release/1 2.2_46_se/configuration/guide/swipv6.html#wp1091926.

Cisco. "Catalyst 6500 Software Configuration Guide - Configuring Denial of Service (DoS) Protection - CoPP." http://www.cisco.com/en/US/docs/switches/lan/catalyst6500/ios/12.2SXF/native/configu ration/guide/dos.html.

Cisco. "Catalyst 6500 Software Configuration Guide - Configuring PFC QoS." http://www.cisco.com/en/US/docs/switches/lan/catalyst6500/ios/12.2SX/configuration/g uide/qos.html.

Cisco. "Catalyst 6500 Software Configuration Guide - IPv6 ACL Compression." http://www.cisco.com/en/US/docs/switches/lan/catalyst6500/ios/12.2SXF/native/configu ration/guide/acl.html#wp1090842.

Cisco. "Catalyst 6500 Virtual Switching System 1440." http://www.cisco.com/en/US/products/ps9336/index.html.

Cisco. "Cisco DHCPv6 Server in IOS." http://www.cisco.com/en/US/docs/ios/ipv6/configuration/guide/ip6-dhcp_ps6441_TSD_Products_Configuration_Guide_Chapter.html#wp1323295.

Cisco. "Cisco First Hop Security." http://www.cisco.com/en/US/docs/ios/ipv6/configuration/guide/ip6-first_hop_security.html.

Cisco. "Cisco IOS IPv6 Configuration Guide - HSRP for IPv6." http://www.cisco.com/en/US/docs/ios/ipv6/configuration/guide/ip6-fhrp.html#wp1055254.

Cisco. "Cisco IOS IPv6 Configuration Guide - Implementing IPv6 Multicast - SSM Mapping." http://www.cisco.com/en/US/docs/ios/ipv6/configuration/guide/ip6-multi-cast_ps10591_TSD_Products_Configuration_Guide_Chapter.html#wp1058805.

Cisco. "Cisco IPv6." http://www.cisco.com/web/solutions/netsys/ipv6/index.html.

Cisco. "Cisco IPv6 Multicast."
http://www.cisco.com/en/US/products/ps6594/products_ios_protocol_group_home.html.

Cisco. "Cisco IPv6 Start Here Guide and Roadmap."
http://www.cisco.com/en/US/docs/ios/ipv6/configuration/guide/ip6-roadmap.html.

Cisco. "Cisco Network Management and Automation."
http://www.cisco.com/en/US/products/sw/netmgtsw/index.html.

Cisco. "Cisco Network Registrar."
http://www.cisco.com/en/US/products/sw/netmgtsw/ps1982.

Cisco. "Design Zone for Campus - Routed Access Layer using EIGRP or OSPF."
http://www.cisco.com/en/US/netsol/ns815/networking_solutions_program_home.html.

Cisco. "Enterprise QoS SRND."
http://www.cisco.com/en/US/docs/solutions/Enterprise/WAN_and_MAN/QoS_SRND/Q
oS-SRND-Book.html.

Cisco. "Medianet Campus QoS Design 4.0."
http://www.cisco.com/en/US/docs/solutions/Enterprise/WAN_and_MAN/QoS_SRND_4
0/QoSCampus_40.html.

Cisco. "Migrate Standalone Cisco Catalyst 6500 Switch to VSS."
http://www.cisco.com/en/US/products/ps9336/products_tech_note09186a0080a7c74c
.shtml.

Cisco. "Routed Access Q&A."
http://www.cisco.com/en/US/netsol/ns340/ns394/ns147/ns17/netqa0900aecd8045965a
.html.

Cisco. "Routing in the Wiring Closet White Paper."
http://www.cisco.com/en/US/netsol/ns340/ns394/ns147/ns17/networking_solutions_
white_paper0900aecd804c6e73.shtml.

Davies, Joseph. *Understanding IPv6*, second edition. (ISBN-10: 0-7356-2446-1. ISBN-13:
978-0-7356-2446-7).

Deering, S. and Hinden, R. RFC 2460, "Internet Protocol, Version 6 (IPv6) Specification."

Hinden, R. and Deering, S. RFC 3513, "Internet Protocol Version 6 (IPv6) Addressing
Architecture."

Hogg, Scott and Vyncke, Eric. *IPv6 Security*. (ISBN-10: 1-58705-594-5. ISBN-13:978-1-
58705-594-2).

McCann, J., Deering, S., and Mogul, J. RFC 1981, "Path MTU Discovery for IP version 6."

Microsoft. "Microsoft–Cisco ISATAP White Paper." http://www.microsoft.com/downloads/details.aspx?FamilyId=B8F50E07-17BF-4B5C-A1F9-5A09E2AF698B&displaylang=en.

Microsoft. "Microsoft IPv6 Home." http://technet.microsoft.com/en-us/network/bb530961.aspx.

Microsoft. "Microsoft Teredo Overview." http://technet.microsoft.com/en-us/library/bb457011.aspx.

Microsoft. "Microsoft Windows Server 2008 - DHCP Server." http://technet.microsoft.com/en-us/library/cc896553%28WS.10%29.aspx.

Narten, T., E. Nordmark, W. Simpson, and H. Soliman. RFC 4861, "Neighbor Discovery for IP version 6 (IPv6)." http://www.ietf.org/rfc/rfc4861.txt.

Popoviciu, Ciprian P.; Eric Levy-Abegnoli, and Patrick Grossetete. *Deploying IPv6 Networks.* ISBN-10: 1-58705-210-5. ISBN-13: 978-1-58705-210-1.

Savola, P. RFC 3627, "Use of /127 Prefix Length Between Routers Considered Harmful."

Savola, P. RFC 3956, "Embedding the Rendezvous Point (RP) Address in an IPv6 Multicast Address."

Szigeti, Tim and Christina Hattingh. *End-to-End QoS Network Design*. (ISBN-10: 1-58705-176-1. ISBN-13: 978-1-58705-176-0(.

Templin, F., T. Gleeson, and D. Thaler. RFC 5214, "Intra-Site Automatic Tunnel Addressing Protocol (ISATAP)."

Van de Velde, G., C. Popoviciu, T. Chown, O. Bonnes, and C. Hahn. RFC 5375, "IPv6 Unicast Address Assignment Considerations.

Chapter 7

Deploying Virtualized IPv6 Networks

This chapter covers the following objectives:

- **Virtualization overview:** This section provides an overview of the benefits, types, and impact of virtualization on designing and deploying IPv6 networks.

- **Network virtualization:** This section provides a detailed step-by-step design, configuration for integrating IPv6 among the various network virtualization techniques such as switch virtualization, and network segmentation. Understanding the different types of network virtualization designs and their requirements is key as network architects integrate IPv6.

- **Network services virtualization:** This section extends network virtualization techniques to Layers 4–7 services, including firewall, server load balancing, and monitoring servers.

- **Desktop virtualization:** Extending IPv6 and virtualization beyond the network to the compute resources. This section outlines desktop virtualization design considerations with IPv6.

This chapter covers the design and implementation techniques of deploying IPv6 in a virtualized network. The first section provides an overview of virtualization along with the different types of virtualization techniques. The subsequent sections cover in detail the design, configuration, and verification of network services and desktop IPv6 virtualization techniques.

The network virtualization section provides details on how to interconnect IPv6 networks across a Multiprotocol Label Switching (MPLS) backbone using 6PE and 6vPE technology. It also provides an overview of services virtualization, its benefits, and how to design, configure, and verify multicontext IPv6 firewalls on a Cisco ASA 5580. The last two sections focus on the desktop and server virtualization technologies but not on deployment because most of the thin-client products do not support IPv6 today.

Virtualization Overview

Today's enterprises require their IT infrastructure to be agile to support a dynamic business model but at the same time focus on enabling new business applications with reduced costs. Virtualization is one such technique that helps enterprises leverage their existing infrastructure to the changing business demands that require enabling new applications. Virtualization also brings about a fundamental change in the way IT managers think about compute, network, and storage resources. Virtualization enables the abstraction of hardware resources from the provided services, which enable the focus of IT to shift from the technology to the services that the technology provides.

The following sections outline the business benefits of enabling virtualization and categorizes virtualization across network, server (compute), and storage infrastructure.

Virtualization Benefits

Virtualization is not a new concept. For example, it has been available in mainframes for a few decades. The same concept still applies today and is used to abstract many of the physical resources in the personal computer that we use today. Virtualization offers the following benefits:

- **Helps reduce total cost of ownership through improved IT infrastructure efficiency:** As computing power grows, it runs the risk of being underutilized. Virtualization enables more optimal use of the hardware resources as opposed to investing in dedicated resources for every application.

- **Saves power and cooling resources:** By leveraging the existing infrastructure, virtualization helps reduce power and cooling requirements. These savings enable the creation of environmentally friendly networks and infrastructure.

- **Increases network flexibility through resource sharing:** Virtualization technology enables several distinct applications to safely share the same physical hardware.

- **Improves resource segmentation:** Applications that require segmentation for compliance, auditing, or performance purposes can be deployed on a virtualized infrastructure so that the applications can be logically segregated and have specific resource controls enabled for each application.

Virtualization Categories

Typically, when IT architects use the term *virtualization*, they are mostly talking about server virtualization, but virtualization is something that is beyond just compute. Virtualization extends beyond servers (compute) to the network, storage, and desktop resources. Table 7-1 outlines the four basic categories of virtualization.

As enterprise customers look toward network, server, and desktop virtualization, they can extend these virtualization techniques for both IPv4- and IPv6-enabled networks.

Table 7-1 *Categories of Virtualization*

Category	Definition	Benefits
Network virtualization	Network virtualization includes Switch virtualization: Techniques like device pooling (Virtual Switching System - VSS) and Virtual Device Context (VDC). Network segmentation: Enables combining different resources in a network by splitting the available bandwidth into independent channels that can be assigned to different hosts. Network services virtualization: Extending virtualization beyond network devices (routers and switches) to L4–L7 service nodes.	Improved security: Separation of data paths enable traffic from one segment to not be seen on another network segment. Broadcasts will be contained to the local network. The internal network structure will not be visible from the outside. Reduced congestion: Improved performance is achieved because on a segmented network, there are fewer hosts per sub-network, thus minimizing local traffic. Network problems contained: Limits the effect of local failures on other parts of network. Increased operational efficiency: Improved service node utilization. Resource allocation: Allocates resources to each instance of the services device depending on application needs.
Server virtualization	Server virtualization enables running multiple instances of virtual servers on a single physical server. Server virtualization is driven by hypervisors like VMware ESX, Xen, Linux KVM, and so on.	Server consolidation • Improved disaster recovery mechanisms • Reduced downtime with virtual machine mobility • Reduced time to deploy new services and applications
Desktop virtualization	Desktop virtualization refers to the deployment of a client operating system in a virtual machine located in the data center on a hypervisor-based system.	Simpler provisioning of new desktops • Reduced downtime in the event of server or client hardware failures • Lower cost of deploying new applications • Desktop image-management capabilities • Enables protection of intellectual property

continues

Table 7-1   *Categories of Virtualization   (continued)*

Category	Definition	Benefits
Storage virtualization*	Storage virtualization combines physical storage from multiple network storage devices to appear as a single storage device.	Saves storage costs through optimized storage usage • Provides better disaster recovery with distributed storage and allows enterprises to use cheaper storage

Storage virtualization is mentioned here for completeness. This chapter does not discuss storage virtualization in detail.

Network Virtualization

The following sections look at how to enable IPv6 in a network virtualization solution. Network virtualization includes the following aspects:

- Switch virtualization

- Network segmentation

- Network services virtualization

The next sections describe these in greater detail.

Switch Virtualization

Switch virtualization is the capability for multiple physical switches to behave like a single physical entity. Two key switch virtualization techniques are as follows:

- **Device pooling (VSS):** Technologies like Virtual Switching System (VSS) enable network administrators to simplify their network by logically combining two physical switches into a single management domain. In addition to simplified management plane, VSS also enables active-active data paths, thereby eliminating the need for Spanning Tree by deploying Multi-chassis EtherChannels (MEC). Details on how to configure and deploy VSS in an IPv6 network are covered at length in Chapter 6, "Deploying IPv6 in Campus Networks."

- **Virtual Device Contexts (VDC) on Nexus 7K:** VDCs enable network administrators to segment a single switch into multiple virtual contexts with independent management planes and policies across various network segments/applications. Chapter 9, "Deploying IPv6 in the Data Center," outlines IPv6 configuration on the Nexus 7K.

Network Segmentation

The following sections provide an overview of the network segmentation technologies, including Virtual Router Forwarding (VRF), IPv6 Layer 3, and Layer 2 Virtual Private

Networks (6PE/6VPE, VPLS). These sections also provide detailed design and configuration for integrating IPv6 networks across an already-existing IPv4/MPLS network. The following list defines the key network segmentation technologies described in these sections:

- **Virtual Router Forwarding (VRF):** VRF is used for separating different networks segments (that is, voice and guest) on the same device.

- **Transporting IPv6 across MPLS backbone (6PE/6VPE):** 6PE is used to carry IPv6 over an MPLS network, and 6VPE is used to carry IPv6 over an MPLS Virtual Private Network (VPN).

- **Virtual Private LAN Services (VPLS):** VPLS can be used to interconnect geographically dispersed multiple-point IPv6 networks (Layer 2 VPNs).

Virtual Routing and Forwarding (VRF-Lite)

Typically, VRFs are associated with MPLS for large enterprise and service provider networks. However, VRF is not completely dependent on MPLS configuration, even though the two technologies work very well with each other. Based on Cisco terminology, deploying VRF configuration without having the need for an MPLS is known as VRF-Lite or Multi-VRF. This section provides details on how to leverage VRF-Lite technology to isolate IPv4 and IPv6 traffic along with maintaining separate routing tables for each of these networks.

VRF-Lite works at Layer 3 and allows multiple instances of a routing table with the same or overlapping IP address ranges to exist within the same router. In the case of VRF-Lite, multiple routing tables with multiple forwarding instances are created with dedicated interfaces assigned to each VRF. This is a simple concept to grasp as long as each of the VRFs is maintained in isolation. However, routing traffic from one VRF to another is more complex.

Figure 7-1 outlines an enterprise network with multiple IP subnets that are completely isolated from each other that is, placed in separate VRFs. As the network architect looks to integrate an IPv6 host network with complete traffic and route isolation from the remaining corporate network, VRF-Lite provides a simple but powerful solution for such environments.

The enterprise campus network hosts three networks:

- **VLAN 10 (VRF - RED):** Hosts in VRF Red have IPv6 addresses only. They are isolated into a separate VLAN 10 and are trunked to the upstream distribution switch using 802.1Q trunking. Users in VRF Red are connected through the access layer switch in Building 3. The Red network includes 2001:DB8:CAFE:2::/64.

- **VLAN 20 (VRF - BLUE):** Hosts in VRF Blue are dual-stack with both IPv4 and IPv6 addresses. The users in VRF Blue are connected through the access layer switch in Building 2. The Blue network includes IPv4:192.168.1.0/24 & IPv6 2001:DB8:CAFE:1::/64.

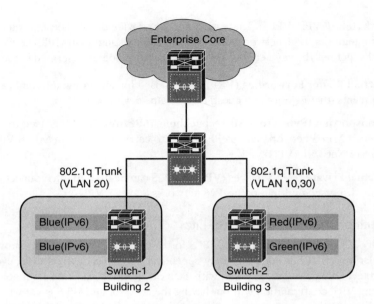

Figure 7-1   *Enterprise Campus with VRF-Lite*

■   **VLAN 30 (VRF - GREEN):** Hosts in VRF Green are IPv4 hosts only that are potentially going to migrate to IPv6. The users in VRF Green are connected through the access layer switch in Building 3. The Green network includes 202.10.12.0/24.

Buildings 2 and 3 are connected to the aggregation switch (Virtual Switching System in
this case) through 802.1Q trunk links. All users in these VRFs rely on the same physical
network infrastructure for connectivity, but the traffic from each VRF is isolated from
the others for security reasons. The configuration in Example 7-1 outlines the switch-1
and switch-2 configurations.

Example 7-1   *Configuring VRF on Switches*

```
switch-1#
!
vrf definition BLUE
 rd 100:3
 route-target export 100:3
 route-target import 100:3
!
 address-family ipv4
 exit-address-family
!
```

```
 address-family ipv6
 exit-address-family
! /* VRF BLUE with IPv4 and IPv6 Addresses */
interface VLAN 20
 vrf forwarding BLUE
 ip address 192.168.1.1 255.255.255.0
 ipv6 address 2001:DB8:CAFE:1::1/64
!
interface GigabitEthernet1/3
 switchport
 switchport mode access
 switchport access vlan 20
!
!/* For the trunk on switch -1 */
interface GigabitEthernet1/3
 switchport
 switchport mode trunk
 switchport trunk allowed 20
!
switch-2#
vrf definition GREEN
 rd 100:2
 route-target export 100:2
 route-target import 100:2
 !
 address-family ipv4
 exit-address-family
!
vrf definition RED
 rd 100:1
 route-target export 100:1
 route-target import 100:1
 !
 address-family ipv6
 exit-address-family
!/* VRF RED with IPv6 address */
interface VLAN 10
 vrf forwarding RED
 ipv6 address 2001:DB8:CAFE:2::1/64
!
interface GigabitEthernet1/1
 switchport
 switchport mode access
 switchport access vlan 10
```

continues

Example 7-1   *Configuring VRF on Switches   continued*

```
!
interface GigabitEthernet1/2
 switchport
 switchport mode access
 switchport access vlan 10
! /* VRF GREEN with IPv4 Addresses */
interface VLAN 30
 vrf forwarding GREEN
 ip address 202.10.12.1 255.255.255.0
!
interface GigabitEthernet1/5
 switchport
 switchport mode access
 switchport access vlan 30
!
```

Note   When assigning an interface to a VRF, IOS automatically deletes any preconfigured IP address to remove that route from the global table. Now, when an IP address is assigned to this interface, its network gets added to the specific routing table for that VRF.

After the VRF and the interfaces associated with the VRF are configured, the administrator can use the **show vrf** command to validate the configuration.

Example 7-2   *Displaying* **show vrf** *Information*

```
switch-2# show vrf
  Name                          Default RD        Protocols    Interfaces
  GREEN                         100:2             ipv4         Gi1/5
  RED                           100:1             ipv6         Gi1/1
                                                              Gi1/2
```

Note   Similar to VLANs, VRFs are only locally significant to the router. A similar configuration would need to be done on the distribution switch for each of the three VRFs.

Being locally significant to the router, VRF-Lite information cannot be carried across the entire network, because the Multi-VRF provides each VRF domain with its own set of interfaces, routing table, and forwarding tables. Thus, it enables the extension of the label-switched paths to the Customer Edge (CE) routers. As shown in Figure 7-2, this allows each CE router to act as several different CEs. Thus, the network architects can leverage MPLS VPN technology to map VRF-Lite to a VPN-ID and carry it across the core of the network.

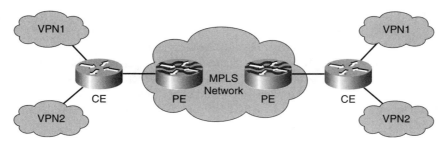

Figure 7-2   *CE Router Acting as a Virtual CE*

Transporting IPv6 Across the MPLS Backbone

Large enterprise IT infrastructures have evolved to behave as service providers within the organization, servicing multiple geographically dispersed business units. Such enterprises leverage MPLS as the underlying technology to help deliver an L3 VPN solution to different geographical sites. In addition to providing L3 VPN capability, MPLS also provides traffic engineering capabilities, which help the IT organization to control and drive different VPN traffic across different links and charge the costs of the long-distance links back to the business unit. As these organizations look toward enabling IPv6 in their network, they need to connect IPv6 domains (network islands) across an MPLS network. In the following sections, we discuss how network architects can extend VRF-Lite (which has local significance) across the entire network. Cisco 6PE and 6VPE allows the network architects to add IPv6 services into an existing IPv4 MPLS infrastructure.

6PE

When Border Gateway Protocol (BGP) peers set up sessions between themselves, they send an OPEN message containing optional parameters. One optional parameter is capabilities. Possible capabilities are multiprotocol extensions, route refresh, outbound route filtering (ORF), and so on. When the BGP peers exchange the multiprotocol extension capability, they exchange Address Family Identifier (AFI) and Subsequent Address Family Identifier (SAFI) numbers and thus identify the capability of the peering BGP router. See Table 7-2.

Table 7-2   *BGP AFI and SAFI Values*

BGP Attributes	Details
Address Family Identifier (AFI)	1: IPv4 2: IPv6
Subsequent Address Family Identifier (SAFI)	1: Unicast 2: Multicast 3: Unicast and Multicast 4: MPLS Label 128: MPLS-labeled VPN

IPv6 in BGP is implemented through Multi-Protocol BGP (MP-BGP) (RFC 4760), as are MPLS and VPNs through two new attributes: MP_UNREACH_NLRI and MP_REACH_NLRI. MP_UNREACH_NLRI carries the destinations that are not reachable, while MP_REACH_NLRI carries the destinations that are reachable. As these attributes are optional so the allow the speaker to talk to the other BGP routers which don't support these capabilities, this allows backward compatibility as the BGP speakers without these attributes can speak to the BGP speakers with these attributes.

If BGP is carrying IPv6 route information, AFI equals 2 and SAFI equals 1 for unicast, and SAFI equals 2 for multicast. This way, the 6PE routers convey their IPv4 addresses as the BGP next-hop for the advertised IPv6 prefixes. The IPv4 address of the egress 6PE router is encoded as an IPv4-mapped IPv6 address (::FFFF:<IPv4 address of BGP next-hop>) in the BGP next-hop field. In addition, the ingress 6PE router binds a label to the IPv6 prefix. The SAFI used in MP-BGP is "label" (value 4). The label binding is piggybacked along the prefix information in the MP_REACH_NLRI attribute.

The IPv4-mapped IPv6 addresses allow a 6PE router that has to forward an IPv6 packet to automatically determine the IPv4-enabled Label Switched Path (LSP) to use for a particular IPv6 destination by looking at the MP-BGP routing information. The IPv4-enabled LSPs can be established using Label Distribution Protocol (LDP) or Resource Reservation Protocol - Traffic Engineering (RSVP-TE).

When IPv6 packets are tunneled through an IPv4 core network, the ingress 6PE router directly performs label imposition on the IPv6 header. The ingress 6PE router first imposes an inner label advertised by egress 6PE using MP-BGP. This label indicates to the egress 6PE router that the packet is an IPv6 packet. The ingress 6PE router also imposes an outer label that corresponds to the IPv4-signaled LSP starting on the ingress 6PE router and ending on the egress 6PE router. Figure 7-3 shows the 6PE network.

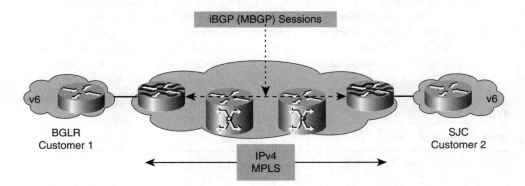

Figure 7-3   *6PE Network*

In Example 7-3, the routing protocol between the PE and CE is Routing Information Protocol next generation (RIPng). Both the PE and the CE devices are Virtual Switching Systems (VSS). The following steps explain how to configure PE and CE routers for 6PE:

Step 1.   Configure the CE interface, as shown in Example 7-3.

Example 7-3 *CE Router Interface Configuration*

```
BGLR-CE:                          # Bangalore CE Router

ipv6 unicast-routing
!
interface Loopback0
 ipv6 address 2001:DB8:CAFE:1:1::1/128
!
interface Port-channel30
 description to PE-VSS-core-BGLR
 ipv6 address 2001:DB8:CAFE:2::1/64          #Assign IPv6 address
  !
interface TenGigabitEthernet1/7/1
  channel-group 30 mode on
!
interface TenGigabitEthernet1/7/1
  channel-group 30 mode on
!
SJC-CE:                           # SanJose CE Router

ipv6 unicast-routing
!
interface Loopback0
 ipv6 address 2001:DB8:CAFE:1:2::1/128
!
interface Port-channel30
 description to PE-VSS-core-BGLR
 ipv6 address 2001:DB8:CAFE:3::1/64          #Assign IPv6 address
!
interface TenGigabitEthernet1/7/1
  channel-group 30 mode on
!
interface TenGigabitEthernet1/7/1
  channel-group 30 mode on
    !
```

Step 2.   After you have configured the CE interfaces, you need to configure the PE router interfaces for connectivity to the P routers and CE routers, as shown in Example 7-4.

Example 7-4 *PE Router Interface Configuration*

```
BGLR-CE:                          # Bangalore CE Router

ipv6 unicast-routing
```

continues

Example 7-4   *PE Router Interface Configuration*   *continued*

```
!
interface Loopback0
 ipv6 address 2001:DB8:CAFE:1:1::1/128
!
interface Port-channel30
 description to PE-VSS-core-BGLR
 ipv6 address 2001:DB8:CAFE:2::1/64          #Assign IPv6 address
   !
interface TenGigabitEthernet1/7/1
   channel-group 30 mode on
!
interface TenGigabitEthernet1/7/1
   channel-group 30 mode on
!
SJC-CE:                                 # SanJose CE Router

ipv6 unicast-routing
!
interface Loopback0
 ipv6 address 2001:DB8:CAFE:1:2::1/128
!
interface Port-channel30
 description to PE-VSS-core-BGLR
 ipv6 address 2001:DB8:CAFE:3::1/64          #Assign IPv6 address
!
interface TenGigabitEthernet1/7/1
   channel-group 30 mode on
!
interface TenGigabitEthernet1/7/1
   channel-group 30 mode on
     !
```

Step 3.   After you have established the basic configuration between the PE and CE, you need to configure the routing protocol. Example 7-5 shows that the routing protocol used is RIPng.

Example 7-5   *CE Routing Protocol Configuration*

```
BGLR-PE:                        # Bangalore PE Router

ipv6 unicast-routing
!
int loopback0
 ip address 10.10.10.1 255.255.255.255
!
```

```
interface Portchannel10
 description interface to P network
 ip address 10.1.2.1 255.255.255.0
 mpls ip
 !
interface PortChannel30
 description interface to VSS-CE BGLR
 ipv6 address 2001:DB8:CAFE:2::2/64
 ipv6 enable
!
interface TenGigabitEthernet1/7/1
   channel-group 30 mode on
!
interface TenGigabitEthernet2/7/1
   channel-group 30 mode on
!
SJC-PE:                           # SanJose PE Router

ipv6 unicast-routing
!
int loopback0
 ip address 10.10.10.4 255.255.255.255
 !
interface Portchannel10
 description interface to P network
 ip address 10.1.5.1 255.255.255.0
 mpls ip
!
interface PortChannel30
 description interface to VSS-CE SJC
 no ip address
 ipv6 address 2001:DB8:CAFE:3::2/64
 ipv6 enable
 !
!Interface assignment to port-channels removed for brevity
BGLR-CE:                          # Bangalore CE Router

ipv6 unicast-routing
!
interface Loopback0
   ipv6 rip customer enable
!
interface Port-channel30
   ipv6 rip customer  enable
 !
```

continues

Example 7-5   *CE Routing Protocol Configuration   continued*

```
ipv6 router rip customer
!
SJC-CE:                                    # SanJose CE Router

ipv6 unicast-routing
!
interface Loopback0
 ipv6 rip customer enable
!
interface Port-channel30
 ipv6 rip customer  enable
!
ipv6 router rip customer
    !
```

Step 4.   After you establish the CE-PE connectivity, you are left with the configuration (routing) on the PE routers. The configuration in Example 7-6 assumes that the P routers in the network are already configured.

Example 7-6   *PE Routing Configuration*

```
BGLR-PE:                       # Bangalore PE Routing Configuration

interface PortChannel30
 ipv6 rip customer enable
!
router bgp 100
 neighbor 10.10.10.4 remote-as 100
 neighbor 10.10.10.4 update-source Loopback0
 no auto-summary
!
 address-family ipv6
  neighbor 10.10.10.4 activate
  neighbor 10.10.10.4 send-community both
  neighbor 10.10.10.4 send-label
  redistribute connected
  redistribute rip customer
 exit-address-family
!
ipv6 router rip customer
 redistribute bgp 100
!
SJC-PE:                        # SanJose PE Routing Configuration

interface PortChannel30
```

```
 ipv6 rip customer enable
!
router bgp 100
 neighbor 10.10.10.1 remote-as 100
 neighbor 10.10.10.1 update-source Loopback0
!
 address-family ipv6
  neighbor 10.10.10.1 activate
  neighbor 10.10.10.1 send-community both
  neighbor 10.10.10.1 send-label
  redistribute connected
  redistribute rip customer
  no synchronization
 exit-address-family
!
ipv6 router rip customer
 redistribute bgp 100
    !
```

Step 5. Configure an internal routing protocol—Open Shortest Path First (OSPF) in this case—at the PE and P routers. Example 7-7 shows the OSPF configuration at the BGLR_PE and P routers.

Example 7-7 *BGLR-PE and P Router OSPF Configuration*

```
BGLR-PE# show running | beg router ospf
router ospf 100
 log-adjacency-changes
 network 10.1.2.0 0.0.0.255 area 0
 network 10.10.10.0 0.0.0.255 area 0
!
/* Bangalore P Router */
BGLR-P# show running ¦ begin ospf 100
router ospf 100
 log-adjacency-changes
 network 10.1.2.0 0.0.0.255 area 0
 network 10.1.4.0 0.0.0.255 area 0
 network 10.10.10.0 0.0.0.255 area 0
    !
```

The **debug** output shown in Example 7-8 helps ensure the verification of the 6PE configuration.

Example 7-8   *BGP Exchange Output Using* debug ip bgp

```
Additionally you c BGLR-PE# debug ip bgp


! BPG negotiation, state moving from Idle to Active
*Jul 23 05:36:28.563: BGP: 10.10.10.4 went from Idle to Active
*Jul 23 05:36:28.563: BGP: 10.10.10.4 open active, local address 10.10.10.1
!Output omitted for brevity


! BGP sending OPEN ,capability exchange and other messages
*Jul 23 05:36:28.575: BGP: 10.10.10.4 OPEN has CAPABILITY code: 1, length 4
*Jul 23 05:36:28.575: BGP: 10.10.10.4 OPEN has MP_EXT CAP for afi/safi: 1/1
*Jul 23 05:36:28.575: BGP: 10.10.10.4 rcvd OPEN w/ optional parameter type 2
(Capability) len 6
!Output omitted for brevity
*Jul 23 05:36:28.575: BGP: 10.10.10.4 OPEN has CAPABILITYcode: 128, length 0
*Jul 23 05:36:28.575: BGP: 10.10.10.4 OPEN has ROUTE-REFRESH capability(old) for
all address-families
*Jul 23 05:36:28.575: BGP: 10.10.10.4 rcvd OPEN w/ optional parameter type 2
(Capability) len 2
*Jul 23 05:36:28.575: BGP: 10.10.10.4 OPEN has CAPABILITY code: 2, length 0
*Jul 23 05:36:28.575: BGP: 10.10.10.4 OPEN has ROUTE-REFRESH capability(new) for
all address-families
BGP: 10.10.10.4 rcvd OPEN w/ remote AS 100


! BGP moved to Established
*Jul 23 05:36:28.575: BGP: 10.10.10.4 went from OpenSent to OpenConfirm
*Jul 23 05:36:28.579: BGP: 10.10.10.4 went from OpenConfirm to Established

*Jul 23 05:36:28.579: %BGP-5-ADJCHANGE: neighbor 10.10.10.4 Up
!Output omitted for brevity
```

Additionally, you can look at the output of the **show ip bgp unicast neighbors** command to verify MP-BGP for IPv6. Example 7-9 shows the command output and the route information.

Example 7-9   show ip bgp unicast neighbors *Command Output*

```
BGLR-PE# debug ip bgp


! BPG negotiation, state moving from Idle to Active
*Jul 23 05:36:28.563: BGP: 10.10.10.4 went from Idle to Active
*Jul 23 05:36:28.563: BGP: 10.10.10.4 open active, local address 10.10.10.1
!Output omitted for brevity


! BGP sending OPEN ,capability exchange and other messages
*Jul 23 05:36:28.575: BGP: 10.10.10.4 OPEN has CAPABILITY code: 1, length 4
```

```
*Jul 23 05:36:28.575: BGP: 10.10.10.4 OPEN has MP_EXT CAP for afi/safi: 1/1

*Jul 23 05:36:28.575: BGP: 10.10.10.4 rcvd OPEN w/ optional parameter type 2
(Capability) len 6

!Output omitted for brevity

*Jul 23 05:36:28.575: BGP: 10.10.10.4 OPEN has CAPABILITYcode: 128, length 0

*Jul 23 05:36:28.575: BGP: 10.10.10.4 OPEN has ROUTE-REFRESH capability(old) for
all address-families

*Jul 23 05:36:28.575: BGP: 10.10.10.4 rcvd OPEN w/ optional parameter type 2
(Capability) len 2

*Jul 23 05:36:28.575: BGP: 10.10.10.4 OPEN has CAPABILITY code: 2, length 0

*Jul 23 05:36:28.575: BGP: 10.10.10.4 OPEN has ROUTE-REFRESH capability(new) for
all address-families

BGP: 10.10.10.4 rcvd OPEN w/ remote AS 100


! BGP moved to Established

*Jul 23 05:36:28.575: BGP: 10.10.10.4 went from OpenSent to OpenConfirm

*Jul 23 05:36:28.579: BGP: 10.10.10.4 went from OpenConfirm to Established


*Jul 23 05:36:28.579: %BGP-5-ADJCHANGE: neighbor 10.10.10.4 Up

!Output omitted for brevity

BGLR-PE# show ip bgp ipv6 unicast neighbors          #BGLR-PE


BGP neighbor is 10.10.10.4,  remote AS 100, internal link
  BGP version 4, remote router ID 10.10.10.4
  BGP state = Established, up for 00:06:21
  Last read 00:00:15, last write 00:00:17, hold time is 180, keepalive interval
is 60 seconds
  Neighbor capabilities:
    Route refresh: advertised and received(new)
    Address family IPv4 Unicast: advertised and received
    Address family IPv6 Unicast: advertised and received
    ipv6 MPLS Label capability: advertised and received
!Output omitted for brevity
  For address family: IPv6 Unicast
  BGP table version 5, neighbor version 5/0
  Output queue size : 0
  Index 1, Offset 0, Mask 0x2
  1 update-group member
  Community attribute sent to this neighbor
  Sending Prefix & Label

                                Sent        Rcvd
  Prefix activity:              - - - -     - - - -
    Prefixes Current:           1           1 (Consumes 76 bytes)
    Prefixes Total:             2           2
    Implicit Withdraw:          1           1
    Explicit Withdraw:          0           0
```

continues

Example 7-9   show ip bgp unicast neighbors *Command Output   continued*

```
      Used as bestpath:              n/a              1
      Used as multipath:             n/a              0
!Output omitted for brevity
BGLR-PE# show ipv6 route     2001:DB8:CAFE:3::1/64  # Route to SJC

Routing entry for 2001:DB8:CAFE:3::/64
  Known via "bgp 100", distance 200, metric 0, type internal
  Redistributing via rip customer
  Route count is 1/1, share count 0
  Routing paths:
    10.10.10.4%Default-IP-Routing-Table indirectly connected
      MPLS Required
      Last updated 00:07:51 ago
! show ipv6 cef , please note the imposition of two labels
BGLR-PE# show ipv6 cef 2000:CAFE:3::/64
2000:CAFE:3::/64
  nexthop 10.1.2.2 Ethernet0/0 label 18 17
```

6VPE

6VPE carries IPv6 in VPNs across an MPLS backbone. An IPv6 VPN works in the same way as the IPv4 MPLS VPN. This basically gives a smooth migration path for the service providers who have deployed IPv4 MPLS VPNs by just upgrading the IOS version on the PE routers. This allows service providers to avoid any changes to the core routers.

A simplified network with just two sites of a company ABC—SanJose (SJC) and Bangalore (BGLR)—to explore the concept is used. Figure 7-3 shows a sample network to help you understand 6VPE.

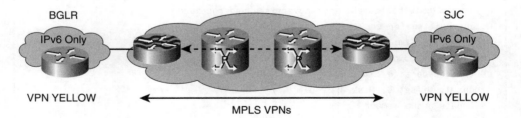

Figure 7-4   *6VPE Sample Network*

Figure 7-3 is a basic network that demonstrates 6VPE. In Example 7-10, customer ABC corresponds to VRF ABC-vrf on the PE routers. The following steps and configurations on the PE and CE routers are required:

Step 1.   Configure the CE routers, as shown in Example 7-10.

Example 7-10 *BGLR CE Router Configuration*

```
BGLR-CE:                        # Bangalore CE Router

 !
 ipv6 unicast-routing
 !
 interface Loopback0
  ip address 10.10.10.10 255.255.255.255
  ipv6 address 2001:DB8:CAFE:1:1::1/128
 !
 interface Portchannel30
  description interface to PE BGLR
  ipv6 address 2001:DB8:CAFE:2::1/64
 !
 /* Assignment of interfaces to channel-group same as 6 PE hence skipped */
 SJC-CE:                        # SanJose CE Router

 !
 ipv6 unicast-routing
 !
 interface Loopback0
  ip address 10.10.10.11 255.255.255.25
  ipv6 address 2001:DB8:CAFE:1:2::1/128
 !
 interface Portchannel30
  description interface to PE BGLR
  ipv6 address 2000:DB8:CAFE:3::1/64
     !
```

Step 2. After configuring the CE interfaces, enable the 6VPE configuration and configure router interfaces for connectivity to the P routers and CE routers, as
shown in Example 7-11.

Example 7-11 *PE Router IP Address and 6VPE Configuration*

```
BGLR-PE:                        # Bangalore PE Router 6VPE Config

 ipv6 unicast-routing
 !
 vrf definition ABC-vrf
  rd 100:1
  !
  address-family ipv6
   route-target both 100:1
  exit-address-family
 !
```

continues

Example 7-11   *PE Router IP Address and 6VPE Configuration   continued*

```
mpls label protocol ldp
!
int loopback0
 ip address 10.10.10.1 255.255.255.255
!
interface Portchannel10
 description interface to P network
 ip address 10.1.2.1 255.255.255.0
 mpls ip
!
interface Portchannel30
 description interface to CE-BGLR
 vrf forwarding ABC-vrf
 ipv6 address 2001:DB8:CAFE:2::2/64
 ipv6 enable
!
SJC-PE:                                 # SanJose PE Router 6VPE Config

ipv6 unicast-routing
!
vrf definition ABC-vrf
 rd 100:1
 !
 address-family ipv6
  route-target both 100:1
 exit-address-family
!
mpls label protocol ldp
!
int loopback0
 ip address 10.10.10.4 255.255.255.255
 !
interface Portchannel10
 description interface to P network
 ip address 10.1.5.1 255.255.255.0
 mpls ip

interface Portchannel30
 description interface to CE SJC
 vrf forwarding ABC-vrf
 ipv6 address 2001:DB8:CAFE:3::2/64
 ipv6 enable
    !
```

Step 3.   Configure the routing protocol. In Example 7-12, the routing protocol used is
Border Gateway Protocol (BGP).

Example 7-12   *CE Routing Configuration*

```
BGLR-CE:                         # Bangalore CE Router

!/* Note: This bgp session will also negotiate exchange if IPv4 AF */
router bgp 65000
 no synchronization
 bgp log-neighbor-changes
 neighbor 2001:DB8:CAFE:2::2 remote-as 100
 no auto-summary
 !
 address-family ipv6
  neighbor 2001:DB8:CAFE:2::2 activate
  network 2001:DB8:CAFE:1:1::1/128
 exit-address-family
!
SJC-CE:                          # SanJose CE Router

router bgp 65000
 no synchronization
 bgp log-neighbor-changes
 neighbor 2001:DB8:CAFE:3::2 remote-as 100
 no auto-summary
 !
 address-family ipv6
  neighbor 2001:DB8:CAFE:3::2 activate
  network 2001:DB8:CAFE:1:2::1/128
  no synchronization
 exit-address-family
!
    !
```

Step 4.   Enable the routing configuration on the PE routers. Example 7-13 shows the
enablement of the routing configuration on both the PE routers.

Example 7-13   *PE Routing Configuration*

```
BGLR-PE:                         #Bangalore PE Routing Configuration

router ospf 100
 log-adjacency-changes
 network 10.1.0.0 0.0.255.255 area 0
 network 10.10.10.0 0.0.255.255 area 0
```

continues

Example 7-13 *PE Routing Configuration   continued*

```
!
router bgp 100
 bgp log-neighbor-changes
 neighbor 10.10.10.4 remote-as 100
 neighbor 10.10.10.4 update-source Loopback0
 !
 address-family ipv4
  no neighbor 10.10.10.4 activate
  no auto-summary
  no synchronization
 exit-address-family
 !
 address-family vpnv6
  neighbor 10.10.10.4 activate
  neighbor 10.10.10.4 send-community both
 exit-address-family
 !
 address-family ipv6
  redistribute connected
  no synchronization
 exit-address-family
 !
 address-family ipv6 vrf ABC-vrf
  neighbor 2001:DB8:CAFE:2::1 remote-as 65000
  neighbor 2001:DB8:CAFE:2::1 activate
  override
  redistribute connected
  no synchronization
 exit-address-family
!
SJC-PE:                         #SanJose PE Routing Configuration
router ospf 100
 log-adjacency-changes
 network 10.1.0.0 0.0.255.255 area 0
 network 10.10.10.0 0.0.255.255 area 0
 !
router bgp 100
 bgp log-neighbor-changes
 neighbor 10.10.10.1 remote-as 100
 neighbor 10.10.10.1 update-source Loopback0
 !
  address-family ipv4
   no auto-summary
   no synchronization
```

```
 exit-address-family
 !
 address-family vpnv6
  neighbor 10.10.10.1 activate
  neighbor 10.10.10.1 send-community both
 exit-address-family
 !
 address-family ipv6 vrf ABC-vrf
  neighbor 2001:DB8:CAFE:3::1 remote-as 65000
  neighbor 2001:DB8:CAFE:3::1 activate
  redistribute connected
  no synchronization
 exit-address-family
!
```

After configuring the 6VPE, you are ready to verify that the 6VPE network is working. To verify the 6VPE configuration, you need to start by verifying the VRF (customer) configured on the PE routers, as shown in Example 7-14.

Example 7-14   *Verification of Customer VRF and Other Basic Parameters*

```
BGLR-PE# show vrf ipv6
  Name                           Default RD        Protocols    Interfaces
  ABC-vrf                        100:1             ipv6         Po30
BGLR-PE# show vrf ipv6 interfaces
Interface              VRF                         Protocol    Address
Po30                   customer-vrf                up
2001:DB8:CAFE:2::2
BGLR-PE# show ip bgp all neighbors
!Output omitted for brevity
For address family: VPNv4 Unicast
!Output omitted for brevity
For address family: VPNv6 Unicast

BGP neighbor is 10.10.10.4,  remote AS 100, internal link
  BGP version 4, remote router ID 10.10.10.4
  BGP state = Established, up for 00:03:35
  Last read 00:00:30, last write 00:00:44, hold time is 180, keepalive interval
is 60 seconds
  Neighbor capabilities:
    Route refresh: advertised and received(new)
    Address family VPNv6 Unicast: advertised and received

!Output omitted for brevity
```

continues

Example 7-14   *Verification of Customer VRF and Other Basic Parameters   continued*

```
BGLR-PE# show bgp vpnv6 unicast vrf customer-vrf 2001:DB8:CAFE:1:2::1/128
BGP routing table entry for [100:1]2001:DB8:CAFE:1:2::1/128, version 7
Paths: (1 available, best #1, table customer-vrf)
  Advertised to update-groups:
        1
  65000
    ::FFFF:10.10.10.4 (metric 22) from 10.10.10.4 (10.10.10.4)
        Origin IGP, metric 0, localpref 100, valid, internal, best
        Extended Community: RT:100:1
        mpls labels in/out nolabel/19
! show ipv6 and the imposition of two labels
BGLR-PE#show ipv6 cef vrf customer-vrf 2000:CAFE:1:2::1/128
2000:CAFE:1:2::1/128
  nexthop 10.1.2.2 Portchannel10 label 18 19
BGLR-PE#
```

To verify the routes at the PE and CE, you can use the **show ipv6 route vrf** *vrf name* command at the PE routers and the **show ipv6 route** command at the CE routers, as shown in Example 7-15.

Example 7-15   **show ipv6 route vrf** *vrf name Command Output*

```
BGLR-PE# show ipv6 route vrf customer-vrf
IPv6 Routing Table - customer-vrf - 6 entries
Codes: C - Connected, L - Local, S - Static, U - Per-user Static route
       B - BGP, M - MIPv6, R - RIP, I1 - ISIS L1
       I2 - ISIS L2, IA - ISIS interarea, IS - ISIS summary, D - EIGRP
       EX - EIGRP external
B    2001:DB8:CAFE:1:1::1/128 [20/0]
     via FE80::A8BB:CCFF:FE00:6500, Port-channel30
B    2001:DB8:CAFE:1:2::1/128 [200/0]
     via 10.10.10.4%Default-IP-Routing-Table, indirectly connected
C    2001:DB8:CAFE:2::/64 [0/0]
     via Port-channel10, directly connected
L    2001:DB8:CAFE:2::2/128 [0/0]
     via Port-channel10, receive
B    2001:DB8:CAFE:3::/64 [200/0]
     via 10.10.10.4%Default-IP-Routing-Table, indirectly connected
L    FF00::/8 [0/0]
     via Null0, receive
BGLR-CE# show ipv6 route
IPv6 Routing Table - Default - 6 entries
Codes: C - Connected, L - Local, S - Static, U - Per-user Static route
       B - BGP, M - MIPv6, R - RIP, I1 - ISIS L1
```

```
          I2 - ISIS L2, IA - ISIS interarea, IS - ISIS summary, D - EIGRP
          EX - EIGRP external
LC  2001:DB8:CAFE:1:1::1/128 [0/0]
      via Loopback0, receive
B   2001:DB8:CAFE:1:2::1/128 [20/0]
      via FE80::A8BB:CCFF:FE00:6601, Port-channel30
C   2001:DB8:CAFE:2::/64 [0/0]
      via Ethernet0/0, directly connected
L   2001:DB8:CAFE:2::1/128 [0/0]
      via Ethernet0/0, receive
B   2001:DB8:CAFE:3::/64 [20/0]
      via FE80::A8BB:CCFF:FE00:6601, Port-channel30
L   FF00::/8 [0/0]
      via Null0, receive
```

To get the exchange information of the BGP 6VPE verification, enable debugging, as shown in Example 7-16.

Example 7-16   debug bgp all *Command Output*

```
/* Negotiation of BGLR PE with the SJC PE router */

BGLR-PE# debug bgp all


! BPG negotiation, state moving from Idle to Active
*Jul 24 18:21:19.225: BGP: 10.10.10.4 went from Idle to Active
*Jul 24 18:21:19.229: BGP: 10.10.10.4 open active, local address 10.10.10.1
*Jul 24 18:21:19.229: BGP: 10.10.10.4 read request no-op
*Jul 24 18:21:19.229: BGP: 10.10.10.4 went from Active to OpenSent

! BGP sending OPEN ,version, Autonomous system number and other messages
*Jul 24 18:21:19.229: BGP: 10.10.10.4 sending OPEN, version 4, my as: 100, hold-
time 180 seconds
*Jul 24 18:21:19.237: BGP: 10.10.10.4 send message type 1, length (incl. header) 45

! BGP receiving OPEN with capabilities
*Jul 24 18:21:19.241: BGP: 10.10.10.4 rcv message type 1, length (excl. header) 26
*Jul 24 18:21:19.241: BGP: 10.10.10.4 rcv OPEN, version 4, holdtime 180 seconds
*Jul 24 18:21:19.241: BGP: 10.10.10.4 rcv OPEN w/ OPTION parameter len: 16
*Jul 24 18:21:19.241: BGP: 10.10.10.4 rcvd OPEN w/ optional parameter type 2
(Capability) len 6
*Jul 24 18:21:19.241: BGP: 10.10.10.4 OPEN has CAPABILITY code: 1, length 4
*Jul 24 18:21:19.241: BGP: 10.10.10.4 OPEN has MP_EXT CAP for afi/safi: 2/128
```

continues

Example 7-16   debug bgp all *Command Output   continued*

```
*Jul 24 18:21:19.241: BGP: 10.10.10.4 rcvd OPEN w/ optional parameter type 2
(Capability) len 2
*Jul 24 18:21:19.241: BGP: 10.10.10.4 OPEN has CAPABILITY code: 128, length 0
*Jul 24 18:21:19.241: BGP: 10.10.10.4 OPEN has ROUTE-REFRESH capability(old) for
all address-families
*Jul 24 18:21:19.241: BGP: 10.10.10.4 rcvd OPEN w/ optional parameter type 2
(Capability) len 2
*Jul 24 18:21:19.241: BGP: 10.10.10.4 OPEN has CAPABILITY code: 2, length 0
*Jul 24 18:21:19.241: BGP: 10.10.10.4 OPEN has ROUTE-REFRESH capability(new) for
all address-families
BGP: 10.10.10.4 rcvd OPEN w/ remote AS 100
*Jul 24 18:21:19.241: BGP: 10.10.10.4 went from OpenSent to OpenConfirm


! BGP moved to Established
*Jul 24 18:21:19.241: BGP: 10.10.10.4 went from OpenConfirm to Established
*Jul 24 18:21:19.241: %BGP-5-ADJCHANGE: neighbor 10.10.10.4 Up
/* Negotiation with the BGLR CE router */

BGLR-PE#

! BPG negotiation, sending OPEN, version and other parameters
*Jul 24 18:22:00.321: BGP: 2001:DB8:CAFE:2::1 went from Active to OpenSent
*Jul 24 18:22:00.321: BGP: 2001:DB8:CAFE:2::1 sending OPEN, version 4, my as: 100,
holdtime 180 seconds
*Jul 24 18:22:00.329: BGP: 2001:DB8:CAFE:2::1 send message type 1, length (incl.
header) 45
! BPG receiving OPEN with other parameters
*Jul 24 18:22:00.337: BGP: 2001:DB8:CAFE:2::1 rcv message type 1, length (excl.
header) 34
*Jul 24 18:22:00.337: BGP: 2001:DB8:CAFE:2::1 rcv OPEN, version 4, holdtime 180
seconds
*Jul 24 18:22:00.337: BGP: 2001:DB8:CAFE:2::1 rcv OPEN w/ OPTION parameter len: 24
*Jul 24 18:22:00.337: BGP: 2001:DB8:CAFE:2::1 rcvd OPEN w/ optional parameter type
2 (Capability) len 6
*Jul 24 18:22:00.337: BGP: 2001:DB8:CAFE:2::1 OPEN has CAPABILITY code: 1, length 4
*Jul 24 18:22:00.337: BGP: 2001:DB8:CAFE:2::1 OPEN has MP_EXT CAP for afi/safi: 1/1
*Jul 24 18:22:00.337: BGP: 2001:DB8:CAFE:2::1 rcvd OPEN w/ optional parameter type
2 (Capability) len 6
*Jul 24 18:22:00.337: BGP: 2001:DB8:CAFE:2::1 OPEN has CAPABILITY code: 1, length 4
*Jul 24 18:22:00.337: BGP: 2001:DB8:CAFE:2::1 OPEN has MP_EXT CAP for afi/safi: 2/1
*Jul 24 18:22:00.337: BGP: 2001:DB8:CAFE:2::1 rcvd OPEN w/ optional parameter type
2 (Capability) len 2
*Jul 24 18:22:00.337: BGP: 2001:DB8:CAFE:2::1 OPEN has CAPABILITY code: 128,
length 0
*Jul 24 18:22:00.337: BGP: 2001:DB8:CAFE:2::1 OPEN has ROUTE-REFRESH
capability(old) for all address-families
*Jul 24 18:22:00.337: BGP: 2001:DB8:CAFE:2::1 rcvd OPEN w/ optional parameter type
2 (Capability) len 2
```

```
*Jul 24 18:22:00.337: BGP: 2001:DB8:CAFE:2::1 OPEN has CAPABILITY code: 2, length 0
*Jul 24 18:22:00.337: BGP: 2001:DB8:CAFE:2::1 OPEN has ROUTE-REFRESH
capability(new) for all address-families
BGP: 2001:DB8:CAFE:2::1 rcvd OPEN w/ remote AS 65000
! BGP going to Established state with the peer and then declaring Adjacency to UP
*Jul 24 18:22:00.337: BGP: 2001:DB8:CAFE:2::1 went from OpenSent to OpenConfirm
*Jul 24 18:22:00.341: BGP: 2001:DB8:CAFE:2::1 went from OpenConfirm to Established
*Jul 24 18:22:00.341: %BGP-5-ADJCHANGE: neighbor 2001:DB8:CAFE:2::1 vpn vrf cus-
tomer Up
```

Virtual Private LAN Services

Virtual Private LAN Services (VPLS) enables Layer 2 multipoint-to-multipoint communication over an MPLS network. It enables geographically dispersed sites to share an Ethernet broadcast domain by interconnecting sites through pseudo-wires. Technologies that enable this interconnectivity include Ethernet over MPLS (EoMPLS), L2TPv3, and generic routing encapsulation (GRE) tunneling. The two IETF drafts that track VPLS include RFC 4761, "Virtual Private LAN Services (VPLS) Using BGP for Auto-Discovery and Signaling" and RFC 4762, "Virtual Private LAN Services (VPLS) Using Label Distribution Protocol (LDP) Signaling."

Being a Layer 2 technology, VPLS works the same for interconnecting IPv6 networks as it does for connecting IPv4 domains. In this section, only a sample configuration for Layer 2 interconnectivity is highlighted that does not go into the details of VPLS.

In the VPLS topology shown in Figure 7-5, the customer has three sites connected over the network. The three PE routers are connected in a full mesh.

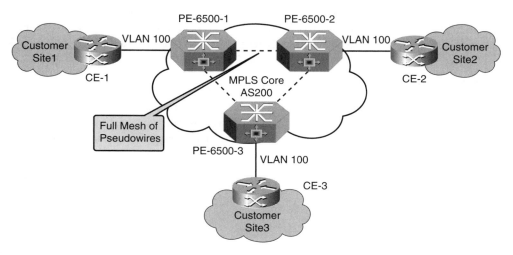

Figure 7-5   *Sample Network for VPLS Topology*

The sample configuration for one of the PE routers (PE-6500-1) is given in Example 7-17. For other routes, the configuration is the same except for the IP addresses.

Example 7-17   *VFI Configuration*

```
Router#
!
 l2 vfi customer manual
! Create a vpn id and configure the vpn neighbors
vpn id 100
 neighbor 20.20.20.20 encapsulation mpls
 neighbor 30.30.30.30 encapsulation mpls
!
interface loopback 0
ip address 10.10.10.10 255.255.255.255
!
interface fastethernet1/0
 switchport
 switchport mode dot1qtunnel
 switchport access vlan 100
!
interface vlan 100
 no ip address
 xconnect vfi customer
```

The VPLS provides a Layer 2 service and consists of six components: attachment circuit, Packet Switched Network (PSN), pseudo-wires, autodiscovery, autoconfiguration, and Virtual Switching Instance (VSI). From the perspective of IPv6, this service is transparent. In the case of Data Center Interconnect, the VPLS provides the Layer 2 path across the geographically separated data centers. Refer to Chapter 9 for more details.

Network Services Virtualization

Network services refer to firewall, load balancing, monitoring, and other Layer 4–7 services required in the network. At the time of this writing, the support for IPv6 on some of these devices is limited. We recommend that you check the latest configuration for the following devices:

■   Cisco firewalls (ASA family, including ASA 5500 and Firewall Service Module [FWSM])

■   Cisco ACE

■   Cisco Intrusion Detection Service Module

In the following sections, we focus on the various aspects of virtualization and use the Cisco ASA 5500 solution that supports IPv6 in a virtual context to understand network services virtualization.

Virtualized Firewall

Virtualization is an abstraction layer that decouples the security policies from the physical hardware to deliver greater network resource utilization and flexibility. Virtualization enables multiple virtual machines with heterogeneous security policies to run in isolation, side by side on the same physical firewall hardware module. Each virtual context has its own set of virtual interfaces upon which the security policies can be applied. These security contexts see a consistent, normalized set of hardware regardless of the physical components. Each security context is an independent firewall with its own configuration, security policy, interfaces, and administrators.

A key benefit of the security contexts is the ease of configuration and management that comes with the security policy being configured around the logical virtual firewall. This breaks down the complex firewall with many interfaces and configuring security policies on them into manageable pieces of smaller firewalls and less complicated policies. This avoids mistakes leading to vulnerabilities and security holes.

Cisco Adaptive Security Appliance (ASA) Virtualization Architecture

Today Cisco firewalls support virtual firewalls, where each virtual firewall is called a *context* because it is one partition or instance of a fully functional firewall. Figure 7-6 shows the different contexts, which are emulated by a single-firewall CPU.

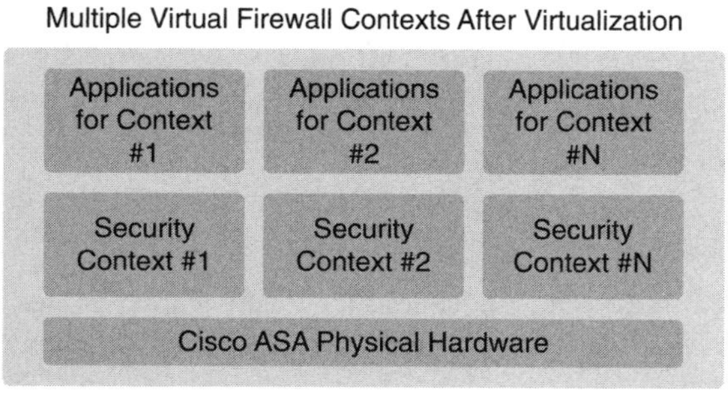

Multiple Virtual Firewall Contexts After Virtualization

- Hardware independent of each security virtual context
- Cisco ASA shared resources can be classified to each security context
- Each security context can be managed separately
- Ease of management
- Decentralized administration/management
- Less prone to configuration errors

Figure 7-6   *Cisco ASA After Virtualization*

Traditionally, firewalls provide a Layer 3 hop or the routed mode. In this mode, the ASA acts as the default gateway for the protected hosts. Cisco ASA also provides the transparent mode (Layer 2 mode), which acts like a "bump in the wire." With virtualization, the ASA is split into multiple security contexts; the details are discussed in the following sections. Figure 7-7 shows how a single Cisco ASA can be organized into multiple security contexts—both routed and transparent.

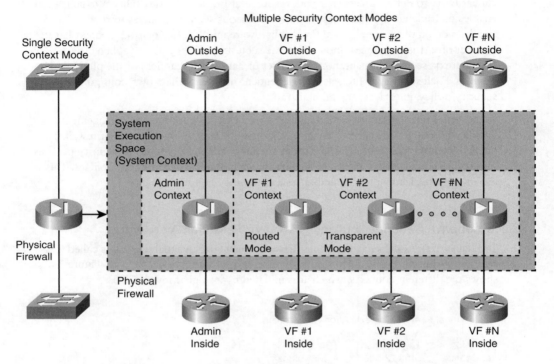

Figure 7-7   *Cisco ASA Multiple-Context Logical Diagram*

Understanding Virtual Contexts on the Cisco ASA

The following sections explain virtual contexts and guidelines for allocating appropriate resources to each of these virtual contexts. The administrator can configure the following different types of contexts on the Cisco ASA:

■ System context

■ Admin context

■ User contexts

The following sections define each context.

System Context (System Execution Space)

The system context, also called the system execution space, is not a true context in itself, but is used for defining and configuring other user contexts. This context enables the administrator to create a context and allocate interfaces and system resources to each of the contexts. The administrator can configure the following types of features in the system execution space. Figure 7-6 shows the various contexts along with the system context:

- Firewall startup configuration file

- Firewall mode (routing or transparent)

- Context definitions (configuration files, interface allocation, or mapping)

- Saving crash information

- Firewall system clock

- Firewall license activation key

Admin Context

The admin context, shown earlier in Figure 7-6, has all the features of a regular virtual context but in addition also defines the interfaces used by the system context when loading a software image or configuration file from the TFTP server. Because the system context does not directly have access to any physical interfaces, it uses the network resources of the admin context. The admin context is configured like any other context and has all the capabilities of any user context.

User Contexts

Each user context, shown earlier in Figure 7-6, is an independent virtual firewall with its own set of security policies that are configured independently of the other user contexts. Each user context can either be in "routed" or "transparent" mode with its own set of security policies, network addressing, access control, and so on. All the security features that can be configured on a single-firewall platform can be configured on a user context. Each virtual firewall that exists in this security context (also known as virtual contexts) includes the following:

- Collection of logical interfaces

- Security parameters for each interface

- Global data, state information, and statistics, which apply to the virtual firewall (security context), accessed and referenced by a unique, virtual firewall identifier

- A configurable, enforced subset of the total system hardware resources

Configuring Multiple Contexts on the Cisco ASA

This section describes configuring different contexts and basic IPv6 on the Cisco ASA virtual firewall. Figure 7-8 shows a network diagram using an admin context named Admin and two user contexts: Red and Blue.

In Figure 7-9, the Admin context uses IPv4, but the other context uses IPv6 for addressing. The configuration examples that follow show how to convert and configure Cisco ASA devices in multiple mode (virtual firewall).

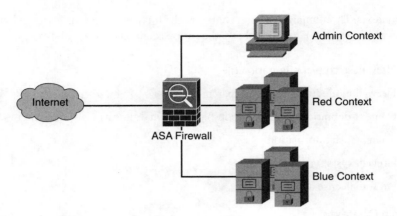

Figure 7-8   *ASA Firewall Network*

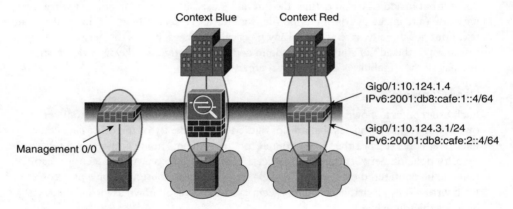

Figure 7-9   *Cisco ASA Context Example*

To enable multiple context mode, use the commands shown in Example 7-18. Different contexts can be created only after the multiple contexts mode has been enabled. The **no** form of the command can be used to disable multiple contexts. Changing the context mode requires a reboot.

Example 7-18   *Enabling Multiple Context Mode*

```
ciscoasa(config)# mode multiple
WARNING: This command will change the behavior of the device
WARNING: This command will initiate a Reboot
Proceed with change mode? [confirm]

Convert the system configuration? [confirm]

!
```

```
The old running configuration file will be written to flash

The admin context configuration will be written to flash

The new running configuration file was written to flash
Security context mode: multiple
***
*** —- SHUTDOWN NOW —-
***
*** Message to all terminals:
***
***    change mode
Process shutdown finished
Rebooting.....
Restarting system.
!Output omitted for brevity

Creating context 'admin'... Done. (1)
*** Output from config line 34, "admin-context admin"

Cryptochecksum (changed): 85ac17c5 76153dab e815c777 22b18a8d

*** Output from config line 36, "  config-url flash:/admi..."

Cryptochecksum (changed): 487a8b1e 3574c5d7 dc07697e 6349934f
Type help or '?' for a list of available commands.
ciscoasa>
```

After the Cisco ASA has been configured in multiple mode, the service context can be configured and addresses assigned. Before going into the context mode, the user should configure the interface and allocated resources to the context based on the service level agreements (SLA); this includes allocation of the interface, the configuration URL, allocation of the Intrusion Prevention System (IPS) sensor, and joining of the failover groups. Example 7-19 explains the context configuration.

Example 7-19   *Configuring a Multicontext Firewall*

```
ciscoasa# conf t
ciscoasa(config)# context Red
Creating context 'Red'... Done. (2)
ciscoasa(config-ctx)# config-url disk0:/Red.cfg

WARNING: Could not fetch the URL disk0:/Red.cfg
INFO: Creating context with default config
```

continues

Example 7-19 *Configuring a Multicontext Firewall continued*

```
ciscoasa(config-ctx)# allocate-interface GigabitEthernet0/0
ciscoasa(config-ctx)# allocate-interface GigabitEthernet0/1
ciscoasa(config-ctx)# context Blue

Creating context 'Blue'... Done. (3)
ciscoasa(config-ctx)# config-url disk0:/Blue.cfg
WARNING: Could not fetch the URL disk0:/Blue.cfg
INFO: Creating context with default config
ciscoasa(config-ctx)# context admin
ciscoasa(config-ctx)# allocate-interface GigabitEthernet0/3

/* Make sure that the contexts are created and interfaces assigned */
ciscoasa# sh context
Context Name      Class        Interfaces           URL
*admin            default      Management0/0         disk0:/admin.cfg
 Red              default      GigabitEthernet0/0,   disk0:/Red.cfg
                               GigabitEthernet0/1
 Blue             default      GigabitEthernet0/3    disk0:/Blue.cfg
Ciscoasa(config-ctx)# int GigabitEthernet0/0
ciscoasa(config-if)# no shutdown
ciscoasa(config-if)# int GigabitEthernet0/1
ciscoasa(config-if)# no shutdown
ciscoasa(config-if)# int GigabitEthernet0/2
ciscoasa(config-if)# no shutdown
ciscoasa(config-if)# int GigabitEthernet0/3
ciscoasa(config-if)# no shutdown
```

The next step in the configuration of contexts is the firewall interface and different features, including failover, routing, access lists, and other ASA features. Example 7-20 explains the configuration of interfaces, static routing, and failover.

Example 7-20 *Configuring the Firewall Interface and Failover Options*

```
/* Red Context Config */

ASA Version 8.2(2) <context>
!
hostname Red
enable password 8Ry2YjIyt7RRXU24 encrypted
passwd 2KFQnbNIdI.2KYOU encrypted
names
!
interface GigabitEthernet0/0
```

```
 nameif Outside
 security-level 0
 ip address 202.1.1.1 255.255.255.0 standby 202.1.1.2
 ipv6 address 2001:db8:cafe:1::1/64 standby 2001:db8:cafe:1::2
!
interface GigabitEthernet0/1
 nameif Inside
 security-level 100
 ip address 10.1.1.1 255.255.255.0 standby 10.1.1.2
 ipv6 address 2001:db8:cafe:2::1/64 standby 2001:db8:cafe:2::2
!
pager lines 24
mtu Outside 1500
mtu Inside 1500
ipv6 route Outside ::/0 2001:db8:cafe:1::10
!Output omitted for brevity
System Context Failover Config:

failover
failover lan unit primary
failover lan interface FO-LINK GigabitEthernet0/2
failover link FO-LINK GigabitEthernet0/2
failover interface ip FO-LINK 2001:db8:cafe:5::1/64 standby 2001:db8:cafe:5::2
!
```

Configuring IPv6 Access Lists

The configuration of IPv6 access lists is similar to the IPv4 access lists, and it involves the creation of the access control entry (ACE) followed by the application of the access list to an interface. Following are the guidelines and limitations that apply to IPv6 access lists:

- The IPv6 **access-list** command is similar to the IPv4 **access-list** command except for the **ipv6** keyword.

- The traffic that is allowed by default differs from product to product. For example, for the access lists on the ASA, all packets from the outside to the interface are denied until specific access lists are configured. On FWSM (Firewall Services Modules), all traffic is denied from any to any interface until access lists are applied.

- The **object-group** command can be used to configure the object group that can be used in the **access-list/ipv6 access-list** command.

Example 7-21 shows the creation of access list ACL_IN, which allows the 2001:db8:cafe:2::/64 and 2001:db8:cafe:3::/64 to any hosts followed by the application of the access-list on the inside interface.

Example 7-21 *IPv6 Access List Configuration and* **show access-list** *Commands*

```
ciscoasa/Red# conf t
ciscoasa/Red(config)#ciscoasa/Red(config)# ipv6 access-list ACL_IN permit ip
2001:db8:cafe:2::/64 any
ciscoasa/Red(config)# ipv6 access-list ACL_IN permit ip 2001:db8:cafe:3::/64 any
ciscoasa/Red(config)# access-group ACL_IN in interface inside
ciscoasa/Red# show access-list ACL_IN
ipv6 access-list ACL_IN; 2 elements; name hash: 0xc0a1e5cd
ipv6 access-list ACL_IN line 1 permit ip 2001:db8:cafe:2::/64 any (hitcnt=0)
0xb72c7224
ipv6 access-list ACL_IN line 2 permit ip 2001:db8:cafe:3::/64 any (hitcnt=0)
0x83b1bec0
# Access list configuration with object-groups
ciscoasa/Red(config)# object-group network out_net
ciscoasa/Red(config-network)# network-object 2001:db8:cafe:10::/64
ciscoasa/Red(config-network)# exit
ciscoasa/Red(config)# object-group network in_net
ciscoasa/Red(config-network)# network-object 2001:db8:cafe:2::/64
ciscoasa/Red(config-network)# exit
ciscoasa/Red(config)# ipv6 access-list ACL_OUT permit ip object-group out_net
object-group in_net
ciscoasa/Red(config)# exit
ciscoasa/Red# show access-list ACL_OUT
ipv6 access-list ACL_OUT; 1 elements; name hash: 0x21ec8810
ipv6 access-list ACL_OUT line 1 permit ip object-group out_net object-group in_net
0x912c1636
ipv6 access-list ACL_OUT line 1 permit ip 2001:db8:cafe:10::/64
2001:db8:cafe:2::/64 (hitcnt=0) 0x984c7723
ciscoasa/Red#
```

Note For stepwise configuration of Cisco ASA firewalls, refer to the following configuration guide:
http://www.cisco.com/en/US/docs/security/asa/asa82/configuration/guide/config.html.

Desktop Virtualization

The ever-changing business workspace continues to evolve from the current desktop, with local compute and productivity applications, to centralized compute in the data center, with desktop virtualization reducing desktop management costs. With desktop virtualization, the end host desktop is decoupled from the underlying hardware and operating system on the client machine. Based on where the client desktop environment is actually running, there are two categories of virtual desktop:

■ **Server-based computing:** In this model, the server host operating system and installed applications run in a virtual memory space (for example, Microsoft Terminal

Services) or dedicated virtual machines running on a hypervisor (for example, VMware vSphere with VMware View). Remote users use a remote display protocol to access the server, such as Microsoft Remote Desktop Protocol (RDP) and Citrix Independent Computing Architecture (ICA).

■ **Client-based computing:** In this model, the client can locally run a guest operating system and application in a virtual machine, or the application can be locally run or even streamed from the data center. Examples of client-based computing include VMware Fusion (Client hypervisor for Apple Mac OS X) and Microsoft App-V (Application virtualization/streaming).

The following section provides the linkage of IPv6 with desktop virtualization designs and design considerations that need to be kept in mind for thin-client vendors as they enable IPv6 on their devices.

IPv6 and Desktop Virtualization

IPv6 as an underlying IP technology supports desktop virtualization by supporting auto-configuration of thin clients and providing a larger address space. With the deployment of thin clients, enterprises need twice the number of IP addresses in their network: one for the thin client and one for the actual compute system (that is, the virtual machine on a server).

Only a minority of thin-client hardware/software and display protocols support IPv6, and other vendors are looking to support IPv6 in the future. For those vendors that support IPv6, there are usually three areas where IPv6 deployment for desktop virtualization needs to be considered:

■ **Zero/thin/thick-client configuration:** Thin clients support IPv6 addressing through Stateless Address Autoconfiguration (SLAAC) or Dynamic Host Configuration Protocol version 6 (DHCPv6) and static IPv6 configuration. The DHCP server needs to provide a path to the firmware TFTP or boot the server using DHCP options.

■ **Connection broker/portal/gateway:** Virtual Desktop Interface (VDI) environments use connection brokers, and server-based computing (SBC) environments often use portals or gateways to perform authentication, entitlement, and provisioning of desk-tops/sessions to clients. If the connection broker is configured for "tunnel" or "proxy" mode, where the broker acts on behalf of the back-end desktop (virtual machine or SBC session), the connection broker and supporting display protocols must support IPv6.

■ **Virtual machine/physical computer/blade PC:** In Hosted Virtual Desktop (HVD) environments such as VMware View and Citrix XenDesktop, virtual machines are used to act as the client's desktop. These virtual machines must support IPv6 through the virtual machine operating system TCP/IP stack (for example, Windows 7 virtual machine) and through an "agent" that is running on the virtual machine. The remote client will connect to the virtual machine using a variety of display protocols, including Microsoft Remote Desktop Protocol (RDP), Citrix Independent

Computing Architecture (ICA), and Teradici PC over IP (PCoIP). These display protocols must support IPv6 for the client to successfully connect to the virtual machine over IPv6, and only a few do. Additionally, display protocols can be used to connect directly to physical computers or blade PCs running Oracle Solaris, Linux, Microsoft Windows, Apple Mac OS, and so on. Today, Microsoft RDP and Virtual Network Computing (VNC) operate over IPv6 and can be used to connect remotely to most operating systems.

The next section describes a desktop virtualization scenario using Oracle Sun Ray.

Desktop Virtualization Example: Oracle Sun Ray

This section demonstrates desktop virtualization using the Oracle Sun Ray thin client. Figure 7-10 shows the network topology used for this example.

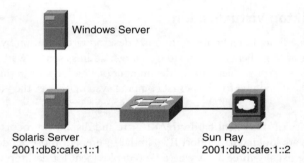

Figure 7-10 *Sun Ray Thin-Client Solution Topology*

The first step is to configure the thin client (in this case, the Sun Ray Integrated Display) for IPv6 configuration. A detailed step-by-step configuration of the Sun Ray client is available at the Oracle Wikis Home website (http://wikis.sun.com/display/SRSS4dot2/Sun+Ray+Client+Boot+Process).

For the GUI configuration, refer to "How to Set DTU Configuration Parameters" on the Oracle Home website (http://wikis.sun.com/display/SRSS4dot2/How+to+Set+DTU+Configuration+Parameters+%28Pop-up+GUI%29).

In this topology, Sun Ray is configured with an IPv6 address of 2001:db8:cafe:1::1. After the Solaris server is configured to connect with the client over IPv6, the server downloads its firmware and the mapping of the virtual machine. After the connectivity is enabled over IPv6, the administrator can use the Sun Ray Administration GUI to validate the IPv6 address, firmware version, and connectivity. Example 7-22 shows the logging output for the Sun Ray connection session.

Example 7-22 *Logging Output for Sun Ray Connection*

```
Jul 18 17:15:56 GSBU-TME-SOLARIS utauthd: [ID 715959 user.info]
Worker0 NOTICE: CLAIMED by StartSession.m5 NAME: pseudo.00144fad725b
PARAMETERS: {stealProtected=true,
terminalIPA=2001:db8:cafe:1:0:0:0:2, type=pseudo,

 fw=GUI4.2_77_2009.10.19.17.01,Boot:2.0; 2007.08.17-17:32:09-PDT,
state=disconnected, cause=insert, doamgh=true, barrierLevel=420,
lockaction=disconnect, rawId=00144fad725b,
terminalCID=IEEE802.00144fad725b, MTU=1500, tokenSeq=1,
firstServer=20010db8cafe0001-01, namespace=IEEE802,

keyTypes=dsa-sha1-x1,dsa-sha1, ddcconfig=1,
clientRand=ZfbRy4BLiO8ZAE2SEu5gXV6okILcQvtx/pJxHPKREUi,
id=00144fad725b, realIP=20010db8cafe0001-02,
startRes=1280x1024:1280x1024, useReal=true, event=insert,
sn=00144fad725b, rawType=pseudo, hw=SunRayP8-270, initState=1,
usersession=false, _=1}
```

Server Virtualization

Server virtualization is a mainstream method for moving bare-metal server operating systems into virtual machines. VMware vSphere, Citrix XenServer, and Microsoft Hyper-V are the leading server virtualization infrastructure products on the market. As it relates to IPv6, there are two critical areas of these server virtualization platforms that need to support IPv6: the hypervisor OS and the management tools.

As of this writing, the server virtualization platform with the most robust IPv6 support is VMware vSphere 4.1 with ESX/ESXi Hypervisor. Most of the VMware vSphere 4.1 components such as the hypervisor OS (ESX/ESXi) and vCenter support IPv6. Chapter 12, "Walk Before Running: Building an IPv6 Lab and Starting a Pilot," shows an example of how to enable IPv6 on these components.

Summary

In this chapter, you learned about the design and implementation techniques of deploying IPv6 in a virtualized network. You learned how to interconnect IPv6 networks across an MPLS backbone using 6PE and 6VPE technology. You learned about services virtualization, its benefits, and how to design, configure, and verify multicontext IPv6 firewalls on the Cisco ASA 5580. You also learned about desktop and server IPv6 virtualization techniques.

Additional References

Cisco. Deploying Secure Multi-Tenancy into Virtualized Data Centers:
http://www.cisco.com/en/US/partner/docs/solutions/Enterprise/Data_Center/
Virtualization/securecldeployg.html.

Cisco. Implementing IPv6 over MPLS:
http://www.ciscosystems.ch/en/US/docs/ios/ipv6/configuration/guide/
ip6-over_mpls_ps6922_TSD_Products_Configuration_Guide_Chapter.html.

Cisco. Network Considerations to Optimize Virtual Desktop Deployment:
http://www.cisco.com/en/US/prod/collateral/switches/ps5718/ps4324/
white_paper_c11-531553_ns725_Networking_Solutions_White_Paper.html.

Durand, A., P. Fasano, and D. Lento. RFC 3053, "IPv6 Tunnel Broker." http://
www.rfc-editor.org/rfc/rfc3053.txt.

Carpenter, B. and K. Moore. RFC 3056, "Connection of IPv6 Domains via IPv4 Clouds."
http://www.rfc-editor.org/rfc/rfc3056.txt.

Vixie, P. and D. Wessels. RFC 2756, "Hyper Text Caching Protocol (HTCP/0.0)."
http://www.rfc-editor.org/rfc/rfc2756.txt.

Gillgan, R. and E. Nordmark. RFC 2893, "Transition Mechanisms for IPv6 Hosts and
Routers." http://www.rfc-editor.org/rfc/rfc2893.txt.

Handley, M., D. Thaler, and R. Kermode. RFC 2776, "Multicast-Scope Zone
Announcement Protocol (MZAP)." http://www.rfc-editor.org/rfc/rfc2776.txt.

Nordmack, E. and R. Gilligan. RFC 4213, "Basic Transition Mechanisms for IPv6 Hosts
and Routers." http://www.rfc-editor.org/rfc/rfc4213.txt.

De Clercq, J., D. Ooms, M. Carugi, and F. Le Faucheur. RFC 4659, "BGP-MPLS IP Virtual
Private Network (VPN) Extension for IPv6 VPN." http://www.rfc-editor.org/rfc/rfc4659.txt.

Templin, F., T. Gleeson, and D. Thaler. RFC 5214, "Intra-Site Automatic Tunnel
Addressing Protocol (ISATAP)." http://www.rfc-editor.org/rfc/rfc5214.txt.

Durand, A., P. Fasano, I. Guardini, and D. Lento. RFC 3053, "IPv6 Tunnel Broker."
http://www.rfc-editor.org/rfc/rfc3053.txt.

Chapter 8

Deploying IPv6 in WAN/Branch Networks

This chapter covers the following subjects:

WAN/branch deployment overview: This section describes the single-tier, dual-tier, and multitier branch deployment models.

General WAN/branch IPv6 deployment considerations: Details on generic IPv6 considerations that apply to any of the WAN/branch deployment models are presented.

WAN/branch implementation example: Detailed configuration information is provided for a WAN/branch design that combines elements of the single-tier, dual-tier, and multitier profiles.

WAN/branch deployment over native IPv6: Configuration details are shown for branch-to-WAN head-end deployments, where the Internet Protocol used between sites is IPv6 instead of IPv6-over-IPv4 shown in other examples.

This chapter focuses on providing you with various options for connecting branch offices to the regional or headquarters site using IPv6. As has been discussed in other chapters, there are times when IPv6 needs to be encapsulated into IPv4 to traverse the WAN transport. This happens most often because of the lack of native IPv6 support by the WAN provider and not by lacking features or capabilities of the networking gear. There are a wide variety of deployment options in WAN/branch scenarios that can provide you with a way to provide IPv6 connectivity to branch users and access applications and services located at the main site and beyond.

Native IPv6 deployment is also discussed in this chapter. When port-to-port IPv6 access is available by the WAN service provider, the dependency for encapsulating IPv6 into IPv4 IPsec or SSL is no longer present. IPv6 over IPsec can be deployed today between Cisco IOS branch routers and the WAN head-end routers.

WAN/Branch Deployment Overview

The following sections provide a high-level overview of the three most commonly deployed Cisco branch profiles and the associated WAN head-end. These sections provide a basic understanding of how IPv6 can be integrated into the following branch profiles:

- Single-tier profile

- Dual-tier profile

- Multitier profile

Single-Tier Profile

The single-tier branch profile is a fully integrated design and based on the Cisco Dynamic Multipoint Virtual Private Network (DMVPN) solution. The requirements for LAN and WAN connectivity and security are met by a single Integrated Services Router (ISR). More information about the Cisco ISR platform can be found in the references section of this chapter. Figure 8-1 shows a high-level view of the single-tier branch profile.

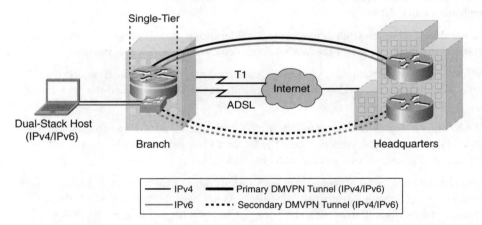

Figure 8-1   *Single-Tier Profile Overview*

The single-tier uses a single ISR and is used to provide WAN connectivity through a T1/E1 line to an Internet service provider (ISP). This T1/E1 is used as the primary link to the headquarters (HQ) site. For WAN redundancy, a backup connection is made through asymmetric digital subscriber line (ADSL). There are many alternatives that can be used in this design, such as a different WAN media type and VPN type.

IPv4 and IPv6 connectivity to the HQ site is provided by IPv4 IPsec using DMVPN technologies (DMVPN supports both IPv4 and IPv6-over-IPv4 IPsec). DMVPN works by encapsulating both IPv4 and IPv6 traffic into a generic routing encapsulation (GRE) tunnel, encrypted by IPv4 IPsec and forwarded between sites. The DMVPN tunnels traverse the T1 link as the primary path and establish backup tunnels over the ADSL link.

All traffic leaving the branch traverses the VPN connections to the HQ, including the Internet-bound traffic. Generally, Cisco does not recommend the use of split tunneling at the branch site. If the customer requires split tunneling (that is, Internet traffic leaves the branch directly while corporate-bound traffic traverses the VPN connection), Cisco recommends a careful analysis and testing of the routing and the security implications of such a deployment.

LAN connectivity is provided by an integrated switch module (EtherSwitch Service Module). Dual-stack (running both an IPv4 TCP/IP stack and IPv6 TCP/IP stack) is used on the VLAN interfaces at the branch.

In addition to all the security policies in place at the HQ, local security for both IPv4 and IPv6 is provided by a common set of infrastructure security features and configurations. Additionally, an integrated firewall such as the Cisco IOS Firewall or the Cisco IOS Zone-based Firewall is used. Quality of service (QoS) for IPv4 and IPv6 is integrated into a single policy.

The obvious disadvantage of the single-tier profile is the lack of router and switch redundancy. There is redundancy for the link to the Internet and the VPN connections to HQ. However, because there is a single integrated switch and single router, if either component fails, the site is completely disconnected from HQ. The dual-tier or multitier profile is the solution for customers requiring additional redundancy for the network components (switches, routers, firewalls, and HQ connections).

Dual-Tier Profile

The dual-tier profile separates the routing and switching roles in the branch and provides device and link redundancy for the branch routers.

Figure 8-2 shows a high-level view of the dual-tier profile.

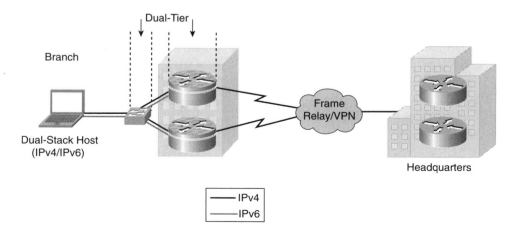

Figure 8-2 *Dual-Tier Profile Overview*

There are three primary differences between the single-tier and dual-tier profile:

- Redundancy
- Scalability
- WAN transport

Redundancy

The dual-tier separates the LAN (switch) and WAN (router) components to offer fault tolerance. A single switch or multiple switches can be used to provide LAN access in the branch. There are two WAN routers redundantly connected to the Frame Relay cloud (or other WAN/VPN type), in addition to being redundantly connected to the LAN switch.

Scalability

The dual-tier scales better because the single-tier is pretty much an "everything but the kitchen sink" approach. In other words, every network role required in the branch is performed by the ISR. This is great for cost and manageability but can limit availability and scalability. The larger the branch and the more services enabled on the ISR, the higher the risk gets for overextending the performance capabilities of the ISR. This can be alleviated by using a more powerful ISR model, but this does not help with the fault-tolerance requirement. If additional LAN switches are needed at the branch, the Catalyst switches can be used together using the Cisco StackWise technology.

WAN Transport

The WAN connections in the dual-tier model can use Frame Relay, point-to-point IPsec VPN, DMVPN, Multiprotocol Label Switching (MPLS), or whatever WAN type is available. IPv6 is fully supported over Frame Relay in Cisco IOS, and therefore there is no need to run tunnels of any kind between the branch and HQ. This is a great advantage for deployment and management because dual-stack is used all the way from the hosts in the branch LAN across the WAN and into the HQ network. This greatly eases the operational aspects of deploying IPv6 in the branch because no special tunnel considerations (such as availability, security, QoS, and multicast) need to be made.

Security for the dual-tier profile is the same as for the single-tier with the exception that both routers in the dual-tier provide security services.

Multitier Profile

The goal of the multitier profile is complete separation of roles and to offer device and link redundancy at each tier or layer in the branch network. Basically, the multitier is a combination of the single-tier and dual-tier with an additional focus on availability, scalability, and more robust firewall services. The multitier, for the most part, looks like a small campus deployment, and both very often use the same or similar products, design concepts, and configurations. The differences between a small campus and the multitier are more around the presence of the firewall and WAN routers in the multitier example.

Figure 8-3 shows a high-level view of the multitier profile.

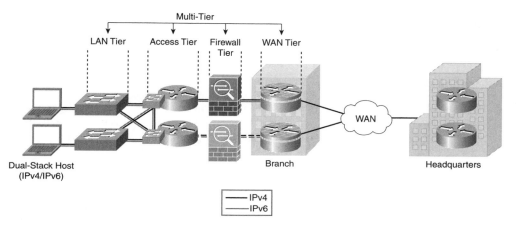

Figure 8-3   *Multitier Profile Overview*

Figure 8-3 shows how the tiers or roles are distributed. Several changes are evident with the multitier versus the dual-tier:

- **Firewall tier:** Firewall services are now separated from the WAN routers. The Cisco ASA 5500 series is shown here and is providing stateful firewall services for both IPv4 and IPv6. The second ASA (the bottom ASA in Figure 8-3) is in stateful failover mode. In a stateful failover configuration, the ASA is operating in an active/standby (shown in Figure 8-3) or active/active mode.

- **Access tier:** The access tier is used for internal service and VLAN termination for the LAN tier. The access tier is like a campus distribution layer in many ways.

- **LAN tier:** The LAN tier is the same as with the dual-tier LAN switch. There are just more of them to account for the larger-scale requirements that are most likely found in a larger branch.

General WAN/Branch IPv6 Deployment Considerations

Some general considerations apply to the deployment profiles described in this chapter. The following sections describe the general considerations to take into account when deploying IPv6 in a branch network, regardless of the deployment profile being used. If a specific consideration should be understood, the specific profile is called out, along with the consideration for that profile.

The branch IPv6 profiles described in this chapter leverage the existing Cisco branch network design best practices as the foundation for all aspects of the deployment. The IPv6 components of the profiles are deployed in the same way as IPv4 whenever possible.

It is critical to understand the Cisco branch design best practice recommendations before deploying IPv6 in the branch profiles described in this chapter. The Cisco branch design best practice documents can be found under the "Branch Office" and "WAN" sections at http://www.cisco.com/en/US/netsol/ns816/networking_solutions_program_home.html.

Addressing

In most cases, the use of a /64 prefix on point-to-point (P2P) links is just fine. IPv6 was designed to have a large address space, and even with the poor address management in place, the customer should not experience address constraints.

Some network administrators think that a /64 prefix for P2P links is a waste of address space. There has been quite a bit of discussion within the IPv6 community about the practice of using longer prefixes for P2P links. For those network administrators who want to more tightly control the address space, it is safe to use a /126 prefix on P2P links in much the same way as /30 is used with IPv4. A /127 prefix can be used if you are aware of the potential address overlap with special use addresses. IPv6 address considerations can be found in RFC 5375 at http://www.ietf.org/rfc/rfc5375.txt.

The P2P configurations shown in this chapter use a /64 prefix. The assignment of end-host IPv6 addresses is done either by using Stateless Address Autoconfiguration (SLAAC) (see RFC 4862, "IPv6 Stateless Address Autoconfiguration"), which advertises an IPv6 prefix (through an RA) on the router subinterface for the VLAN where PCs are located, or through stateful DHCPv6. The options for Domain Name System (DNS) server and domain name are assigned using stateless DHCPv6 or stateful DHCPv6. The configurations for the SLAAC, stateless, and stateful DHCPv6 will be shown later in the chapter.

More information can be found on IPv6 addressing services at the following URL: http://www.cisco.com/en/US/docs/ios/ipv6/configuration/guide/15_0/ipv6_15_0_book .html.

Physical Connectivity

Considerations for physical connectivity with IPv6 are the same as with IPv4, plus five additional elements:

- **Sufficient bandwidth:** One important factor for deployment of any new technology, protocol, or application is to ensure that there is a sufficient amount of bandwidth for both existing and new traffic. This issue is especially true with the branch because, in many cases, the connections to the WAN are low-speed links and the reliance on QoS to solve bandwidth problems goes only so far. Bandwidth requirements for IPv6 are outside the scope of this chapter because there are many variables to account for and should therefore be considered on a case-by-case basis.

- **Maximum transmission unit (MTU) and fragmentation:** The minimum MTU size for IPv6 is 1280 bytes. If the link layer does not support the MTU requirement, link-layer fragmentation and reassembly must be provided and be transparent to IPv6. A good starting point for understanding MTU and Path MTU Discovery (PMTUD) for IPv6 is with RFC 2460 (http://www.ietf.org/rfc/rfc2460.txt) and RFC 1981 (http://www.ietf.org/rfc/rfc1981.txt).

- **IPsec VPN:** When IPsec is used with GRE or manual tunnels, it is important to account for how to adjust the MTU value on the routers to ensure that the router is not forced to perform fragmentation of the IPv4 traffic because of the IPsec header and the additional tunnel overhead. By manually configuring the MTU values prior to IPv6 encapsulation, the MTU requirements can be met for IPv6 without fragmentation concerns. More information on this can be found in any of the IPsec design guides at http://www.cisco.com/en/US/tech/tk583/tk372/tech_design_guides_list.html.

- **IPv6 over wireless LANs (WLAN):** IPv6 should operate correctly over WLAN access points in much the same way as IPv6 operates over Layer 2 switches. However, there are considerations to IPv6 with WLAN environments such as managing WLAN devices (APs and controllers) through IPv6 and controlling IPv6 traffic through AP or controller-based QoS, VLANs, and access control lists (ACL). IPv6 must be supported on the AP and controller devices to take advantage of these more intelligent services on the WLAN devices. At the time of writing this chapter, Cisco does not yet have robust IPv6 support on its WLAN product family.

- **IPv6 phone ports:** It is important to point out that Cisco supports the use of IPv6-enabled hosts that are directly attached to Cisco IP Phone ports. These IP phone ports are switch ports and operate in much the same way as plugging the host directly into a Catalyst Layer 2 switch.

In addition to the previous considerations, Cisco recommends that a thorough analysis of the existing traffic profiles, memory use, and CPU use on both the hosts and network equipment, and the service level agreement (SLA) language, be completed prior to implementing any of the IPv6 models described in this chapter.

VLANs

VLAN considerations for IPv6 are mostly the same as for IPv4. When dual-stack configurations are used, both IPv4 and IPv6 traverse the same VLAN. For the current VLAN design recommendations, refer to the Cisco branch–LAN design best practice documents at http://www.cisco.com/en/US/docs/solutions/Enterprise/Branch/Overview.html.

The use of IPv6 on data VLANs that are trunked along with voice VLANs (behind IP phones) is fully supported. Care must be taken to ensure that the correct firmware and proper Cisco Unified Communications Manager configurations are made to ensure that the data and voice VLANs do not allow IPv6 router advertisements (multicast-based) to be bled between VLANs.

For more information on IPv6 and Cisco IP Phones and how to best support VLANs for those endpoints, refer to the section "Unified Communications Endpoints" at http://www.cisco.com/en/US/docs/voice_ip_comm/cucm/srnd/ipv6/ipv6srnd.html. For information on how to deploy IPv6 on the Cisco Unified Communications Manager, refer to http://www.cisco.com/en/US/docs/voice_ip_comm/cucm/srnd/ipv6/ipv6srnd.html.

Routing

Choosing an interior gateway protocol (IGP) to run in the branch network is based on a variety of factors: Platform capabilities, IT staff expertise, and the size of network are just a few. In this chapter, the IGP for both IPv4 and IPv6 is Enhanced IGRP (EIGRP). Open Path Shortest First version 2 (OSPFv2) for IPv4 and OSPFv3 for IPv6 can also be used.

As previously mentioned, every effort to implement the current Cisco branch design best practices has been made. Both the IPv4 and IPv6 IGPs have been tuned according to the current best practices for the branch. It should be one of the top priorities of any network design to ensure that the IGPs are tuned to provide a stable, scalable, and fast-converging routing protocol.

EIGRP has been configured to provide authentication for both IPv4 and IPv6 adjacencies and updates.

High Availability

Many aspects of High Availability (HA) are not applicable to or are outside the scope of this chapter. Many of the HA requirements and recommendations are met by leveraging the existing Cisco branch design best practices. The primary HA components described in this chapter are

- **Redundant WAN connections:** The deployment of redundant WAN links can vary greatly from customer to customer. Some customers deploy a T1 with a backup connection over a different connection, such as a broadband DSL connection. Redundant Frame Relay connections and/or MPLS connections are also quite common.

- **Redundant routing and forwarding paths:** This is accomplished by leveraging EIGRP for IPv4 and IPv6. In some cases, Equal Cost Multi-Path (ECMP) is used, and in other cases (IPsec GRE and manual tunnels), one path is preferred over another, but the secondary path is available for redundancy.

- **High availability of the first-hop gateways:** This level of HA applies to any branch and/or WAN head-end connection where there are two or more routers. HSRPv2 for IPv4 and IPv6 can provide first-hop gateway redundancy in this chapter. Cisco also supports gateway load balancing protocol (GLBP) for IPv4 and IPv6.

QoS

Cisco recommends that QoS policies be implemented in an application- or service-dependent methodology instead of a protocol- (IPv4 or IPv6) dependent methodology. Basically, if the existing QoS policy has specific classification, policing, and queuing for an application, that policy should treat the IPv4 and IPv6 traffic for that application equally.

The key consideration as far as Modular QoS CLI (MQC) is concerned is the removal of the **ip** keyword in the QoS **match** and **set** statements when IPv6 QoS is required.

Table 8-1 shows the modification in the QoS syntax to support IPv6 and IPv4.

There are QoS features that work for both IPv6 and IPv4 but require no modification to the command-line interface (CLI), for example, Weighted Random Early Detection (WRED), policing, and Weighted Round Robin (WRR).

Cisco provides an extensive collection of QoS recommendations for the WAN/branch. See the references section at the end of this chapter for a complete list.

Table 8-1 *QoS Syntax Modifications*

IPv4-Only QoS Syntax	IPv4/IPv6 QoS Syntax
match ip dscp	match dscp
match ip precedence	match precedence
set ip dscp	set dscp
set ip precedence	set precedence

Security

Many of the common threats and attacks on existing IPv4 campus networks also apply to IPv6. Unauthorized access, spoofing, routing attacks, viruses, worms, denial of service (DoS), and man-in-the-middle attacks are just a few that plague both IPv4 and IPv6.

There are many new threats with IPv6 that do not exist with IPv4 or they operate differently from IPv4. There are inherent differences in how IPv6 handles neighbor and router advertisement and discovery, headers, and even fragmentation. Based on all of these variables and possibilities, IPv6 security is an involved topic in general, and detailed security recommendations and configurations are outside the scope of this chapter. There are numerous efforts both within Cisco and the industry to identify, understand, and resolve IPv6 security threats. There is an excellent Cisco Press book dedicated to the topic of IPv6 security: *IPv6 Security*, by Scott Hogg and Eric Vyncke. (See the "Additional References" section at the end of this chapter for more information.)

This chapter points out some possible areas to address within the branch and gives basic examples of how to provide basic protection of IPv6 dual-stack and tunneled traffic.

> **Note** The examples given in this chapter are in no way meant to be recommendations or guidelines, but rather are intended to challenge you to carefully analyze your own security policies as they apply to IPv6 in the branch/WAN.

General security considerations for network device protection that apply to branch profiles are as follows:

■ **Controlling management access to the branch routers and switches:** All the branch/WAN routers and switches for each profile have configurations in place to provide management access protection to the devices. All routers have loopback interfaces configured for management and routing purposes.

To more tightly restrict access to a particular switch/router through IPv6, an ACL is used to permit access to the management interface (line vty) by way of the loopback interface. The permitted source network is from the enterprise IPv6 prefix. To make ACL generation more scalable for a wide range of network devices, the ACL definition can permit the entire enterprise prefix as the primary method for controlling management access to the device instead of filtering to a specific interface on the device. The IPv6 prefix used in this enterprise site (for example only) is 2001:db8:cafe::/48. See Example 8-1.

Example 8-1 *Router VTY Configuration*

```
interface Loopback0
 ipv6 address 2001:DB8:CAFE:1F3::9/128
!
ipv6 access-list MGMT-IN
remark Permit MGMT only to Loopback0
permit tcp 2001:DB8:CAFE::/48 host 2001:DB8:CAFE:1F3::9
deny ipv6 any any log-input
!
line vty 0 4
session-timeout 3
access-class MGMT-IN-v4 in
password 7 08334D400E1C17
ipv6 access-class MGMT-IN in          #Apply IPv6 ACL to restrict
                                      #access
logging synchronous
login local
exec prompt timestamp
transport input ssh
```

■ **Controlling access through HTTP:** At the time of this writing, Cisco IOS does not support the use of IPv6 HTTP ACLs to control access to the device. This is important because switches and routers that currently use **ip http access-class** ACLs for

IPv4 do not have the same level of protection for IPv6. This means that subnets or users who were previously denied access through HTTP/HTTPS for IPv4 now have access to the switch or router through IPv6.

- **Control Plane Policing (CoPP):** CoPP protects the router by preventing DoS or unnecessary traffic from negatively impacting CPU resources. Priority is given to important control plane/management traffic. The configuration of CoPP is based on a wide variety of factors, and no single deployment recommendation can be made because the specifics of the policy are determined on a case-by-case basis. You can find more information about CoPP at http://www.cisco.com/en/US/docs/ios/12_3t/12_3t4/feature/guide/gtrtlimt.html.

- **Controlling ingress traffic from the branch LAN:** Filter which prefixes are allowed to source traffic. This is most commonly done on ingress on the LAN or subinterface on the branch router. Controlling IPv6 traffic based on source prefix can help protect the network against basic spoofing.

Example 8-2 shows a basic ACL example: applied ingress on a branch router's LAN interface.

Example 8-2   *Basic Branch LAN Ingress ACL*

```
ipv6 access-list DATA_LAN-v6
remark PERMIT ICMPv6 PACKETS FROM HOSTS WITH PREFIX 2001:DB8:CAFE:1004::/64
permit icmp 2001:DB8:CAFE:1004::/64 any
remark PERMIT IPv6 PACKETS FROM HOSTS WITH PREFIX 2001:DB8:CAFE:1004::64
permit ipv6 2001:DB8:CAFE:1004::/64 any
remark PERMIT ICMPv6 PACKETS SOURCED BY HOSTS USING LINK-LOCAL
permit icmp FE80::/10 any
remark PERMIT DHCPv6 ALL-DHCP-AGENTS REQUESTS FROM HOSTS
permit udp any eq 546 any eq 547
remark DENY ALL OTHER IPv6 PACKETS AND LOG
deny ipv6 any any log-input
!
interface GigabitEthernet0/0.104
 description VLAN-PC
 ipv6 traffic-filter DATA_LAN-v6 in
```

Cisco IOS IPv6 ACLs contain implicit permit entries for IPv6 neighbor discovery. If **deny ipv6 any any** is configured, the implicit neighbor discovery entries are overridden. It is important that if a manually configured catch-all **deny** statement is used for logging purposes, the following two permit entries must be added back in: **permit icmp any any nd-na** and **permit icmp any any nd-ns**.

- **IPv6 stateful firewall services:** Firewalls provide a stateful security inspection for IPv6 traffic entering or leaving a branch network. At the time of this writing, the Cisco ASA 5500 Series, Cisco IOS Firewall, and Cisco IOS Zone-based Firewall support IPv6 inspection at various levels. It is critical that you consult with Cisco documentation, a Cisco account team, and/or a Cisco partner to understand which Cisco Firewall solution is appropriate for the customer environment.

■ **Disabling unused services:** Many services, such as HTTP server, are supported for IPv4 and IPv6. Enabling or disabling these services generally applies to both protocols. It is a long-standing recommendation to disable any services that are not in use.

Multicast

IPv6 multicast is an important service for any enterprise network design. One of the most important factors to IPv6 multicast deployment is to ensure that host/group control is handled properly in the branch LAN. Multicast Listener Discovery (MLD) in IPv6 is the equivalent to Internet Group Management Protocol (IGMP) in IPv4. Both are used for host multicast group membership control. MLD snooping is the ability to control the distribution of multicast traffic only to the ports that have listeners. Without it, multicast traffic meant for only a single receiver (or group of receivers) would be flooded to all ports on the branch LAN switch belonging to the same VLAN. In the branch LAN, it is important that the switches support MLD snooping for MLD version 1 and/or version 2.

Today, Cisco IOS supports the following Protocol Independent Multicast (PIM) implementations: PIM-SM, PIM-BSR, PIM-SSM, Bidirectional PIM, Embedded-RP, and Multiprotocol BGP for the IPv6 Multicast Address Family.

There are several documents on Cisco.com and within the industry that describe IPv6 multicast in detail. Other than generic references to the commands that are used to enable IPv6 multicast and requirements for Embedded-RP definition, no other configuration notes are made in this chapter. For more information, refer to the following URLs:

■ **Cisco IPv6 multicast:**
http://www.cisco.com/en/US/technologies/tk648/tk828/tk363/technologies_white_
paper0900aecd8014d6dd.html

■ **Cisco IOS IPv6 multicast configuration:**
http://www.cisco.com/en/US/tech/tk828/technologies_white_paper09186a0080203
f7a.shtml

Management

Management for IPv6 is under development and has a long way to go. Many of the traditional management tools used in IPv4 also support IPv6. In this chapter, the only considerations for management of the branch network are related to basic control of management services (Telnet, SSH, and SNMP). All the IPv6-enabled devices in the two branch profiles described are manageable over IPv6 through the previously mentioned services except SNMP.

The deployment of Simple Network Management Protocol (SNMP) for IPv6 is the same as with IPv4. In the branch profiles described in this chapter, SNMPv3 (AuthNoPriv) can provide polling capabilities for the Cisco Network Management Systems (NMS) servers located in the HQ data center. Here is an example of the SNMPv3 configuration used in the branch routers in this chapter:

```
snmp-server contact John Doe - ipv6rocks@example.com
snmp-server group IPv6-ADMIN v3 auth write v1default
snmp-server user jdoe IPv6-ADMIN v3 auth md5 cisco1234
```

If information needs to be sent to a Cisco NMS server, an SNMP host can be defined. The host can be defined to send SNMP information over IPv4 and/or IPv6:

```
snmp-server host 2001:DB8:CAFE:100::60 version 3 auth jdoe
```

Another area of management that must be thoroughly researched is that of address management. The process of assigning large hexadecimal addresses to many network devices should, at some point, be automated or at least made more user-friendly than it is today.

Today, one way to help with the deployment of address prefixes on a Cisco router is through the use of the general prefix feature. This feature enables the customer to define a prefix or prefixes in the global configuration of the router with a user-friendly name. That user-friendly name can be used on a per-interface basis to replace the usual IPv6 prefix definition on the interface. The general prefix feature is most applicable in deployments where there is or can be frequent changes in the address prefix, such as during a pilot or in early production when the final IPv6 address policy is not fully nailed down. The following is an example of how to use the general prefix feature:

Step 1.   Define the general prefix:

br1-1(config)# **ipv6 general-prefix BRANCH-1 2001:DB8:CAFE::/48**

Step 2.   Configure the general prefix named BRANCH-1 on a per-interface basis:

br1-1(config-if)# **ipv6 address BRANCH-1 ::1005:0:0:0:1/64**

Step 3.   Verify that the general prefix was correctly assigned to the interface:

```
br1-1# show ipv6 interface g1/0.100
GigabitEthernet1/0.100 is up, line protocol is up
  IPv6 is enabled, link-local address is FE80::217:94FF:FE90:2829
  No Virtual link-local address(es):
  Description: DATA VLAN for Computers
  Global unicast address(es):
   2001:DB8:CAFE:1005::1, subnet is 2001:DB8:CAFE:1005::/64
```

You can find more information on the general prefix feature at the Cisco IOS IPv6 documentation page at http://www.cisco.com/en/US/docs/ios/ipv6/configuration/guide/ip6-addrg_bsc_con_ps10591_TSD_Products_Configuration_Guide_Chapter.html#wp1132473.

Cisco supports the management of IPv6-enabled network devices through a variety of network management products to include DNS, DHCPv6, device management and monitoring, and network management, troubleshooting, and reporting. You can find more

information on the various Cisco Network Management solutions at
http://www.cisco.com/en/US/products/sw/netmgtsw/index.html.

Chapter 11, "Managing IPv6 Networks," goes into greater detail on IPv6 management.

Scalability and Performance

This chapter is not meant to analyze scalability and performance information for the various platforms tested. The coverage of scale and performance is more focused on general considerations when planning and deploying IPv6 in the branch versus a platform-specific view.

Scalability and performance considerations for the branch network devices are as follows:

- **Traffic utilization:** In IPv6 implementations, it is common to see a change in traffic utilization ratios on the branch network links. As IPv6 is deployed, IPv4 traffic utilization is often reduced as users leverage IPv6 as the transport for applications that were historically IPv4-only. There is often a slight increase in overall network utilization, which usually derives from control traffic for routing and, if deployed, tunnel overhead.

- **Routing/forwarding:** It is important to understand the routing and forwarding capabilities of the branch routers. If the existing branch router is already running at high CPU and memory utilization rates for the handling of IPv4 routing tables and updates, it is a bad idea to add IPv6 to the existing router. If the routing platform is hardware based, the impact is less of a concern.

- **ACL processing:** It is imperative that the deployment of ACLs be carefully planned. IPv6 ACLs in the branch routers are used for QoS (classification and marking of ingress packets from the access layer), for security (controlling DoS, snooping, and unauthorized access for ingress traffic in the access layer), and for a combination of QoS + security to protect the control plane of the router from attack. The router can also provide Cisco IOS stateful firewalling services, intrusion detection systems/intrusion prevention systems (IDS/IPS), and voice services for IPv4 and new services for IPv6. Advanced services that are added to the branch router should support both IPv4 and IPv6. Performance will be impacted with all these added services plus the newly enabled IPv6 configuration.

Cisco has an IPv4/IPv6 performance comparison document that goes into some detail on these topics at http://www.cisco.com/web/strategy/docs/gov/IPv6perf_wp1f.pdf.

WAN/Branch Implementation Example

Much of the configuration and design among the three different WAN/branch deployment profiles is similar. The largest variables are usually the number of devices within a branch for high-availability purposes and the scale of the overall environment.

The implementation example given in this chapter combines properties from each of the three WAN/branch profiles so that you can get a basic understanding of the various tiers, network roles, and specific products and features when configured for IPv6 support.

Throughout the remainder of this chapter, the example topology is called the "hybrid branch example," or HBE. Again, this is just an example configuration that is meant to combine elements from each of the three WAN/branch profiles and is not meant to be a recommended best practice design.

Figure 8-4 shows the high-level overview of the HBE environment.

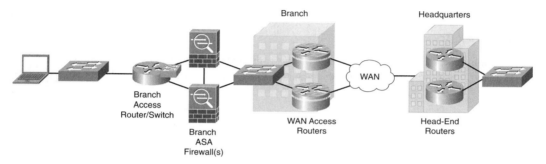

Figure 8-4   *Hybrid Branch Example Overview*

The HBE has the flexibility to run almost any WAN type to include Frame Relay, MPLS, point-to-point IPsec VPN, DMVPN, and so on. In this example, the branch has redundant WAN access routers that connect to the HQ through redundant head-end routers. Behind the WAN access routers in the branch there is a Cisco ASA 5500 series firewall. Optionally a redundant ASA can be added for additional availability. There is a Cisco ISR series router with either a built-in Cisco EtherSwitch Module or a separate Catalyst switch that can connect local host resources such as PCs, printers, and other network-attached resources.

Additional devices might be required to meet the business requirements for each branch, such as additional routers, switches, and other network devices that can augment the high-availability, security, or robust network services goals of the branch.

Note   The configurations shown are not full-device configurations but rather snippets of the full configuration and reveal only the most relevant portions of the IPv6 side of the deployment.

Tested Components

Table 8-2 lists the components that were used and tested in the hybrid branch example.

Table 8-2   *HBE-Tested Components*

Role	Hardware	Software
Router	Integrated Services Router: 2800 and 3800 Series	Advanced Enterprise Services 15.0.1M1
Switch	Cisco Catalyst 3750E/3560E	12.2(46)SE
Firewall	Cisco ASA 5510	8.2(2)
Host devices	Various laptops—PC	Microsoft Windows Vista, Windows 7

Network Topology

Figure 8-5 serves as a reference for all the configurations for the HBE. The figure shows the IPv6 addressing layout for the branch and HQ connections.

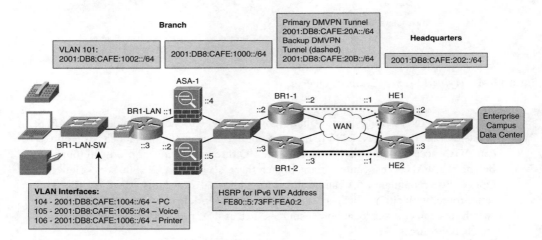

Figure 8-5   *HBE IPv6 Addressing Details*

The following sections discuss the physical and logical connectivity of the WAN access, branch LAN, and firewalls.

WAN Connectivity

The HBE uses the Dual DMVPN Cloud Topology with spoke-to-spoke support, as outlined in the Cisco DMVPN Design Guide at http://www.cisco.com/en/US/docs/solutions/Enterprise/WAN_and_MAN/DMVPDG.html.

The Dual DMVPN Cloud Topology has each branch site configured with a primary (solid lines between branch and HW) and secondary (dashed lines) DMVPN tunnel configuration. Each tunnel configuration is on a separate IPv4 and IPv6 network. The IGP is tuned to prefer one tunnel over another, and if the primary tunnel fails, the IGP reconverges and traffic flows between the branch routers and the secondary head-end router using the secondary tunnel configuration.

The HBE could easily use a traditional Frame Relay, MPLS, or point-to-point IPsec VPN as well. DMVPN was selected for this example to give the reader a usable configuration for Cisco DMVPN support with IPv6.

Being that this is just an example and that there are many variables that could influence how this network is connected and configured, a simplistic approach was taken for addressing and physical connectivity. The important thing to take away from the HBE shown here is that most things are the same as with IPv4. The goal is to illustrate the minor syntax adjustments.

Branch LAN Connectivity

The LAN connectivity between the WAN access routers and the Cisco ASA is through a Catalyst switch. Each router is configured as a Hot Standby Router Protocol (HSRP) group member for both IPv4 and IPv6. The Cisco ASA has a default route to the HSRP standby address.

The LAN access router and ASA connect to each other using the EtherSwitch Module in the router. Alternatively a dedicated Catalyst switch could be used.

The LAN access portion of the branch uses a Catalyst switch to provide network access for hosts, IP phones, and printers. There are three VLANs in use in the HBE that are used for host access:

- **VLAN 104:** Used as the PC data VLAN. IPv4 addressing is provided by a local DHCP pool on the router. IPv6 addressing is provided by the branch router using SLAAC, and DNS/domain name are provided by a local DHCP pool for IPv6. Optionally, full DHCP for IPv4 and IPv6 can be used at the HQ site.

- **VLAN 105:** Used as the voice VLAN. IPv4 addressing is provided by a local DHCP pool on the router to include any voice-specific options (TFTP server). IPv6 addressing is provided by stateful DHCPv6. Optionally, stateless DHCP IPv6 can be used.

- **VLAN 106:** Used as the printer VLAN. IPv4 addressing is provided by a local DHCP pool on the router. The print server cards located in the branch automatically receive an IPv6 address from the router interface through stateless autoconfiguration. Optionally, full DHCP for IPv4 and IPv6 can be used at the HQ site.

Firewall Connectivity

Depending on the branch design and the security policy, a dedicated firewall might or might not be deployed. Some sites deploy a firewall at the branch if local Internet access for that branch is permitted (split-tunneling scenario) or if the firewall itself is used as the branch VPN device. Also, firewall support on the WAN access routers can be enabled to offer perimeter protection instead of using a dedicated ASA.

In the HBE, the Cisco ASA Firewall is used and configured in a basic way. There is an "outside" interface and an "inside" interface. The Cisco ASA can be deployed as a single standalone firewall with no redundancy, or the ASA can be configured in a stateful failover deployment, where a second ASA is deployed and used as standby unit (as shown earlier in Figure 8-4).

The Cisco ASA can be deployed in a *routed mode* or a *transparent mode* (sometimes known as *bridge mode*). Routed mode is what is used in this chapter and is the most popular of the deployment choices. Routed mode, simply put, is where the ASA has distinct Layer 3 interfaces, each on a different IPv4 and IPv6 network, and acts as a routed hop in the network (static and dynamic routing is supported in this mode). Transparent mode has the ASA in a Layer 2 configuration where packets are bridged across and inspected; the ASA is basically a bump-in-the-wire. These are oversimplified explanations of the routed and transparent modes, and the reader should fully understand the differences of each and their pros/cons. More information on routed and transparent mode can be found at http://www.cisco.com/en/US/docs/security/asa/asa83/configuration/guide/fwmode.html.

Head-End Configuration

The HBE WAN configuration begins at that headquarters site, where there are two Cisco routers acting as head-end termination points for the Dual DMVPN Cloud Topology.

Note   Depending on the size/scale requirements, the platform and model of the router may vary. Work with a Cisco account team and/or Cisco partner to determine the most appropriate product to fill this role.

The two head-end routers (HE1 and HE2) have connections to the ISP through Fast Ethernet connections but could just as easily be T1/E1, DS3, and any other connection option. Fast Ethernet was the option selected to generate the configurations for this chapter.

DMVPN is the VPN technology that carries both IPv4 and IPv6. The DMVPN configuration used in this chapter uses Phase 3 of Cisco IOS support for DMVPN. The following three phases are defined for DMVPN:

- **Phase 1:** Hub-and-spoke capability only

- **Phase 2:** Initial spoke-to-spoke capability

- **Phase 3:** Support for IPv6 and enhancements for spoke-to-spoke to support larger-scale nonbroadcast multiaccess (NBMA) networks

More information on the theory, operation, and configuration of DMVPN for IPv6, Phase 3 enhancements, and next hop resolution protocol (NHRP) operation can be found at the following URLs:

- **Implementing DMVPN for IPv6:**
  http://www.cisco.com/en/US/docs/ios/ipv6/configuration/guide/ip6-dmvpn_ps10591_TSD_Products_Configuration_Guide_Chapter.html

- **Shortcut switching enhancements for NHRP:**
  http://www.cisco.com/en/US/docs/ios/ipaddr/configuration/guide/iad_nhrp_dmvpn.html#wp1072593

- **Configuring NHRP:**
  http://cisco.com/en/US/docs/ios/ipaddr/configuration/guide/iad_cfg_nhrp.html#wp1078234

You need to configure different features and values for the DMVPN configuration such as keys, hold times, and so on.

HE1 and HE2 have one tunnel configuration each. HE1 is the primary head-end, and because this a dual DMVPN cloud configuration, the tunnel used on HE1 is in a different IPv4 and IPv6 network than the tunnel used by HE2. One thing to note is that when IPv6 multicast is enabled on a router, Protocol Independent Multicast (PIM) uses tunnel numbers 0 and 1 to communicate with rendezvous points (RP) and tunnel sources. It is recommended to use tunnel numbers beginning at 2.

The configuration for HE1 is shown in Example 8-3. The configuration for HE2 is identical with the exception of different IPv4 and IPv6 addressing and route preference. The configuration for HE2 is not shown.

Example 8-3 *HE1 Configuration*

```
ipv6 unicast-routing
ipv6 cef
!
crypto isakmp policy 1       #Set ISAKMP Policy using pre-shared
                            #keys
 encr aes 256
 authentication pre-share
 group 2
!
crypto isakmp key CISCO address 0.0.0.0 0.0.0.0
crypto isakmp key CISCO address ipv6 ::/0  #Pre-share key for
                                          #any (::/0) peer
!
crypto ipsec transform-set HUB esp-aes 256 esp-sha-hmac
!
```

continues

Example 8-3 *HE1 Configuration   continued*

```
crypto ipsec profile HUB
 set transform-set HUB
!
interface Tunnel2                     #If deployed, PIMv6 uses
                                      #tunnel 0 and 1 by default
                                      #so it is recommended to start
                                      #at 2

 description DMVPN Tunnel 1
 ip address 10.126.1.1 255.255.255.0
 no ip redirects
 no ip unreachables
 no ip proxy-arp
 ipv6 address 2001:DB8:CAFE:20A::1/64
 ipv6 mtu 1416                        #Set MTU to account for
                                      #Tunnel/IPSec overhead
 ipv6 eigrp 10                        #Enable IPv6 EIGRP
 ipv6 hold-time eigrp 10 35
 no ipv6 next-hop-self eigrp 10
 no ipv6 split-horizon eigrp 10
 ipv6 nhrp authentication CISCO       #Set authentication string
                                       #for NHRP
 ipv6 nhrp map multicast dynamic      #Automatically add routers to
                                       #NHRP mappings
 ipv6 nhrp network-id 10              #Enables NHRP on interface
 ipv6 nhrp holdtime 600
 ipv6 nhrp redirect                   #Phase 3 NHRP redirect for
                                       #spoke-to-spoke

 tunnel source Serial1/0
tunnel mode gre multipoint            #Multipoint GRE to support
                                       #multiple end-points

tunnel key 10
tunnel protection ipsec profile HUB  #Apply IPSec profile
!
interface GigabitEthernet2/0          #LAN interface to HQ network
 description to HQ
 ip address 10.123.1.2 255.255.255.0
 ipv6 address 2001:DB8:CAFE:202::2/64
 ipv6 eigrp 10
 standby version 2
 standby 2 ipv6 autoconfig
 standby 2 priority 120
 standby 2 preempt delay minimum 30
 standby 2 authentication CISCO
 standby 2 track 2 decrement 90
```

```
!
interface FastEthernet0/0
 description to ISP
 ip address 172.16.1.1 255.255.255.252
!
ip route 0.0.0.0 0.0.0.0 172.16.1.2
!
ipv6 router eigrp 10                      #Enable EIGRP for IPv6
 no shutdown
```

Branch WAN Access Router Configuration

The branch routers have serial (T1/E1) connections to the ISP. Again, these connections can be broadband (DSL/cable/wireless), Ethernet, DS3, and so on. The branch WAN access routers have IPv4-only connectivity to the ISP and should have ACLs permitting access to/from the ISP for only the necessary ports/protocols required to establish DMVPN connectivity to the head-end routers. (This assumes that no split tunneling is allowed.) The IPv6 portion of the configuration is similar to that of the head-end, where the IPv6 configuration applies to the local branch Ethernet interface and the DMVPN tunnel interfaces.

Both branch WAN access routers (BR1-1 and BR1-2) are configured nearly identically. The differences are in the unique IPv4 and IPv6 addressing, routing preferences, and HSRP preferences. The configuration for BR1-1 is shown in Example 8-4 (only one of the two DMVPN tunnel configurations is shown).

Example 8-4 *BR1-1 Configuration*

```
ipv6 unicast-routing
ipv6 cef
!
crypto isakmp policy 1
 encr aes 256
 authentication pre-share
 group 2
!
crypto isakmp key CISCO address 0.0.0.0 0.0.0.0
crypto isakmp key CISCO address ipv6 ::/0
!
crypto ipsec transform-set SPOKE esp-aes 256 esp-sha-hmac
!
crypto ipsec profile SPOKE
 set transform-set SPOKE
!
interface Tunnel2
```

continues

Example 8-4   *BR1-1 Configuration   continued*

```
 description to HUB
  ip address 10.126.1.2 255.255.255.0
  no ip redirects
  no ip unreachables
  no ip proxy-arp
  ipv6 address 2001:DB8:CAFE:20A::2/64
  ipv6 mtu 1416
  ipv6 eigrp 10
  ipv6 hold-time eigrp 10 35
  no ipv6 next-hop-self eigrp 10
  no ipv6 split-horizon eigrp 10
  ipv6 nhrp authentication CISCO
  ipv6 nhrp map 2001:DB8:CAFE:20A::1/64 172.16.1.1
  ipv6 nhrp map multicast 172.16.1.1
  ipv6 nhrp network-id 10
  ipv6 nhrp holdtime 600
  ipv6 nhrp nhs 2001:DB8:CAFE:20A::1
  ipv6 nhrp shortcut
  tunnel source Serial1/0
  tunnel mode gre multipoint
  tunnel key 10
  tunnel protection ipsec profile SPOKE
interface Serial1/0
  description to ISP
  ip address 172.16.1.9 255.255.255.252
 !
interface GigabitEthernet2/0
  description to BRANCH LAN
  ip address 10.124.1.2 255.255.255.0
  negotiation auto
  ipv6 address 2001:DB8:CAFE:1000::2/64
  ipv6 eigrp 10
  standby version 2
  standby 1 ip 10.124.1.1
  standby 1 priority 120
  standby 1 preempt delay minimum 30
  standby 1 authentication CISCO
  standby 1 track 1 decrement 90
  standby 2 ipv6 autoconfig
  standby 2 priority 120
  standby 2 preempt delay minimum 30
  standby 2 authentication CISCO
  standby 2 track 2 decrement 90
 !
```

```
router eigrp 10
 network 10.0.0.0
!
ip route 0.0.0.0 0.0.0.0 172.16.1.10
!
ipv6 router eigrp 10
 no shutdown
```

Branch Firewall Configuration

As was previously mentioned, the Cisco ASA firewall deployment in the HBE is simple and meant only as a reference for you. Many customers avoid the cost and management of a branch firewall because they believe the branch is a trusted site connected to the HQ through a trusted private WAN or VPN link. Because of this, the customer often configures some ACLs on the WAN access router to protect against basic attacks. The common thinking is that because the branch is configured to not enable direct Internet access by branch users, no comprehensive firewall policies are required, and the cost and complexity of deploying a dedicated firewall (and redundant pair of them) are avoided.

This chapter is not meant to argue the values of having a dedicated branch firewall but rather offers a basic design and configuration example if you do plan to include a dedicated Cisco ASA Firewall as a part of your branch design.

The following configuration is for a Cisco ASA Firewall running version 8.2(2), and there are two firewalls for redundancy sake. The firewalls are configured for a routed mode deployment.

Because the application types and ACL options are so diverse from customer to customer, no comprehensive security policies are provided in this chapter. Rather, a basic ACL example is shown for reference.

Note   As was previously mentioned, only relevant portions of the IPv6 side of the configurations are shown. The Cisco ASA configurations shown in this section are not complete as they relate to including all the necessary configurations to fully deploy a product-quality firewall in the branch. You should not assume that the configurations are best practices for the Cisco ASA or for security in general.

The configuration example begins with defining an alias that associates an IPv6 prefix with a user-defined name; prefix 2001:DB8:CAFE:1003::/64 is known as "BR1-LAN." Another alias is created for associating a full IPv6 address with a user-defined name (in this case, a server located at the branch that is IPv6-enabled).

The "outside" and "inside" interfaces are defined with the security level, IPv4 addresses, and IPv6 addresses. The **standby** keyword defines the peer address of the redundant ASA Firewall.

An example object group is configured (this is not required) for RDP using TCP port 3389. This object group is used by the ACL, permitting any source from 2001:DB8:CAFE::/48 to the previously defined branch server (Br1-v6-Server) over RDP. The configured ACLs are applied inbound on the "outside" interface.

At the time of this writing, the Cisco ASA supports dynamic routing only for IPv4 IGPs. For IPv6, static routing must be used. The example shown has a route configured for the inside branch LAN networks as well as the network between the Cisco ASA and the EtherSwitch Module located in the BR1-LAN router. This route uses one of the aliases defined previously. A static default route is configured for the outside interface, and the next hop is defined as the HSRP virtual link-local address of both the branch WAN access routers.

Interface GigabitEthernet0/3 will be used as the failover interface, and this ASA (ASA-1) is configured to be the primary unit. On the failover interface, the administrator must choose between defining an IPv4 or IPv6 address; both are not supported. In this case, an IPv6 address was used for the failover interface IP address.

Finally, Secure Shell (SSH) is permitted on the "inside" interface from the prefix shown.

Note   Configurations for the Cisco ASA are shown through the command-line interface (CLI). Alternatively, the configurations can be deployed through the Cisco Adaptive Security Device Manager (ASDM) GUI.

Example 8-6   *ASA-1 Configuration*

```
name 2001:db8:cafe:1003:: BR1-LAN description VLAN on EtherSwitch
name 2001:db8:cafe:1004:9db8:3df1:814c:d3bc Br1-v6-Server
!
interface GigabitEthernet0/0
 description TO WAN
 nameif outside
 security-level 0
 ip address 10.124.1.4 255.255.255.0 standby 10.124.1.5
 ipv6 address 2001:db8:cafe:1000::4/64 standby 2001:db8:cafe:1000::5
!
interface GigabitEthernet0/1
 description TO BRANCH LAN
 nameif inside
 security-level 100
 ip address 10.124.3.1 255.255.255.0 standby 10.124.3.2
 ipv6 address 2001:db8:cafe:1002::1/64 standby 2001:db8:cafe:1002::2
!
interface GigabitEthernet0/3
 description LAN Failover Interface
```

```
!
object-group service RDP tcp
 description Microsoft RDP
 port-object eq 3389
!
ipv6 route inside BR1-LAN/64 2001:db8:cafe:1002::3
ipv6 route inside 2001:db8:cafe:1004::/64 2001:db8:cafe:1002::3
ipv6 route inside 2001:db8:cafe:1005::/64 2001:db8:cafe:1002::3
ipv6 route inside 2001:db8:cafe:1006::/64 2001:db8:cafe:1002::3

#Default route to HSRP address on WAN access routers
ipv6 route outside ::/0 fe80::5:73ff:fea0:2
ipv6 access-list v6-ALLOW permit icmp6 any any
ipv6 access-list v6-ALLOW permit tcp 2001:db8:cafe::/48 host Br1-v6-Server object-
group RDP
failover
failover lan unit primary
failover lan interface FO-LINK GigabitEthernet0/3
failover interface ip FO-LINK 2001:db8:cafe:1001::1/64 standby
2001:db8:cafe:1001::2
access-group v6-ALLOW in interface outside
ssh 2001:db8:cafe::/48 inside
```

Example 8-7 output shows the summary of the failover interface (G0/3) configuration.

Example 8-7 *ASA-1* show failover interface *Command Output*

```
asa-1# show failover interface
        interface FO-LINK GigabitEthernet0/3
                System IP Address: 2001:db8:cafe:1001::1/64
                My IP Address   : 2001:db8:cafe:1001::1
                Other IP Address : 2001:db8:cafe:1001::2
```

A general view of the failover state and configuration is shown in Example 8-8. The output shows that this ASA is the primary unit and is active. Interface information for both the "outside" and "inside" interfaces is shown. The information shows the IPv4 and IPv6 address information that is used on both interfaces for failover tracking.

Example 8-8 *ASA-1* show failover *Command Output*

```
asa-1# show failover
Failover On
Failover unit Primary
Failover LAN Interface: FO-LINK GigabitEthernet0/3 (up)
Unit Poll frequency 1 seconds, holdtime 15 seconds
```

continues

Example 8-8 *ASA-1 show failover Command Output   continued*

```
Interface Poll frequency 5 seconds, holdtime 25 seconds
Interface Policy 1
Monitored Interfaces 2 of 160 maximum
Version: Ours 8.2(2), Mate 8.2(2)
Last Failover at: 05:15:12 UTC Apr 12 2010
        This host: Primary - Active
                Active time: 48 (sec)
                slot 0: ASA5520 hw/sw rev (2.0/8.2(2)) status (Up Sys)
                   Interface outside (10.124.1.4/fe80::21e:7aff:fe81:8e2c): Normal
                   Interface inside (10.124.3.1/fe80::21e:7aff:fe81:8e2d): Normal
                slot 1: ASA-SSM-4GE hw/sw rev (1.0/1.0(0)10) status (Up)
        Other host: Secondary - Standby Ready
                Active time: 261 (sec)
                slot 0: ASA5520 hw/sw rev (2.0/8.2(2)) status (Up Sys)
                   Interface outside (10.124.1.5/fe80::21d:a2ff:fe59:5fe4): Normal
                   Interface inside (10.124.3.2/fe80::21d:a2ff:fe59:5fe5): Normal
                slot 1: ASA-SSM-4GE hw/sw rev (1.0/1.0(0)10)
status (Up)
```

The output in Example 8-9 shows the connection state of the firewall. There is a TCP connection between a host on the outside and a host on the inside over TCP port 23 (Telnet).

Example 8-9 *Connection State of the Firewall*

```
asa-1# show conn
6 in use, 13 most used
TCP outside 2001:db8:cafe:1000::2:23 inside
2001:db8:cafe:1004:c53c:2d6a:ccef:f2c5:1044, idle 0:02:49, bytes 115, flags UIO
```

EtherSwitch Module Configuration

The EtherSwitch Module is an optional component and can be replaced with a traditional Catalyst switch. It is shown in this chapter to give you a view of the configuration that is almost identical to that of a Catalyst 3560/3750 switch. The EtherSwitch Module used in this example is an NME-16ES-1G.

In the HBE, the EtherSwitch Module connects the branch LAN access router and the two ASA firewalls. Before enabling IPv6 features and functionality on the EtherSwitch Module, the Switch Database Management (SDM) template needs to be configured to support both IPv4 and IPv6. The three SDM templates that support IPv4 and IPv6 are

- Dual IPv4 and IPv6 default template

- Dual IPv4 and IPv6 routing template

- Dual IPv4 and IPv6 VLAN template

The dual IPv4 and IPv6 SDM template configuration is defined from the global configuration mode as follows:

```
BR1-EtherSwitch(config)#sdm prefer dual-ipv4-and-ipv6 {default | routing | vlan}
```

The device needs to be rebooted for the changes to take effect. After the EtherSwitch Module has rebooted, the **show sdm prefer** command (shown in Example 8-10) can verify that the correct SDM template is in use.

Example 8-10   *EtherSwitch Module* **show sdm prefer** *Command Output*

```
BR1-EtherSwitch# show sdm prefer
The current template is "desktop IPv4 and IPv6 default" template.
The selected template optimizes the resources in
the switch to support this level of features for
8 routed interfaces and 1024 VLANs.

number of unicast mac addresses:                    2K
number of IPv4 IGMP groups + multicast routes:      1K
number of IPv4 unicast routes:                      3K
number of directly-connected IPv4 hosts:            2K
number of indirect IPv4 routes:                     1K
number of IPv6 multicast groups:                    1.125k
number of directly-connected IPv6 addresses:        2K
number of indirect IPv6 unicast routes:             1K
number of IPv4 policy based routing aces:           0
number of IPv4/MAC qos aces:                        0.5K
number of IPv4/MAC security aces:                   1K
number of IPv6 policy based routing aces:           0
number of IPv6 qos aces:                            0.625k
number of IPv6 security aces:                       0.5K
```

More information on the SDM template configuration can be found at http://www.cisco.com/en/US/docs/switches/lan/catalyst3560/software/release/12.2_25_see/configuration/guide/swsdm.html#wp1077854.

The IPv6 portion of the EtherSwitch Module configuration is straightforward. In the HBE, there are only three interfaces that are in use on the module. There is the EtherSwitch-to-router internal interface (GigabitEthernet 1/0/2) and two Ethernet interfaces connecting the two Cisco ASA firewalls.

At the time of this writing, the Cisco ASA does not yet support dynamic routing for IPv6, so a default static route is configured on the module that points to the failover IPv6 address of the Cisco ASA. Optionally, EIGRP for IPv6 is enabled so that the default route can be advertised to the internal "BR1-LAN" router and so that all internal routes on that device can be advertised to the EtherSwitch Module. Static routes on "BR1-LAN" and the

EtherSwitch Module work as well. The configuration for the EtherSwitch Module is shown in Example 8-11.

Example 8-11   *EtherSwitch Module Configuration*

```
ipv6 unicast-routing
!
interface FastEthernet1/0/1
 description TO ASA-1
 switchport access vlan 101
!
interface FastEthernet1/0/2
 description TO ASA-2
 switchport access vlan 101
!
interface GigabitEthernet1/0/2      #Interface connecting to
                                    #branch LAN access
                                    #router (EtherSwitch internal
                                    #interface)
 description to BR1-LAN
 no switchport
 ip address 10.124.4.2 255.255.255.0
 ipv6 address 2001:DB8:CAFE:1003::2/64
 ipv6 eigrp 10                      #Optional - dynamic routing
                                    #for IPv6 inside the branch
!
interface Vlan101
 ip address 10.124.3.3 255.255.255.0
 ipv6 address 2001:DB8:CAFE:1002::3/64    #VLAN for network
                                              #connecting ASA
 ipv6 eigrp 10
!
ipv6 route ::/0 2001:DB8:CAFE:1002::1      #Default route pointing
                                              #to ASA
ipv6 router eigrp 10                 #Enable EIGRP for IPv6
 redistribute static                #Redistribute default route
                                    #to LAN router
 passive-interface Vlan101          #Do not attempt adjacency on
                                    #VLAN101
```

Branch LAN Router Configuration

The BR1-LAN branch LAN access router (configuration shown in Example 8-12) acts as a Layer 3 distribution device for the branch. BR1-LAN terminates the VLAN trunks from the Layer 2 access switch (BR1-LAN-SW) that the individual hosts connect to. In addition to basic L3 termination and routing, the BR1-LAN router provides basic addressing services to IPv6-attached hosts through stateless DHCPv6 (RFC 3736) and provides stateful DHCPv6 relay functionality (RFC 3315). With stateless DHCPv6, the router provides IPv6 addressing services through SLAAC (RFC 4862), but other information, such as DNS name and DNS server, is provided through a stateless DHCPv6 pool (G0/0.104 example). With stateful DHCPv6 relay, the router forwards on the DHCP requests to a defined DHCPv6 server (G0/0.105 example).

Example 8-12 *BR1-LAN Configuration Example*

```
ipv6 unicast-routing
ipv6 cef
!
ipv6 dhcp pool DATA_W7                      #DHCPv6 pool name
 dns-server 2001:DB8:CAFE:102::8            #Primary IPv6 DNS server
 domain-name cisco.com                      #DNS domain name passed
                                            #to client
!
interface GigabitEthernet0/0
 description to BR1-LAN-SW
 no ip address
 duplex auto
 speed auto
!
interface GigabitEthernet0/0.104
 description VLAN-PC
 encapsulation dot1Q 104
 ip address 10.124.104.1 255.255.255.0
 ipv6 address 2001:DB8:CAFE:1004::1/64      #Client uses SLAAC
                                            #with this prefix
 ipv6 nd other-config-flag         #Set flag in RA to instruct
                                   #host how to obtain "other"
                                   #information such as domain
 ipv6 dhcp server DATA_W7          #Use DHCP pool above for
                                   #options
 ipv6 eigrp 10
!
interface GigabitEthernet0/0.105
 description VLAN-PHONE
 encapsulation dot1Q 105
 ip address 10.124.105.1 255.255.255.0
 ipv6 address 2001:DB8:CAFE:1005::1/64
 ipv6 nd prefix 2001:DB8:CAFE:1005::/64 0 0 no-autoconfig #Do
                                           #not use prefix for
                                           #autoconfiguration
 ipv6 nd managed-config-flag       #Set flag in RA to instruct
```

continues

Example 8-12 *BR1-LAN Configuration Example   continued*

```
                                    #host to use DHCPv6
 ipv6 dhcp relay destination 2001:DB8:CAFE:102::9      #Relay for
                                                       #DHCPv6 server
 ipv6 eigrp 10
 interface GigabitEthernet0/0.106
 description VLAN-PRINTER
 encapsulation dot1Q 106
 ip address 10.124.106.1 255.255.255.0
 ipv6 address 2001:DB8:CAFE:1006::1/64
 ipv6 eigrp 10
!
interface GigabitEthernet1/0
 description TO ETHERSWITCH MODULE
 ip address 10.124.4.1 255.255.255.0
 ipv6 address 2001:DB8:CAFE:1003::1/64
 ipv6 eigrp 10
!
ipv6 router eigrp 10
 no shutdown
```

The BR1-LAN-SW Catalyst switch is configured with an interface connected to the BR1-LAN router and is configured for IEEE 802.1Q trunking. VLANs 104–106 are carried over the trunk link. No relevant IPv6 configurations are made on the BR1-LAN-SW except that a management interface is defined that is reachable over both IPv4 and IPv6. The configuration for the BR1-LAN-SW device is not shown.

WAN/Branch Deployment over Native IPv6

At the time of this writing, it is rare for an enterprise to have full end-to-end reachability over native IPv6 from a branch site to a WAN head-end. As more and more service providers deploy IPv6 services to their customers, the enterprise can use IPv6 as the means of transporting encrypted IPv6 traffic between sites and leave behind the IPv6-in-IPv4 encrypted tunnel deployments that have been discussed in this chapter thus far.

Cisco supports the deployment of IPsec over IPv6 in Cisco IOS. The following section provides a basic configuration example of how to deploy IPsec over IPv6 on Cisco IOS between two routers.

Figure 8-6 shows a network topology of two routers connected to the Internet through IPv6. In this case, the routers are not running dual-stack (IPv4 and IPv6) but they could be; instead they are IPv6-only routers with IPv6-only devices attached.

The configuration is straightforward and closely resembles that of a point-to-point IPsec configuration over IPv4. The differences are mostly with the addressing for the interfaces.

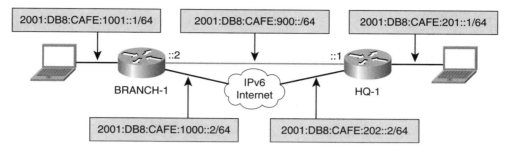

Figure 8-6 *IPsec VPN over IPv6 Internet*

Example 8-13 shows the basic configuration on the HQ-1 router. The Internet security association and key management protocol (ISAKMP) and IPsec policy information is the same as what was used in the HBE discussed earlier. The difference comes in the tunnel configuration. The tunnel source and destination are now IPv6 addresses instead of IPv4, as shown previously. Also, the tunnel mode is now using IPsec over IPv6 transport. Finally, the serial interface has an IPv6 address that is used for the connection to the IPv6-enabled ISP. Unicast Reverse Path Forwarding (uRPF) is enabled to help with spoofing. In a production deployment, there would be a set of ACLs used to enable only certain protocols and source/destinations (between branch and HQ) ingress on the serial interface.

Example 8-13 *HQ-1 Configuration*

```
ipv6 unicast-routing
ipv6 cef
!
crypto isakmp policy 1
 encr aes 256
 authentication pre-share
 group 2
crypto isakmp key CISCO address ipv6 ::/0
!
crypto ipsec transform-set HUB esp-aes 256 esp-sha-hmac
!
crypto ipsec profile HUB
 set transform-set HUB
!
interface Tunnel2
 no ip address
 ipv6 address 2001:DB8:CAFE:900::1/64
 ipv6 eigrp 10
 tunnel source 2001:DB8:CAFE:202::2      #Source is now using IPv6
 tunnel mode ipsec ipv6                  #IPSec over IPv6 tunnel mode
```

continues

Example 8-13 *HQ-1 Configuration   continued*

```
   tunnel destination 2001:DB8:CAFE:1000::2  #Dest. now using IPv6
   tunnel protection ipsec profile HUB
   !
interface GigabitEthernet1/0
 description LAN
 no ip address
 ipv6 address 2001:DB8:CAFE:201::1/64
 ipv6 eigrp 10
!
interface Serial2/0
 description to ISP
 no ip address
 ipv6 address 2001:DB8:CAFE:202::2/64       #v6 connection to ISP
 ipv6 verify unicast reverse-path                 #uRPF for IPv6
 !
ipv6 route ::/0 2001:DB8:CAFE:202::1              #Default to ISP
ipv6 router eigrp 10
 eigrp router-id 1.1.1.2
```

Example 8-14 shows the configuration for BRANCH-1. It is similar to the configuration for HQ-1, with the exception of addressing and the IPsec profile name.

Example 8-14 *BRANCH-1 Configuration*

```
ipv6 unicast-routing
ipv6 cef
!
crypto isakmp policy 1
 encr aes 256
 authentication pre-share
 group 2
crypto isakmp key CISCO address ipv6 ::/0
!
crypto ipsec transform-set SPOKE esp-aes 256 esp-sha-hmac
!
crypto ipsec profile SPOKE
 set transform-set SPOKE
!
interface Tunnel2
 no ip address
 ipv6 address 2001:DB8:CAFE:900::2/64
 ipv6 eigrp 10
 tunnel source 2001:DB8:CAFE:1000::2
 tunnel mode ipsec ipv6
```

```
 tunnel destination 2001:DB8:CAFE:202::2
 tunnel protection ipsec profile SPOKE
!
interface GigabitEthernet1/0
 description LAN
 no ip address
 ipv6 address 2001:DB8:CAFE:1001::1/64
 ipv6 eigrp 10
!
interface Serial2/0
 description to ISP
 no ip address
 ipv6 address 2001:DB8:CAFE:1000::2/64
 ipv6 verify unicast reverse-path
!
ipv6 route ::/0 2001:DB8:CAFE:1000::1
ipv6 router eigrp 10
 eigrp router-id 1.1.1.3
```

Example 8-15 shows the status of the ISAKMP peers and security association (SA) state.

Example 8-15   *ISAKMP Peer and SA Output on HQ-1*

```
HQ-1# show crypto isakmp peers
Peer: 2001:DB8:CAFE:1000::2 Port: 500 Local: 2001:DB8:CAFE:202::2
 Phase1 id: 2001:DB8:CAFE:1000::2


HQ-1# show crypto isakmp sa
IPv4 Crypto ISAKMP SA
dst              src              state          conn-id status


IPv6 Crypto ISAKMP SA

 dst: 2001:DB8:CAFE:1000::2
 src: 2001:DB8:CAFE:202::2
 state: QM_IDLE          conn-id:   1002 status: ACTIVE

 dst: 2001:DB8:CAFE:202::2
 src: 2001:DB8:CAFE:1000::2
 state: QM_IDLE          conn-id:   1003 status: ACTIVE
```

Summary

This chapter describes how to deploy IPv6 in the branch network. The branch profiles described were the single-tier, dual-tier, and multitier. The configuration example was based on a hybrid branch example that included elements of each of the three tiers. In addition to IPv6-over-IPv4 VPN solutions, a native IPv6 IPsec example was given for those customers who have service provider support for end-to-end IPv6 transport. The profiles described are certainly not the only ways to deploy IPv6 in this environment, but they provide options that can be leveraged based on the branch environment.

Additional References

Many notes and disclaimers in this document discuss the need to fully understand the technology and protocol aspects of IPv6. There are many design considerations associated with the implementation of IPv6 that include security, QoS, availability, management, IT training, and application support.

The following references are a few of the many that provide more details on IPv6, Cisco design recommendations, products and solutions, and industry activity:

Popoviciu, Ciprian P., Eric Levy-Abegnoli, and Patrick Grossetete. *Deploying IPv6 Networks*. Cisco Press. (ISBN10: 1-58705-210-5; ISBN13: 978-1-58705-210-1).

Hogg, Scott and Eric Vyncke. *IPv6 Security*. Cisco Press. (ISBN10: 1-58705-594-5; ISBN13: 978-1-58705-594-2).

Szigeti, Tim and Christina Hattingh. *End-to-END QoS Network Design*. Cisco Press. (ISBN10: 1-58705-176-1; ISBN13: 978-1-58705-176-0).

Cisco. Cisco IOS IPv6 Configuration Guide:
http://www.cisco.com/en/US/docs/ios/ipv6/configuration/guide/15_0/ipv6_15_0_book
.html.

Cisco. Design Zone for Branch:
http://www.cisco.com/en/US/netsol/ns816/networking_solutions_program_home.html.

Cisco. Deploying IPv6 in Unified Communications Networks with Cisco Unified Communications Manager:
http://www.cisco.com/en/US/docs/voice_ip_comm/cucm/srnd/ipv6/ipv6srnd.html.

Cisco. IPsec Design Guides:
http://www.cisco.com/en/US/tech/tk583/tk372/tech_design_guides_list.html.

Cisco. Cisco IOS Control Plane Policing:
http://www.cisco.com/en/US/docs/ios/12_3t/12_3t4/feature/guide/gtrtlimt.html.

Cisco. Enterprise QoS Solution Reference Network Design Guide:
http://www.cisco.com/en/US/docs/solutions/Enterprise/WAN_and_MAN/QoS_SRND/
QoS-SRND-Book.html.

Cisco. Cisco IOS IPv6 Multicast Technologies:
http://www.cisco.com/en/US/technologies/tk648/tk828/tk363/technologies_white_paper
0900aecd8014d6dd.html.

Cisco. Cisco IOS IPv6 Multicast Configuration:
http://www.cisco.com/en/US/tech/tk828/technologies_white_paper09186a0080203f7a
.shtml.

Cisco. Cisco Implementing IPv6 Multicast:
http://www.cisco.com/en/US/docs/ios/ipv6/configuration/guide/
ip6-multicast_ps10591_TSD_Products_Configuration_Guide_Chapter.html.

Cisco. Defining and Using IPv6 General Prefixes:
http://www.cisco.com/en/US/docs/ios/ipv6/configuration/guide/
ip6-addrg_bsc_con_ps10591_TSD_Products_Configuration_Guide_Chapter
.html#wp1132473.

Cisco. Network Management and Automation:
http://www.cisco.com/en/US/products/sw/netmgtsw/index.html.

Cisco. Dynamic Multipoint VPN (DMVPN) Design Guide:
http://www.cisco.com/en/US/docs/solutions/Enterprise/WAN_and_MAN/DMVPDG.html.

Cisco. Cisco IOS Release 15.0 - Implementing Dynamic Multipoint VPN for IPv6:
http://www.cisco.com/en/US/docs/ios/ipv6/configuration/guide/
ip6-dmvpn_ps10591_TSD_Products_Configuration_Guide_Chapter.html.

Cisco. Shortcut Switching Enhancements for NHRP in DMVPN Networks:
http://www.cisco.com/en/US/docs/ios/ipaddr/configuration/guide/iad_nhrp_dmvpn.html
#wp1072593.

Cisco. Configuring NHRP:
http://cisco.com/en/US/docs/ios/ipaddr/configuration/guide/iad_cfg_nhrp.html#wp1078
234.

Cisco. Catalyst 3560 Switch Configuration Guide: Configuring SDM Templates:
http://www.cisco.com/en/US/docs/switches/lan/catalyst3560/software/release/12.2_25_
see/configuration/guide/swsdm.html#wp1077854.

Cisco. Branch Routers (including ISR):
http://www.cisco.com/en/US/products/ps10906/Products_Sub_Category_Home.html.

Savola, P. RFC 3627, "Use of /127 Prefix Length Between Routers Considered Harmful."
http://www.ietf.org/rfc/rfc3627.txt.

Hinden, R. and S. Deering. RFC 3513, "Internet Protocol Version 6 (IPv6) Addressing
Architecture." http://www.ietf.org/rfc/rfc3513.txt.

Savola, P. and B. Haberman. RFC 3956, "Embedding the Rendezvous Point (RP) Address
in an IPv6 Multicast Address." http://www.ietf.org/rfc/rfc3956.txt.

Deering, S. and R. Hinden. RFC 2460, "Internet Protocol, Version 6 (IPv6) Specification."
http://www.ietf.org/rfc/rfc2460.txt.

Thomson, S., T. Narten, and T. Jinmei. RFC 4862, "IPv6 Stateless Address Autoconfiguration." http://www.ietf.org/rfc/rfc4862.txt.

Droms, R. RFC 3736, "Stateless Dynamic Host Configuration Protocol (DHCP) Service for IPv6." http://www.ietf.org/rfc/rfc3736.txt.

McCann, J., S. Deering, and J. Mogul. RFC 1981, "Path MTU Discovery for IP version 6." http://www.ietf.org/rfc/rfc1981.txt.

Arkko, J. (Ed.), J. Kempf, and P. Nikander. RFC 3971, "SEcure Neighbor Discovery (SEND)." http://www.ietf.org/rfc/rfc3971.txt.

Templin, F., T. Gleeson, M. Talwar, and D. Thaler. RFC 4214, "Intra-Site Automatic Tunnel Addressing Protocol (ISATAP)." http://www.ietf.org/rfc/rfc4214.txt.

Van de Velde, G., T. Chown, O. Bonness, and C. Hahn. RFC 5375, "IPv6 Unicast Address Assignment Considerations." http://www.ietf.org/rfc/rfc5375.txt.

Chapter 9

Deploying IPv6 in the Data Center

This chapter covers the following subjects:

- **Designing and implementing a dual-stack data center:** This section describes design and implementation considerations for deploying IPv6 in the access, aggregation, and core layers of the data center.

- **Implementing IPv6 in a virtualized data center:** This section describes considerations for implementing IPv6 in a virtualized data center.

- **Implementing IPv6 for the SAN:** This section describes the implementation of IPv6 in a storage-area network.

- **Designing IPv6 data center interconnect:** This section describes design considerations for IPv6 in a data center interconnect scenario.

The deployment of IPv6 in a data center environment is often the most overlooked and underestimated areas in an enterprise. There are several similarities between the campus and data center as they relate to routing and switching, but that is where the similarities end. Many customers are unprepared for the extensive amount of research, assessment time, and the wide range of product and technologies used in the data center that will be impacted by IPv6 deployment.

In addition to the traditional requirements for routing and switching, data centers also require the following:

- Network, security, and performance services in the form of service modules and/or appliances

- Storage-area networks (SAN) such as Fibre Channel, Ethernet, and Fiber Channel over Ethernet (FCoE) attached storage systems and switches

- Data center virtualization, including server, network, and storage virtualization technologies

- Device, operating system, and application management, including the following:

  - Out-of-band server management (also called lights-out management [LoM]) such as Hewlett-Packard Integrated Lights Out (iLO) or Dell Remote Assistance Card (DRAC)

  - CiscoWorks LAN Management Solution, Microsoft System Center, and other management systems for full end-to-end device, OS, and application management

- Device and site disaster recovery and high availability, including the following:

  - Data Center Interconnect (DCI), which connects two or more data centers using a diverse number of transport technologies to enable Layer 2 and Layer 3 adjacencies for services and applications such as clusters and live virtual machine movement (for example, VMware vMotion and Microsoft Hyper-V Live Migration)

  - Global and site load balancing

  - Stateless and/or stateful failover of network and security devices such as firewalls and other services

- Server farms that house a wide range of applications such as the following:

  - Mission-critical applications (for example, SAP, Oracle, other line-of-business applications)

  - Virtual Desktop Infrastructure (VDI)

  - Messaging and collaboration (for example, Microsoft Exchange)

  - File and print

  - DNS and DHCP

  - Specialized grid computing applications

This chapter examines some, but not all, of these elements as they relate to IPv6 deployment. IPv6 support is fairly mature in the routing and switching space but is nonexistent or spotty in other areas such as services, mission-critical applications, and across any product or technology operating above Layer 3.

Of all the areas within the enterprise, the data center is the most complicated and technology/product diverse, and it is critical for you to establish and maintain a gap list of what does and what does not support IPv6 and work with vendors to close these gaps.

Designing and Implementing a Dual-Stack Data Center

The focus of this section is to look at the three network tiers of the data center (access, aggregation, and core) and walk through the design considerations and implementation examples of enabling dual-stack (IPv4/IPv6) in those tiers. Many of the concepts, products, features, and configurations used in this section equally apply to the internal data center and the external Internet-facing data center. However, some concepts such as service provider peering, Internet-facing link configuration, multihoming, and Internet data center availability are not discussed. Many of those design elements are still being worked out, tested, and validated by Cisco and enterprise and service provider customers.

> **Note**   In this chapter, you see references to a wide range of products and technologies from Cisco and other vendors. It is not the goal of this chapter to explain what these products and technologies are and how they operate, but rather to include them as a reference for how they might be deployed with IPv6. Many of these products and technologies are powerful and flexible. Therefore, the design and implementation considerations can be numerous, and those included in this chapter are not meant to be the only way to use them.

The three network tiers of the data center are the access layer, aggregation layer, and core layer. There are other tiers within the data center relevant to things like storage and applications, but the network tiers are what will be discussed in the following section.

Figure 9-1 is a high-level view of the three data center network tiers discussed and includes a few of the typical Cisco products you can find in each tier. Again, there are many combinations of products and topologies, and this view is only one example.

Figure 9-1 has a few combinations in the access layer, and this is typical in many data centers because some data center switching products can be used for different purposes or areas of the data center. There might be some servers connected to Catalyst products such as the Catalyst 6500, 4900M/4948E, and/or Nexus 5000 and 2000 through 10/100/1000 or even 10-Gbps Ethernet. In other areas of the data center, the customer might have the Cisco Unified Computing System (UCS), which includes the Fabric Interconnect (FI) and the blade chassis, which can run a server virtualization solution such as VMware ESX. Within this environment, the Nexus 1000 product family can be deployed that has a Virtual Ethernet Module (VEM) that runs on each VMware ESX host and the Virtual Supervisor Module (VSM) that manages the VEMs. When virtualized server and network components are merged, it often becomes difficult to delineate where the "true" access layer is. Many times, customers will consider the Nexus 1000 VEM or the UCS Fabric Interconnect as their access layer. Regardless of the layer association, these products share common features that connect hosts to the network, which is the primary goal of the access layer.

The aggregation layer is the point in the data center where all the access layer uplinks are terminated or "aggregated." In addition to terminating the access layer uplinks, network and application services are often located in the aggregation layer and include services such as security (for example, Cisco ASA or IDS/IPS), networking monitoring (for example, Cisco NAM), server load balancing, management systems, and so on. This aggregation/services layer can use appliances or service modules and most often leverages the large-scale and virtualization capabilities of the Nexus 7000 and the long-standing Catalyst 6500.

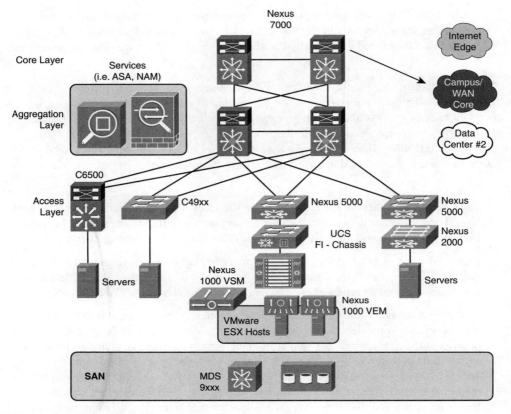

Figure 9-1 *High-Level Data Center Topology*

The core layer is used to connect the aggregation layers(s) to the rest of the network, which can include the Internet edge, campus and WAN cores, and one or multiple data centers through various data center interconnect technologies.

The following sections discuss how IPv6 can be deployed in each data center network tier and will use simple topologies that focus on the concepts versus specific product combinations. Most of, if not all, the Cisco data center switching products discussed have a similar look and feel, so product-specific IPv6 configurations are not included.

Data Center Access Layer

As mentioned previously, the access layer has one goal: : to physically or virtually connect hosts to the network. Many types of hosts and many Cisco products can connect these hosts to the network physically and virtually. For IPv6 in the data center access layer, there are just a few considerations, and most of those considerations are shared with the campus access layer. Some of the considerations for IPv6 in the access layer include, but are not limited to

- **IPv6 multicast:** If hosts connected to the access layer switch need to receive IPv6 multicast, the switch needs to support IPv6 Multicast Listener Discovery (MLD) version 1 and version 2 snooping. This enables the Layer 2 hardware-supported constraint of multicast to only those ports that need to receive the multicast packets.

- **IPv6 QoS:** IPv6 quality of service (QoS) classification/marking might or might not take place at the access layer. Some customers perform QoS classification/marking in the access layer, aggregation layer, or even further into the network. If it is required in the access layer, IPv6 packets should be classified and marked, allow re-marking of the packets, and trust markings that took place on the host.

- **IPv6 security:** A variety of security-related features and technologies can be enabled in the access layer and include access control lists (ACL), control-plane policing, first-hop security tools such as rogue-RA protection, and other features more protocol-independent such as private VLANs.

- **IPv6 management:** It is important to have device-level and systemwide management support over IPv6. It is quite common to have Simple Network Management Protocol (SNMP), Secure Shell (SSH)/Telnet, HTTP, and other management access protocols supported at a device-management level. It is equally important for the "manager of manager" or systemwide management tools to have rich support for IPv6-enabled endpoints and IPv6-specific feature capabilities.

- **Performance:** Many vendors, including Cisco, have historically had a policy of halving the performance of some platforms for IPv6 (that is, the IPv6 packet-per-second rate is 50 percent of IPv4). This policy was justified in the past, but as higher amounts of data and with more users coming online with IPv6-enabled endpoints and applications, it is obvious that IPv6 must have equal or better performance than IPv4 in next-generation platforms.

Although other considerations come into play depending on how a particular access layer design looks, the ones in the preceding list are considered the important items that you should evaluate carefully.

Configuring Access Layer Devices for IPv6

Configuration of data center access layer switches for IPv6 is straightforward and generally trivial. Unless a routed access design is used, a specialized configuration for IPv6 is unnecessary. Many of the configurations made for IPv4 equally apply to IPv6.

The example configuration shown in Example 9-1 is basic and includes a few items that can be included in a typical data center access layer switch. The example is of a Catalyst 6500 that has 10-Gbps uplinks to a pair of Nexus 7000 switches located in the aggregation layer (only one uplink is shown), and there are multiple host links connecting to servers (only one shown). The access layer can have various access layer switch models, as shown earlier in Figure 9-1, and some of the syntax will change based on switch model and OS version, but the concepts are the same.

Example 9-1 *Data Center Access Layer Configuration*

```
vlan 14
 name WebSVR
!
interface TenGigabitEthernet2/1
 description to N7k-agg-1
 switchport
 switchport trunk encapsulation dot1q
 switchport trunk allowed vlan 10-14,30,31
 switchport mode trunk
 spanning-tree guard loop
 mls qos trust dscp
!
interface GigabitEthernet1/31
 description W2K8 Server
 switchport
 switchport access vlan 14
 switchport mode access
 spanning-tree portfast edge
 spanning-tree bpduguard enable
 mls qos trust dscp
 !
interface GigabitEthernet1/48
 description to OOB-NETWORK
 ipv6 address 2001:DB8:CAFE:100::14/64

!
ipv6 route ::/0 GigabitEthernet1/48 FE80::211:BCFF:FEC0:C800
```

In addition to physical access layer switches, virtual switches are used in server virtualization deployments using hypervisors such as VMware ESX, Microsoft Hyper-V, Xen, and others. These software-based virtual switches are often looked at as a "virtual access layer," where virtual machines (VM) connect to the virtual switch inside the host. More advanced software-based virtual switches such as the Cisco Nexus 1000v operate much like a traditional physical switch to include transparently forwarding IPv6 frames. The Cisco Nexus 1000v also supports IPv6 for management access, as seen in Example 9-2.

Example 9-2 *Cisco Nexus 1000v IPv6 Management*

```
ip host Nexus1000v-1 172.16.100.18 2001:db8:cafe:100::18


vrf context management
  ip route 0.0.0.0/0 172.16.100.1
```

```
 ipv6 route 0::/0 fe80::0211:bcff:fec0:c800 mgmt0

interface mgmt0
  ip address 172.16.100.18/24
  ipv6 address 2001:0db8:cafe:0100::0018/64
```

NIC-Teaming Considerations

Another consideration applicable to the access layer is for hosts connecting to the access layer using network interface card (NIC) teaming. NIC teaming is when two or more physical NICs on a server are logically bonded together to act as a single interface. This provides increased throughput to the server and offers higher availability for the physical ports on the server.

It is dangerous to assume that every NIC-teaming vendor has native support for IPv6. A common issue around NIC-teaming-enabled hosts is when IPv6 is not supported natively in the NIC-teaming software, but the administrator already has IPv6 enabled (before creating the team) or by manually adding IPv6 addressing to the team interface later on. Depending on the operating system, things can go wrong regarding the normal and expected operation of IPv6. One example is when IPv6 is manually added to a NIC team interface, as seen in Example 9-3.

Example 9-3   *Microsoft Windows Static Addressing of Team - IPv6 Not Supported*

```
netsh interface ipv6> add address "Local Area Connection" 2001:db8:cafe:10::7
Ok.
netsh interface ipv6>sh add
Querying active state...
Interface 10: Local Area Connection
Addr Type  DAD State  Valid Life  Pref. Life  Address
---------  ---------  ----------  ----------  ----------------------
Manual     Duplicate  infinite    infinite 2001:db8:cafe:10::7
```

Example 9-3 shows the Microsoft Windows Server 2008 command prompt output where a NIC team has been created previously and now a static IPv6 address is configured on that team interface (Interface 10: "Local Area Connection"). Because the NIC-teaming software in this example does not understand IPv6 and no error is triggered; however, this causes an issue with IPv6. The issue occurs when the Microsoft Windows TCP/IP stack (this occurs in other operating systems as well) accepts the IPv6 address but cannot control the new virtual adapter (the team software controls it), so the address is assigned to the physical interfaces within the team. The address gets assigned to both physical interfaces inside the team, which triggers Duplicate Address Detection (DAD). A DAD state of "Duplicate" is seen in the output. This will break IPv6 connectivity.

It is imperative that you research which NIC-teaming vendors support IPv6 and determine whether a new NIC card is required, or whether just a software update needs to be performed. Example 9-4 shows a command prompt output that illustrates the adapter information when NIC-teaming software supports IPv6. Alternatively this can be done through the Network Properties interface within Microsoft Windows.

Example 9-4   *Microsoft Windows Static Addressing of Team - IPv6 Supported*

```
Ethernet adapter DC-ACCESS-1:                    #Physical Interfaces- Pre Team

   Connection-specific DNS Suffix  . :
   Autoconfiguration IP Address. . . : 169.254.25.192
   Subnet Mask . . . . . . . . . . . : 255.255.0.0
   IP Address. . . . . . . . . . . . : fe80::204:23ff:fec7:b0d7%12
   Default Gateway . . . . . . . . . : fe80::212:d9ff:fe92:de76%12

Ethernet adapter DC-ACCESS-2:
   Connection-specific DNS Suffix  . :
   IP Address. . . . . . . . . . . . : 172.16.10.20
   Subnet Mask . . . . . . . . . . . : 255.255.255.0
   IP Address. . . . . . . . . . . . : 2001:db8:cafe:10::20

   IP Address. . . . . . . . . . . . : fe80::204:23ff:fec7:b0d6%11

   Default Gateway . . . . . . . . . : fe80::212:d9ff:fe92:de76%11


Ethernet adapter TEAM-1:                         #Team Interface - Post Team

   Connection-specific DNS Suffix  . :
   IP Address. . . . . . . . . . . . : 172.16.10.20
   Subnet Mask . . . . . . . . . . . : 255.255.255.0
   IP Address. . . . . . . . . . . . : 2001:db8:cafe:10::20
   IP Address. . . . . . . . . . . . : fe80::204:23ff:fec7:b0d6%13

   Default Gateway . . . . . . . . . : fe80::212:d9ff:fe92:de76%13


Interface 13: TEAM-1
Addr Type  DAD State   Valid Life   Pref. Life   Address
---------  ---------   ----------   ----------   ---------------------------
Public     Preferred   4m11s        4m11s        2001:db8:cafe:10::20

Link       Preferred   infinite     infinite     fe80::204:23ff:fec7:b0d6
```

Example 9-4 shows two physical interfaces (DC-ACCESS-1 and DC-ACCESS-2) before the teaming interface has been created. TEAM-1 is the new NIC-teaming interface and has a single IPv4 address and IPv6 address. With full IPv6 support on this NIC team, the IPv6 address passes DAD and is enabled for use (in "preferred" status).

Data Center Aggregation Layer

The data center aggregation layer, as its name implies, is the point in which the various access layer switches meet and are "aggregated" into a smaller number of very powerful data center switches. The aggregation layer is sandwiched in between the access and core layers and provides external connectivity to those hosts residing in the access layer by linking those hosts to the outside (for example, Internet edge, WAN, or campus) through the core layer. Besides the physical aggregation of links from access layer switches and the logical aggregation of VLANs, many of the application-focused load-balancing, security, and offload services are applied and provided at the aggregation layer. Some of these services include

- Firewall services

- Deep packet inspection/intrusion detection/intrusion prevention services

- Server load-balancing services

- SSL offload services

- Network monitoring and analysis services

Many of these services are provided by hardware such as appliance and/or service module-based products. Because the role of these specialized products operates at or above Layer 3, it is critical that these products support IPv6, not only through basic addressing, routing/forwarding, and management functions, but they must also provide full-service functionality all the way to Layer 7 if that is the role the product fills. Because of this requirement, there are many vendors, including Cisco, that might not have full feature or performance parity for these service products and their associated technologies. You should contact each vendor you do business with so that a list of product support and road-map information can be obtained.

The following section discusses a few of the many high-level considerations that need to be researched when deploying IPv6 in the data center aggregation layer when application services are being applied.

Bypassing IPv4-Only Services at the Aggregation Layer

It is common to have IPv4-only service products at the aggregation layer and also have the need to get IPv6 through the aggregation layer in spite of these non-IPv6-capable products.

Most service modules and appliances can be deployed in what is known as *one-arm mode*. Additionally, some service modules and appliances can be configured to operate in *transparent* (or *bridge*) *mode* and *routed mode*.

Figure 9-2 gives a summary view of these various modes and shows how IPv4 and IPv6 traffic can be processed in each mode.

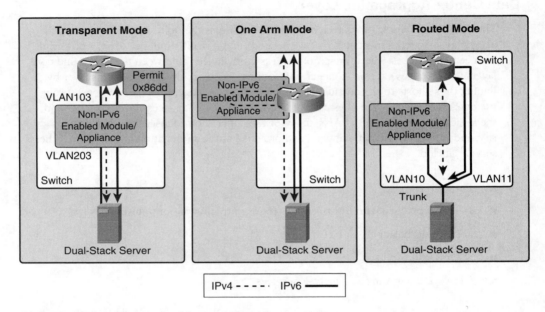

Figure 9-2 *Non-IPv6-Capable Service Products - Options*

Figure 9-2 shows transparent, one-arm, and routed mode examples where an integrated services module or, alternatively, an appliance is deployed, but either does not have IPv6 enabled or cannot support it yet. A dual-stack server is connected to the access layer (not shown) and has connectivity to the aggregation layer switch, where a service module is deployed directly on the aggregation switch (through a Catalyst 6500 with service module), a services chassis design (all modules are located in external services switches that are physically attached to the aggregation layer switch), or an appliance directly attached to the aggregation layer switch.

In each of these cases, IPv6 can be allowed to transit the aggregation layer and these service products, but inspection, load balancing, or any Layers 4–7 service that is provided by the module or appliance is not applied to IPv6 traffic. A few considerations for each mode are as follows:

■ **Transparent mode:** IPv4 traffic is bridged and serviced through the module or appliance, and IPv6 traffic is bridged but *not* serviced through the module or appliance. Basically, an Ethertype ACL is applied to the module or appliance that enables

0x86DD (Ethertype for IPv6). After it is permitted, any traffic matching the Ethertype will be bridged through the device without inspection or processing.

- **One-arm mode:** This mode is the easiest mode to deploy when it comes to allowing IPv6 past the services layer. In one-arm mode, traffic is specifically forwarded to the module or appliance based on the destination IP address of a configured Virtual IP (VIP) address, through Policy-Based Routing (PBR), or through another policy-based mechanism. If there are no IPv6-enabled VIPs, PBR, or other routing policies configured, the IPv6 traffic continues on to the destination with no services applied. Basically, there is nothing to configure to allow IPv6 to reach its destination in this mode.

- **Routed mode:** This mode is the most complex and difficult to deal with because it relates to getting IPv6 traffic to its destination. In routed mode, the module or appliance has Layer 3 awareness, which means that if it is not enabled for or capable of processing IPv6 packets, IPv6 will not be routed through the module or appliance. To circumvent this issue, you must bypass the routed mode module or appliance altogether in one of the following ways:

  - Route IPv6 to a dedicated VLAN or physical Layer 3–enabled port that is connected to the downstream host.

  - Configure the host network interface as a trunk. This allows the tagging of VLANs on the trunk between the downstream host, access layer switch, and aggregation layer switch. One VLAN can be for IPv4 (VLAN 10 in Figure 9-2) and another VLAN for IPv6 (VLAN 11 in Figure 9-2). This option can greatly complicate the deployment and management of IPv6 in the data center.

Deploying an IPv6-Only Server Farm

Another alternative is to deploy an IPv6-only server farm, where only IPv6-enabled network devices, hosts, operating systems, and services are deployed. This is a popular way of deploying IPv6 in the earlier stages of implementation within the enterprise because it allows isolation of IPv6 traffic, IPv6-enabled endpoints, and applications from the existing production IPv4 network. However, over time, this operational model can be costly, both in capital spending and in operational spending, because much of the network devices, operating system licensing cost, endpoint (that is, physical HW for servers) cost, and operational overhead are being duplicated for the two environments. Pursuing a dual-stack server farm within the data center should be the primary goal.

Supporting IPv4-Only Servers in a Dual-Stack Network

There will be cases where most of, if not all, the network has been dual-stack enabled but yet there are still IPv4-only servers in the data center. This could be due to the operating system not being upgraded to an IPv6-capable OS. It could be that the OS can support IPv6 but the application(s) running on that OS are protocol dependent—as in the case where the application has been coded to be aware of IPv4 but not IPv6. Whatever the case, in a minority of deployments, there will be some need to support IPv6 hosts connecting to IPv4-only servers.

Several options can help you solve this issue for a period of time. Some of these options include IPv4/IPv6 proxies, NAT64 (at the time of this writing, NAT64 is in draft form under the BEHAVE working group within the IETF), and SLB64.

Some customers use Apache HTTP proxy functionality to provide HTTP-specific flows to a basic level of service between IPv6 and IPv4 hosts. Others leverage stateless NAT64 as a means to do 1:1 IPv6-to-IPv4 address translation (less useful in the enterprise data center) or stateful NAT64 as a means to do many-to-one or many-to-few IPv6-to-IPv4 address translation (sometimes known as address/port overload). Finally, if both address family translation and server load-balancing services need to be performed, a function known as SLB64 (server load balancing) can be used, where both IPv6-IPv4 translation and SLB are performed simultaneously and on the same box.

Until SLB64 becomes more mainstream from vendors and is ran at higher rates of performance, some customers are looking to glue NAT64 + SLB44 (common server load balancing with IPv4-to-IPv4 translation) together for a period of time.

Regardless of the method used, these options should be seen as interim solutions, and a true native dual-stack data center—including the network, application-aware services, operating systems, and applications—should be the end goal.

Deploying IPv6-Enabled Services at the Aggregation Layer

When IPv6-capable services and devices are in the aggregation layer, most of the design and deployment considerations used with IPv4 are used with IPv6. Feature parity for a given platform can prevent a perfect 1:1 mapping between IPv4 and IPv6, but for the most part, the elements needed for a highly available, secure, and well-managed services layer are the same between to the two protocols.

The following sections describe two examples of deploying IPv6-enabled services at the aggregation layer. The first example uses the Cisco Network Analysis Module (NAM). The second describes deploying Cisco ASA at the data center aggregation layer.

Configuring Cisco Network Analysis Module at the Aggregation Layer

When you deploy the Cisco Network Analysis Module (NAM) at the aggregation layer, you can use it to monitor, report, and troubleshoot both IPv4 and IPv6 traffic going into, out of, and within the aggregation layer or anywhere a data source such as a NetFlow-enabled device is located. The configuration of the Cisco NAM to support the monitoring and reporting of IPv6 traffic is protocol agnostic in nature. The Cisco NAM can be integrated into the Catalyst 6500 or Cisco ISR series and simply needs to have the correct VLAN or interface defined as a data source. This is a protocol-agnostic configuration, as seen in Example 9-5.

Example 9-5   *Catalyst 6500 + Cisco NAM Module Integration Example*

```
6k-agg-1# show module
Mod Ports Card Type                                    Model            Serial No.
--- ----- ------------------------------              ----------       ------------
. . . # Output summarized
  9    8  Network Analysis Module                     WS-SVC-NAM-2     SAD074900GH

!
analysis module 9 management-port access-vlan 16
!
monitor session 5 source vlan 10
monitor session 5 destination analysis-module 9 data-port 1
```

Example 9-5 shows a Catalyst 6500 acting as a services chassis in the aggregation layer
and has a Cisco NAM-2 Module in slot 9. The configuration identifies the NAM module
slot and the management port VLAN. Within the Cisco NAM or the Catalyst 6500, the
monitor configuration is defined. In this example, the source monitor port is VLAN 10
and the destination is the Cisco NAM in slot 9 data port 1. The Cisco NAM interface
shows the same monitor configuration in Figure 9-3.

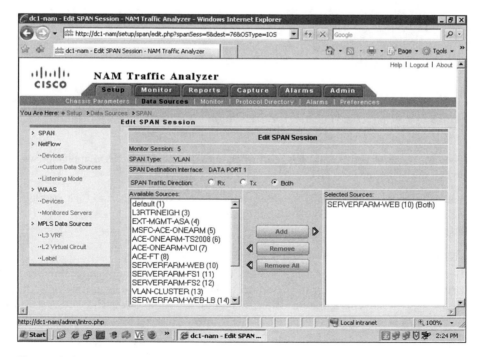

Figure 9-3   *Cisco NAM Monitor Source Configuration*

After the data source(s) have been configured, the NAM can monitor, report, and perform packet captures of data traversing the data source(s). Depending on the version of the NAM you have, the interface may look slightly different. Figure 9-4 shows the detail view of the conversation between a host 2001:db8:cafe:10:da61 and other hosts with an application protocol breakdown.

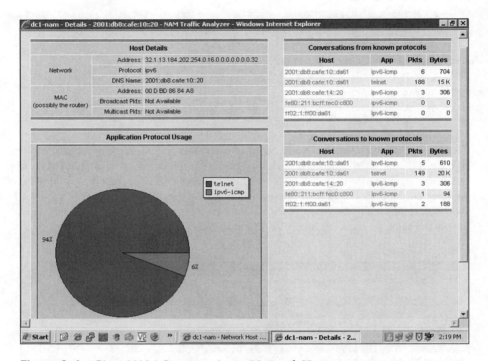

Figure 9-4   *Cisco NAM Conversations - Network Hosts*

The same type of configuration is used when integrating a Cisco NAM appliance with a switch in the aggregation layer or other location.

You can find more information regarding the Cisco NAM products and their configuration at http://www.cisco.com/en/US/products/ps5740/ Products_Sub_Category_Home.html.

Configuring Cisco ASA at the Aggregation Layer

Deploying the Cisco ASA at the data center aggregation layer is another example. Usually the physical setup of the Cisco ASA will remain the same in an IPv4-only, dual-stack, or IPv6-only configuration. The virtual or logical setup of the Cisco ASA will also be similar, if not the same, depending on the features deployed.

There are many ways of deploying the physical links and the VLAN configurations that run over them. Figure 9-5 shows a basic topology using a pair of Nexus 7000 data center switches at the aggregation layer and a pair of ASA 5580s (in transparent mode) connected to each Nexus 7000.

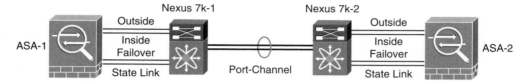

Figure 9-5 *Nexus 7000 Aggregation Switches and ASA Connections*

In Figure 9-5, there are four physical links that connect the Cisco ASA to the Nexus 7000. The outside (VLAN 114) and inside (VLAN 115) links are 10-Gbps Ethernet links that are configured as VLAN trunks for multiple VLANs and are used for inspection of traffic into and out of the aggregation layer. The failover (VLAN 116) and state link (VLAN 117) interfaces are 1-Gbps Ethernet links used for stateful failover of the Cisco ASAs.

Example 9-6 shows part of the physical and VLAN configuration of one of the Nexus 7000 aggregation switches. This is not an exhaustive example because most of the configuration is related to trunks and port channels that are important but not directly relevant to IPv6 in the context of this chapter.

Example 9-6 *Nexus 7000 Aggregation Layer Switch - Physical/VLAN Example*

```
interface Vlan114

  no shutdown
  description Outside FW VLAN
  ipv6 address 2001:0db8:cafe:0114::0002/64

  hsrp version 2

  hsrp 114 ipv6

    preempt delay minimum 180

    timers  1  3

    ip autoconfig


interface Vlan115

  no shutdown
  description Inside FW VLAN
  ipv6 address 2001:0db8:cafe:0115::0002/64
```

continues

Example 9-6   *Nexus 7000 Aggregation Layer Switch - Physical/VLAN Example continued*

```
    hsrp version 2

    hsrp 115 ipv6

      preempt delay minimum 180

      timers  1  3

      ip autoconfig


interface Ethernet1/2
  description ASA-1-Outside
  switchport
  switchport mode trunk
  switchport trunk allowed vlan 114

  logging event port link-status
  logging event port trunk-status
  no shutdown

interface Ethernet1/3
  description ASA-1-Inside
  switchport
  switchport mode trunk
  switchport trunk allowed vlan 115

  logging event port link-status
  logging event port trunk-status
  no shutdown
interface Ethernet1/4
  description ASA Failover Link
  switchport
  switchport access vlan 116

  no shutdown

interface Ethernet1/5
  description ASA State Link
  switchport
  switchport access vlan 117

  no shutdown
```

There are many configuration elements to a Cisco ASA that serves a data center, and the deployment can be quite complex, with multiple contexts with multiple different features and policies. Example 9-7 is a snippet of a basic Cisco ASA configuration based on Figure 9-5. Note that the Admin context is not shown.

Example 9-7 *Cisco ASA System Configuration Example*

```
firewall transparent
!
interface GigabitEthernet3/0
 description LAN Failover Interface
!
interface GigabitEthernet3/1
 description STATE Failover Interface

interface TenGigabitEthernet5/0
 description N7k1 Outside
!
interface TenGigabitEthernet5/0.114
 vlan 114
!
interface TenGigabitEthernet5/1
 description N7k1 Inside
!
interface TenGigabitEthernet5/1.115
 vlan 115
!
failover
failover lan unit primary
failover lan interface FO GigabitEthernet3/0
failover replication http
failover link STATE GigabitEthernet3/1
failover interface ip FO 2001:db8:cafe:116::1/64 standby 2001:db8:cafe:116::2

failover interface ip STATE 2001:db8:cafe:117::1/64 standby 2001:db8:cafe:117::2

!
context sf-1
  allocate-interface TenGigabitEthernet5/0.114 outside
  allocate-interface TenGigabitEthernet5/1.115 inside
  config-url disk0:/sf-1.cfg
```

In Example 9-7, the physical interfaces are associated with VLAN 114 and 115. The failover configuration includes the failover link and the state link as well as the IPv6 primary and standby addresses. Note that the Cisco ASA uses either IPv6 or IPv4 for the failover configuration, not both. Finally, the interfaces used as outside and inside are defined and allocated to the context sf-1.

Example 9-8 shows a snippet of the configuration in a context (sf-1) on the Cisco ASA.

Example 9-8   *Cisco ASA - Context Configuration Example*

```
firewall transparent
hostname sf-1
!
interface outside
 nameif outside
 security-level 0
!
interface inside
 nameif inside
 security-level 100
!
access-list bpdu ethertype permit bpdu
ipv6 address 2001:db8:cafe:114::5/64 standby 2001:db8:cafe:114::6

ipv6 access-list v6-ALLOW permit ip any any

ipv6 access-list v6-ALLOW permit icmp any any

ipv6 access-list v6-ALLOW permit eigrp any any

access-group bpdu in interface outside
access-group v6-ALLOW in interface outside

access-group bpdu in interface inside
access-group v6-ALLOW in interface inside
```

The configuration for the sf-1 context is straightforward. The firewall is in transparent mode with two interfaces allocated to this context. (Example 9-7 shows t5/0.114 and t5/1.115 as allocated to sf-1.) Because this ASA is in transparent mode, it is necessary to allow bridge protocol data units (BPDU) through. An IPv6 address is assigned to the context, and the IPv6 access list is wide open (permitting any). In transparent mode, Ethertype filters are used for Layer 2 and IPv6 access lists are used for Layer 3. Finally, the access lists are applied to the interfaces.

Other network service products, such as the Cisco intrusion protection system/intrusion detection system (IPS/IDS) solutions, also support IPv6 and are often located in the data center aggregation layer. Whatever the service or device, most of the configuration work related to getting IPv6 enabled is similar to how it is done through IPv4. More information about the Cisco IPS product support for IPv6 can be found at http://www.cisco.com/en/US/docs/security/ips/7.0/configuration/guide/idm/idmguide7.html.

In addition to application services at the aggregation layer, there are also situations where data center–to–data center interconnections are made for the purpose of replicating/connecting storage and networking services such as Layer 2 extensions for clusters and virtual machine mobility (for example, VMware vMotion). All these designs and their deployments need to support IPv6 in much the same way as with IPv4. Some of these elements are discussed later in this chapter.

Data Center Core Layer

A few factors can dictate whether an enterprise has a dedicated data center core layer or whether the data center aggregation layer connects to a campus core. The size of the data center is one driver that can push an enterprise to dedicate a data center core to servicing all the data center aggregation switches. Regardless of the reasoning or even the overall design of the data center core, the IPv6 deployment at this layer is often trivial in design and deployment. Because there is a goal to keep the core layer a fast, controlled, scalable, and stable point in the network, there is rarely a desire to have a bunch of features enabled, services deployed, and noncritical overhead associated with the core layer switches.

Because of the reduction in the number of features needed in the core and overall design, the IPv6 configuration is usually limited to enabling IPv6 addressing on relevant Layer 3 interfaces connecting the core switches with other network blocks (for example, WAN, Internet edge, and campus) and deploying a routing protocol such as Enhanced IGRP (EIGRP) for IPv6, Open Shortest Path First version 3 (OSPFv3), or Intermediate System–to–Intermediate System (IS-IS). Additional technology deployed at the core, such as QoS and device/network security, most often use the same policies that are in place for IPv4.

At this point, you should understand how to configure IPv6 addressing, routing protocols, and management access to Layer 3–enabled devices; therefore, no configuration examples are shown in this section.

Implementing IPv6 in a Virtualized Data Center

If business continuity is a key objective of an organization, it implies that the operations are up and running 24 x 7. To achieve business continuity, some organizations might implement geographic redundancy and maintain multiple data centers located in different geographic regions, each enabled with replicated applications and data.

Virtualization happens in many places such as the network, server, storage, application, desktop, and security. Combining all of these allows a more agile data center environment. This approach is much more cost effective and provides a highly available architecture with better manageability. As data centers are virtualized, the scale and use of IP addresses grow in greater proportion. Some limitations arise with using IPv4 addresses, such as native security support and, most notably, the lack of address space for the rapidly increasing number of connected end devices.

Server virtualization software such as VMware vSphere supports IPv6 today. The solution comprises a number of individual physical and virtual elements, as shown in Figure 9-6.

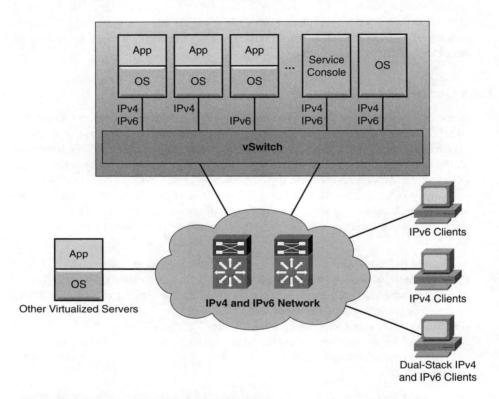

Figure 9-6   *Server Virtualization Using IPv6*

Most of the guest operating systems (operating systems that are virtual machines hosted on a physical server) today are IPv6 ready. Just as in the case of the physical servers, the virtual machines can be configured to use IPv6-only, IPv4-only, or both IPv6 and IPv4, depending on the capability of the operating system of the individual virtual machine. The underlying network should be configured for dual-stack (IPv6 and IPv4) connectivity to ensure access for management, IP-based storage, and migration/backup services.

Server virtualization software such as VMware ESX, Microsoft Hyper V, and Xen support IPv6 and dual-stack for the VMs that run on the hypervisor. In addition to allowing IPv6 to be bridged across the virtual switches on the hypervisor, the management components of the virtualization system should support IPv6. See Chapter 12, "Walk Before Running: Building an IPv6 Lab and Starting a Pilot," for an example of how to configure VMware vSphere, and Hypervisor ESXi for IPv6.

The Cisco Unified Computing System (UCS) is a platform that unites computing capabilities, network, storage access, and server virtualization in a cohesive system. Each UCS system can support thousands of virtual machines, all of which can be IPv6 enabled. The computing system can be IPv6 enabled for the sake of management tools, but much of the operations of a computing platform are IP agnostic and, instead, support the server hardware, power, network access, storage access, and the management of the bare-metal or hypervisor operating system.

Implementing IPv6 for the SAN

The Cisco Multilayer Director Switch (MDS) 9000 provides SAN access features such as Fibre Channel over IP (FCIP) and iSCSI, using IPv4 and IPv6. These services leverage the existing IP-based network to provide Fibre Channel–based services.

FCIP

FCIP enables enterprise networks to extend the reach of Fibre Channel storage-area networks (SAN) using the existing IP network. This proves to be cost effective because extending SANs using dedicated Fibre Channel can be very costly to implement as well as can add management overhead. NX OS supports dual-stack and multiple FCIP tunnels (one tunnel can support both IPv4 and IPv6) on a single physical interface, as illustrated in Figure 9-7.

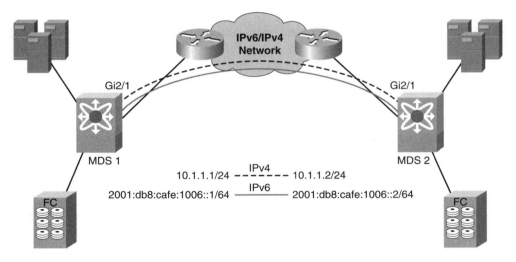

Figure 9-7   *FCIP on MDS Using IPv4 and IPv6*

The first step in configuring IPv6 for FCIP is to enable IPv6 routing and the FCIP features, as shown in Example 9-9.

Example 9-9   *Enabling IPv6 and FCIP on MDS Switches*

```
ipv6 routing
feature fcip
```

After this, configure the Gigabit Ethernet interface on the MDS switches, as illustrated in Examples 9-10 and 9-11.

Example 9-10   *Interface Configuration on MDS 1*

```
interface GigabitEthernet2/1
  ip address 10.1.1.1 255.255.255.0
  ipv6 address 2001:db8:cafe:1006::1/64
  no shutdown
```

Example 9-11   *Interface Configuration on MDS 2*

```
interface GigabitEthernet2/1
  ip address 10.1.1.2 255.255.255.0
  ipv6 address 2001:db8:cafe:1006::2/64
  no shutdown
```

You can verify the connectivity by using the **ping** command, as illustrated in Example 9-12.

Example 9-12   **ping** *Command Output on the MDS*

```
ping ipv6 2001:db8:cafe:1006::1
PING 2001:db8:cafe:1006::1(2001:db8:cafe:1006::1) 56 data bytes
64 bytes from 2001:db8:cafe:1006::1: icmp_seq=1 ttl=64 time=0.636 ms
64 bytes from 2001:db8:cafe:1006::1: icmp_seq=2 ttl=64 time=0.597 ms
64 bytes from 2001:db8:cafe:1006::1: icmp_seq=3 ttl=64 time=0.578 ms
64 bytes from 2001:db8:cafe:1006::1: icmp_seq=4 ttl=64 time=0.590 ms
64 bytes from 2001:db8:cafe:1006::1: icmp_seq=5 ttl=64 time=0.571 ms

—- 2001:db8:cafe:1006::1 ping statistics —-
5 packets transmitted, 5 received, 0% packet loss, time 3996ms
rtt min/avg/max/mdev = 0.571/0.594/0.636/0.031 ms
```

Next, configure the FCIP profiles and FCIP tunnels. In this example, one physical Gigabit Ethernet is being used by two FCIP tunnels. One FCIP tunnel is the existing IPv4 tunnel, and the second FCIP tunnel is the IPv6 tunnel. Different TCP ports can be used to configure multiple FCIP tunnels. For your example, configure a new FCIP tunnel using TCP port 3226. Traffic can be slowly migrated to the IPv6 FCIP tunnel. The FCIP profile and tunnel configuration can be configured as illustrated in Examples 9-13 and 9-14. It is important to point out that while this example has two tunnels (one for each protocol), both IPv4 and IPv6 can be enabled on a single tunnel.

Example 9-13 *Cisco MDS FCIP Configuration on MDS 1 Switch*

```
fcip profile 1
  ip address 10.1.1.1
!
fcip profile 2
  port 3226
  ip address 2001:db8:cafe:1006::1
!
interface fcip1
  use-profile 1
  peer-info ipaddr 10.1.1.2
  write-accelerator
  ip-compression auto
  no shutdown
!
interface fcip2
  use-profile 2
  peer-info ipaddr 2001:db8:cafe:1006::2 port 3226
  write-accelerator
  ip-compression auto
  no shutdown
```

Example 9-14 *Cisco MDS FCIP Configuration on MDS 2 Switch*

```
fcip profile 1
  ip address 10.1.1.2
!
fcip profile 2
  port 3226
  ip address 2001:db8:cafe:1006::2
!
interface fcip1
  use-profile 1
  peer-info ipaddr 10.1.1.1
  write-accelerator
  ip-compression auto
  no shutdown
!
interface fcip2
  use-profile 2
  peer-info ipaddr 2001:db8:cafe:1006::1 port 3226
  write-accelerator
  ip-compression auto
  no shutdown
```

You can verify the FCIP configuration using the **show interface** commands or the **show fcip summary** command, as illustrated in Examples 9-15 and 9-16.

Example 9-16   *Cisco MDS* **show fcip summary** *Command on MDS 1*

```
mds-1# show fcip summary
- - - - - - - - - - - - - - - - - - - - - - - - - - - - - - - - - - - - - - - -
Tun prof    Eth-if    peer-ip        Status T W T Enc Comp  Bandwidth   rtt
                                            E A A            max/min    (us)
- - - - - - - - - - - - - - - - - - - - - - - - - - - - - - - - - - - - - - - -
1   1    GE2/1    10.1.1.2        TRNK  Y Y N   N    A    1000M/500M  1000
2   2    GE2/1    2001:db8:cafe:  TRNK  Y Y N   N    A    1000M/500M  1000
                  1006::2
```

Example 9-17   *Cisco MDS* **show fcip summary** *Command on MDS 2*

```
mds-2# show fcip summary
- - - - - - - - - - - - - - - - - - - - - - - - - - - - - - - - - - - - - - - -
Tun prof    Eth-if    peer-ip        Status T W T Enc Comp  Bandwidth   rtt
                                            E A A            max/min    (us)
- - - - - - - - - - - - - - - - - - - - - - - - - - - - - - - - - - - - - - - -
1   1    GE2/1    10.1.1.1        TRNK  Y Y N   N    A    1000M/500M  1000
2   2    GE2/1    2001:db8:cafe:  TRNK  Y Y N   N    A    1000M/500M  1000
                  1006::1
```

iSCSI

Internet SCSI (iSCSI) is used widely to transport the SCSI protocol over TCP/IP. iSCSI is a standards-based protocol used to carry SCSI commands and the SCSI response. It provides hosts block-level access to storage arrays over a TCP/IP network using a network interface card.

The hosts requires an iSCSI driver that is used to bridge the SCSI and TCP/IP protocols. This driver translates SCSI commands between the host and storage into an iSCSI payload that can be forwarded on the TCP/IP network. It also performs the reverse function of translating the incoming iSCSI payload from the storage to the server into the SCSI command.

Gigabit Ethernet NICs are widely used as a standard connectivity interface for iSCSI on servers because they provide 1-Gbps speed connectivity between host and storage.

The MDS 9000 series switches supports configuration for IPv6 when using iSCSI, as illustrated in Figure 9-8. The Gigabit Ethernet and iSCSI initiator can be configured for IPv6 as shown in Example 9-18.

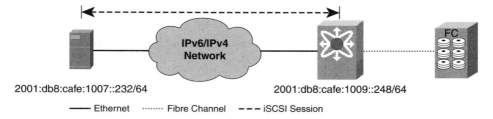

Figure 9-8 *Cisco MDS iSCSI Configuration*

Example 9-18 *Cisco MDS IPv6 Configuration for iSCSI*

```
feature iscsi
ipv6 routing
!
interface GigabitEthernet2/2
  ipv6 address 2001:db8:cafe:1009::248/64
  no shutdown
!
iscsi initiator ip-address 2001:db8:cafe:1007::232
```

Illustrated in Figure 9-9 is an iSCSI Initiator client on a Microsoft Windows Server 2008
R2 host that is using the MDS as the target portal for the iSCSI session.

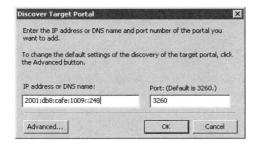

Figure 9-9 *iSCSI Initiator Client*

Cisco MDS Management

Cisco Fabric Manager is the management tool that uses Simple Network Management
Protocol version 3 (SNMPv3) to provide a graphical user interface that displays real-time
views of the devices in the network. The Fabric Manager relies on the underlying operating system's IPv6 configuration. After connectivity is established between the Fabric
Manager server and the MDS switch, the operation of the SNMP get and set operations
is no different than IPv4.

The MDS 9000 Series also provides out-of-band management through the mgmt0 port and in-band management using virtual SAN (VSAN) interfaces, which is also known as IP over FC (IPFC). Figure 9-10 illustrates methods to manage the MDS switch.

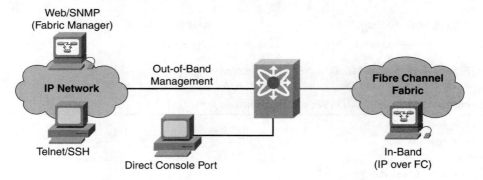

Figure 9-10   *Cisco MDS Management*

All interfaces illustrated in Figure 9-10 capable of IP addressing can use IPv6 and IPv4 addresses. Example 9-19 provides a configuration example of the out-of-band management interface mgmt0 and in-band interface using VSAN 10.

Example 9-19   *Cisco MDS Management-Based Configuration*

```
interface mgmt0
  ipv6 enable
  ip address 10.121.10.20 255.255.255.0
  ipv6 address 2001:db8:cafe:10::20/64
```

Figure 9-11 shows Fabric Manager 4.2 showing the management interface configuration. Fabric Manager can be used to configure the IPv4- and IPv6-specific settings on the MDS such as management, FCIP, and iSCSI.

Designing IPv6 Data Center Interconnect

The following sections introduce LAN extensions, also called Data Center Interconnect (DCI), and describe how they relate to the routing and storage space. The section "FCIP," earlier in this chapter, discussed how storage can be extended across data centers using the Layer 3 network. Similarly, DCI designs and technologies are commonly used to extend subnets across data centers.

DCI is used to extend layer 2 subnets beyond the traditional Layer 3 boundaries of a data center. DCI connects multiple data centers together to highlight the virtualized data center model with application and server mobility. This mobility provides the underlying services for disaster recovery as well as data center migration, consolidation, or planned maintenance.

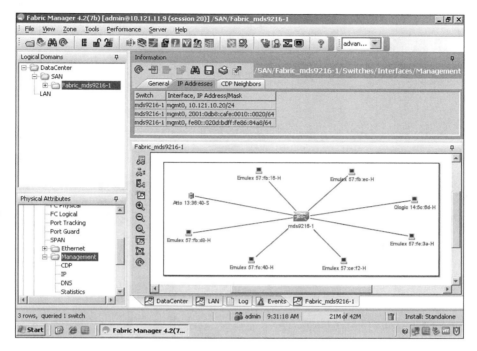

Figure 9-11   *Cisco MDS Fabric Manager: IPv6 Management Configuration*

Design Considerations: Dark Fibre, MPLS, and IP

Different transport alternatives can be used for connecting various data center sites as follows:

- **Dark Fibre (optical):** This is typically a Layer 1 service. This type of service is relatively expensive, but it is popular because it serves to transport various types of traffic such as Ethernet and SAN.

- **Layer 2 network:** In this case, the enterprise sends the provider native Ethernet traffic that will be forwarded to the remote site. Alternatively, an overlay of a Layer 2 VPN solution such as Virtual Private LAN Services (VPLS) can be used, giving the enterprise additional operational flexibility. Regardless of the technology or transport used, IPv6 can run across this Layer 2 network between data centers.

- **Layer 3 network:** Enterprises can also use Layer 3 connectivity from the SP or over the SP. The enterprise edge devices establish a Layer 3 peering with the SP device or to another enterprise edge device across the SP network. An overlay technology is deployed to extend the LAN between various data center sites. A new Cisco innovation for DCI is OTV, or Overlay Transport Virtualization. OTV is basically MAC routing where a MAC address is a destination but using an IP address as a next hop. More information on OTV can be found at http://www.cisco.com/en/US/prod/ switches/ps9441/nexus7000_promo.html.

When Layer 3 awareness comes into the picture, it is critical that IPv6 be supported in the same way IPv4 is, either as a means of transporting the protocol or using the protocol as a means of encapsulation.

Figure 9-12 illustrates at a high-level what these data center connections look like.

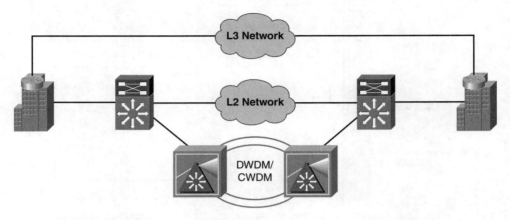

Figure 9-12   *Data Center Interconnect*

DCI Services and Solutions

Ensuring a loop-free LAN extension stretching across the WAN is a crucial part of designing DCI. Table 9-1 lists the solution that can be used at each network layer.

Depending on the design and technologies used with DCI, the configuration can be agnostic to the upper-layer IP protocol version or dependent. Be sure to take IPv6

Table 9-1   *DCI Solutions*

Requirement	Solution
Dark Fibre	Virtual Switching System (VSS) Virtual PortChannel (vPC)
Layer 2	Ethernet over MPLS (EoMPLS) Virtual Private LAN Services (VPLS) Advanced VPLS (A-VPLS)
Layer 3	EoMPLS over Generic Routing Encapsulation (EoMPLSoGRE)
Encryption	IEEE 802.1ae IP Security (IPsec)
Quality of Service (QoS)	Hierarchical QoS (HQoS)

deployment and support into account when you plan and deploy a new service, technology, or design such as DCI.

The configuration of the solutions listed in Table 9-1, if required for IPv6, has been discussed in previous chapters, such as Chapter 8, "Deploying IPv6 in WAN/Branch Networks," for IPsec and Chapter 6, "Deploying IPv6 in Campus Networks," for VSS. For more information on DCI, refer to http://www.cisco.com/go/dci.

Summary

This chapter looks at deploying IPv6 for the data center network. Considerations of designing and implementing dual-stack in the data center were discussed along with an overview. The data center access layer provided example configurations for the Nexus 7000 and 1000v for access layer devices. In the data center aggregation layer, IPv6-enabled NAM services, IPv6 configuration on the Nexus 7000, and ASA configuration examples were highlighted. The data center core layer needs to be simple and is mostly used for Layer 3 IPv6 addressing.

Virtualization plays an important role in the data center to increase performance and high availability. Storage, which is an essential part of the data center, can use IPv6 for FCIP to extend SANs across geographical locations leveraging existing Layer 3 network resources. Configuration examples for FCIP, iSCSI, and SAN management can be used to configure IPv6 in enterprise data centers.

The DCI section provided an overview of different technologies that are used to provide Layer 2 extensions between data centers. These technologies and designs are maturing, and it is important to track where these new trends are going and how IPv6 is supported or is the key element in making them happen.

Additional References

Popoviciu, Ciprian P., Eric Levy-Abegnoli, and Patrick Grossetete. *Deploying IPv6 Networks*. Cisco Press, 2006 (ISBN-10: 1-58705-210-5; ISBN-13: 978-1-58705-210-1).

Cisco Data Center Switches:
http://www.cisco.com/en/US/products/ps9441/Products_Sub_Category_Home.html.

Cisco Catalyst 6500 Series Switches:
http://www.cisco.com/en/US/products/hw/switches/ps708/index.html.

Cisco Catalyst 4900 Series Switches:
http://www.cisco.com/en/US/products/ps6021/index.html.

Cisco Network Analysis Module Products:
http://www.cisco.com/en/US/products/ps5740/Products_Sub_Category_Home.html.

Cisco ASA 5550 Series Products:
http://www.cisco.com/en/US/products/ps6120/index.html.

Cisco ASA 5500 Series Configuration Guide Using the CLI, 8.3: http://www.cisco.com/en/US/docs/security/asa/asa83/configuration/guide/config.html.

Cisco Data Center Interconnect: http://www.cisco.com/en/US/netsol/ns975/index.html.

Cisco MDS 9000 Family NX-OS IP Services Configuration Guide: http://www.cisco.com/en/US/docs/switches/datacenter/mds9000/sw/5_0/configuration/guides/ipsvc/nxos/ipsvc.html.

Data Center Interconnect (DCI): Layer 2 Extension Between Remote Data Center: http://www.cisco.com/en/US/prod/collateral/switches/ps5718/ps708/white_paper_c11_493718.html.

Cisco Nexus 7000: Overlay Transport Virtualization (OTV): http://www.cisco.com/en/US/prod/switches/ps9441/nexus7000_promo.html.

Cisco Nexus 1000V Series Switches: http://www.cisco.com/en/US/products/ps9902/index.html.

Chapter 10

Deploying IPv6 for Remote Access VPN

This chapter covers the following subjects:

- **IPv6 remote access over Cisco AnyConnect:** This section covers providing IPv6 access to enterprise services over a dual-stack SSL VPN session using the Cisco AnyConnect SSL VPN Client.

- **IPv6 remote access over Cisco VPN Client:** This section discusses providing IPv6 access to enterprise services over an IPsec session using the Cisco VPN Client and host-based IPv6 tunnels.

Many IT groups put a lot of effort into providing IPv6 access within the traditional boundaries of their enterprise and often delay supporting those users who work remotely. Traditional encrypted client-based Virtual Private Network (VPN) solutions can be leveraged to provide IPv6 access while a user works remotely, provided that the VPN solution can offer at least one of these three capabilities:

- Enable IPv6 to traverse an IPv4 Secure Socket Layer (SSL) VPN session, and also provide dual-stack support on the VPN termination device.

- Enable IPv6-based tunnels through an established IPv4 IPsec VPN session to an IPv6 tunnel termination point inside the enterprise.

- Provide native IPv6 support between a remote client and the enterprise site over a secured connection (for example, over IPsec or SSL).

The first solution leverages the Cisco AnyConnect SSL VPN Client (SVC) to establish an SSL-over-IPv4 connection to the Cisco Adaptive Security Appliance (ASA). IPv6 is transported between the client and the ASA over the IPv4/SSL connection, and then, after it is terminated on the Cisco ASA, the IPv6 traffic is routed as a native IPv6 packet.

The second solution leverages the Cisco VPN Client to establish an IPsec-over-IPv4 session to one of a few Cisco VPN head-end solutions, such as the Cisco Adaptive Security Appliance (ASA), Cisco IOS router, or Cisco VPN 3000 Concentrator. A tunnel mechanism such as Intra-Site Automatic Tunnel Addressing Protocol (ISATAP), 6to4, or manual-ly configured tunnels encapsulates IPv6 traffic inside of IPv4 and then is injected into the IPsec VPN connection. The Cisco VPN head-end device terminates the IPsec connection, but the IPv6-in-IPv4 tunnel remains and is routed to the tunnel termination device further inside the enterprise network. After the IPv6-in-IPv4 tunnel is terminated, IPv6 is routed as a native IPv6 packet.

The third solution today leverages the capability of Microsoft DirectAccess (DA). Microsoft DA provides IPv6-only remote access capabilities between Microsoft Windows 7 and Windows Server 2008 R2 hosts. Microsoft DA requires IPv6-only con-nectivity between the secured endpoints. If the transport between the endpoints is not IPv6, Microsoft DA attempts to encapsulate IPv6 over a number of tunneling mecha-nisms such as 6to4, Teredo, ISATAP, and IP-HTTPS. There is much to understand with Microsoft DA, but the theory, design, and deployment of Microsoft DA is outside the scope of this chapter. You should refer to the guides at the following Microsoft site to find out whether Microsoft DA is appropriate for your network:

http://technet.microsoft.com/en-us/network/dd420463.aspx

This chapter focuses on the first two solutions: remote access using Cisco AnyConnect and Cisco VPN Client. At the time of this writing, neither offers native remote access support over IPv6 transport, but the AnyConnect solution has this on the road map. You should check with your Cisco account team or the product pages on the Cisco website for the release of AnyConnect access over IPv6 transport.

Remote Access for IPv6 Using Cisco AnyConnect

With the Cisco AnyConnect solution on the Cisco ASA, a user can securely connect to the enterprise site in two ways:

- Clientless SSL VPN

- Cisco AnyConnect VPN Client

The Clientless SSL VPN (also called WebVPN) method enables a user to open a web browser, connect to the Cisco ASA portal, and establish a Transport Layer Security (TLS) connection over IPv4/TCP port 443. From there, the client can access applications that reside inside the enterprise. If the Cisco ASA and the back-end applications accessed through the portal are configured to work over IPv6, the client can access those applica-tions over IPv6. The Clientless SSL VPN configuration is not shown in this chapter. Refer to the Cisco documentation for more information:

> http://www.cisco.com/en/US/docs/security/asa/asa80/asdm60/ssl_vpn_deployment_
> guide/deploy.html#wp1016526

The Cisco AnyConnect VPN Client is an application that is installed on the user's host. The user launches the Cisco AnyConnect VPN Client and establishes Datagram Transport Layer Security (DTLS) over IPv4/UDP port 443 to the Cisco ASA. Although

the traditional TLS over TCP port 443 is supported, DTLS (RFC 4347) helps avoid latency and bandwidth problems normally found in some SSL-only connections by providing
a low-latency path over UDP. This helps with latency-sensitive applications such as voice.
When DTLS is enabled for the Cisco AnyConnect environment, two simultaneous tunnels are used: one for TLS and one for DTLS. If the UDP tunnel is blocked or interrupted,
traffic can traverse the TLS-based tunnel.

Figure 10-1 shows a high-level view of a dual-stack-enabled computer accessing the enterprise corporate network using the SVC. The SVC establishes a DTLS session (over the
IPv4 Internet) to the Cisco ASA. The Cisco ASA is also enabled for dual-stack functionality. After the IPv6 packets from the client traverse the DTLS connection through the
Cisco ASA, the packets are routed to their destination inside the corporate network.

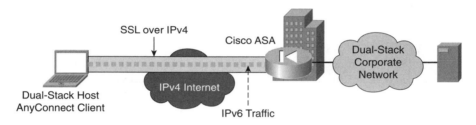

Figure 10-1 *Cisco AnyConnect VPN Client Connection*

Figure 10-2 is an example topology for the configuration shown in this section. The
client has an IPv4 address of 172.16.1.2 and is connected to the IPv4 Internet. The Cisco
ASA connects to the IPv4 Internet through a Cisco router (not shown) that provides
access, basic filtering, and IPv4 Network Address Translation (NAT). The Cisco ASA has
an "outside" IPv4 address of 10.124.1.4 and an "inside" IPv4 address of 10.124.3.1. The
Cisco ASA is dual-stack enabled on the inside and also has an IPv6 address of
2001:DB8:CAFE:1002::1.

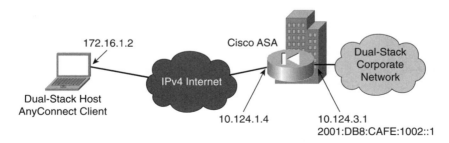

Figure 10-2 *Cisco AnyConnect VPN Client Example Topology*

The Cisco ASA has two pools of addresses for incoming AnyConnect sessions. One is an
IPv4 pool with a range of 10.124.3.30–10.124.3.80. The other is an IPv6 pool providing
50 addresses in the 2001:DB8:CAFE:1002::/64 prefix, with a starting address of

2001:DB8:CAFE:1002::100/64. After a Cisco AnyConnect Client connection is established, the client will be assigned an IPv4 and IPv6 address out of these pools. Also, other network services can be leveraged over either IPv4 or IPv6, such as Domain Name System (DNS), user authorization/authentication, Microsoft Active Directory integration, and so on. Security filtering and inspection are no different in this model than in an IPv4-only model. You would apply security policies for IPv6 at the same point as IPv4 for the internally destined traffic.

The configuration shown in Example 10-1 is a snippet of the full Cisco ASA configuration and is not meant to be a best-practice configuration, but simply one example of how to enable IPv6 support for Cisco AnyConnect. Also note that all of this configuration can be done in the Cisco Adaptive Security Device Manager (ASDM) GUI.

The example shows an "outside" and "inside" interface. The Cisco ASA software requires that basic IPv6 be enabled (through the **ipv6 enable** command) on the outside interface. This is just a software requirement, and this interface is not used to process IPv6 packets for the VPN session. No special security considerations need to be made to protect this interface from IPv6 attack from the Internet because this command is locally significant (although an IPv6 link-local address is created) and no IPv6 access is available (the Internet connection is IPv4-only), and the attacker would need to have direct physical access to this link/port to even have a chance of attacking the link-local address of the outside interface.

Example 10-1   *Cisco ASA AnyConnect Configuration*

```
interface GigabitEthernet0/0
 nameif outside
 security-level 0
 ip address 10.124.1.4 255.255.255.0
 ipv6 enable                          #Software requirement to enable IPv6 on the

                                      #outside interface

!
interface GigabitEthernet0/1
 nameif inside
 security-level 100
 ip address 10.124.3.1 255.255.255.0
 ipv6 address 2001:db8:cafe:1002::1/64

!
ip local pool v4Pool 10.124.3.30-10.124.3.80 mask 255.255.255.0
ipv6 local pool v6Pool 2001:db8:cafe:1002::100/64 50    #v6 pool (50 addresses)

ipv6 route inside ::/0 2001:db8:cafe:1002::3            #default route pointing to

                                                       #next-hop inside enterprise
```

```
!
route outside 0.0.0.0 0.0.0.0 10.124.1.1 1
!
webvpn
 enable outside
 svc image disk0:/anyconnect-win-2.4.1012-k9.pkg 1
 svc enable
group-policy ANYCONNECTGRP internal
group-policy ANYCONNECTGRP attributes
 vpn-tunnel-protocol svc webvpn              #Enable SSL VPN Client and Clientless

 split-tunnel-policy tunnelall               #Prohibit split-tunneling

 webvpn
  svc dtls enable                            #Enable DTLS (TLS over UDP)

  svc keep-installer installed
  svc ask enable default svc timeout 15
group-policy DfltGrpPolicy attributes
 vpn-tunnel-protocol IPSec l2tp-ipsec svc webvpn
 address-pools value v4Pool
 ipv6-address-pools value v6Pool

webvpn
  svc ask enable default svc timeout 15
username sslvpn1 password bzN3HgmMqoLp3Liy encrypted

username sslvpn1 attributes                  #Associate test user with Group Policy

 vpn-group-policy ANYCONNECTGRP

tunnel-group DefaultRAGroup general-attributes
 address-pool v4Pool
tunnel-group DefaultWEBVPNGroup general-attributes
 address-pool v4Pool
tunnel-group ANY-TG type remote-access
tunnel-group ANY-TG general-attributes       #Assign pool/group policy to tunnel grp

 address-pool v4Pool

 ipv6-address-pool v6Pool

 default-group-policy ANYCONNECTGRP
```

After the client has established an active SVC connection to the Cisco ASA, a number of output commands can show sessions and statistics. Example 10-2 shows output from two different commands.

The first output shows the IPv6 pool name, address range, size, and number of addresses in use and available. The output gives the "In Use" addresses and also the "Available Addresses" (output shortened because this is a long list).

The second output shows a summarized output for the **vpn-sessiondb** details, specifically the DTLS-Tunnel status. The output includes the assigned IPv4 and IPv6 address and the public IPv4 address that the client is using to connect with.

Example 10-2   *IPv6 Pool and* **vpn-sessiondb** *Command Output*

```
asa-1# show ipv6 local pool v6Pool
IPv6 Pool v6Pool
Begin Address: 2001:db8:cafe:1002::100

End Address: 2001:db8:cafe:1002::131

Prefix Length: 64
Pool Size: 50

Number of used addresses: 2
Number of available addresses: 48

In Use Addresses:
2001:db8:cafe:1002::100
2001:db8:cafe:1002::101
Available Addresses:
2001:db8:cafe:1002::102
2001:db8:cafe:1002::103
!OUTPUT OMITTED


asa-1# show vpn-sessiondb detail svc
!OUTPUT SUMMARIZED...
DTLS-Tunnel:
  Tunnel ID    : 6.3
  Assigned IP  : 10.124.3.30           Public IP     : 172.16.1.2

  Assigned IPv6: 2001:db8:cafe:1002::100

  Encryption   : AES128                Hashing       : SHA1
  Encapsulation: DTLSv1.0              UDP Src Port  : 4430

  UDP Dst Port : 443                   Auth Mode     : userPassword
  Idle Time Out: 30 Minutes            Idle TO Left  : 30 Minutes
  Client Type  : DTLS VPN Client
```

```
Client Ver    : AnyConnect Windows 2.4.1012
Bytes Tx      : 8720              Bytes Rx      : 26074
Pkts Tx       : 109               Pkts Rx       : 303
Pkts Tx Drop : 0                  Pkts Rx Drop : 0
```

Figure 10-3 shows the Cisco AnyConnect VPN Client statistics for the connection.

Figure 10-3 *Cisco AnyConnect Client Statistics*

The user can now access both IPv4- and IPv6-enabled applications and services through a single AnyConnect SSL session. Support for end-to-end IPv6 access from the user to the ASA head-end using SSL over IPv6 transport is on the product road map and will be available for those customers who need it.

Remote Access for IPv6 Using Cisco VPN Client

The Cisco VPN Client does not have built-in support for IPv6 like the Cisco AnyConnect solution does. However, it is still possible to support IPv6 through a Cisco VPN Client connection by using host-based tunnels (dynamic or static). One example of this is to leverage Intra-Site Automatic Tunnel Addressing Protocol (ISATAP) (RFC 5214) on the remote client along with an established Cisco VPN Client connection. Remember that ISATAP is a host-based tunnel that can provide tunneled IPv6 connectivity between the host and a router, Layer 3 switch, or server. The idea is that after a Cisco VPN Client connection has been made, there should be a routing path between the host and the tunnel endpoint located inside the enterprise network. The Cisco VPN Client enables tunneled traffic through the IPv4 IPsec connection.

Figure 10-4 shows an example topology where there is a remote user connecting to a Cisco IPsec VPN termination device (for example, Cisco IOS, ASA, 3000 Concentrator) over an IPv4 IPsec session. After that connection is made, the ISATAP (or other host tunnel type) tunnel is established between the remote host and the IPv6 tunnel termination point inside the enterprise network. After the ISATAP tunnel has been terminated, the IPv6 traffic can be routed to its destination over a dual-stack or native IPv6-only connection. In this model, IPv6 security access control lists (ACL) and inspection needs to be applied to IPv6 traffic after decapsulation inside the enterprise (that is, the internal IPv6 tunnel termination point).

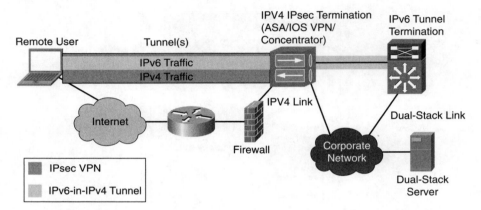

Figure 10-4   *Using the Cisco VPN Client with Host-Based Tunnels*

Note   Chapter 6, "Deploying IPv6 in Campus Networks," goes into much greater detail on the deployment of ISATAP and how to deploy it in a highly available manner for the enterprise.

Example 10-3 shows the basic ISATAP configuration deployed inside the enterprise. A tunnel interface is defined on an internal Cisco IOS router or Layer 3 switch such as a Catalyst 6500 Supervisor 720. An IPv6 prefix is configured, and the interface ID uses a modified EUI-64-derived address (as defined in RFC 4291). This prefix will be used by the ISATAP client after it is connected. The default tunnel behavior in Cisco IOS is to disable router advertisements (RA). Because this tunnel is going to be connecting to multiple endpoints and the IPv6 prefix needs to be learned by those endpoints, RAs need to be sent. This is accomplished by turning off the default suppression of RAs. The tunnel source is the loopback on the router, and there is no tunnel destination because the "isatap" tunnel mode implies multipoint tunnel functionality.

Note   The VPN termination device configuration is not shown because it is transparent to the actual IPv6 traffic.

Example 10-3 *ISATAP Configuration for a Cisco VPN Client*

```
interface Loopback0
 ip address 10.124.109.1 255.255.255.255
!
interface Tunnel4
 no ip address
 no ip redirects
 ipv6 address 2001:DB8:CAFE:1009::/64 eui-64

 no ipv6 nd ra suppress

 tunnel source Loopback0

 tunnel mode ipv6ip isatap
```

As discussed in Chapter 6, ISATAP can learn about the ISATAP router by either using a static configuration or dynamically through a DNS lookup. The static configuration is the recommended way to start because it enables granular control of when, how, and who can leverage ISATAP in the enterprise. The following command is used on a Microsoft Windows operating system and statically identifies the router interface (the loopback interface on the router). This statement can be an IPv4 address or host name (as resolved in DNS). In this example, the **set router 10.124.109.1** statement is the IPv4 address configured on interface Loopback0—the source of the ISATAP tunnel.

```
C:\>netsh interface ipv6 isatap set router 10.124.109.1
Ok.
```

Figure 10-5 shows that the client has a Cisco VPN Client session and that the client address is 10.124.3.30.

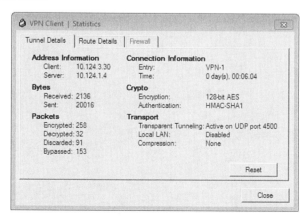

Figure 10-5 *Cisco VPN Client Session*

Example 10-4 is a summarized output from the Microsoft Windows 7 **ipconfig** command. The output shows that the IPv6 address of the client is 2001:db8:cafe:1009:0:5efe:10.124.3.30. The 2001:db8:cafe:1009 is the prefix defined on the Tunnel4 interface from Example 10-4. The 0:5efe is the ISATAP interface identifier as defined in RFC 5214. The 10.124.3.30 is the value that is derived from the client's IPv4 address.

Example 10-4 also shows that the client can successfully ping a host inside the enterprise network.

Example 10-4 *Microsoft Windows* ipconfig *and* **ping** *Output*

```
Tunnel adapter isatap.cisco.com:

   Connection-specific DNS Suffix  . : cisco.com
   IPv6 Address. . . . . . . . . . . : 2001:db8:cafe:1009:0:5efe:10.124.3.30

   Link-local IPv6 Address . . . . . : fe80::5efe:10.124.3.30%13
   Default Gateway . . . . . . . . . : fe80::5efe:10.124.109.1%13

C:\> ping 2001:db8:cafe:1005::1

Pinging 2001:db8:cafe:1005::1 with 32 bytes of data:
Reply from 2001:db8:cafe:1005::1: time=2ms
Reply from 2001:db8:cafe:1005::1: time<1ms
Reply from 2001:db8:cafe:1005::1: time=2ms
Reply from 2001:db8:cafe:1005::1: time=3ms
```

Summary

You need to account for access to IPv6-enabled services and applications from anywhere within and outside of the enterprise. IPv6 access over remote VPN solutions is maturing. Cisco provides IPv6 access over Cisco AnyConnect, which is based on SSL VPN, and this solution enables dual-stack access to the enterprise. If the Cisco VPN Client over IPsec is being leveraged today, it is recommended to move to the Cisco AnyConnect solution. If it is not possible to move to Cisco AnyConnect and IPv6 access is required in the near term, host-based tunnels (ISATAP, 6to4, manual, and so on) can be leveraged to provide a remote client access over the Cisco VPN Client IPsec session.

Additional References

Popoviciu, Ciprian P., Eric Levy-Abegnoli, and Patrick Grossetete. *Deploying IPv6 Networks*. Cisco Press. (ISBN-10: 1-58705-210-5; ISBN-13: 978-1-58705-210-1).

Hogg, Scott and Eric Vyncke. *IPv6 Security*. Cisco Press. (ISBN-10: 1-58705-594-5; ISBN-13: 978-1-58705-594-2).

Microsoft. Microsoft DirectAccess: http://technet.microsoft.com/ en-us/network/dd420463.aspx.

Cisco. Cisco ASA 5500 SSL VPN Deployment Guide, Version 8.x: http://www.cisco.com/en/US/docs/security/asa/asa80/asdm60/ssl_vpn_deployment_ guide/deploy.html.

Cisco. Cisco ASA 5500 SSL VPN Deployment Guide - Clientless SSL Documentation: http://www.cisco.com/en/US/docs/security/asa/asa80/asdm60/ssl_vpn_deployment_ guide/deploy.html#wp1016526.

Rescorla, E. and N. Modadugu. RFC 4347, "Datagram Transport Layer Security."

Templin, F., T. Gleeson, and D. Thaler. RFC 5214, "Intra-Site Automatic Tunnel Addressing Protocol (ISATAP)."

Hinden, R. and S. Deering. RFC 4291, "IP Version 6 Addressing Architecture."

Chapter 11

Managing IPv6 Networks

This chapter covers the following topics:

- **Network management framework: FCAPS:** The chapter starts with an introduction to a management framework that is independent of IPv4 and IPv6. This framework provides the foundation of managing any network infrastructure.

- **IPv6 network management applications:** This section provides information on integrating IPv6 with the existing IPv6 network management applications.

- **IPv6 network instrumentation:** With IPv6 running in conjunction to IPv4, the network infrastructure extends the support of existing built-in tools such as MIBs, NetFlow, IP SLA, and EEM to support IPv6 deployments.

- **IPv6 network management:** Enterprises typically focus on extending their network management infrastructure over IPv6 after they have successfully deployed IPv6 for the end-host connectivity. In this section, we look at various applications that are used for IPv6 network management.

- **IPv6 traffic-monitoring tools:** This section focuses on tools to monitor, capture, and analyze IPv6 tools are needed for troubleshooting and network anomaly detection needs.

Network management and monitoring are essential building blocks and critical parts of operating any enterprise-class network. The primary objective of network management is to support the operational processes of the infrastructure including provisioning, change management, monitoring, reporting, and troubleshooting. This becomes challenging as organizations integrate IPv6 within their existing network infrastructure. As discussed in Chapter 1, "Market Drivers for IPv6 Adoption," IPv6 as such is not a feature but a fundamental rewrite of the IP network layer model. Because IPv6 can coexist with the IPv4 infrastructure for the near future, existing tools, processes, and methodologies must evolve to support heterogeneous IPv4 and IPv6 networks.

Today, existing IPv4 networks are managed with a wide variety of tools ranging from scripts to complex and costly licensed-based and database-driven management applications. Although the vast majority of these tools have grown and matured with the IPv4 network infrastructure they manage, there is no parity between the features used to manage IPv4 and those used for IPv6. To begin with, the following questions need to be kept in mind when extending IPv4 tools to manage dual-stack, hybrid IPv4-IPv6 networks:

- Are the network management applications deployed today capable of managing network infrastructure through IPv4 and IPv6? Which network applications are IPv4-capable-only? And which applications support dual-stack IPv4 and IPv6?

- What devices are currently being managed? Are these devices capable of supporting management through IPv6 either through Simple Network Management Protocol (SNMP) IPv6 extensions or a mixture of other management protocols?

- What is the nature of the Management Information Base (MIB) currently being used? Are they discrete IPv4 and IPv6 MIBs or the newer unified protocol-agnostics MIBs? Does the existing network infrastructure support IPv6 MIBs?

- Will the tools used today fit into the transition plan and a long-term IPv6 "native or "IPv6-only" plan?

This chapter outlines key concepts and identifies tools needed for managing IPv6 deployments. The chapter assists network architects in managing their IPv6 designs and deployments as part of their existing IPv4 network management infrastructure. Table 11-1 lists the capabilities of popular Cisco devices. Throughout this chapter, these features will be discussed in detail; however, the following table provides a good summary of which devices offer these features.

Network Management Framework: FCAPS

To help simplify and standardize network management, network managers have developed a comprehensive framework that addresses the range of management functions required to operate a network environment. This generic framework is independent of IPv4 or IPv6 as such, but it helps outline the foundation of managing any network infrastructure. The framework outlines five management functional areas: Fault, Configuration, Accounting, Performance, and Security Management (FCAPS). This comprehensive framework for network management addresses the wide range of management functions that are required in an operational network environment.

FCAPS was introduced by ISO in its first working draft (N1719). Each functional area can be addressed independently of each other. For example, fault-diagnosing activities required for troubleshooting network problems are very different from configuring network devices as such. The following sections provide an overview of the FCAPS functional areas.

Table 11-1   *IPv6 Capabilities of Popular Cisco Switches*

Management Protocol		Nexus 7000	Catalyst 6500	Catalyst 4900	Catalyst 4500
Monitoring and reporting	SNMP	Y	Y	Y	Y
	Syslog	Y	Y	Y	Y
Network services	NTP	Y	Y	Y	Y
	TFTP	Y	Y	Y	Y
Control and operation	Telnet	Y	Y	Y	Y
	SSH	Y	Y	Y	Y
	HTTP	Y	Y	Y	Y
	Netconf	Y	N	Y	N
MIB		Y	Y	Y	Y
Interface statistics		Y	Y	Y	Y
ICMP		Y	Y	Y	Y
NetFlow		Y	Y	N	Y (Sup 7E)
IPSLA		N	Y	Y	Y

Note   Additional details on the FCAPS framework can be found at http://www.tech-faq.com/fcaps.html.

Fault Management

Fault management is the process of detecting, categorizing, logging, and reporting faults through proactive monitoring or reactive manual detection (for example, a user call to the Help Desk). It also includes the root cause analysis and event correlation.

Configuration Management

Configuration management is the control mechanism and discipline that increase the probability of implementing successful changes in the production network environment. This also includes being able to automatically manage network inventory, software licenses, and system certifications.

Accounting Management

Accounting management refers to a methodology of measuring managed resources and services rendered to end users within a billing period. This includes asset tracking, service-level reporting, and vendor management.

Performance Management

Performance management includes the capability to meet target service levels and to establish a detailed service-level baseline. This functional area also includes capacity planning, network performance analysis, and reporting.

Security Management

Security management includes network encryption, disaster recovery and contingency planning, security alert monitoring, reporting, and policy management.

Table 11-2 summarizes the functional areas, their features, and product examples.

Table 11-2   *FCAPS Summary*

FCAPS Functional Area	Features	Product Examples
Fault	Fault detection and correction Fault isolation and network recovery Alarm handling, alarm filtering, and alarm generation Trouble detection and logging Diagnosis Trouble correction Test and acceptance Network recovery Fault reporting	Cisco Works Tivoli Netview Cisco Fabric Manager for managing storage networks
Configuration	Resource initialization Network provisioning Autodiscovery Backup and restore Database handling Change/inventory management Certifications	Cisco Works Cisco Fabric Manager Cisco Data Center Network Management (DCNM) Network Registrar Network Compliance Manager
Accounting	Usage tracking Billing Asset tracking Service-level management Vendor management	Cisco Works NetFlow Collectors: NetQoS

Table 11-2   *FCAPS Summary*

FCAPS Functional Area	Features	Product Examples
Performance	Baseline definition Capacity planning Performance analysis Monitoring Reporting	Cisco Works NetFlow
Security	Access control Security administration System audit Alert monitoring Encryption Policy management	Cisco ACS (TACACS+/RADIUS)

IPv6 Network Management Applications

A network management system (NMS) is an application that manages the agents and communicates with the agent through a management interface provided by the agent. An NMS is also referred to as the manager.

Enterprise customers integrating IPv6 require the network management applications to help them with the following:

■ Deploy IPv4/IPv6 dual-stack and IPv6-only networks

■ Extend the management of the existing IPv4-only network infrastructure to manage IPv4/IPv6 dual-stack and IPv6-only networks

Cisco offers a broad suite of network management applications that help manage the network infrastructure. In addition to the Cisco offerings of network management applications, third-party network management stations such as HP OpenView and IBM Tivoli can manage Cisco network devices through the built-in instrumentation on routers and switches. On the Cisco side, Cisco LAN Management Station is the leading IPv6 network management station that has three key components: CiscoView, Campus Manager, and Resource Manager (RME).

Table 11-3 summarizes the functions of Cisco LAN Management Station key components.

Table 11-3   *Summary of Cisco LAN Management Solutions Key Components*

Key Component	Features
CiscoView	Configuration and IPv6 address configuration (unicast and multicast) Neighbor discovery of IPv6 neighbors (ND) Router advertisement (RA) Multicast Listener Discovery (MLD) Interface information IPv6 neighbors (ND and RA) Statistics (IPv6 versus IPv4 traffic)
CiscoWorks Campus Manager	IPv6 topology services IPv6 access control lists User tracking
CiscoWorks RME	IPv6 addresses in reports IPv6 support in NetConfig templates **netshow** commands in IPv6 Facility to parse and compare config files for specific IPv6 configlets

IPv6 Network Instrumentation

Fundamentally the network infrastructure has been managed by Cisco or third-party network management applications with the help of open application programming interfaces (API). These APIs have now been extended to assist with the following fault isolation, debugging, and troubleshooting tools:

■ Network device management using SNMP Management Information Base (MIB)

■ IPv6 application visibility and monitoring, including Flexible NetFlow, Sampled Flow (sFLOW), IPFIX, and IPv6 IPSLA

■ Automation using flexible programming with Embedded Event Manager (EEM)

The following sections describe each of these tools in greater detail.

Network Device Management Using SNMP MIBs

A Management Information Base (MIB) provides an abstraction of the network device in the form of an "agent" that can be retrieved by a network management application (for example, CiscoWorks). These management requests can be any one of the previously outlined FCAPS functions, including physical configuration information, historical performance trends, and current physical resources state. The information in a MIB is commonly known as a managed object (MO). Each managed object is represented by a unique identification known as the object identifier (OID).

Figure 11-1 illustrates the logical representation of MIB and the network device. The network device has been split logically into the real resource plane and the management plane. The real resource plane depicts the real entities that are being used for network communications. The management plane shows the managed object that are used to manage the individual resources. The managed objects combined represent the MIB, which in turn represents the device.

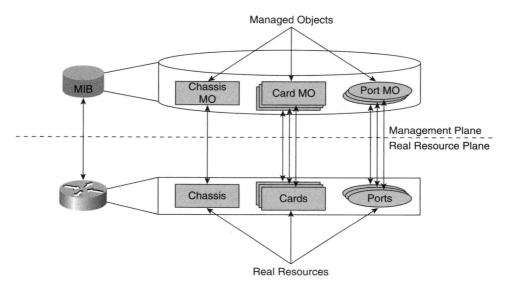

Figure 11-1 *Management Agent and MO*

MIBs are accessed through SNMP for network operations as follows:

■ **Reading a MIB variable:** A network management station (NMS) requests information from the management agent of a network device by specifying an OID. The management agent retrieves the value of the OID and sends the information to the NMS.

■ **Setting a MIB variable:** The NMS sends a value for the OID to the management agent of a network device. The management agent changes the OID to the value requested by the NMS.

Initially, the IETF created protocol-specific MIBs for IPv6 in parity with existing IPv4 MIBs. But as organizations adopted IPv6 in their networks, they required the IETF to define MIBs that are protocol agnostic for ease of integration with their existing IPv4 SNMP infrastructure. Table 11-4 outlines the IPv4 and IPv6 protocol-specific MIB RFCs.

But with increased adoption of dual-stack IPv4-IPv6 network designs, the IETF felt a need to define protocol-agnostic MIBs that outline the same management information independent of the protocol - IPv4 and IPv6. Figure 11-2 shows the evolution of IETF

MIB RFCs from protocol-specific to protocol-agnostic MIBs. The protocol-agnostic MIBs are outlined in the following RFCs:

- RFC 4292, "IP Forwarding Table MIB," provides recommendations to support IP version-independent implementations of the forwarding MIB. This gives a common forwarding MIB framework for IPv4 and IPv6.

- RFC 4293, "Management Information Base for the Internet Protocol (IP)," is a revision of the IP MIB to create a single set of objects to describe and manage IP modules in an IP version-independent manner. It merges RFCs 2465, 2466, and 2011 to increase the manageability of IPv6 devices.

- RFC 4022, "Management Information Base for the Transmission Control Protocol (TCP)," outlines protocol-independent TCP MIBs.

- RFC 4113, "Management Information Base for the User Datagram Protocol (UDP)," outlines protocol-independent UDP MIBs.

Table 11-4   *Protocol-Specific MIBs*

IPv4-Specific RFC	IPv6-Specific RFC	RFC MIB Definition
RFC 2011	RFC 2465	IP/IP Forwarding MIB
RFC 2012	RFC 2452	TCP MIB
RFC 2013	RFC 2454	UDP MIB
RFC 2096 (obsoletes RFC 1354)	—	IP Forwarding Table MIB

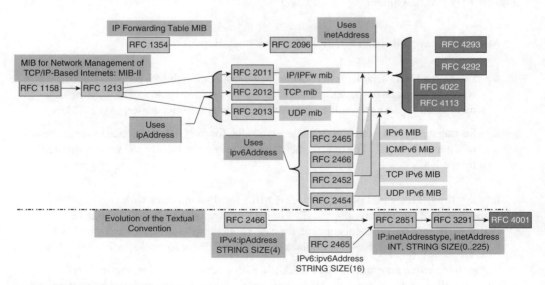

Figure 11-2   *Evolution of MIBs*

> **Note** With the definition of protocol-agnostic MIBs, all Cisco network devices can support protocol-agnostic MIBs.

Relevance of IPv6 MIBs

MIBs are defined in SNMP MIB language and are submitted to the Internet Engineering Task Force (IETF) as RFC documents. Cisco enterprise MIBs comply with the guidelines described in the relevant RFCs unless otherwise noted in the documentation. As RFCs are constantly being updated, so are the MIBs. Generally speaking, the NMS should be using the latest MIBs to ensure maximum network visibility.

If the NMS cannot get the SNMP-requested information from a managed device, such as a Cisco router, the MIB that allows that specific data collection might be missing. Typically, if an NMS cannot retrieve a particular MIB variable, either the NMS does not recognize the MIB variable or the agent does not support the MIB variable. If the NMS does not recognize a specified MIB variable, the MIB might need to be loaded into the NMS, usually by means of a MIB compiler. An NMS administrator might need to load the Cisco MIB or the supported RFC MIB into the NMS to execute a specified data collection. If the agent does not support a specified MIB variable, the version of Cisco IOS or system software needs to be checked. Different MIBs are supported in different software releases. This information is generally available in the release notes.

Approximately 300 RFCs in the first 5000 RFCs contain MIBs. Although discussing all the MIBs is beyond the scope of this book, the focus is only on protocol-agnostic and other MIBs relevant to managing network devices. The MIBs outlined in Table 11-5 are integrated into Cisco products.

Table 11-5 *IPv6 MIB Descriptions*

IPv6-Related MIB	Description	RFC
CISCO-CONFIG-COPY-MIB	MIB for copying a Cisco router's configuration.	Cisco Private MIB
CISCO-CONFIG-MAN-MIB	Configuration management MIB.	Cisco Private MIB
CISCO-DATA-COLLECTION-MIB	Used for collecting data periodically.	Cisco Private MIB
CISCO-FLASH-MIB	Used for managing flash devices.	Cisco Private MIB
CISCO-IETF-IP-FORWARDING-MIB	Used for managing IP routes. This is the Cisco version of IP-FORWARD-MIB.	Cisco Private MIB
CISCO-IETF-IP-MIB	Used for managing IP and ICMP operations. This is the Cisco version of IP-MIB.	Cisco Private MIB

continues

Table 11-5   *IPv6 MIB Descriptions   (continued)*

IPv6-Related MIB	Description	RFC
IP-FORWARD-MIB	Used for managing IP routes.	RFC 4292
IP-MIB	Used for managing IP and ICMP.	RFC 4293
ENTITY-MIB	Used for managing multiple logical entities by a single SNMP agent.	RFC 4133
NOTIFICATION-LOG-MIB	Used for logging SNMP events such as traps and informs.	RFC 3014
SNMP-TARGET-MIB	Used to remotely configure SNMP parameters.	RFC 2273
CISCO-SNMP-TARGET-EXT-MIB	Used to remotely configure SNMP parameters. This is the Cisco version of the SNMP-TARGET-MIB.	Cisco Private MIB
INET-ADDRESS-MIB	Defines textual conventions for defining IP addresses.	RFC 4001
TCP-MIB	Used for managing TCP connections.	RFC 4022
UDP-MIB	Used for managing UDP connections.	RFC 4113

IPv6 Application Visibility and Monitoring

This section provides an overview of features that enable application visibility as well as monitoring tools that can be used with IPv6. The following features are discussed:

- Flexible NetFlow
- IPFIX
- IPv6 SLA

Flexible NetFlow

NetFlow has been shipping on Cisco routers and switches since 1996. This technology is the de facto standard for acquiring IP operational data, enabling network administrators to provide network monitoring, planning, traffic analysis accounting, and security monitoring. NetFlow allows network administrators to better understand

- How to establish a network baseline by monitoring the utilization of network assets

- What, when, where, and how network traffic is flowing

- How to detect and classify security incidents

To maximize the utilization of NetFlow, it is important to understand what features to implement in which layer in an enterprise network, as shown in Figure 11-3.

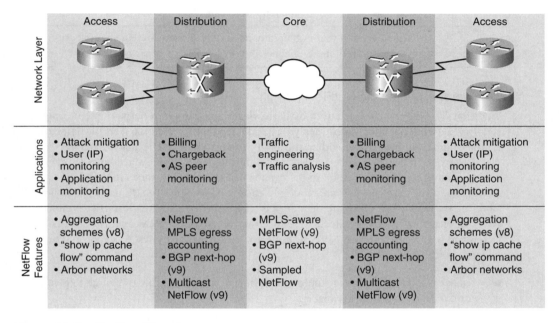

Figure 11-3   *NetFlow Placement*

NetFlow Versions

Over the years, NetFlow has evolved to support new protocols and enhancements, which Table 11-6 summarizes. The latest version of NetFlow v9 provides support for IPv6 along with other additional enhancements. This bookfocuses only on NetFlow v9 (also known as Flexible NetFlow).

Note   For additional information on the different versions of NetFlow, visit http://www.cisco.com/en/US/prod/collateral/iosswrel/ps6537/ps6555/ps6601/prod_white _paper0900aecd80406232.html.

Table 11-6   *NetFlow Export Version Features*

Export Format	Features Supported
Version 9	Supports IPv6. For the purposes of this book, we will be concentrating on version 9. This version also supports Multicast, DoS, BGP next hop, and so on. Defined in RFC 3954.
Version 8	Supports aggregation schemes and reduces resource usage.
Version 5	Most common version generally followed.
Version 1	Original version that is generally used only if there are legacy collection systems that require it.

NetFlow version 9 (Flexible NetFlow [FnF])

Traditionally NetFlow has been used by network administrators for network monitoring, security, network planning, traffic analysis, and IP accounting. Flexible NetFlow improves on the original NetFlow by providing the ability to customize traffic analysis parameters. NetFlow exists in both full and sampled mode. In full mode, NetFlow accounts for every packet coming on the interface up to the capacity of the NetFlow table. In sampled mode, only a subset of packets are randomly chosen (typically a 1-in-32 packet sampling) from the traffic stream, which are then used to characterize the network traffic. Sampled NetFlow enables network architects to reduce the volume of NetFlow export that is collected and sent to the external NetFlow collector for further analytics. It is typically used under two scenarios:

- Capacity planning, where an approximate view of network traffic is enough to give a good indication of traffic capacity.

- Traffic flow monitoring on high-speed interfaces (for example, 10 Gigabit Ethernet), where creating flows for every packet would burden the NetFlow cache and collector.

Key enhancements provided by Flexible NetFlow over traditional NetFlow v5 are outlined in Table 11-7.

The following sections describe full and sampled NetFlow in greater detail.

Full NetFlow

Full NetFlow allows collection updates for every packet that constitutes the identified flow. This is the default NetFlow behavior and helps administrators account for every packet that flows through the particular switch. Because NetFlow is handled by the hardware in higher-end switching and routing products, creating flow records for each flow does not impose a significant impact on the switch (or router) CPU as such. However, the NetFlow flow record export to an external NetFlow collector is still handled by CPU and under high traffic flow volume conditions, the export process can burden the CPU. Based on the flow mask configured at the incoming interface, each flow has a flow entry in the NetFlow hardware table.

Table 11-7   *NetFlow and FNF Comparison*

Traditional NetFlow v5	Flexible NetFlow (FnF)	Benefit
One set of flow information, single cache used by all applications.	Different NetFlow applications are tracked uniquely.	Track security and traffic analysis data separately. Export different flow monitors to different destinations. Detailed analysis for each application.
Single cache used for all flows.	Creates virtual NetFlow caches to provides more flexible network visibility.	Create virtual NetFlow caches. Isolate security or traffic incidents in the network. Customized traffic identification. Nearly 100 percent accuracy in determining and isolating incidents.
Limited data aggregation by using fixed flow fields.	Flow information is user configurable and leverages new data types defined in NetFlow version 9 export.	Ability to select relevant information. New information from Layer 2 and above, including packet sections.

Flow Mask

Flow mask determines the granularity of the statistics gathered. For example, if the flow mask is set to source-only, the NetFlow table contains only one entry per source IP address. NetFlow stores flow in a NetFlow table that can become very large if flow masks are not configured correctly. A flow mask is used to specify the following fields in the incoming packet that NetFlow uses to identify the flow:

- Source and destination IP address

- Source and destination TCP/UDP port number

- IP protocol type, input VLAN, and ToS bit

NetFlow Operation

NetFlow works using seven operational parameters, as shown in Figure 11-4. NetFlow inspects a packet for these seven keys and creates a flow in the NetFlow cache. These flows are then exported to a an external NetFlow collector (for example, CiscoWorks and NetQoS).

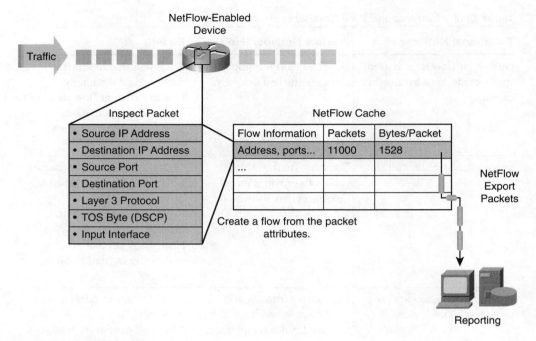

Figure 11-4 *NetFlow Operation*

Note For additional details on available commercial and freeware NetFlow collectors, visit http://www.cisco.com/en/US/prod/collateral/iosswrel/ps6537/ps6555/ps6601/prod_white _paper0900aecd80406232.html.

Sampled NetFlow

Sampled NetFlow is designed to allow the administrator to define a time-based rate or a packet-sampling rate as the means to derive the sampled data. Should time-based sampling be used for export, the administrator would be required to define a "sampling rate." The sampling rate defines the amount of time within a given interval from which the flow information can be collected. Packet-based sampling uses a similar formula in that the number of times sampled is derived by dividing the number of packets in a flow by the sampling rate.

The obvious downside to using sampled NetFlow is that it does not give as accurate a picture of the makeup of the flow. For this reason, sampled NetFlow is often used for purposes where a full view of the data is not required. Use case examples for sampled NetFlow include capacity and network planning. In the sampled mode of operation, the NetFlow engine accounts for M in N packets on the interface (anywhere from 1:2 to 1:8000), up to the capacity of the NetFlow table. Extending on the previous example shown in Figure 11-4, if the ingress interface is a higher-bandwidth interface like 10 GE and beyond (keeping 40 G and 100 G in mind), the recommended mode of operation in that case would be sampled NetFlow because it helps scale to the incoming traffic speeds.

NetFlow Data Export

NetFlow Data Export (NDE) is a control plane process that extracts the NetFlow records and exports them in a specified record format to an external NetFlow collector. The NDE process running on the router/switches will export the NetFlow datagrams from the TCAM table and send these packets using UDP to a configured NetFlow collector. Being UDP based, the network flow data export process lacks an acknowledgment mechanism, thereby leading to a situation where the data export record can be dropped. The NetFlow collector, however, relies on a sequence number in the NetFlow header (the sequence number is very similar to that of a TCP sequence number). The sequence number in the NetFlow data record is equal to the sequence number of the last datagram plus the number of flows in the previous datagram. With the help of the sequence number, the NetFlow collector can then subtract the expected sequence number to determine whether any datagrams were lost in the export process.

The network administrator can provision the NetFlow flow record export to be triggered upon any of the following conditions:

- The interface where the flow is coming in goes down.

- A route flap occurs.

- The entry is manually cleared by the administrator.

- The entry is aged out by the expiration of one of the NetFlow aging timers.

- An aging timer is used to indicate to the NDE process when a flow is ready for export. The flow "aging" is the process of removing stale NetFlow entries when they expire. Only when the flow expires it is removed from the NetFlow table and exported together with its statistics.

Network architects would need to make changes to their existing collector applications to support the different NetFlow v9 formats.

Configuring Flexible NetFlow on Nexus OS

Configuring Flexible Netflow on the Nexus OS is a four step process, illustrated here:

Step 1. Configure the exporter.

Step 2. Configure the flow record.

Step 3. Configure the flow monitor:

Create a new NetFlow cache

Attach the flow record.

Attach the exporter to the cache.

Step 4.   Configure NetFlow on the interface.

The following sections discuss these components in more detail.

Configure the Exporter

The NetFlow data can be accessed through the CLI or an application. The exporter configuration is used to define where the export can be sent, along with the type of transport for the export and properties of the export.

Note   At this time, only IPv4 addresses can be used for NetFlow export destinations.

Configure the Flow Record

A flow record is used to characterize flows in the NetFlow cache. The flow record contains a set of key and nonkey NetFlow field values. Network management applications will support user-defined and predefined flow records based on the type of traffic being monitored.

Configure the Flow Monitor

The flow monitor defines the information stored in the NetFlow cache. The flow monitor contains the flow records.

Configure the Interface

In the final step, the flow monitor is applied to the interface on which traffic is to be analyzed. Example 11-1 demonstrates a simple NetFlow configuration.

Example 11-1   *Cisco Nexus OS Flexible NetFlow Configuration*

```
! Create Exporter
flow exporter my-exporter
destination 1.1.1.1
! Create Flow Record
flow record my-record
match ipv6 destination address
match ipv6 source address
collect counter bytes
! Create Flow Monitor
flow monitor my-monitor
exporter my-exporter
record my-record
! Apply Flow Monitor on interface
int gig3/1
ip flow monitor my-monitor input
```

Configuring Flexible NetFlow for IPv6 on Cisco IOS Devices

NetFlow configuration for IPv6 is similar to IPv4 on IOS, IOS-XE, and IOS-XR with the following caveats:

- NetFlow Export version 9 must be used.

- NetFlow is available for both ingress and egress traffic.

- NetFlow L2 and security monitoring is available in IPv6.

- NetFlow requires an IPv4-based device for data export.

- IPv6 Cisco Express Forwarding (CEF) must be configured.

- IPv6 flows must be configured on the interfaces.

Example 11-2 shows the NetFlow configuration for IPv6 on Cisco IOS.

Example 11-2   *NetFlow Configuration in Cisco IOS Using IPv6*

```
ipv6 unicast-routing
ipv6 cef
ip flow-export destination 172.28.103.122 99
!
interface FastEthernet0/0
 no ip address
 duplex auto
 speed auto
 ipv6 address 2001:DB8:CAFE:155::1/64
 ipv6 enable
 ipv6 flow ingress
 ipv6 flow egress
```

Example 11-3 shows that the output commands are the same as for IPv4.

Example 11-3   show ipv6 flow cache *Command Output*

```
Router-1# show ipv6 flow cache
IP packet size distribution (49990 total packets):
   1-32   64   96  128  160  192  224  256  288  320  352  384  416  448  480
   .000 .000 .000 .999 .000 .000 .000 .000 .000 .000 .000 .000 .000 .000 .000

   512  544  576 1024 1536 2048 2560 3072 3584 4096 4608
   .000 .000 .000 .000 .000 .000 .000 .000 .000 .000 .000

IP Flow Switching Cache, 475168 bytes
  8 active, 4088 inactive, 8 added
```
continues

Example 11-3   show ipv6 flow cache *Command Output   continued*

```
    100 ager polls, 0 flow alloc failures
    Active flows timeout in 30 minutes
    Inactive flows timeout in 15 seconds
IP Sub Flow Cache, 33928 bytes
    12 active, 1012 inactive, 12 added, 8 added to flow
    0 alloc failures, 0 force free
    1 chunk, 1 chunk added
SrcAddress          InpIf      DstAddress        OutIf      Prot SrcPrt DstPrt Packets
2001:DB...:155::2 Fa0/0      FE80::2...E:9478 Local      0x3A 0x0000 0x8800 1
FE80::2...49:1540 Fa0/0      FE80::2...E:9478 Local      0x3A 0x0000 0x8800 1
FE80::2...6E:9478 Local      FE80::2...9:1540 Fa0/0      0x3A 0x0000 0x8800 1
2001:DB...:155::1 Local      2001:DB...155::2 Fa0/0      0x3A 0x0000 0x8100 16K
2001:DB...:155::2 Fa0/0      2001:DB...155::1 Local      0x3A 0x0000 0x8000 35K
FE80::2...49:1540 Fa0/0      FE80::2...E:9478 Local      0x3A 0x0000 0x8700 1
FE80::2...6E:9478 Local      FE80::2...9:1540 Fa0/0      0x3A 0x0000 0x8700 1
```

IPFIX

Internet Protocol Flow Information eXport (IPFIX) is an emerging IETF standard. IPFIX is defined in RFC 3917 and is based on NetFlow version 9. There are some changes in terminology and methods; however, the principles of working are the same as NetFlow version 9. IPFIX is primarily a push protocol. This implies that each sender will periodically send IPFIX messages to the receiver without any intervention by the receiver. The sender can use user-defined data types in its messages, so IPFIX becomes freely extensible and can adapt to different scenarios. Figure 11-5 shows the IPFIX flow.

Similar to Flexible NetFlow, IPFIX requires the following steps for a traffic flow. These steps include the observation, metering process, exporting process, and finally the collecting process. An IP traffic flow is quantified as a group of IP packets going through an observation point with common properties such as

- Header fields (IP address, port numbers, and so on)

- Packet fields (Multiprotocol Label Switching [MPLS] labels and so on)

- Packet treatment fields (next-hop IP address, interface, and so on)

The following sections describe each step of the IPFIX flow shown in Figure 11-5.

Observation Point

An observation point is a location in the network point where packets can be observed, such as an interface. An observation point can be a superset of multiple observation points. For example, an entire line card can be an observation point that would be a superset of the individual observation points of the line card's interfaces.

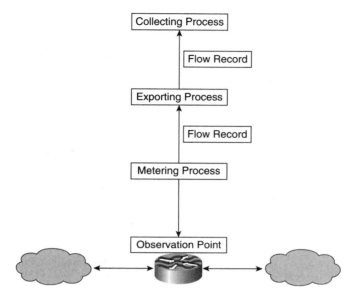

Figure 11-5   *IPFIX Flow*

Metering Process

The observation point classifies the interesting flows and forwards the information to the metering process, which generates the flow records. A flow record contains measured properties and characteristics about a specific flow that was metered at an observation point.

The metering process looks at the packet headers and packet treatments at an observation point. The metering process is responsible for

■ Creating new flow records

■ Updating existing flow records

■ Computing flow statistics

■ Passing flow records to the exporting process

■ Deleting flow records

Exporting Process

Flow records are generated by one or more metering process. The exporting process generates an IPFIX message that carries the flow records of this exporting process. An IPFIX message is encapsulated at the transport layer and sent to the collecting process.

Collecting Process

The collecting process receives the flow records from one or more exporting processes. The collecting process is based on user configuration and can store or further process flow records.

As illustrated in Figure 11-6, the following key enhancements to IPFIX are compared to NetFlow version 9 to make it more robust and efficient:

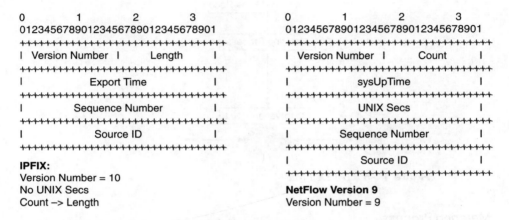

Figure 11-6   *IPFIX and NetFlow Version 9 Packet Differences*

- IPFIX packets are smaller compared to the NetFlow packet size with the removal of the UNIX secs field.

- The IPFIX Length field replaces the Count field in NetFlow v9.

- The IPFIX version type is 10, whereas the NetFlow v9 version type is 9.

IP SLA for IPv6

Traditionally in a network, a network management station (NMS) is deployed in a central location from where it runs tests to other remote locations for connectivity and other management data. As network connectivity and features evolve, the complexity in managing and collecting performance data increases. One way to address this is to introduce NMS appliances or software in different sections of the network, but that can be very expensive and even more difficult to manage.

Cisco IOS IP service-level agreements (SLA) allow the Cisco devices to collect and send performance and management data to an NMS. The CiscoWorks Internetwork Performance Monitor (IPM) tool can be used with IP SLAs to proactively discover and address end-to-end network performance issues.

The IP SLA source is typically a router or a switch running a test toward a destination. The destination can be any IP device. If the destination is a Cisco device, it can be configured as a responder. The responder feature allows the Cisco device to capture data in one direction and send additional data back, such as calculating the transaction time of data moving across the network to determine the performance for both ends. The NMS then collects the SLA data from the Cisco IP SLA device and provides a display of the data.

Cisco IOS IP SLAs use active traffic monitoring to aid in analyzing IP service levels for IP applications and services and measure network performance. Cisco IOS IP SLAs are Layer 2 independent, which provides end-to-end metrics that an end user is likely to experience.

IP SLAs send metrics over SNMP, which makes it accessible by performance-monitoring applications like CiscoWorks Internetwork Performance Monitor (IPM) and other third-party performance management products. Cisco IOS IP SLA operations allow the router to receive alerts when performance drops below a specified level and when problems are corrected. Cisco RTTMON MIB is used for interaction between external NMS applications and the Cisco devices. For a complete description of the object variables, refer to the text of the CISCO-RTTMON-MIB.my file, available from the Cisco MIB website: http://www.cisco.com/public/sw-center/netmgmt/cmtk/mibs.shtml.

Although the complete operation of IP SLAs is beyond the scope of this book, some examples of common scenarios using IPv6 are discussed:

- **ICMP echo operation:** Measures hop-by-hop response times between a Cisco router and any IP device

- **TCP connect operation:** Measures response times for a TCP connect operation between a Cisco device and any IP host

- **UDP echo operation:** Measures response times between Cisco devices

- **UDP jitter operation:** Uses UDP traffic to generate an approximate Voice over IP score as well as to calculate jitter variance for the data

The following sections provide an overview of these IP SLA operations.

ICMP Echo Operation

The ICMP echo operation can be used to monitor end-to-end response time between a Cisco router and devices. This is a very useful tool in troubleshooting network connectivity issues. Figure 11-7 shows that the router calculates the round-trip time by calculating T2-T1. This type of operation will not include the processing time on the target host.

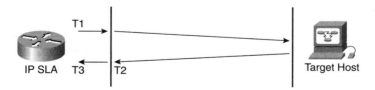

Figure 11-7   *IP SLA ICMP Echo Operation*

Example 11-4 shows the configuration of ICMP echo for IP SLA using IPv6.

Example 11-4   *Cisco IOS IP SLA ICMP Echo Operation Example*

```
ip sla 10
 icmp-echo 2001:db8:cafe:151::10 source-ip 2001:db8:cafe:121::1
 frequency 300
 request-data-size 28
 tag Gateway_WebServer
!
ip sla schedule 10 life forever start-time now
```

Example 11-4 shows an IP SLA operation number 10 that will start immediately and run indefinitely. The operation will generate 28-byte ICMP echoes for destination 2001:db8:cafe:151::10 with a source of 2001:db8:cafe:121::1 after a 300-second interval. Configuring a tag for the SLA operation provides a method of identification. Example 11-5 illustrates the statistics captured for IP SLA.

Example 11-5   *Cisco IP SLA ICMP Echo Statistics*

```
show ip sla statistics 10 details

Round Trip Time (RTT) for        Index 10
Type of operation: icmp-echo
        Latest RTT: NoConnection/Busy/Timeout
Latest operation start time: *01:40:13.920 UTC Tue Jan 18 2011
Latest operation return code: Timeout
Over thresholds occurred: FALSE
Number of successes: 0
Number of failures: 1
Operation time to live: Forever
Operational state of entry: Active
Last time this entry was reset: Never
```

TCP Connect Operation

The Cisco IP SLA TCP connect operation measures the response time taken to perform a TCP connect operation between a Cisco router and devices using IPv6. TCP is a transport layer (Layer 4) Internet protocol that provides reliable full-duplex data transmission. The destination device can be any IPv6 device or an IP SLA responder.

This operation can be used to test virtual circuit availability or application availability. As seen in Figure 11-8, measured connection time is the difference between the times when the ACK and initial SYN were sent, which in this case is T2-T1.

In Example 11-6, we use a host (2001:db8:cafe:101::51) running a Telnet application at the destination router.

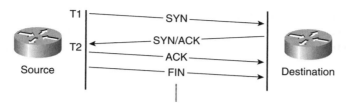

Figure 11-8   *IP SLA TCP Connect Operation*

Example 11-6   *Cisco IOS IP SLA TCP Connect Example Destination*

```
ip sla responder
```

Example 11-7 illustrates the configuration for this operation at the source router. The application is set to start immediately.

Example 11-7   *Cisco IOS IP SLA TCP Connect Example Source*

```
ip sla 10
 tcp-connect 2001:DB8:CAFE:101::51 23
 frequency 30
ip sla schedule 10 life forever start-time now
```

UDP Echo Operation

Just like the ICMP echo operation, the UDP echo operation can be used to monitor end-to-end response time between a Cisco router and devices. This operation can be used for measuring response times and testing end-to-end connectivity. Many applications use UDP for IP services. A UDP echo operation can be used for any networking device that supports RFC 862, "Echo Protocol"; however, we recommend using a Cisco networking device as the destination device.

As illustrated in Figure 11-9, the source router and the responder router are being used to measure UDP echoes. The processing delay on the source can be calculated as T5-T4, and the processing delay on the destination can be calculated as T3-T2. The total delay can be calculated as T2+T4-T1-T3. On loaded interfaces, queuing delay might become a problem; otherwise, it is negligible.

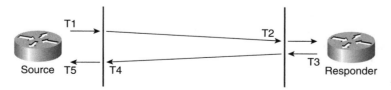

Figure 11-9   *IPSLA UDP Echo Operation*

The configuration of a UDP echo operation, as illustrated in Figure 11-9, can be achieved with the **ip sla responder** command for the responder. Example 11-8 illustrates the configuration of the source router.

Example 11-8   *Cisco IOS IP SLA UDP Echo Operation Example Source Router*

```
ip sla 10
 udp-echo 2001:DB8:CAFE:101::51 5000
 frequency 5
ip sla schedule 10 life forever start-time now
```

UDP Jitter Operation

The UDP jitter operation is used to monitor real-time applications such as Voice over IP (VoIP), video over IP, or real-time conferencing, as shown in Figure 11-10. This single operation can capture at the same time the delay, jitter, and loss in both directions. A comprehensive report of information is contained in the output. This operation can also be used to simulate the IPv6 service you are planning to provide.

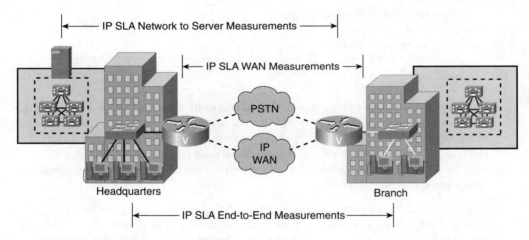

Figure 11-10   *Use of IP SLA UDP Jitter Operation*

Jitter is the measure of variance in delay of a packet sent from the source to the destination. When multiple packets—for example, a VoIP stream—are sent consecutively, the timing in receiving the packets should be constant in a stable network, as seen in Figure 11-10 between end-to-end IP phones. If there are delays in the network, the arrival delay between the packets might increase. This is known as a positive jitter, which indicates that the time between receiving the packets is increasing. The reverse is known as negative jitter. In a VoIP stream, which by nature is a delay-sensitive network application, a positive jitter is undesirable and a value of 0 is ideal.

The UDP jitter operation generates simulated UDP traffic. By default, 10 UDP packets, each with a payload of 10 bytes, are generated every 10 ms, and the operation is repeated every 60 seconds. Each of these parameters is user configurable. Before configuring a UDP jitter operation on the source device, the IP SLA's responder must be enabled on the destination device. The IP SLA responder feature is only available in a Cisco IOS device. Example 11-9 illustrates a configuration for UDP jitter IP SLA operation.

Example 11-9   *Cisco IOS IP SLA UDP Jitter Operation Example Router B (Source)*

```
ip sla 10
udp-jitter 2001:DB8:CAFE:101::51 65051
ip sla schedule 10 life forever start-time now
```

Example 11-10 shows the output of the **show ip sla detail** command. The output provides a comprehensive report on metrics such as

- **Delay:** The delay values will report the round-trip time delay in milliseconds or microseconds per the configuration after the operation has finished execution.

- **Jitter:** This output will give tremendous output on positive and negative jitter, which is easy to understand in the **show** output.

- **Packet:** Four types of packet loss or assimilated events can be measured with IP SLA:

  - **Packet loss:** Packet loss can be in the direction from the source to destination (notified in MIB as packetLossSD) or in the reverse direction, from destination to source (notified in MIB as packetLossDS).

  - **Tail drop:** We know it has been dropped, but we do not know in which direction. This is when the last packet(s) of the test streams were dropped, because in this case, we do not receive the sequence numbers. In older releases, this is called Packet MIA, for missing in action. In the MIB, the notation PacketMIA is still in use.

  - **Packet late arrival:** The packet did arrive, but so late that the underlying application probably considered it as dropped, or at least not useful. Think about a VoIP application. If one packet arrives much later than expected, it is too late because the conversation keeps going. This packet is assimilated to a drop.

  - **Packet misordering:** The packets arrived but not in the right order. This might or might not be considered as a packet drop (packetOutOfOrder).

Example 11-10   *Cisco IOS IP SLA UDP Jitter Statistics*

```
c38d14-1# show ip sla sta 1 details
IPSLAs Latest Operation Statistics
IPSLA operation id: 10
Type of operation: udp-jitter
        Latest RTT: 1 milliseconds
Latest operation start time: 15:16:59.005 UTC Thu Jan 5 2010
Latest operation return code: OK
```

continues

Example 11-10   *Cisco IOS IP SLA UDP Jitter Statistics   continued*

```
RTT Values:
        Number Of RTT: 1000              RTT Min/Avg/Max: 1/1/2 milliseconds
Latency one-way time:
        Number of Latency one-way Samples: 0
        Source to Destination Latency one way Min/Avg/Max: 0/0/0 milliseconds
        Destination to Source Latency one way Min/Avg/Max: 0/0/0 milliseconds
        Source to Destination Latency one way Sum/Sum2: 0/0
        Destination to Source Latency one way Sum/Sum2: 0/0
Jitter Time:
        Number of SD Jitter Samples: 999
        Number of DS Jitter Samples: 999
        Source to Destination Jitter Min/Avg/Max: 0/1/1 milliseconds
        Destination to Source Jitter Min/Avg/Max: 0/1/1 milliseconds
        Source to destination positive jitter Min/Avg/Max: 1/1/1 milliseconds
        Source to destination positive jitter Number/Sum/Sum2: 29/29/29
        Source to destination negative jitter Min/Avg/Max: 1/1/1 milliseconds
        Source to destination negative jitter Number/Sum/Sum2: 29/29/29
        Destination to Source positive jitter Min/Avg/Max: 1/1/1 milliseconds
        Destination to Source positive jitter Number/Sum/Sum2: 22/22/22
        Destination to Source negative jitter Min/Avg/Max: 1/1/1 milliseconds
        Destination to Source negative jitter Number/Sum/Sum2: 22/22/22
        Interarrival jitterout: 0         Interarrival jitterin: 0
        Over thresholds occurred: FALSE
Packet Loss Values:
        Loss Source to Destination: 0         Loss Destination to Source: 0
        Out Of Sequence: 0      Tail Drop: 0      Packet Late Arrival: 0
Packet Skipped: 0
Voice Score Values:
        Calculated Planning Impairment Factor (ICPIF): 0
        Mean Opinion Score (MOS): 0
Number of successes: 120
Number of failures: 0
Operation time to live: Forever
Operational state of entry: Active
Last time this entry was reset: Never
```

Automation Using Flexible Programming with Embedded Event Manager

EEM (Embedded Event Manager) is a flexible programmable policy-based framework that allows an administrator to customize a script to invoke an action based on a given set of events occurring. Figure 11-11 illustrates the framework of the EEM process in the Cisco Catalyst and Cisco Nexus switches.

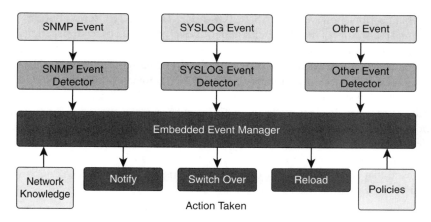

Figure 11-11   *EEM Process in the Catalyst 6500*

The essence of how EEM operates is summarized as follows:

Step 1.   A system event occurs and is picked up by an event detector. For example, an event could be a specific syslog message, when a certain command is executed on the CLI, if a given counter exceeds a set threshold, or when a linecard is inserted. EEM incorporates a number of event detectors that are subsystem processes designed to monitor the system for those key events.

Step 2.   The given event detector alerts the EEM subsystem and passes relevant information to it regarding the event. A predefined script that is created by the administrator and registered with EEM is started, which will use the event information to invoke a given action on the switch.

EEM provides two types of scripts that can be used as the criteria for invoking actions based on given events occurring:

■   **Applet:** This script is run through the CLI.

■   **TCL script:** Support for TCL in the Catalyst 6500 EEM subsystem is based on TCL version 8.3.4. This is the same version of TCL used for TCL Shell in the Cisco router IOS. While applet-based scripts provide an easy option from which to load a script onto the switch, it is with TCL where the more flexible (and powerful) scripts can be developed. Both script options are discussed in more detail later in this section.

The EEM architecture incorporates two operational levels within which a TCL script can run. These levels, in many respects, provide a mechanism to protect the switch from user-based scripts inadvertently accessing system resources that could override the integrity of a running system.

Cisco mandatory scripts run in Full TCL mode. This mode provides full access to all the switch resources.

User-built scripts, however, run in Safe TCL mode. The Safe TCL script mode of operation runs the script inside a "safe interpreter," isolating it from other applications. The execution of scripts in Safe TCL mode is under the control of a master interpreter, allowing it to control the service requests made by the running script. The Safe TCL mode allows Cisco to disable or customize individual TCL commands, thus providing a means to protect the system from a runaway script. This mode also allows the administrator to disable user-based TCL scripts from the CLI using a single command. It is possible to modify a Cisco mandatory policy, but doing so requires the user to move the modified policy to the user directory and run it in Safe TCL mode. Furthermore, an additional level of security is implemented for those scripts that invoke a CLI command. EEM provides a command that allows the specification of the IOS user-id, allowing a TACACS+ command authorization service to be used.

Environment variables are commonly used by this Safe TCL scripting feature. An environment variable is a global variable that is set outside of the TCL script, but one that can be referenced from within the script. These variables provide a useful vehicle for the script to learn more about the system within which it is operating and to learn more about the environment that triggered an event. The following types of environment variables exist:

- **User-defined environment variables:** Defined by a user

- **Cisco-defined environment variables:** Either defined by Cisco or created for a specific policy

The Event Manager environment command is used to set environment variables on the switch. All Cisco-defined environment variables start with an underscore (_). This is a reserved character and cannot be used by a user when defining variables. There are a number of Cisco-defined environment variables available, all of which are documented in the IOS manuals on Cisco.com. You can find EEM scripts on Cisco.com at http://tinyurl.com/2dvjvnu.

IPv6 Network Management

Table 11-8 outlines the three main categories of IPv6 network management transport: monitoring and reporting, network services, and access control and operations. Cisco offers a broad range of features and functionalities in Cisco IOS, Cisco Nexus OS, Cisco IOS-XE, and Cisco IOS-XR that help migrate customers from an IPv4-only management network to a dual-stack/hybrid IPv4-IPv6 management network.

By default, IPv6 routing is disabled in Cisco IOS Software. To use the IPv6 management features, an IPv6 communication path must be available between the source and destination for the network management information.

Table 11-8 *IPv6 Network Management Summary*

IPv6 Network Management	Transport
Monitoring and reporting	SNMP
	Syslog
	ICMP
Network services	TFTP
	NTP
Access control and operations	Telnet
	SSH
	HTTP

Monitoring and Reporting

In the following sections, various methods to monitor as well as provide reporting are discussed. Earlier in this chapter, MIBs were discussed in great detail, while these sections will discuss configuring SNMP to access those MIBs. Syslog provides network administrators with the ability to identify network events. Finally, these sections will discuss ICMP, which is used to check reachability.

SNMP over IPv6

An IPv6 host can perform queries and receive SNMP notifications from a Cisco IOS device. As we discussed earlier in the MIBs section, the SNMP agent and MIBs embedded in the Cisco switches/routers have been enhanced to support IPv6. For more secure SNMP configuration, Triple Data Encryption Standard (3DES) and Advanced Encryption Standard (AES) have also been provided to encrypt SNMP packets.

For basic configuration, an SNMP community string is required. Optionally for security, an access list restricting specific hosts using the community to access the Cisco device as well as read and write or read-only permission for the MIBs accessible to the community can also be configured.

In Example 11-11, a host 2001:db8:cafe:151::51 is being used to receive Open Shortest Path First (OSPF) notifications using a community string named public.

Example 11-11 *SNMP over IPv6 Configuration*

```
snmp-server community public RW
snmp-server enable traps ospf
snmp-server host 2001:DB8:CAFE:151::51 public
```

Syslog over IPv6

The syslog process on Cisco routers/switches allows users to log syslog messages to external syslog servers and host with IPv6 addresses. As of Cisco IOS Release 12.4(4)T and 12.2(33)SRC/12.2(33)SXH, IPv6 addresses can be used to configure syslog. Syslog on IOS can be configured as follows:

```
logging host ipv6 2001:DB8:CAFE:151::62
```

Syslog services on Cisco NX OS can be configured as follows:

```
logging server 2001:DB8:CAFE:151::62
```

ICMPv6

Internet Control Message Protocol (ICMP) functions the same way in IPv6 as it does in IPv4. ICMP generates informational and error messages, and ICMP packets in IPv6 are used in the IPv6 neighbor discovery process, MTU discovery, and Multicast Listener Discovery (MLD). As illustrated in Figure 11-12, ICMP for IPv6 is defined by a value of 58 in the Next Header field.

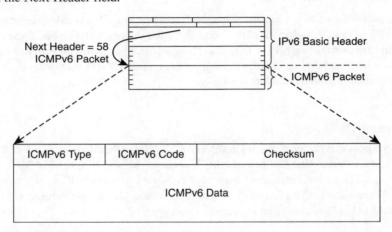

Figure 11-12   *ICMPv6 Packet Type*

Example 11-12 shows a sample **ping** command.

Example 11-12   *IPv6* ping *Command Output*

```
Router# ping ipv6 2001:DB8:CAFE:155::6509

Type escape sequence to abort.
Sending 5, 100-byte ICMP Echos to 2001:DB8:CAFE:155::6509, timeout is 2 seconds:
!!!!!
Success rate is 100 percent (5/5), round-trip min/avg/max = 0/0/4 ms
Router#
```

You also can view ICMP for IPv6 debugs for troubleshooting purposes, as shown in Example 11-13.

Example 11-13 *IPv6 ICMP Debugs*

```
Router# debug ipv6 icmp
6w3d: ICMPv6: Sending echo request to 2001:DB8:CAFE:155::6509
6w3d: ICMPv6: Received echo request from 2001:DB8:CAFE:152::3550
6w3d: ICMPv6: Sending echo reply to 2001:DB8:CAFE:152::3550
6w3d: ICMPv6: Received echo reply from 2001:DB8:CAFE:151::6513
6w3d: ICMPv6: Received echo reply from 2001:DB8:CAFE:155::6509
6w3d: ICMPv6: Sending echo request to 2001:DB8:CAFE:155::6509
```

Network Services

In the following sections, we look at tools that allow you to provide various services to Cisco network devices. These services allows you to upload and download images and configuration files as well as sync clocks of network devices.

TFTP

Cisco device IOS supports file downloading and uploading using IPv6 as a protocol in the same manner as IPv4. For example:

```
copy running-config tftp://2001:DB8:CAFE:151::51/running-config
```

In NX OS–based devices, such as the MDS 9500 directors, IPv6 is supported for TFTP and other applications in the same manner as Cisco IOS.

NTP

Network Time Protocol (NTP) is a protocol for syncing clocks of various network devices. NTP provides an accurate and reliable time reference necessary for financial and legal transactions. NTP also aids in troubleshooting to determine time of failures. All Cisco IOS–and NX OS–based devices support NTP.

NTP runs over UDP, which in turn runs over IP. In a network, one device usually gets the time from an NTP authoritative time source and distributes this time across the network.

Cisco IOS features NTP version 4 (NTPv4). NTPv4 supports IPv6 and provides other enhancements over previous NTP versions. The most significant enhancement in NTPv4 is the use of specific multicast groups that leverage site-local IPv6 multicast addresses. This enables automatic configurations of NTP servers to achieve best accuracy at a low bandwidth cost.

Configuring NTP using IPv6 on NX OS peers or servers remains the same as IPv4:

```
ntp server 2001:0DB8:151:0:0:0:0:3555 version 4
ntp peer 2001:0DB8:151:0:0:0:0:6509 version 4
```

The following shows the configuration of NTP version 4 with site-local IPv6 multicast addresses:

```
interface fastethernet 0/1
ntp multicast FF02::1:FF0E:8C4E
```

Access Control and Operations

The following sections focus on how to access and operate network devices using IPv6. Telnet, SSH, and HTTP are discussed.

Telnet

To enable Telnet access to a Cisco IOS device, a vty interface and password must be created. An IPv6 Telnet connection can be initiated from the Cisco IOS device, and an IPv6 Telnet client can establish a Telnet session to the Cisco IOS device. The Telnet feature functions in the same manner in IPv6 as it does in IPv4. Example 11-14 illustrates configuring Telnet access using IPv6.

Example 11-14   *IPv6 Telnet Configuration*

```
ipv6 unicast-routing
!
interface gigabitethernet1/1
 ipv6 address 2001:DB8:CAFE:155::6509/64
 ipv6 enable
!
line vty 0 4
 login
 password cisco
```

To verify this configuration, use a Telnet client or telnet from another router, as shown in Example 11-15.

Example 11-15   *Telnet Using IPv6*

```
Router_A# telnet 2001:db8:cafe:155::6509
Trying 2001:DB8:zCAFE:155::6509 ... Open


User Access Verification
```

```
Password:
Router_B>en
Password:
Router_B#
```

The output of the **show sessions** command would also give you information about an IPv6 connection, as illustrated in Example 11-16.

Example 11-16 show sessions *Output Showing IPv6 Sessions*

```
show sessions

Conn Host                   Address              Byte  Idle Conn Name
*  1 2001:0db8:20:1::12 2001:0db8:20:1::12      0       0 2001:0db8:20:1::12
```

SSH

The Secure Shell (SSH) server and client features in Cisco routers and switches enable a device to create a secure and encrypted connection. Cisco routers and switches also feature SSH version 2, which further provides additional SSH debug enhancements and Virtual Router Forwarding (VRF)–aware SSH. The SSH configuration remains the same for IPv6 as it does in IPv4 with the following requirements:

- Either a local username and password or authentication, authorization, and accounting (AAA) should be configured.

- The domain name must be configured.

- An SSH key needs to be generated.

SCP can be used for copying images and configuration files after SSH has been configured. As illustrated in Example 11-17, SSH for IPv6 can be configured for IOS.

Example 11-17 *IOS IPv6 SSH Configuration*

```
ipv6 unicast-routing
aaa new-model
user cisco password cisco
interface gigabitethernet1/1
 ipv6 address 2001:DB8:CAFE:155::6509/64
 ipv6 enable
 exit
ip domain-name cisco.com
crypto key generate
line vty 0 4
 transport input ssh
```

Example 11-18 illustrates SSH configuration for NX OS.

Example 11-18   *NX OS IPv6 SSH Configuration*

```
ipv6 routing
ssh key rsa
feature ssh
```

HTTP

The HTTP server in Cisco IOS Software can service requests from both IPv6 and IPv4 HTTP clients. The HTTP client in Cisco IOS Software supports sending requests to both IPv4 and IPv6 HTTP servers. When you use the HTTP client, URLs with literal IPv6 addresses must be formatted using the rules listed in RFC 2732. To use a literal IPv6 address in a URL, the literal address should be enclosed in brackets ([ ]). For example, the literal IPv6 address 2001:db8:cafe:1001::4507 would be represented as http://[2001:db8:cafe:1001::4507].

Figure 11-13 illustrates using HTTP with IPv6.

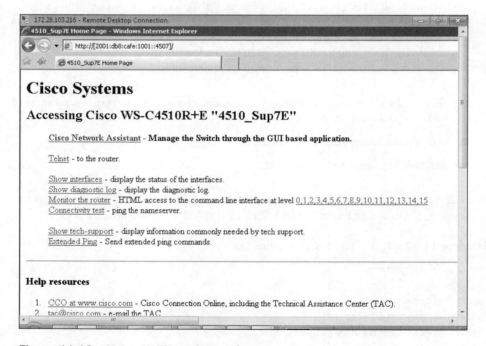

Figure 11-13   *Using HTTP with IPv6 for Cisco Device Access*

IPv6 Traffic-Monitoring Tools

The following sections introduce various tools to monitor IPv6 traffic. We begin by look-ing at tools to capture traffic for analysis. The Mini Protocol Analyzer can be used to analyze captured traffic on the Catalyst 6500 switch itself. Finally, we discuss how you can analyze traffic at the VLAN level on the Nexus 7000.

SPAN, RSPAN, and ERSPAN

Switch Port ANalyzer (SPAN) is an efficient, high-performance traffic-monitoring system. It duplicates network traffic to one or more monitor interfaces as it traverses the switch. This feature is widely used for troubleshooting connectivity issues and calculating net-work utilization and performance, among many others. There are three types of SPANs supported in Cisco products (including Cisco Catalyst 6500, 4500E, and 3750 switches and Cisco Nexus switches), which are illustrated in Figure 11-14:

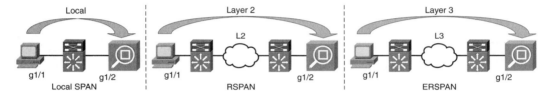

Figure 11-14 *Types of SPAN*

- **Local SPAN:** Mirrors traffic from one or more interfaces on the switch to one or more interfaces on the same switch.

- **Remote SPAN (RSPAN):** Mirrors traffic from one or more interfaces on the switch to a special RSPAN VLAN, which carries the traffic across a Layer 2 switched network to one or more other switches. The other switch duplicates the traffic from the RSPAN VLAN to one or more of its local interfaces.

- **Encapsulated Remote SPAN (ERSPAN):** Mirrors traffic from one of more interfaces on a switch to an IP generic routing encapsulation (GRE) tunnel. This traffic is carried across an arbitrary Layer 3 network to another device. This is only supported on the Catalyst 6500 and Nexus 7000 series switches.

The following section provides examples to configure SPAN, RSPAN, and ERSPAN ses-sions. You also learn about using a mini protocol analyzer for troubleshooting in the Catalyst 6500 series.

Configuring SPAN Types

Local SPAN configuration consists of a single "monitor session" specifying the SPAN source and destination as shown here. Example 11-19 illustrates configuring SPAN on Cisco IOS Release 12.2(18)SXF and earlier.

Example 11-19   *Local SPAN Configuration on Cisco IOS Release 12.2(18)SXF and Earlier*

```
monitor session 1 source int fa 4/1
monitor session 1 destination int fa 2/2
```

In Cisco IOS 12.2(33)SXH, the configuration for SPAN changed to what is illustrated in Example 11-20.

Example 11-20   *Local SPAN Configuration on Cisco IOS Release 12.2(33)SXH and Beyond*

```
monitor session 1 type local
 source int fa 4/1
 destination int fa 2/2
```

Configure RSPAN keeping the following limitations in mind:

- The original VLAN ID of the monitored traffic is not preserved across an RSPAN session.

- Bridge protocol data unit (BPDU) class frames are not captured using RSPAN.

Examples 11-21 and 11-22 show how to configure RSPAN across two switches using a VLAN dedicated for RSPAN.

Example 11-21   *Remote SPAN Configuration Example - Switch 1*

```
vlan 120
 remote-span
 exit
monitor session 1 source int fa1/1
monitor session 1 destination remote vlan 120
```

Example 11-22   *Remote SPAN Configuration Example - Switch 2*

```
vlan 120
 remote-span
 exit
monitor session 1 source remote vlan 120
monitor session 1 destination interface int fa 3/12
```

For configuring ERSPAN, it is recommended to use dedicated loopback IP interfaces on both the source and destination ERSPAN devices. ERSPAN is configured using the SPAN subconfiguration mode. On the ERSPAN source device, define the ERSPAN source session. The system activates an ERSPAN source session only after you have defined a SPAN source, an ERSPAN destination IP address, an ERSPAN ID, and an origin IP address. The ERSPAN tunnel is in "shutdown" mode by default, and the **no shut** command needs to be applied before exiting the SPAN configuration mode. The following is an example of ERSPAN at the source.

Note   At the time of this writing, only IPv4 addresses can be used for ERSPAN configuration.

Mini Protocol Analyzer

The Mini Protocol Analyzer can be used for troubleshooting in the Catalyst 6500 series. The Mini Protocol Analyzer captures traffic from a SPAN session and stores the captured packets in a local memory buffer. The captured data can then be displayed on the console, stored to a local file system, or exported to an external server.

The Mini Protocol Analyzer is configured, as shown in Example 11-23.

Example 11-23   *Cisco IOS Mini Protocol Analyzer for Catalyst 6500*

```
monitor session 2 type capture
buffer-size 65535
 source interface Fa4/2
```

For example, a packet is configured with the source IPv6 address of 2001:db8:cafe:155::4001 and a destination IPv6 address of 2001:db8:cafe:155::6509. These types of packets are sent from a packet generator to the FastEthernet 4/2 interface on the Catalyst 6500 switch.

To turn on the capture of packets on the switch, the monitor capture session has to be started and stopped. In Example 11-23, there were 100 IPv6 packets generated from a packet generator with a source address of 2001:db8:cafe:0155::4001 and a destination address of 2001:db8:cafe:0155::6509. The monitor capture session was started with an option to capture 100 packets and stop automatically with a notification on the console. The **show monitor capture buffer detail dump** command lists the captured packets on the console. The capture on the Catalyst switch shows the packet content in hex. The hex value contains, among other information, the source and destination address highlighted in the **show** output in Example 11-24.

Example 11-24   *Cisco IOS Mini Protocol Analyzer Output Example*

```
6509_A# monitor capture start for 100 packets
6509_A#
```

continues

Example 11-24 *Cisco IOS Mini Protocol Analyzer Output Example   continued*

```
*Mar  8 01:39:27.012: %SPAN-5-PKTCAP_START: Packet capture session 2 started

*Mar  8 01:39:55.913: %SPAN-5-PKTCAP_STOP: Packet capture session 2 ended as the
specified number of packets are captured, 100 packets captured
6509_A# show monitor capture buffer detail dump nowrap 256

   1       Arrival time : 01:39:42.997 UTC Mon Mar 8 2010
           Packet Length : 60 , Capture Length : 60
           len 60  ,   0000.0300.0100   0000.0300.0000   86DD
6030000000063BFF20010DB8CAFE01550000000000000400120010DB8CAFE0155000000000000006509000
102030405
   2       Arrival time : 01:39:42.997 UTC Mon Mar 8 2010
           Packet Length : 60 , Capture Length : 60
           len 60  ,   0000.0300.0100   0000.0300.0000   86DD
6030000000063BFF20010DB8CAFE01550000000000000400120010DB8CAFE0155000000000000006509000
102030405
   3       Arrival time : 01:39:42.997 UTC Mon Mar 8 2010
           Packet Length : 60 , Capture Length : 60
           len 60  ,   0000.0300.0100   0000.0300.0000   86DD
6030000000063BFF20010DB8CAFE01550000000000000400120010DB8CAFE0155000000000000006509000
102030405
   4       Arrival time : 01:39:42.997 UTC Mon Mar 8 2010
           Packet Length : 60 , Capture Length : 60
           len 60  ,   0000.0300.0100   0000.0300.0000   86DD
6030000000063BFF20010DB8CAFE01550000000000000400120010DB8CAFE0155000000000000006509000
102030405
   5       Arrival time : 01:39:42.997 UTC Mon Mar 8 2010
           Packet Length : 60 , Capture Length : 60
           len 60  ,   0000.0300.0100   0000.0300.0000   86DD
6030000000063BFF20010DB8CAFE01550000000000000400120010DB8CAFE0155000000000000006509000
102030405
   6       Arrival time : 01:39:42.997 UTC Mon Mar 8 2010
           Packet Length : 60 , Capture Length : 60
           len 60  ,   0000.0300.0100   0000.0300.0000   86DD
6030000000063BFF20010DB8CAFE01550000000000000400120010DB8CAFE0155000000000000006509000
102030405
```

VLAN Access Control List (VACL) Capture

VACL capture provides a more granular method of network traffic analysis. This feature provides the ability to filter and move VLAN traffic. This feature does not provide the ability to select ingress or egress traffic like SPAN ports, but instead forwards all traffic matching the filtering criteria that is specified using access control entries (ACE). The VACL capture functionality is currently supported on the Catalyst 6500 and Nexus 7000 platforms. Some differences between VACL and SPAN are shown in Table 11-9.

Table 11-9 *Differences Between VACL Capture and SPAN*

VACL	SPAN
Captures traffic-based ACEs, which allow selected traffic to be captured.	Captures all traffic from source interface or multiple source interfaces.
VACL capture for IPv6 is currently supported in Nexus OS only.	SPAN is available on all Cisco switching platforms.
Enforced in hardware.	SPAN/RSPAN requires ASIC hardware resources for mirroring data.
Only one session can be configured.	SPAN enables multiple sessions.
Traffic that matches VACL capture is sent to all configured interfaces.	Different SPAN sessions enable capturing traffic from one interface and sending it to another interface.

Configuring a VACL capture involves

- Configuring an IP access list.
- Assigning that IP access list to a VACL access map.
- Applying the access map to filter VLANs.
- Configuring the interfaces to capture.

Example 11-25 shows a VACL capture for IPv6.

Example 11-25 *VACL Capture for IPv6 on NX OS*

```
ipv6 access-list vacl
  10 permit tcp any any eq www
vlan access-map vacl 10
        match ipv6 address vacl
        action forward
vlan filter vacl vlan-list 200,300
```

Summary

In this chapter, we took a closer look at managing different design IPv6 options. The chapter outlines the FCAPS framework and maps it to the different network management applications. The network infrastructure supports built-in instrumentation (MIBs), which enables being managed by Cisco and third-party network management applications. Cisco switches and routers support NetFlow, IP SLA, and EEM capabilities, which enable easier fault isolation and provide better network visibility.

NetFlow enables network administrators to look at the network holistically and to determine usage and impacts of network change or security incidents, as well as to improve the performance of the network. Only NetFlow v9 supports IPv6 and is currently being evolved to an IETF standard, IPFIX.

IP SLA is a probe mechanism that simulates different traffic patterns to help with fault isolation across the entire network. Key IPv6 IP SLA probes include IP echo, UDP echo, TCP, and jitter operations, which provide performance and management data for the network.

The IPv6 network management section explains the methodology by which access and management methods such as SNMP, Telnet, SSH, and syslog, used with IPv4, can still be used with IPv6 with minimal configuration changes.

In the end, network tools such as SPAN, the Mini Protocol Analyzer, and VACL capture are discussed to aid in troubleshooting.

All the information discussed in this chapter would allow a network administrator to migrate management tasks from IPv4 to IPv6 and use tools to troubleshoot if necessary.

Additional References

Cisco. Cisco IOS Configuration Guide: http://www.cisco.com/en/US/products/ps6350/tsd_products_support_configure.html.

Cisco. Cisco Nexus 7000 Series Switches Configuration Guides: http://www.cisco.com/en/US/products/ps9402/products_installation_and_configuration_guides_list.html.

Cisco. Cisco MDS 9000 NX-OS and SAN-OS Software Configuration Guides: http://www.cisco.com/en/US/products/ps5989/products_installation_and_configuration_guides_list.html.

Cisco. Catalyst 6500 Release 12.2SXH and Later Software Configuration Guide: http://www.cisco.com/en/US/docs/switches/lan/catalyst6500/ios/12.2SX/configuration/guide/book.html.

Haberman, B. RFC 4294, "IP Forwarding Table MIB." http://tools.ietf.org/html/rfc4292.

Hinken, R., et. al. RFC 2732, "Format for Literal IPv6 Addresses in URLs." http://tools.ietf.org/html/rfc2732.

S. Routhier, Ed. RFC 4293, "Management Information Base for the Internet Protocol." http://tools.ietf.org/html/rfc4293.

Bierman, A. RFC 4133, "SNMP Entity MIB". http://tools.ietf.org/html/rfc4133.

Kavasseri, R. RFC 3014, "SNMP Notification MIB." http://tools.ietf.org/html/rfc3014.

Levi, D., et. al. RFC 2273, "SNMPv3 Applications." http://tools.ietf.org/html/rfc2273.

Daniele M., et. al. RFC 4001, "Textual Conventions for Internet Network Addresses." http://tools.ietf.org/html/rfc4001.

Raghunarayan, R. RFC 4022, "Management Information Base for the Tranmission Control Protocol." http://tools.ietf.org/html/rfc4022.

Fenner B., et al. RFC 4113, "Management Information Base for the User Datagram Protocol." http://tools.ietf.org/html/rfc4113.

Chapter 12

Walk Before Running: Building an IPv6 Lab and Starting a Pilot

This chapter covers the following subjects:

- **Sample lab topology:** Create a simple topology that can be used when a near-real production environment is not replicated in the lab.

- **Sample lab addressing:** Create a simple IPv6 addressing plan that is more about the thought process of addressing hierarchy, rather than a baseline plan you should use as is.

- **Configuring the networking devices:** Use the configurations shown throughout this book as a baseline for configuring the networking devices inside the lab/pilot.

- **Operating system, application, and management deployment:** A network is useless without applications. This section shows some example ways to get operating systems, sample applications, and OS/Hypervisor/Application management tools deployed.

- **Moving to a pilot:** Not everything about IPv6 deployment is technical. There are political and business processes that are needed. This section summarizes a few of these considerations.

Very few IT projects are successful without first having a detailed plan, common goals that are shared across IT, and considerable time getting the IT staff comfortable with the new technologies, protocols, equipment, and processes. The deployment of IPv6 in the enterprise is no different than the role of any other major technology initiative; it requires planning and hands-on experience to avoid many pitfalls during pilot and production phases.

Many overlook the lab and pilot phases of an IPv6 deployment because they think "How different can it be from IPv4?" It is true that there are many similarities between IPv4 and IPv6 and that the deployments, especially with dual-stack, are nearly identical from a design standpoint. However, there are enough differences between the two protocol versions to warrant a serious hands-on view of how IPv6 is configured and how hosts, operating systems, and applications work with it.

This chapter discusses considerations for building an IPv6-focused lab that can support testing of the following:

■ Layer 2 configuration/operation (for example, MLD Snooping)

■ Layer 3 configuration/operation (for example, addressing and routing)

■ WAN/branch connectivity (for example, WAN transport options)

■ Internet connectivity and security (for example, establishing IPv6 Internet access and firewall and remote access VPNs)

■ Operating system configuration (for example, client and server OS)

■ Active Directory, DNS, and DHCP

■ Application testing (for example, file server, web server, and server virtualization access/management)

Using the considerations found in the previous bullets and the design and configuration information from the other chapters in this book, we work through building a basic lab or pilot environment. This lab or pilot can be used to solidify your understanding of IPv6 and see how to deploy it in your own network.

Sample Lab Topology

There are nearly an endless number of possibilities when building a lab. In this chapter, a sample lab topology is provided and discussion, testing, and configuration points are made based on it.

In Figure 12-1, a logical view of the sample lab topology is shown. It is a logical view because some components shown in the diagram are a single device that has been logically separated to fill a role in different places (Layer 2 switch through VLANs). Also, a single physical host (server hardware) has been virtualized to provide virtual machines (VM) in different parts of the network.

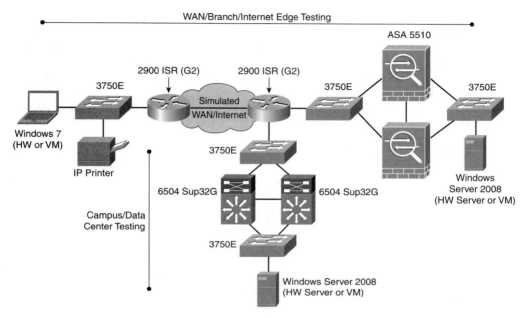

Figure 12-1 *High-Level Topology of the Lab*

The inventory used in the sample topology includes

- One Cisco Catalyst 3750E-48TD

- Two Cisco 2911 ISR G2 routers

- Two Cisco Catalyst 6504 switches with Supervisor 32G

- Two Cisco ASA 5510s

- One server-class hardware platform with VMware vSphere 4.1 with ESXi

- One 4-port 10/100/1000 network interface card (NIC)

- vSphere 4.1 hosting the following VMs:

  - VMware vCenter on Microsoft Windows 2008 R2 64-bit

  - Microsoft Windows Server 2008 R2 64-bit (AD/DNS/DHCP)

  - Microsoft Windows Server 2008 R2 64-bit (Internet simulator)

  - Microsoft Windows 7 Enterprise 32-bit

  - Various Linux VMs

- One IPv6-enabled printer (in the lab, there is a Brother MFC 7840W)

The physical layout of the lab looks different than the logical topology because there is one Cisco Catalyst 3750E-48TD that has multiple VLANs. (The VLANs are locally significant and are not trunked or used outside of the switch.) The VLANs are configured to break the switch up so that different parts of the network can use the same switch for lab purposes without having to purchase a different switch for each area. Also, there is one physical server-class hardware platform that is used with a 4-port 10/100/1000 NIC that is physically cabled to different ports on the Cisco Catalyst 3750E-48TD so that various VMs can access those ports and VLANs.

Ideally, it is best to get the same infrastructure components that you use in your production network into the lab so that you have direct experience with the same gear you have in production. This includes mimicking as much of your topology as you can. The topology and gear used in this chapter are one of an endless number of ways to get a lab built.

The physical topology is referenced in Figure 12-2.

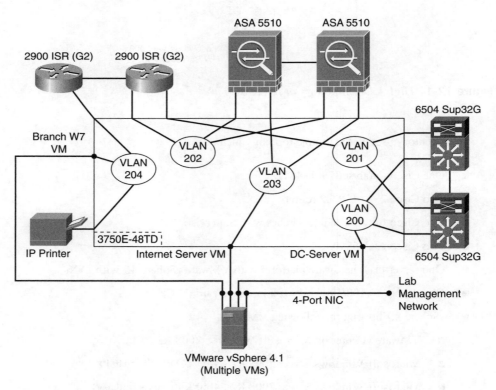

Figure 12-2   *Physical Topology of the Lab*

With this simplistic but functional lab layout, it is time to create an IPv6 addressing scheme for use in the lab, configure gear, install operating systems, set up applications, and prepare to run some tests.

Sample Lab Addressing

The lab IPv6 addressing scheme can be extravagant if the lab is large enough, or it can be simple. Most of the time, an organization does not use its lab to do its IPv6 address planning for the production network simply because of the size of the environment. One exception is that the lab can reveal whether the production network can use /64s on point-to-point links rather than /126s, /127s, or other prefixes. Also, an organization can experiment with very complex 64-bit interface IDs rather than with a more simple one (for example, 2001:DB8:CAFE:100:6500:ABFD:1928:3746 vs. 2001:DB8:CAFE:100::1) when assigning addresses to networking devices. Most find that the complex addressing does not buy them much from a security standpoint and causes an additional operational burden. The point is that this lab can be used to try out all kinds of interesting possibilities, but it might not be sufficient to nail down a large-scale production IPv6 addressing plan.

It is always a good idea to plan for the expansion of the lab. In many cases, other IT groups find out about the lab, realize that they need to test their own components for IPv6, and want to add to the environment. Because of this, it is a good idea to lay out a basic addressing plan that can be used to allow growth and also provide some basic education on how to lay out a production IPv6 address plan. The following addressing layout is basic and not based on any best practice, but it does give you an idea of how an IPv6 prefix can be chopped up for lab use or even as a starter reference for production.

Starting IPv6 prefix:

2001:db8:cafe::/48 (company prefix, using RFC 3849 prefix)
    /50 - Theatre (US, EMEA, APAC, spare)
       /51 - Region (West/East)
          /55 - City/site (Denver, SFO, NYC, and so on), 16 cities per region
            /64 - Link prefix at each site (512 /64s used)

An example of this addressing hierarchy is as follows (note: nonzero prefixes are shown):

Company - 2001:db8:cafe::/48
  USA - 2001:db8:cafe::/50
    West - 2001:db8:cafe::/51
      San Jose, CA (HQ) - 2001:db8:cafe::/55
       Campus - 2001:db8:cafe::/64 - cafe:ff::/64
       Data center - 2001:db8:cafe:100::/64 - cafe:1f2::/64
       Loopback range - 2001:db8:cafe:1f3::/128 (out of /64)
      WAN core/DMZ - 2001:db8:cafe:200::/55
(Sites are **Los Angeles, CA** - 2001:db8:cafe:400::/55
branches)
      San Diego, CA - 2001:db8:cafe:600::/55
      Seattle, WA - 2001:db8:cafe:800::/55
      Las Vegas, NV - 2001:db8:cafe:a00::/55
      Phoenix, AZ - 2001:db8:cafe:c00::/55
      Salt Lake City, UT - 2001:db8:cafe:e00::/55
      Denver, CO - 2001:db8:cafe:1000::/55
      and so on

This is just one of many ways that you can create an addressing plan for use in the lab. Additional considerations for addressing include how to set up and test multihoming scenarios, how to set up BGP filtering with different prefixes to different providers, how to best aggregate routes, and so on.

Configuring the Networking Devices

The configuration of the networking devices depends on the types of enterprise deployment scenarios and the type of testing that needs to be completed. This book has provided a comprehensive set of configurations that you can reference when building the configurations for the lab. Because of easy-to-use configuration references in previous chapters, no per-device configuration samples are shown in this chapter. A reference to where usable configurations can be found in this book is shown in Table 12-1.

Table 12-1 *Cisco Networking Device Configuration References*

Section of Lab	Chapter Reference
Campus/data center	Chapter 6, "Deploying IPv6 in Campus Networks" Chapter 9, "Deploying IPv6 in the Data Center"
WAN/branch/Internet edge	Chapter 8, "Deploying IPv6 in WAN/Branch Networks" Chapter 10, "Deploying IPv6 for Remote Access"

Operating System, Application, and Management Deployment

After the network devices have been connected and configured with IPv6 functionality and end-to-end connectivity has been verified, it is time to set up the endpoints, operating systems, applications, and any management tools or systems needed in the lab. In the lab diagram shown in Figure 12-1, the only operating system installations that need to be made are Microsoft Windows 7, Microsoft Windows Server 2008 R2, and VMware vSphere 4.1 with Hypervisor ESXi. In most enterprise labs, a much wider range of operating systems, such as Linux and hypervisor solutions such as Microsoft Hyper-V, would be installed. For the sake of clarity and brevity, only Microsoft Windows operating systems are installed.

The installation of the operating systems will begin with VMware vSphere 4.1 and installing the Hypervisor ESXi 4.1 on the server hardware. The installation of VMware vSphere and ESXi is straightforward, and instructions for planning and deployment of the VMware environment can be found at the VMware vSphere support center: http://www.vmware.com/support/product-support/vsphere.

The area of focus for this chapter is the IPv6 configuration for ESXi so that the host can be connected to and managed by VMware vCenter and the VMware Infrastructure Client (VI Client) over IPv6.

Figure 12-3 shows the ESXi console that is used for the installation of ESXi in the lab.

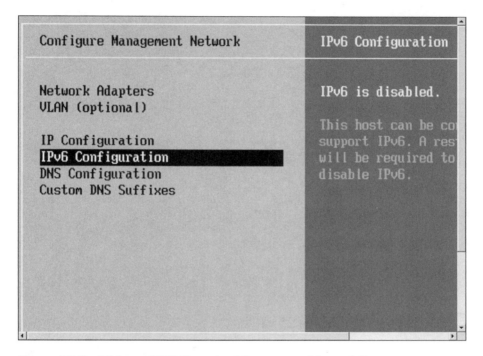

Figure 12-3 *VMware ESXi Console - Management Network Screen*

From the main console screen (shown in Figure 12-3) and under Configure Management Network, select IPv6 Configuration.

By default, IPv6 is not enabled on VMware ESXi, so it needs to be enabled before any other IPv6 functions are configured. Figure 12-4 shows the screen where IPv6 is enabled.

When IPv6 has been enabled in the console, you must reboot the host. After the host has been rebooted, the other IPv6 configuration parameters are available for use. Figure 12-5 shows the static definition of the IPv6 address for the ESXi host. In the lab, the first-hop routers (the VLAN interfaces on the two Catalyst 6504s) will send router advertisements (RA) that this host will use as the default gateway (the RA will be the Hot Standby Router Protocol [HSRP] or Gateway Load Balancing Protocol [GLBP] IPv6 virtual IP address). Optionally, the HSRP or GLBP IPv6 virtual IP address can be statically defined here.

In addition to the static addressing, the Domain Name System (DNS) IPv6 address can be defined so that this host can leverage an IPv4- and/or IPv6-enabled DNS server for name resolution. This step can also be configured in the host properties in vCenter. Figure 12-6 shows the DNS definition for the host.

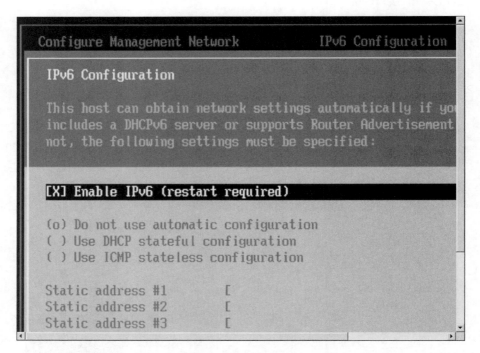

Figure 12-4   *VMware ESXi Console - Enable IPv6*

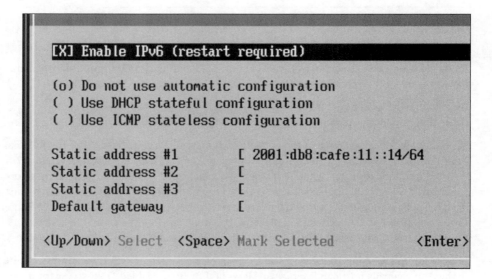

Figure 12-5   *VMware ESXi Console - IPv6 Static Address*

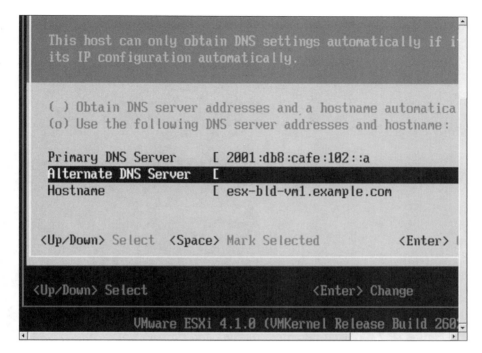

Figure 12-6 *VMware ESXi Console - DNS Definition*

Now that the ESXi host is online and has IPv6 configured, a VMware vCenter VM can be built (or another vCenter installation can manage this host). Figure 12-7 shows the Add Host Wizard from the VMware vCenter VM (running on Microsoft Windows Server 2008 R2 Enterprise Edition) that was built to manage the ESXi host.

In Figure 12-7, the vCenter Add Host Wizard has the host field populated with the IPv6 address that was previously defined for the ESXi host. If DNS or a local host file has been configured for name resolution, the name of the ESXi host can be used here instead of the IPv6 address. After the credentials have been provided, vCenter will begin connecting to and adding the ESXi host to its database.

Figure 12-8 shows that the new host (2001:db8:cafe:11::14) has been added to the data center list along with two other IPv6-enabled hosts (not referenced in this chapter).

At this point, there is a fully functional lab network built and a usable VMware vCenter and Hypervisor ESXi host built from which all other VMs can be deployed.

A Microsoft Windows Server 2008 R2 VM is built and will be used for a new Active Directory (AD), DNS, and Dynamic Host Configuration Protocol (DHCP) deployment. To keep things simple, this same VM will have the web server role enabled so that the Windows 7 clients can access the default web page and the FTP server over IPv6.

By default, IPv6 is enabled and functional on Microsoft Windows Vista, Windows 7, and Windows Server 2008 and 2008 R2. For the Windows Server in the lab, a static address is defined and the DNS server entry is pointing to itself using the loopback address of ::1, as seen in Figure 12-9.

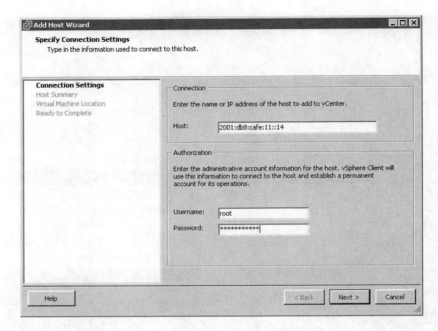

Figure 12-7   *VMware vCenter Console - Add Host Wizard*

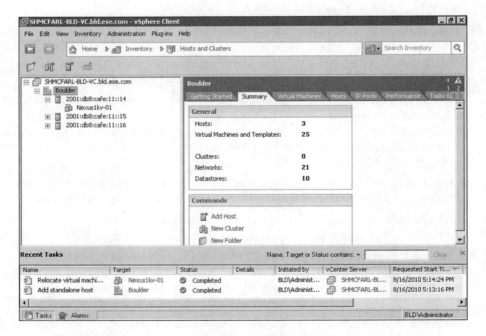

Figure 12-8   *VMware vCenter Console - IPv6-Enabled Hosts*

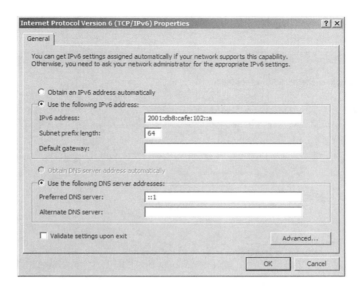

Figure 12-9   *Microsoft Windows Server 2008 R2 - Static IPv6 Address*

After the Windows Server 2008 R2 VM has been built, AD and DNS have been configured, and the various roles such as DHCP and web server have been installed, it is time to configure DHCP for IPv6 address allocation so that the Windows 7 clients can receive centralized IPv6 addressing.

The Microsoft Windows Server 2008 DHCP role offers two modes: stateless and stateful. Stateless allows the client to receive IPv6 addressing through some other means of assignment such as IPv6 autoconfiguration from the local router, but the DHCP options come from the Microsoft Windows Server running DHCP. Stateful-only mode is similar to what is used already in IPv4-based DHCP deployments, where the client receives both addressing and options through the DHCP server. The choice can be changed later if the stateless mode needs to be disabled or reenabled. In the lab environment, stateless mode is left enabled in case it needs to be tested later on.

Figure 12-10 shows the screen where a choice can be made about stateless or stateful mode.

The next steps in defining a DHCP IPv6 scope are nearly identical to the steps used to create an IPv4 scope. Scope name, address range, and exclusions are the required steps.

Figure 12-11 shows the first screen in the DHCP New Scope Wizard.

The initial test of DHCP in this lab is to ensure that the Microsoft Windows 7 client can receive an IPv6 address through DHCP on the same VLAN. The first scope is for the VLAN 102 using prefix 2001:db8:cafe:102::/64, which is on the same network as the DHCP server itself. The Windows 7 client will initially be configured to connect to VLAN 102 to ensure that it gets an address, can join the domain, and test basic access.

Figure 12-12 shows the scope prefix of 2001:db8:cafe:102::/64.

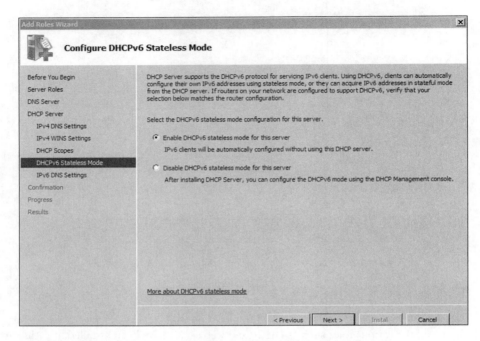

Figure 12-10   *DHCP Server - Stateless or Stateful-Only Mode*

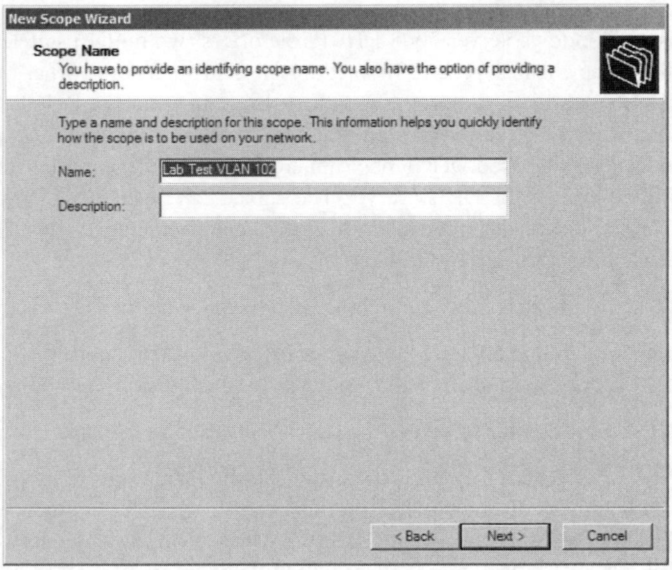

Figure 12-11   *DHCP for IPv6 New Scope Wizard - Scope Name*

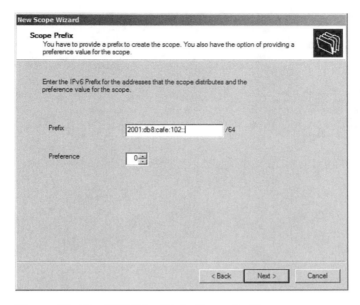

Figure 12-12   *DHCP for IPv6 - Scope Prefix*

The next step is to enter an address exclusion range so that DHCP does not assign addresses in this range. For the sake of this lab, no exclusions were added.

The scope is now completed, and additional DHCP server options such as domain search list and other options can be configured for the clients.

AD, DNS, and DHCP have all been configured with basic parameters, and now the Microsoft Windows 7 VM can be built and connected to the VLAN 102 network inside of vCenter.

When the Windows 7 VM is powered on, it will obtain an IPv6 address from the DHCP server. Figure 12-13 shows the DHCP Management Console on the Microsoft Windows Server 2008 R2 VM. The Windows 7 client successfully received an IPv6 address from the DHCP server, as shown in this figure.

A few basic tests can be executed to ensure that the Windows 7 client can communicate with the Windows 2008 R2 server. An FTP session is established between the Windows 7 client and the Windows server, as seen in Figure 12-14.

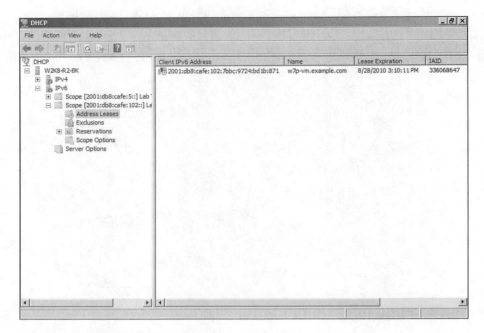

Figure 12-13   *DHCP for IPv6 - Successful Address Assignment*

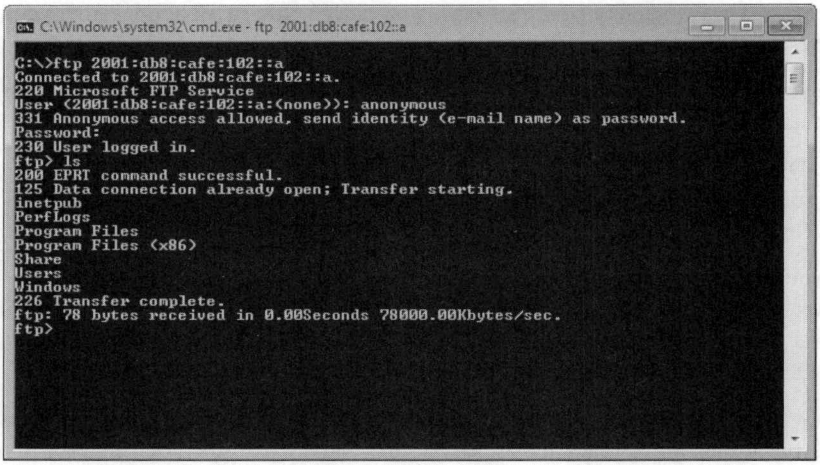

Figure 12-14   *FTP over IPv6 Test*

A drive is mapped from the Windows 7 client to a network share on the Windows 2008 R2 server over IPv6 (the server name is used instead of the literal IPv6 address). Also, a new DNS AAAA record is created to test that new DNS entries can be resolved by the client. In Figure 12-15, a new entry of **test** is entered into DNS, and it resolves to the address of the server.

Figure 12-15 *New DNS AAAA Record*

The client can then open a web browser, enter **http://test.example.com**, and reach the Internet Information Service (IIS) default website at 2001:db8:cafe:102::a. The Windows 7 client now has an open FTP session, a mapped network drive, and an HTTP session all over IPv6. Figure 12-16 shows the active TCP sessions on the Windows 7 client.

Figure 12-16 *Active TCP Sessions over IPv6*

The Windows 7 client can now have its network port association moved to the WAN/branch section of the lab. DHCPv6 Relay can be enabled on the branch router interface so that the client can obtain a new DHCP lease from the DHCP server over the WAN link. Refer to Chapters 6 and 8 for examples on configuring DHCPv6 Relay.

Also, located in the branch section of the lab is the IPv6-enabled printer that can be used for other testing. The Brother MFC 7840W (a small-office multifunction printer/copier/scanner) is used for the testing. The MFC 7840W supports IPv6, as seen in Figure 12-17, and is using 2001:db8:cafe:1000::5, which is the prefix assigned to this branch link.

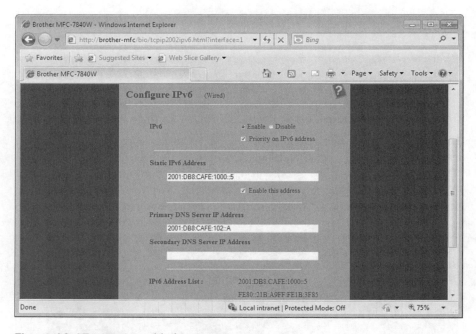

Figure 12-17 *IPv6-Enabled Printer Setup*

At this point, the network is configured, there are hosts such as the Windows 7 and Windows Server 2008 R2 VMs, and other endpoints such as the IPv6-enabled printer are connected. Another VM can be created so that there is a server and/or client located out in the Internet edge portion of the lab network. This VM can be used to simulate an Internet server for external access, a VPN client for Cisco AnyConnect SSL VPN client testing, and inbound port filter testing for the Cisco ASA.

Basic testing has been completed, and now the lab is ready for more comprehensive testing and application deployment.

Moving to a Pilot

The start of a pilot most often involves bringing IPv6 into the production network at some level or perhaps allows access from the production network into the lab environment. This is where more operational IT issues get tested and resolved, such as exposing day-to-day operations and support to IPv6-enabled endpoints, management applications, patching/updates, and help desk issues.

The most critical element of a pilot is more political than technical. It is imperative that a cross-functional virtual team of IT representatives be involved in the planning and rollout of the pilot. If the network team pushes IPv6 into pilot without the knowledge of the desktop, security, operations, applications/data center teams, or other IT groups, the pilot will fail.

A few actions that should be taken to successfully plan for and execute a successfully pilot include

- Create a cross-IT virtual team (VT).

- Set expectations and goals for the pilot with input from the VT and senior management.

- Decide whether the pilot runs on the production network or whether selected users of the pilot are funneled into the lab.

- Don't be afraid to back out and try again with a new plan. It is better to experiment and find a workable solution now versus when moving to full production.

- Don't be afraid to take risks and try new things. It is a pilot, so if expectations are set properly with all involved, any outages or issues should have limited to no impact on production traffic.

- Seek help. There are many resources on the Internet that can help you nail down configurations and tests and troubleshoot issues. Always reach out to your vendors for help, and if they won't help, find other vendors.

- Immediately file bugs with vendors so that they have as much time as they can get to resolve the bugs before you are ready for production. Support for Cisco can be accessed through the support site on Cisco.com, by calling TAC directly, or through the account team: http://www.cisco.com/cisco/web/support/index.html.

- Learn. That is the purpose of a lab and a pilot. This should be a less stressful process than managing a production environment, so take some time, enjoy learning something new, and come out of the pilot with a well-documented plan for moving to production.

Summary

The success of most IT projects can be boiled down to how well they were planned, tested, and piloted. It is critical to the success of any IPv6 rollout to establish a lab and work through the network configurations, application deployment, operating system nuances, and management of the entire environment. The lessons learned from the lab directly translate into a more streamlined pilot. Every pilot should involve representatives from all areas of IT, with a clear set of goals and expectations. With an IT staff that feels a part of the process, a sense of ownership, and a playbook of lessons learned from the lab and pilot, a successful production rollout is easily within reach.

Additional References

Cisco. Cisco Catalyst 3750E Series Switches: http://www.cisco.com/en/US/products/ps7077/index.html.

Cisco. Cisco Branch ISR Routers: http://www.cisco.com/en/US/products/ps10906/Products_Sub_Category_Home.html.

Cisco. Cisco Catalyst 6500 Series Switches: http://www.cisco.com/en/US/products/hw/switches/ps708/index.html.

Cisco. Cisco ASA 5500 Series Adaptive Security Appliances: http://www.cisco.com/en/US/products/ps6120/index.html.

Cisco. Cisco Support Tools: http://www.cisco.com/cisco/web/support/index.html.

Microsoft. Microsoft Windows Server 2008 R2: http://www.microsoft.com/windowsserver2008/en/us/default.aspx.

Microsoft. Microsoft Windows 7: http://www.microsoft.com/windows/windows-7/default.aspx.

Microsoft. Microsoft IPv6: http://technet.microsoft.com/en-us/network/bb530961.aspx.

Huston, G., A. Lord, and P. Smith. RFC 3849, "IPv6 Address Prefix Reserved for Documentation." http://www.ietf.org/rfc/rfc3849.txt.

VMware. VMware vSphere 4: http://www.vmware.com/products/vsphere/ and http://www.vmware.com/support/product-support/vsphere.

Index

B

C

W-X-Y-Z

FREE Online Edition

Your purchase of **IPv6 for Enterprise Networks** includes access to a free online edition for 45 days through the Safari Books Online subscription service. Nearly every Cisco Press book is available online through Safari Books Online, along with more than 5,000 other technical books and videos from publishers such as Addison-Wesley Professional, Exam Cram, IBM Press, O'Reilly, Prentice Hall, Que, and Sams.

SAFARI BOOKS ONLINE allows you to search for a specific answer, cut and paste code, download chapters, and stay current with emerging technologies.

Activate your FREE Online Edition at www.informit.com/safarifree

> **STEP 1:** Enter the coupon code: FBDRSZG.

> **STEP 2:** New Safari users, complete the brief registration form.
> Safari subscribers, just log in.

If you have difficulty registering on Safari or accessing the online edition, please e-mail customer-service@safaribooksonline.com